AI-Driven Strategies for Inclusive and Sustainable Urbanization

This book explores the transformative potential of artificial intelligence (AI) in reshaping urban development practices. Its objective is to provide a comprehensive overview of the latest advancements in AI-driven strategies for urban development and governance, with a focus on promoting inclusivity, sustainability, and resilience in cities worldwide. This book studies how AI technologies can be utilized to tackle the complex challenges encountered in urban areas, spanning ethical, social, and environmental implications across urban governance and beyond.

The in-depth analysis in this book uncovers the potential of AI in addressing longstanding challenges and seizing new opportunities in urban contexts, offering insights into wide-ranging applications. For the use of AI in urban planning, the authors showcase applications that help reduce environmental impact while enhancing accessibility for underserved communities by analyzing real-time data on land use, transportation, and population needs. Another topic in this book examines AI-powered urban mobility systems, utilizing software that integrates real-time data to create adaptive transportation networks. These systems offer efficient, eco-friendly travel solutions tailored to diverse populations, including individuals with disabilities, by dynamically adjusting routes and services. Additionally, this book delves into digital inclusion and accessible technologies in smart cities, highlighting software that prioritizes accessibility and digital inclusion, ensuring that all residents, regardless of ability, can fully participate in urban life. The interdisciplinary approach allows readers to understand how different fields, such as technology, urban planning, and social policy, intersect and shape AI-driven urban development. By weaving together insights from these diverse areas, this book demonstrates how AI can address real-world challenges, from improving infrastructure to fostering sustainability and inclusivity in cities. This perspective helps readers grasp the broader impact of AI, showing how it can enhance various aspects of urban life, including social equity and environmental resilience.

Through interdisciplinary research, case studies, and expert insights, this book aims to educate students in higher learning and inspire policymakers, urban planners, and practitioners to leverage AI technologies in addressing urban challenges and build better cities for all residents.

AI-Driven Strategies for Inclusive and Sustainable Urbanization

Edited by
Mazni Omar, Samsul Ariffin Abdul Karim,
Amirulikhsan Zolkafli, and Mazida Ahmad

CRC Press
Taylor & Francis Group
Boca Raton London New York

CRC Press is an imprint of the
Taylor & Francis Group, an **informa** business

Designed cover image: @Shutterstock

First edition published 2026
by CRC Press
2385 NW Executive Center Drive, Suite 320, Boca Raton FL 33431

and by CRC Press
4 Park Square, Milton Park, Abingdon, Oxon, OX14 4RN

CRC Press is an imprint of Taylor & Francis Group, LLC

ISBN: 978-1-041-04872-5 (hbk)
ISBN: 978-1-041-04869-5 (pbk)
ISBN: 978-1-003-63037-1 (ebk)

DOI: 10.1201/9781003630371

Typeset in Palatino
by codeMantra

Contents

Preface

Urbanization is accelerating at an unprecedented rate, reshaping the global landscape and redefining the future of human habitation. By 2050, nearly 70% of the world's population will reside in urban areas, a seismic demographic shift that brings both extraordinary opportunities and formidable challenges. Cities, as engines of economic growth and innovation, are central to human progress. Yet, rapid urbanization has exacerbated critical issues such as infrastructure strain, environmental degradation, social inequality, and resource scarcity. Traditional urban planning methods, reliant on static models and fragmented data, struggle to address the dynamic, interconnected complexities of modern cities. In this context, AI emerges not merely as a technological tool but also as a transformative scientific paradigm, one that offers data-driven precision, predictive analytics, and adaptive solutions to reimagine urban ecosystems. This book, *AI-Driven Strategies for Inclusive and Sustainable Urbanization*, explores how AI, grounded in rigorous scientific methodologies, can align urban development with the United Nations' Sustainable Development Goals (SDGs), fostering cities that are resilient, equitable, and harmonious with planetary boundaries.

The scientific method, rooted in observation, hypothesis testing, and iterative learning, helps to provide a robust framework for addressing urbanization's multifaceted challenges. AI, as a product of advanced computational science, embodies this approach. By leveraging machine learning algorithms, big data analytics, and the Internet of Things (IoT), AI transforms raw urban data into actionable insights. For instance, predictive modeling enables cities to anticipate traffic congestion, energy demand, or flood risks with unprecedented accuracy, moving urban planning from reactive crisis management to proactive, evidence-based governance. These models are validated through real-world pilot studies and iteratively refined using feedback loops, a hallmark of the scientific process. Consider the application of reinforcement learning in optimizing public transportation networks. By simulating millions of scenarios, AI systems identify optimal routes, schedules, and resource allocations that minimize emissions and maximize accessibility. Similarly, computer vision algorithms analyze satellite imagery to monitor deforestation, urban sprawl, or air quality, providing empirical evidence to guide policy decisions. These technologies exemplify how AI integrates the scientific principles of reproducibility, scalability, and empirical validation into urban governance.

The SDGs, adopted by all UN Member States in 2015, provide a universal blueprint for achieving a sustainable future by 2030. AI's role in advancing these goals is both profound and multifaceted. SDG 11: Sustainable Cities and Communities (Indicator 11.2.1: Access to safe and affordable public transport) emphasizes inclusive, safe, resilient, and sustainable urban development. AI contributes through innovations such as smart mobility systems that reduce congestion and emissions, disaster resilience tools that predict and mitigate climate risks, and cultural heritage preservation technologies that balance growth with conservation. For example, Barcelona's AI-driven traffic management system reduced travel delays by 21% while lowering CO_2 emissions, directly supporting SDG 11's targets for sustainable transport and reduced environmental impact. Similarly, Jakarta's flood prediction models, powered by machine learning, enable adaptive infrastructure planning that safeguards vulnerable communities.

SDG 9: Industry, Innovation, and Infrastructure (Indicator 9.1.1: Proportion of the rural population living within 2 km of an all-weather road) underscores the need for sustainable industrialization and technological advancement. Here, AI modernizes infrastructure through predictive maintenance systems that preempt failures in bridges, railways, and energy grids. Rotterdam's port, for instance, uses AI to predict equipment malfunctions, reducing downtime by 30% and enhancing operational efficiency. AI also drives circular economy initiatives, such as Amsterdam's AI-guided robotic waste sorting systems, which achieve 95% recycling accuracy, aligning with SDG 9's focus on sustainable infrastructure and resource efficiency.

Education and equity are central to SDG 4: Quality Education (Indicator 4.4.1: Proportion of youth/adults with ICT skills), which AI advances by democratizing access to digital literacy and personalized learning. In urban contexts, AI-powered platforms tailor educational content to diverse populations, bridging skill gaps in marginalized communities. Natural language processing (NLP) tools analyze social media to design targeted public awareness campaigns on sustainability practices, fostering informed citizen engagement. These efforts ensure that AI-driven urbanization does not widen the digital divide but instead promotes equitable access to technology, a cornerstone of inclusive progress.

Climate action, as outlined in SDG 13: Climate Action (Indicator 13.2.1: Integration of climate change measures into national policies), is another critical arena where AI demonstrates its scientific rigor. Carbon footprint modeling tools analyze emissions across supply chains, guiding cities like Stockholm toward carbon-neutral urban planning. Neural networks forecast renewable energy output from solar and wind sources, enabling smart grids to dynamically balance supply and demand. Such innovations not only mitigate climate change but also enhance urban resilience, ensuring cities adapt to environmental shocks while minimizing ecological disruption.

However, the integration of AI into urban systems is not without ethical complexities. Algorithmic bias, often rooted in historical data reflecting systemic inequalities, risks perpetuating discrimination in housing, policing, or resource allocation. A scientific approach demands rigorous bias audits, diverse data sampling, and transparent model architectures to ensure fairness. Data privacy, another pressing concern, necessitates advanced cryptographic techniques like federated learning, where AI models train on decentralized data without compromising individual anonymity. The digital divide remains a stark reality, with over 3 billion people lacking internet access, thus disproportionately affecting low-income urban populations. Scientific innovation must prioritize inclusive design, such as Mumbai's AI-enabled SMS-based grievance redressal system, which bypasses smartphone dependency to engage marginalized communities. These ethical considerations are not ancillary but integral to aligning AI with the SDGs' ethos of "leaving no one behind."

Malaysia has made notable strides in aligning its urbanization strategies with the SDGs. Under SDG 11, the country's *Kuala Lumpur Smart City 2025* initiative leverages AI and IoT to optimize public transport and reduce traffic congestion, directly addressing Indicator 11.2.1. The Mass Rapid Transit system in Kuala Lumpur, enhanced by AI-driven predictive maintenance, has improved service reliability and ridership by 18% since 2022. Additionally, Malaysia's Low Carbon Cities Framework integrates AI to monitor and reduce urban carbon emissions, contributing to SDG 13. As of 2023, 35 cities nationwide have adopted smart grids and energy-efficient systems, cutting energy consumption by 12% in participating municipalities.

In line with SDG 9, Malaysia's National Fourth Industrial Revolution Policy (4IR) prioritizes AI-driven infrastructure innovation. The Penang Smart Parking system, powered by AI and IoT, has reduced traffic congestion by 25% in George Town, exemplifying progress toward Indicator 9.1.1. Furthermore, the government's MyDigital Initiative aims to equip 80% of Malaysians with digital literacy skills by 2025 (Indicator 4.4.1), with AI-powered e-learning platforms already reaching over 1.2 million rural students. Despite these achievements, challenges persist. Urban-rural disparities in digital access and uneven adoption of green technologies highlight the need for inclusive policies. Malaysia's 12th Malaysia Plan (2021–2025) addresses these gaps by allocating RM15.1 million to smart city projects and RM10 million to AI research, ensuring that technological advancements align with equitable development.

This book, *AI-Driven Strategies for Inclusive and Sustainable Urbanization*, serves as both a scholarly resource and a call to action. It examines AI's potential to enhance participatory governance, strengthen environmental sustainability, and support equitable infrastructure development. Through interdisciplinary research bridging computer science, urban ecology, and social sciences, the text advocates for context-specific AI solutions that reflect local needs and global sustainability targets. Case studies, such as Singapore's Virtual Urban Laboratory—a "digital twin" platform simulating energy use and traffic patterns—illustrate how computational physics and real-time data can revolutionize policy testing. Cape Town's AI-driven water crisis management during its 2018 drought demonstrates how predictive analytics can allocate resources equitably, prioritizing vulnerable neighborhoods. Medellín's social urbanism initiatives, which use AI to map crime hotspots and socioeconomic disparities, exemplify the fusion of data science and social justice.

The path forward requires a tripartite alliance of science, policy, and ethics. Governments must adopt agile regulatory frameworks, such as the EU's AI Act, which classifies systems by risk levels to balance innovation with public safety. Global collaboration is essential to sharing datasets, algorithms, and best practices, particularly for transnational challenges like climate migration or pandemic response. Equally critical is fostering digital literacy among citizens and policymakers, ensuring informed participation in shaping AI technologies that reflect communal aspirations.

As cities evolve into complex living laboratories, AI stands as a cornerstone of scientific urban governance. By embedding SDG principles into algorithmic design, cities can harness AI not merely for efficiency but for equity, resilience, and regeneration. This book is a testament to the transformative power of interdisciplinary innovation roadmap for researchers pioneering ethical AI methodologies, policymakers championing inclusive governance, and citizens advocating for technologies that serve the collective good. Together, we can build cities where science serves humanity, and sustainability is not a distant goal but a lived reality for generations to come.

Acknowledgments

The editors would like to express their gratitude to all the contributing authors for their superb efforts and dedication in preparing and reviewing high-quality manuscripts for the book, and to all reviewers for reviewing all manuscripts and providing very constructive feedback. The editors would also like to express their appreciation to the Consortium of Geomatics for Disaster Risk Reduction (GeoDRR) team, funded by Erasmus+ [617841-EPP-1-2020-1-PL-EPPKA2-CBHE-JP], for their invaluable support and contributions to this book project. Finally, special thanks go to Taylor and Francis/CRC Press staff for their support towards the publication of this book. The Second Editor was fully supported by the Ministry of Higher Education (MOHE) of Malaysia through the Fundamental Research Grant Scheme [FRGS/1/2023/ICT06/UMS/02/1] (New Scattered Data Interpolation Scheme Using Quasi Cubic Triangular Patches for RGB Image Interpolation). Finally, a special thank you goes to the School of Computing and School of Quantitative Sciences for their tremendous computing facilities support.

Mazni Omar
Samsul Ariffin Abdul Karim
Amirulikhsan Zolkafli
Mazida Ahmad
March 10, 2025

Editors

Mazni Omar is an Associate Professor at the School of Computing (SOC) and a Research Fellow at the Institute for Advanced and Smart Digital Opportunities (IASDO) at Universiti Utara Malaysia (UUM). She holds professional certifications in software testing, specifically CTFL and CTFL-AT. With a focus on software engineering, her research interests encompass agile project management, software process, software quality, and data mining using AI techniques. She has contributed significantly to her field, with numerous articles published in esteemed journals, proceedings, and book chapters. She has also secured research grants from diverse sources, including universities, national and international agencies, and industry partners. Collaborating extensively with Asian universities, including those in Indonesia and Pakistan, she actively participates in Erasmus+ CBHE and Erasmus+ KA107 Mobility Projects involving Asian and European universities. Dr. Mazni's research extends beyond computing to encompass social sciences applications related to the human aspects of software engineering. She serves on the editorial board of the Scopus-indexed *Journal of Information and Communication Technology (JICT)*.

Samsul Ariffin Abdul Karim is an Associate Professor with the School of Quantitative Sciences, UUM College of Arts and Sciences, Universiti Utara Malaysia (UUM), Malaysia. He earned a PhD in mathematics at Universiti Sains Malaysia (USM). He is a Professional Technologist registered with the Malaysia Board of Technologists (MBOT), no. Perakuan PT21030227. His research interests include numerical analysis, machine learning, approximation theory, optimization, science, and engineering education as well as wavelets. He has published more than 180 papers in journals and conference proceedings, including five edited conference volumes and 80 book chapters. He received the Effective Education Delivery Award and Publication Award (Journal and Conference Paper) on UTP Quality Day 2010, 2011, and 2012. He is a Certified WOLFRAM Technology Associate, Mathematica Student Level. He has published 13 books with Springer Publishing, including eight books in the Studies in Systems, Decision and Control (SSDC) series, three books with Taylor & Francis/CRC Press, one book with IntechOpen, and one book with UTP Press. He received the Book Publication Award on UTP Quality Day 2020 for the book *Water Quality Index*

(WQI) Prediction Using Multiple Linear Fuzzy Regression: Case Study in Perak River, Malaysia, published by SpringerBriefs in Water Science and Technology in 2020.

Amirulikhsan Zolkafli is a Senior Lecturer at Universiti Utara Malaysia (UUM), where he serves as a faculty member in the School of Computing, contributing significantly to the fields of geographic information systems and information technology. He earned a PhD in geographic information systems at the University of Queensland, Australia. With a robust academic background and a passion for research, he has published numerous papers in reputable journals, focusing on participatory GIS approaches and practical solutions in various areas. In addition to his research contributions, he is dedicated to teaching and mentoring students, fostering a dynamic and engaging learning environment. He is also a member of an Erasmus+ research team that has successfully designed a master's program on geoinformatics for disaster risk reduction. His commitment to education and scholarly excellence is reflected in his active participation in various academic conferences and workshops. He continually seeks to bridge the gap between theoretical knowledge and real-world application. His work not only advances academic understanding but also has a tangible impact on industry practices. Beyond his academic and research endeavors, he is actively involved in community service, striving to make a positive difference both within and outside the university.

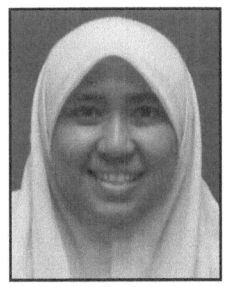

Mazida Ahmad is an Associate Professor in the School of Computing, Universiti Utara Malaysia. With a degree from International Islamic University Malaysia, a master's of real-time software engineering from Universiti Teknologi Malaysia, and a PhD from Universiti Sains Malaysia, Mazida has been serving Universiti Utara Malaysia for approximately 15 years. She teaches courses on advanced systems analysis and design, information system development, information technology project management, knowledge management, and management information systems. Her research areas include knowledge management, software engineering, and IT in education. She is currently involved in numerous international collaborations, such as International Research Collaboration with Universitas Komputer, Telkom University, and Universitas Kuningan in Indonesia, the International Credit Mobility (ICM) program with University West Attica, Greece, and Capacity Building in the field of Higher Education (CBHE) project with European and Asian universities.

Contributors

Nurzulaikha Abdullah
Faculty of Data Science and
    Computing
Universiti Malaysia Kelantan
Kota Bharu, Kelantan,
    Malaysia

Mazida Ahmad
School of Computing
Universiti Utara Malaysia
Sintok, Kedah, Malaysia

Hamzah Alaidaros
Faculty of Computer Science and
    Engineering
Al-Ahgaff University
Mukalla, Yemen

Omar Naji Mohammed Al-Jamili
School of Computing
Universiti Utara Malaysia
Sintok, Kedah, Malaysia

Abdullah Almogahed
Faculty of Computer Sciences and
    Information Technology
Universiti Tun Hussein Onn
    Malaysia
Batu Pahat, Johor, Malaysia

Chrissanthi Angeli
School of Engineering, Department
    of Electrical and Electronics
    Engineering
University of West Attica
Egaleo, Athens, Greece

Mohd Azmeer Abu Bakar
School of Humanities
Universiti Sains Malaysia
Minden, Penang, Malaysia

Manee Sangaran Diagarajan
School of Engineering, Faculty of
    Innovation and Technology
Taylor's University
Subang Jaya, Selangor, Malaysia

Salmah Fattah
Network Engineering Programme
Faculty of Computing and
    Informatics
Universiti Malaysia Sabah
Kota Kinabalu, Sabah, Malaysia

Abdul Rehman Gilal
Knight Foundation School of
    Computing and Information
    Sciences
Florida International University
Miami, Florida, United States of
    America

Ruqaya Gilal
Institute for Advanced and Smart
    Digital Opportunities (IASDO)
School of Computing
Universiti Utara Malaysia
Sintok, Kedah, Malaysia

Ilyas Ahmad Huqqani
School of Humanities
Universiti Sains Malaysia
Minden, Penang, Malaysia

Huda Ibrahim
Institute for Advanced and Smart
    Digital Opportunities (IASDO)
School of Computing
Universiti Utara Malaysia
Sintok, Kedah, Malaysia

Mohd Hakimi Aiman Ibrahim
Faculty of Data Science and
    Computing
Universiti Malaysia Kelantan
Kota Bharu, Kelantan, Malaysia

Noni Harianti Junaidi
Faculty of Administrative Science
    and Policy Studies
Universiti Teknologi MARA
Kota Samarahan, Sarawak, Malaysia

Samsul Ariffin Abdul Karim
Institute of Strategic Industrial
    Decision Modelling (ISIDM)
School of Quantitative Sciences
UUM College of Arts & Sciences
Universiti Utara Malaysia
Sintok, Kedah Darul Aman,
    Malaysia

Tan Mou Leong
School of Humanities
Universiti Sains Malaysia
Minden, Penang, Malaysia

Mohd Amirul Mahamud
School of Humanities
Universiti Sains Malaysia
Minden, Penang, Malaysia

Haythem Nakkas
School of Computing
University of Portsmouth
Portsmouth, United Kingdom

Mazni Omar
Institute for Advanced and Smart
    Digital Opportunities (IASDO)
School of Computing
Universiti Utara Malaysia
Sintok, Kedah, Malaysia

Afrodite Papagiannopoulou
School of Engineering, Department
    of Electrical and Electronics
    Engineering
University of West Attica
Egaleo, Athens, Greece

Muhammad Wafiy Adli Ramli
School of Humanities
Universiti Sains Malaysia
Minden, Penang, Malaysia

Fakhitah Ridzuan
Faculty of Data Science and
    Computing
Universiti Malaysia Kelantan
Kota Bharu, Kelantan, Malaysia

Muhamad Danish Saiful Rizal
Faculty of Data Science and
    Computing
Universiti Malaysia Kelantan
Kota Bharu, Kelantan, Malaysia

Dani Salleh
Institute of Local Government
    Studies (ILGS)
School of Government
Universiti Utara Malaysia
Sintok, Kedah, Malaysia

Narimah Samat
School of Humanities
Universiti Sains Malaysia
Minden, Penang, Malaysia

Kamal Imran Mohd Sharif
School of Technology Management
   and Logistics
Universiti Utara Malaysia
Sintok, Kedah, Malaysia

Asni Tahir
Preparatory Centre for Science and
   Technology
Universiti Malaysia Sabah
Kota Kinabalu, Sabah, Malaysia

Siti Hasnah Tanalol
Preparatory Centre for Science and
   Technology
Universiti Malaysia Sabah
Kota Kinabalu, Sabah, Malaysia

Murugan Thangiah
School of Liberal Arts and Sciences,
   Faculty of Innovation and
   Technology
Taylor's University
Subang Jaya, Selangor, Malaysia

**Chockalingam Aravind
Vaithilingam**
School of Engineering, Faculty of
   Innovation and Technology
Taylor's University
Subang Jaya, Selangor, Malaysia

Amirulikhsan Zolkafli
School of Computing
Universiti Utara Malaysia
Sintok, Kedah, Malaysia

1

AI-Driven Strategies: An Overview Towards Inclusive and Sustainable Urbanization

Mazni Omar and Samsul Ariffin Abdul Karim

1.1 Introduction to Urbanization and Artificial Intelligence (AI)

With the vast majority of people around the globe currently residing in urban centres, urbanization is profoundly altering societies across the world. Cities serve as the engines of economic development, technological progress, and cultural development. Nevertheless, uncontrolled urban expansion also puts pressure on resources, exacerbates environmental issues, and worsens social inequalities (Bush & Doyon, 2019). These issues can only be tackled with the use of creative solutions that are in compliance with the sustainable development goals (SDGs).

The rise of artificial intelligence (AI) has led to the changes in analysis, modelling, and optimization approaches, whereby AI is increasingly being used for rapid and sustainable development of urban cities. The employment of AI in urban planning is likely to alter the fundamental concepts of metropolitan planning and management. With rapid urbanization, cities are faced with complex problems such as traffic congestion, resource allocation, and extreme weather management. AI provides creative solutions by improving the data analysis scope and capabilities, enabling urban planners to make educated decisions that improve urban infrastructure and quality of life.

Using historical trends, AI-assisted predictive analytics can build forecasts, enabling city planners to respond to challenges before they arise. For instance, predictive models can cross-analyse datasets pertaining to demographics, environmental conditions, and even public sentiment conveyed via social media posts, to identify potentially adverse trends. Machine learning (ML) algorithms, for example, can be trained to analyse data from sensors, GPS devices, and social networks to project future traffic conditions. This provides an opportunity to take targeted measures such as adjusting signal timings, changing traffic policies, and even taking legal action (Marchau et al., 2008).

DOI: 10.1201/9781003630371-1

With the introduction of ML as a branch of AI, one can foresee the development of urban and regional planning paradigms being incorporated with models that auto-update with newfound information. Urban regions can have their patterns analysed and subsequently frame zoning policies that not only cater to the residents but also improve service delivery by utilizing clustering algorithm. One such case is in Los Angeles, California, where the parking data's dynamic processes aid in predicting the current state of availability. This way, drivers are given information during real time which reduces the traffic congestions caused by drivers circling the streets in search of a parking space while also improving the overall usefulness of the parking facilities (Sadaf et al., 2023).

The integrated development of urban intelligent systems is also augmented by AI with the use of intelligent traffic control systems. For instance, in Barcelona, Spain, an AI-based traffic control system is used whereby camera and monitoring sensors are actively watching the road. Using the collected data, this technology can change the traffic signal light periods automatically in order to reduce the congestion of road traffic and improve the movement of vehicles. This introduction of technology in Barcelona has reduced traffic congestion in the city by 25%, which has led to shorter travelling times and significantly improved the air quality of the city (Rodriguez-Rey et al., 2022).

The optimization of public transport networks through the application of AI is crucial as well. Intelligent public transport systems include real-time public transport routing, in which AI processes user and traffic data to allow transport agencies to change routes and schedules on the fly. In London, an AI system known as "Bus Priority" is used, which interacts with traffic lights and gives signals to buses, which leads to better use of public transport and reduced travel times. As a result, there has been a major increase in the use of public transport, which leads to less usage of cars and the emission of greenhouse gases (GHG) (Cheng et al., 2023). The GHG emission issue is significant in Cheng's work for various global cities including Barcelona, London, and Los Angeles. It stems from the integration of AI in urban planning, which reveals the benefits of predictive analytics and ML in traffic control. AI's role fundamentally changes data into some actionable information, developing publicly sophisticated infrastructure and enabling further informed situations, posing infrastructural problems around the world. The central issues of urbanization necessitate propelling AI's role to resolve urban planning problems by configuring more usable and green cities.

1.2 AI in Smart Urban Planning

Planning is necessary for the provision of sustainable cities as workable and sustainable urban environments. This is the foundation of urban development. Traditional approaches to urban planning often neglect the fast paced and very complex nature of contemporary urban environments due to increased urbanization, resource availability, and climatic concerns. Thus, the adoption of AI-based tools in urban planning has shifted the decision-making process towards data-driven predictive scenario modelling (Kamrowska-Załuska, 2021). With AI-powered software, urban planners are able to view, analyse, and predict future trends, therefore creating opportunities for better adapted, sustainable, and resilient urban infrastructure.

AI possesses unique abilities for processing vast datasets, identifying patterns, and simulating complex metropolitan systems. As AI is being embedded in urban planning processes, cities can enhance land use, transportation systems, energy consumption, and waste management while furthering inclusiveness and sustainability (Al-Raeei, 2024). Predictive analytics equip consultants to plan for population growth, infrastructure development, and environmental effects, offering proactive rather than reactive measures.

For instance, the Sidewalk Labs, a subsidiary of Alphabet Inc., set out to showcase the potential of AI for the future of urban planning in Toronto, Canada. The programme utilized generative design algorithms to evaluate energy-efficient, environmentally friendly metropolitan layouts and performed analyses on optimizing accessibility. Using sophisticated analytics, the researchers discovered the best configurations for building location, improved public transit networks, and incorporated green areas. These efforts led to an impressive 30% decrease in carbon emissions, illustrating how AI-driven metropolitan design can address environmental issues while focusing on sustainability and liveability (Lifelo et al., 2024).

In addition, a case study in South Korea's Songdo International Business District demonstrates the integration of AI and Internet of Things (IoT) technology in the creation of a smart city from the bottom up. AI algorithms analyse a wide range of data streams from traffic sensors, waste management systems, and energy grids to ensure that urban systems operate seamlessly. For example, Songdo's smart traffic management system modifies traffic flows dynamically to reduce congestion and carbon emissions. To ensure environmental sustainability, the city also uses AI-driven waste management operations, which optimize recycling and disposal systems. Songdo serves as a global model for sustainable urban development, demonstrating how AI can construct smart, efficient, and environmentally friendly communities (Fang et al., 2023).

AI is radically changing urban planning by offering revolutionary tools and approaches guided by data-driven insights. Real-world applications, such as Sidewalk Labs and Songdo, demonstrate AI's capacity to handle difficult urban issues, improve sustainability, and promote equitable development. Nevertheless, integrating AI into urban planning requires resident support to make cities more adaptable, responsive, and resilient to future uncertainties.

As urban areas expand and adapt, AI integration will be critical for creating cities that not only fulfil today's expectations but also foresee tomorrow's issues. The future of urban planning is in the combination of human innovation and AI-driven solutions, ensuring that cities remain lively, sustainable, and inclusive for years to come.

1.3 AI in Sustainable Resource Management

Sustainable cities rely on effective management of their resources. Cities are built with advanced infrastructure and systems that accommodate a growing population that requires more resources, such as energy and water, and has to deal with waste management. In these cases, the AI has positioned itself as a revolutionary component by providing improved methods for resource management. Through the optimization method through AI predictive insights, operational capabilities can be improved, costs decreased, and city environmental objectives can be achieved. These technologies are making fundamental changes for improving operational processes, offering unprecedented possibilities for sustainable cities of the future.

AI's capability is not limited to enhancements in resource efficiency. Rashid and Kausik (2024) have illustrated how AI fosters innovation using ML algorithms, neural networks (NNs), and big data analytics. AIs learn to capture and analyse large volumes of data, empowering them to directly resolve inefficiencies at their origins. Also, AI is capable of recognizing sufficient utilization and supply patterns, along with predicting demand, which enables the resource management to shift from reactive to proactive approaches.

As an example, predictive analytics can analyse a combination of weather phenomena, population activity, and energy economic activity to forecast the energy usage to enhance grid operators' allocation of electricity. Similarly, AI-based water management systems can predict a multitude of phenomena such as droughts and leaks in pipelines, while timing urban and rural water supply to the most optimal points, thus eliminating the unnecessary usage of water. Additionally, AI real-time optimization systems, integrated with IoT systems and sensors, can react to the cities' statuses such as resources monitored, track locations with excessive usage, and allocate immediate remedial measures.

1.3.1 Energy Management

The use of AI technologies in energy management is not only confined to smart grids but also reaches residential, commercial, and industrial systems. AI based building energy management systems used powered IoT devices and ML algorithms to control energy use in cities (Ali et al., 2024). These systems improve efficiency by altering the operation of HVAC systems, raising illumination through motion and daylight sensors and carrying out energy audits to identify inefficiencies and recommend changes. In the same way, AI enables energy optimization in industrial settings during the manufacturing process, in predictive maintenance that decreases downtime, and in the use of energy throughout the supply network.

AI is critical in the integration of renewable sources into the power system. With the analysis of specific weather conditions, expected energy output, and the energy storage systems are purposely optimized, AI increases the dependability and stability of renewable energy resources. In addition, AI takes management of microgrids one step further by controlling the local consumption and production of energy, which lowers the need for central power systems. In addition, demand response programmes powered by AI allow users to alter their energy consumption at any point, which saves costs and is good for the environment (Stecuła et al., 2023). Along with smart home gadgets, variable tariffs, and local energy trading systems, AI encourages energy saving activities and participation in environmental protection.

The application of AI to manage energy results in achieving remarkable improvements from economic and ecological perspectives. AI helps in cutting GHG emission, improving the use of renewable resources, promoting sustainable approaches, and helping to meet climate targets. Most importantly, it enables the advancement of green technologies, facilitates innovation, and transitions society towards a world where energy production and consumption are always environmentally friendly. As these technologies become common in cities and industries, AI will be increasingly applied for solving energy challenges and creating a greener and more resilient future.

1.3.2 Water Conservation

Conservation of water is necessary in every area that may have a need for sustainable growth, specifically for the ongoing problems created by global warming, overpopulation, and limited resources. Cities are now managing these challenges through the implementation of AI technologies, which are redefining how AI is used in the monitoring, allocation, and optimization of water resources. AI's effectiveness in preventing wasteful water usage, improving operational effectiveness, and providing equal opportunities to this resource is well documented (Sakkaravarthy et al., 2024). These problems can be countered with the aid of these AI tools, enabling cities to proactively manage water in a manner that is greater than the challenges that may be faced in the future.

The configuration of Barcelona's smart water network is a notable illustration of AI use in the management and conservation of water resources because it enables the monitoring of water distribution in real time. Such AI technologies are beneficial in detecting and identifying leaks, inefficiencies, and irregular activities within the water distribution network, thus enabling efficient and effective repairs. Furthermore, analytics are also used to forecast water consumption on the premise of weather patterns, urban population trends, and economic activities. In light of such initiatives, it is astonishing to note that Barcelona stands out with a 20% decrease in water waste, which serves as a benchmark for effective urban water management globally (Bibri & Krogstie, 2020). The performance of the city demonstrates the capacity of AI to resolve persistent issues and enhance the supply of water in highly urbanized areas.

Singapore serves as an important case study for the application of AI in urban areas with specific challenges to water management. Due to very few natural sources of freshwater, Singapore greatly depends on innovative approaches such as water recycling and desalination. AI systems greatly facilitate these processes by analysing renowned datasets to ensure effective generation and distribution of desalinated water. The systems monitor water quality, water consumption, and surrounding conditions so that the operations can be altered in real time, thus minimizing resource and energy waste. Moreover, the application of AI on the water management infrastructure in Singapore has increased its resilience to any potential water crises while placing Singapore at the forefront of global water governance (Susantono & Li, 2021).

AI systems augment world society in a myriad of ways. Activating such systems helps communities identify and fix leaks, as well as, other inefficiencies in real time. This further assists in saving resources and reduces expenditure on a greater scale (Suryavanshi et al., 2024). Decision-makers obtain predictive analytics to make better estimates concerning allocation of resources. Additionally, AI operates towards sustainability by optimizing highly energy consuming activities such as water treatment and desalination, which reduces GHG and other environmental impacts (Sayed et al., 2023). AI applications are responsive to different urban settings, which makes it easier to deal with challenges related to dilapidated buildings, rampant urban sprawl, and changing weather patterns.

Looking onward, the importance of AI in water preservation as this technology improves is expected to increase. The future AI systems are likely to employ even more sophisticated algorithms by integrating data received from IoT devices, satellite images, and ML modelling to boost the levels of accuracy and effectiveness. Such improvements will enable urban centres to construct more robust water systems capable of withstanding the increasing stress that accompanies population and climate change.

1.3.3 Waste Management

Modern waste management systems are increasingly using AI to promote circular economies. In Seoul, convolutional neural networks (CNNs) are used to categorize and sort garbage, considerably increasing recycling efficiency and minimizing contamination in recycling streams. By automating these procedures, AI guarantees that more materials are recycled and repurposed, reducing the environmental effect of urban waste (Lakhouit, 2025). These technologies show how AI may change traditional trash management approaches into more sustainable alternatives.

Furthermore, AI-driven optimization models improve garbage collection routes, lowering fuel consumption and operational expenses. Advanced systems analyse material flow patterns and provide data-driven plans for reuse and recycling. For example, predictive analytics may detect trends in garbage creation, allowing cities to execute targeted solutions (Menezes et al., 2024). These advances connect with the global sustainability goals by minimizing waste, encouraging resource recovery and lowering the environmental impact of urban waste systems.

AI technologies are redefining how cities manage energy, water, and waste, paving the way for sustainable resource management. These achievements highlight AI's critical role in helping cities to accomplish sustainability goals effectively and fairly (Kulkov et al., 2024). Cities that incorporate AI technology into their resource management procedures may save money, preserve resources, and contribute to global sustainability goals. As cities expand, adopting AI-driven resource management systems will be critical to establishing resilient and sustainable communities.

Beyond immediate issues, AI offers a platform for long-term sustainability planning. Its capacity to analyse large amounts of information and deliver actionable insights means that cities are better prepared to respond to changing conditions. By adopting AI technology, cities may build a more sustainable and inclusive future, safeguarding the well-being of present and future generations.

1.4 AI for Social Inclusion and Equity

Urbanization frequently exacerbates social inequities, disproportionately hurting marginalized communities. AI has the ability to close these gaps by encouraging diversity, improving accessibility, and ensuring that resources are dispersed properly. Cities may address structural imbalances and strengthen social connections by strategically implementing AI technology (Ortega-Fernández et al., 2020), resulting in more inclusive urban settings.

AI's capacity to analyse huge datasets and provide practical answers creates new prospects for addressing long-standing social issues. By identifying patterns and forecasting future trends, AI assists policymakers in more efficiently allocating resources and addressing the core causes of inequality. This proactive approach guarantees that urban growth benefits everyone, producing a more balanced and equitable future (Choudhury, 2024).

1.4.1 Accessibility

Identifying and acknowledging the emerging needs within an expanding urban populace can be aided by the use of AI technologies. Urban AI tools enable accessibility for disabled individuals through analysis of urban design and forecasting scenarios. Singapore, for example, has adapted so-called digital twin technologies that monitor the comprehensive metrics on the ease of access. With the aid of these technologies, planners can detect and correct weaknesses in the urban fabric so the developments meet the universal design criteria (Yan et al., 2023).

Certain AI specialized tools enhanced mobility for the disabled by allowing customization of parameters for the AI to select the most appropriate route while providing instructions such as which direction to turn that can be understood by a blind user, or using voice for a wheelchair bound person. These developments make it possible for disabled persons to independently navigate the streets confidently, making urban environments more inclusive (Muhmad Kamarulzaman et al., 2023).

The integration of AIs into tools and applications makes urban living simpler and much more convenient. As such, AI does not need to be viewed as the end, but rather as a strong asset to the residents of various abilities. Urban planners and developers stand to gain a lot by employing such technologies because public space and transportation infrastructure can be improved to such levels that everyone can actively participate in city life, regardless of their personal physical limitations. These advancements enable a step towards truly inclusive cities to be constructed.

1.4.2 Digital Equity

Access to digital technologies and infrastructure remains a major hurdle for effective inclusive urban development, especially for the underserved groups. This divide not only reduces the chances for these groups but also increases social and economic problems. Bridging the gap through AI systematized education is fundamental for these communities and particularly underserved areas. For instance, India's Digital Saksharta Abhiyan uses AI to assess a region's lack of access to the digital world and administers training to rectify these inequalities. With these systematic efforts, the marginalized are being provided with the much-needed skills that will help in employment, greater economic inclusion, and reduced inequality (Pérez-Escolar & Canet, 2023).

AI is changing the way essential services are delivered to remote and underserved communities, and is further advanced by the provision of digital literacy services. There has been growing use of Chatbots and Virtual Assistants as they help provide multilingual support in services. These tools ensure that more users, regardless of their literacy levels, are able to make use of the services being offered. With such tools, underserved members of society can access vital services such as healthcare, education, and even government services. By eliminating language obstacles, AI ensures that justice is achieved in the provision of services while making it possible for underserved communities to flourish in this digital age (Olugboja & Agbakwuru, 2024).

This application of AI sheds light on its promise for fostering achievement in development by bridging the gaps in access to technology and other critical services. The further development of AI in education, medicine, and other fields provides the opportunity for greater participation of marginalized people in the digital economy. The impacts of the advancement are not just individual in nature; they support a new approach to urban planning and development that is more equitable and sustainable for everyone.

1.5 AI in Participatory Governance

The advancement of technologies like AI is transforming participatory governance by facilitating citizen co-participation in the formulation and implementation of urban policies. AI systems that aggregate public opinions from webinars, forum discussions, social media, and polls have made it possible to monitor sentiments and even formulate policies. In Barcelona, for example, citizens can use AI tools to both submit ideas and vote on them, which promotes great transparency and accountability in the municipal officials' processes (Alahi et al., 2023).

AI enables cities to aggregate and process large amounts of public opinions in a shorter period of time. This results in policies that are more accommodating to basic necessities of resolving urban problems. This method ensures active participation of the entire population in urban development as opposed to being a privilege of a certain group.

In addition, the integration of AI tools by local governments improves democracy through greater participation and accountability of citizens. AI systems allow for public participation in decision-making, which helps cities craft more effective and fair policies that engage and concern the citizenship. Such methods ensure that urban development is participatory, transparent, and addresses the needs of all parties involved (Ganeshu et al., 2023).

1.6 AI for Climate Sustainability

AI is becoming a critical tool for dealing with climate change problems affecting urban areas. Cities are now applying AI technologies to predict, prevent, and tackle climate change issues to ensure eco-friendly operations. With AI's ability to perform real-time analysis and provide predictions, cities must adopt informed policies that lessen their adverse impacts on the environment.

AI's ability to scan historical data to assess climate change is also one of its critical functions. In cities affected by heatwaves and floods, such as Amsterdam, AI-based technology can be used to issue alerts once the water levels and meteorological conditions surpass a dangerous set point.

This technology allows planners to take active countermeasures that mitigate destruction and save lives (Jamei et al., 2017).

AI has also made significant contribution to the efforts aimed at greater energy efficiency and GHG reduction. AI-enabled construction and business systems proactively suggest changes by observing energy patterns in order to minimize energy consumption. Smart AI-enabled grids use computer processing to redress the equilibrium of energy supply and consumption which encourages the usage of green energy and decreases fossil fuel dependence. For instance, Copenhagen now uses an AI-run district heating system that automatically sets the energy distribution parameters based on weather forecasts and energy consumption, thus drastically reducing carbon emissions (Addad & Al-Taani, 2024).

AI aids in urban green planning as it enables cities to utilize their resources more efficiently. The use of AI in satellite image analysis helps track the condition of greenery in cities and marks out areas that could be enhanced through afforestation. This information allows urban planners to build appropriate infrastructural nature-based solutions, such as green roofs and urban forests. Such developments assist in reducing the urban heat island effects and improving air quality. These examples demonstrate how AI tools can be used for fostering economic growth whilst preserving the natural environment.

1.7 Applications of AI Algorithms in Urban Sustainability

AI technology has demonstrated to be an enabling factor for urban sustainability by aiding with resource allocation, decision-making, and social equity distribution. ANNs are used extensively for supervision and inspection of urban services such as water and electricity supply (Krishnan et al., 2022). Application of ANNs leads to better allocation of resources and minimization of waste. CNNs can also be applied in these contexts as they are critical for visual data processing such as in trash sorting and disaster risk area mapping (Al Shafian & Hu, 2024). These inventions, if adopted, will improve recycling activities and cities' responsiveness greatly.

Decision tree can also be useful in the allocation of resources and modelling climates (Shaamala et al., 2024). For instance, city planners can examine historical records and predict future needs for countering possible adverse changes. On the other hand, the application of generative adversarial networks (GANs) facilitates urban expansion simulation tremendously for planning purposes through synthetic datasets thus improving disaster management and sustainable growth (Akhyar et al., 2024).

Multi-agent systems are particularly advantageous for studying complex urban interactions such as traffic flows and resource distribution. They also allow resource allocation to be done better through enhanced collaboration among all stakeholders (García-Valls et al., 2018). Similarly, systems that are based on reinforcement learning can also control supply and demand by adjusting those in real time, especially for renewable energy (Stavrev & Ginchev, 2024).

Sentiment analysis and other forms of natural language processing (NLP) technology play a critical through understanding public opinion that should be incorporated in formulating socially responsive policies (Saul et al., 2013). Technology makes it possible for city administrations to formulate policies aimed at social equity. For example, measuring people's opinions and feelings about certain urban interventions provide information for social inclusion policies to increase trust towards the government and participation.

The above examples of embedding AI algorithms into urban networks exemplify their efficient solving of complex issues. Decreased operating costs and environmental impacts are achieved by using ANN, CNN, and reinforcement learning. In addition, predicted and actual scenarios for decision-making in urban development projects are provided through GANs and decision trees. On the other hand, NLP, sentiment analysis, multi-agent systems, and other AI technologies enhance participation and ensure the creation of sustainable urban areas. Table 1.1 provides some examples of the AI algorithms that can be used in the urban context.

In conclusion, AI algorithms are essential for achieving urban sustainability. By referring to Table 1.1, it is evident that each algorithm can contribute uniquely to optimizing resources, enhancing governance, and fostering inclusivity. As cities continue to grow, integrating AI technologies will be critical to addressing present and future urban challenges, paving the way for smarter, more sustainable cities (Bibri et al., 2024).

TABLE 1.1

Potential of AI Algorithms for Urban Sustainability

No.	Example of Algorithm	Applications	Purpose
1	Artificial neural networks (ANNs)	Monitoring and controlling water and energy distribution systems, forecasting urban resource needs (Krishnan et al., 2022)	Ensure sustainability by monitoring and controlling essential urban utilities
2	Convolutional neural networks (CNNs)	Waste sorting, urban planning, visual data analysis, and disaster risk mapping (Al Shafian and Hu, 2024)	Improve efficiency and accuracy in data-intensive tasks like visual recognition and classification
3	Decision trees	Resource allocation in water networks, climate modelling, and decision support systems in urban governance (Shaamala et al., 2024)	Support informed decision-making through predictive analytics and scenario planning

(Continued)

TABLE 1.1 (*Continued*)

Potential of AI Algorithms for Urban Sustainability

No.	Example of Algorithm	Applications	Purpose
4	Generative adversarial networks (GANs)	Urban climate modelling, simulation of urban expansion, and generating synthetic data for urban planning scenarios (Akhyar et al., 2024)	Generate realistic models and simulations for better urban planning and disaster preparation
5	Multi-agent systems	Modelling complex interactions in urban ecosystems, such as traffic flow and collaborative resource sharing (García-Valls et al., 2018)	Facilitate collaboration and coordination in complex, multi-stakeholder urban environments
6	Natural language processing (NLP)	Policy development analysis, citizen feedback analysis, and automated content summarization for urban inclusion (Saul et al., 2013)	Enhance communication and policymaking by understanding and processing textual data
7	Reinforcement learning	Energy grid optimization, transportation routing, and dynamic demand–supply balancing in urban planning (Stavrev and Ginchev, 2024)	Optimize resource allocation and enhance real-time decision-making in dynamic urban systems
8	Sentiment analysis	Analysing public opinion for social inclusion initiatives and improving citizen engagement strategies (Malek et al., 2021)	Gauge public sentiment to drive inclusive and socially responsive urban strategies

1.8 Issues and Challenges

AI is revolutionizing urban development, climate change adaptation, resource allocation, ethical governance, and social integration. However, alongside these great transformations that AI can bring, there are potential issues that can arise due to inadequate data quality, ethical bias, and lack of infrastructure integration (Dwivedi et al., 2021), as well as the need for diversified and multidisciplinary collaboration (Brown et al., 2023).

Predictive analytics and insights derived from spatial data modelling make AI a powerful tool in urban planning development. However, most cities—especially developing ones—do not have access to quality data or the systems required to collect it properly, which renders urban challenges even harder to solve (Elmes et al., 2020). The organizational effort it takes to incorporate AI systems into a city's existing planning framework and infrastructure is also an obstacle, and it is conceivable that moving towards AI-driven processes may deepen existing inequalities while failing to meet the needs of marginalized populations (Haque & Sharifi, 2024).

AI has enabled dramatic improvements in the management of resources, particularly in the areas of energy, water, and waste. However, there are still some challenges to overcome. AI infrastructures are often biased due to the data they are trained on, leading to disparities in resource allocation. For instance, energy optimization algorithms are likely to give precedence to cities over rural areas because data is more accessible in metropolitan regions (Meiser & Zinnikus, 2024). Another issue is the ability of AI systems to scale up. Some models may work well in one region but need extensive modifications for others, which raises the issue of the potential environmental costs of training AI models. AI can be beneficial when it comes to aiding with conservation issues; however, the computational difficulties involved result in high energy expenditure and carbon emissions (Bolón-Canedo et al., 2024).

AI tools can be used for natural disaster forecasting, improving rapid action to rescue victims. On the other hand, the reliability of AI predictions is constrained by its dependence on historical data (Urban et al., 2016). Ethical issues may also emerge when AI-driven processes are guided by zero-sum decision making, as this inevitably has a negative effect on some individuals (York et al., 2023). Another challenge that emerges as a result of over-reliance on technology for climate change adaptation stems from new forms of risk. For example, inadequate system management and man-made disasters during harsh climatic conditions can put greater population segments at risk (Kuruppu & Willie, 2015).

AI applications also raise important ethical concerns regarding their use. These ethical challenges relate to fairness, bias, justice, transparency, responsibility, and even privacy. AI systems are often referred to as "black boxes," as their decision-making processes are impossible to determine. Such opacity undermines trust and accountability, particularly for AI uses in public policy (Land & Aronson, 2020). Privacy is another crucial consideration given that AI systems, particularly those controlling video surveillance, need to gather vast amounts of information, increasing the risk of violating privacy rights. This is a significant challenge as policymakers must establish effective norms of ethical conduct. As this is rarely done at a speed that matches the technological sophistication of AI, this delay leads to the absence of clear recommendations for the ethical use of AI (González-Gonzalo et al., 2022).

While the use of AI for social inclusion has some benefits, it also comes with some challenges. It can single out underserved groups and tailor solutions for them, which would increase the overall inclusion (Malek et al., 2021). However, the digital divide remains a substantial challenge, given that AI-infused solutions are typically designed without incorporating diverse cultures (Timmons et al., 2023). Fundamental participatory design is critical for social inclusion. Nevertheless, qualitative engagement is hard to achieve because of the existing power relations and the distribution of resources (De Weger et al., 2018).

The division of AI issues into separate sub problems reveals various AI-adoption problems in different fields. Such integration of disciplines is particularly needed among urban designers, climate specialists, IT professionals, and policymakers. Unfortunately, cross-functional coordination tends to slow down progress due to missing skillsets. Developing and applying AI solutions requires a special expertise that is still lacking in urban planning and environmental protection fields (Kaginalkar et al., 2021).

Balancing these diverse concerns will require a wide-ranging approach. Cities should ensure that robust systems for data collection and management are put in place to offer high-quality datasets. The design of AI systems should be equitable and actively target the alleviation of the disadvantages suffered by the underrepresented people. There is a shared responsibility among the government, the industry, and universities to foster multidisciplinary partnerships and holistic AI approaches. Policy framers need to cultivate rigorous ethical standards that emphasize and uphold progressiveness, answerability, and fairness. Public campaigns could help in building the trust needed for the responsible use of AI, while fostering an understanding of its ability within communities. In order to mitigate the negative effects of AI on the environment, practices like the development of algorithms and hardware that consume less power should be adopted. Finally, overcoming the digital divide will require focused policies and initiatives that target resource-deprived communities and ensure equitable availability of AI tools and technologies.

AI can be used by policymakers to lessen social disparities in cities. From increasing accessibility and closing the digital gap to participatory governance and climate change mitigation, AI provides the means to build more equitable, sustainable, and inclusive metropolitan communities. These improvements illustrate the role AI can play in strengthening social capital, lowering the carbon footprint, and ensuring equal opportunities for everyone. AI can target the existing gaps in service delivery, healthcare, education, and information to make society more inclusive.

AI has the potential to address urban planning, resource management, climate adaption, ethical governance, and social inclusion problems comprehensively. However, to achieve these ambitious objectives, it must be implemented in a controlled and responsible manner. By fostering collaboration, ensuring justice, and establishing strong ethical frameworks, society can better harness AI's potential.

1.9 Conclusion

AI has the potential to help addressing social gaps and promote equality in urban areas. AI narrows the gap in accessibility, increases engagement in governance, and tackles climate challenges which makes it possible to build cities that are inclusive and sustainable. These accomplishments highlight the ability of technology to build social capital, mitigate the negative effects of urbanization on the environment, and guarantee that no marginalized group in society. AI can bridge the gap in service provision, health care, education, and information provision in order to advance an inclusive society.

The application of AI in access improvement is especially important in the context of different urban social groups because it enables equal participation. Smart assistive technologies used in smart city infrastructure and communications can help remove physical and virtual barriers of the disabled, poor, elderly, and other at-risk populations. Such creations will enable greater economic, social and cultural participation of citizens in designing future city.

The rise in population requires the application of AI tools during the planning and development of cities. In order to have all groups on par without any unfair advantage, there must be accessibility of AI resources to everyone; thus, planners and policymakers need to ensure fairness in AI resources utilization. When applying AI techniques in urban settings, issues of data governance, algorithmic bias, and digital skills gap should take into considerations. This enables the approach towards managing social inequalities while simultaneously advancing AI-driven technology that is more progressive in nature.

By utilizing AI that encourages social equity and enhances climate mitigation, cities are able to portray an ideal world that is equally beneficial for all people regardless of their lifestyles. With AI, it becomes easier to design urban systems that are more responsive to the impacts of climate change, population diversity, and other types of social inequalities to create sustainable cities.

References

Addad, M., & Al-Taani, S. (2024). Leveraging AI for energy-efficient smart cities: Architectural and urban planning solutions for sustainable growth - A comparative case study of Amman city and international examples. *Journal of Civil Engineering and Architecture*, *18*(12). https://doi.org/10.17265/1934-7359/2024.12.006.

Akhyar, A., Asyraf Zulkifley, M., Lee, J., Song, T., Han, J., Cho, C., Hyun, S., Son, Y., & Hong, B.-W. (2024). Deep artificial intelligence applications for natural disaster management systems: A methodological review. *Ecological Indicators*, *163*, 112067. https://doi.org/10.1016/J.Ecolind.2024.112067.

Al Shafian, S., & Hu, D. (2024). Integrating machine learning and remote sensing in disaster management: A decadal review of post-disaster building damage assessment. *Buildings*, *14*(8), 2344. https://doi.org/10.3390/Buildings14082344.

Alahi, M. E. E., Sukkuea, A., Tina, F. W., Nag, A., Kurdthongmee, W., Suwannarat, K., & Mukhopadhyay, S. C. (2023). Integration of IoT-enabled technologies and artificial intelligence (AI) for smart city scenario: Recent advancements and future trends. *Sensors*, *23*(11), 5206. https://doi.org/10.3390/S23115206.

Ali, D. M. T. E., Motuzienė, V., & Džiugaitė-Tumėnienė, R. (2024). AI-driven innovations in building energy management systems: A review of potential applications and energy savings. *Energies, 17*(17), 4277. https://doi.org/10.3390/En17174277.

Al-Raeei, M. (2024). The smart future for sustainable development: Artificial intelligence solutions for sustainable urbanization. *Sustainable Development*. https://doi.org/10.1002/Sd.3131.

Barthel, S., Isendahl, C., Vis, B. N., Drescher, A., Evans, D. L., & Van Timmeren, A. (2019). Global urbanization and food production in direct competition for land: Leverage places to mitigate impacts on SDG2 and on the earth system. *The Anthropocene Review, 6*(1–2), 71–97. https://doi.org/10.1177/2053019619856672.

Bibri, S. E., & Krogstie, J. (2020). The emerging data–driven smart city and its innovative applied solutions for sustainability: The cases of London and Barcelona. *Energy Informatics, 3*(1), 5. https://doi.org/10.1186/S42162-020-00108-6.

Bibri, S. E., Krogstie, J., Kaboli, A., & Alahi, A. (2024). Smarter eco-cities and their leading-edge artificial intelligence of things solutions for environmental sustainability: A comprehensive systematic review. *Environmental Science and Ecotechnology, 19*, 100330. https://doi.org/10.1016/J.Ese.2023.100330.

Bolón-Canedo, V., Morán-Fernández, L., Cancela, B., & Alonso-Betanzos, A. (2024). A review of green artificial intelligence: Towards a more sustainable future. *Neurocomputing, 599*, 128096. https://doi.org/10.1016/J.Neucom.2024.128096.

Brown, S.-A., Sparapani, R., Osinski, K., Zhang, J., Blessing, J., Cheng, F., Hamid, A., Mohamadipour, M. B., Lal, J. C., Kothari, A. N., Caraballo, P., Noseworthy, P., Johnson, R. H., Hansen, K., Sun, L. Y., Crotty, B., Cheng, Y. C., Echefu, G., Doshi, K., & Olson, J. (2023). Team principles for successful interdisciplinary research teams. *American Heart Journal Plus: Cardiology Research and Practice, 32*, 100306. https://doi.org/10.1016/J.Ahjo.2023.100306.

Bush, J., & Doyon, A. (2019). Building urban resilience with nature-based solutions: How can urban planning contribute? *Cities, 95*, 102483. https://doi.org/10.1016/j.cities.2019.102483.

Cheng, G., Liu, X., & Pei, Y. (2023). A review of research on public transport priority based on CiteSpace. *Journal of Traffic and Transportation Engineering (English Edition), 10*(6), 1118–1147. https://doi.org/10.1016/J.Jtte.2023.04.008.

Choudhury, D. (2024). Collage urbanism: Creating sustainable cities through equitable urban resources for good health. In *Developments in Environmental Science* (pp. 595–630). https://doi.org/10.1016/B978-0-443-21948-1.00028-5.

De Weger, E., Van Vooren, N., Luijkx, K. G., Baan, C. A., & Drewes, H. W. (2018). Achieving successful community engagement: A rapid realist review. *BMC Health Services Research, 18*(1), 285. https://doi.org/10.1186/S12913-018-3090-1.

Dwivedi, Y. K., Hughes, L., Ismagilova, E., Aarts, G., Coombs, C., Crick, T., Duan, Y., Dwivedi, R., Edwards, J., Eirug, A., Galanos, V., Ilavarasan, P. V., Janssen, M., Jones, P., Kar, A. K., Kizgin, H., Kronemann, B., Lal, B., Lucini, B., … Williams, M. D. (2021). Artificial intelligence (AI): Multidisciplinary perspectives on emerging challenges, opportunities, and agenda for research, practice and policy. *International Journal of Information Management, 57*, 101994. https://doi.org/10.1016/J.Ijinfomgt.2019.08.002.

Elmes, A., Alemohammad, H., Avery, R., Caylor, K., Eastman, J., Fishgold, L., Friedl, M., Jain, M., Kohli, D., Laso Bayas, J., Lunga, D., Mccarty, J., Pontius, R., Reinmann, A., Rogan, J., Song, L., Stoynova, H., Ye, S., Yi, Z.-F., & Estes, L. (2020). Accounting for training data error in machine learning applied to earth observations. *Remote Sensing, 12*(6), 1034. https://doi.org/10.3390/Rs12061034.

Fang, B., Yu, J., Chen, Z., Osman, A. I., Farghali, M., Ihara, I., Hamza, E. H., Rooney, D. W., & Yap, P.-S. (2023). Artificial intelligence for waste management in smart cities: A review. *Environmental Chemistry Letters*, *21*(4), 1959–1989. https://doi.org/10.1007/S10311-023-01604-3.

Ganeshu, P., Fernando, T., & Keraminiyage, K. (2023). Barriers to, and enablers for, stakeholder collaboration in risk-sensitive urban planning: A systematised literature review. *Sustainability*, *15*(5), 4600. https://doi.org/10.3390/Su15054600.

García-Valls, M., Dubey, A., & Botti, V. (2018). Introducing the new paradigm of social dispersed computing: Applications, technologies and challenges. *Journal of Systems Architecture*, *91*, 83–102. https://doi.org/10.1016/J.Sysarc.2018.05.007.

González-Gonzalo, C., Thee, E. F., Klaver, C. C. W., Lee, A. Y., Schlingemann, R. O., Tufail, A., Verbraak, F., & Sánchez, C. I. (2022). Trustworthy AI: Closing the gap between development and integration of AI systems in ophthalmic practice. *Progress in Retinal and Eye Research*, *90*, 101034. https://doi.org/10.1016/J.Preteyeres.2021.101034.

Haque, Md. N., & Sharifi, A. (2024). Who are marginalized in accessing urban ecosystem services? A systematic literature review. *Land Use Policy*, *144*, 107266. https://doi.org/10.1016/J.Landusepol.2024.107266.

Jamei, E., Mortimer, M., Seyedmahmoudian, M., Horan, B., & Stojcevski, A. (2017). Investigating the role of virtual reality in planning for sustainable smart cities. *Sustainability*, *9*(11), 2006. https://doi.org/10.3390/Su9112006.

Kaginalkar, A., Kumar, S., Gargava, P., & Niyogi, D. (2021). Review of urban computing in air quality management as smart city service: An integrated IoT, AI, and cloud technology perspective. *Urban Climate*, *39*, 100972. https://doi.org/10.1016/J.Uclim.2021.100972.

Kamrowska-Załuska, D. (2021). Impact of AI-based tools and urban big data analytics on the design and planning of cities. *Land*, *10*(11), 1209. https://doi.org/10.3390/Land10111209.

Krishnan, S. R., Nallakaruppan, M. K., Chengoden, R., Koppu, S., Iyapparaja, M., Sadhasivam, J., & Sethuraman, S. (2022). Smart water resource management using artificial intelligence—A review. *Sustainability*, *14*(20), 13384. https://doi.org/10.3390/Su142013384.

Kulkov, I., Kulkova, J., Rohrbeck, R., Menvielle, L., Kaartemo, V., & Makkonen, H. (2024). Artificial intelligence - driven sustainable development: Examining organizational, technical, and processing approaches to achieving global goals. *Sustainable Development*, *32*(3), 2253–2267. https://doi.org/10.1002/Sd.2773.

Kuruppu, N., & Willie, R. (2015). Barriers to reducing climate enhanced disaster risks in least developed country-small islands through anticipatory adaptation. *Weather and Climate Extremes*, *7*, 72–83. https://doi.org/10.1016/J.Wace.2014.06.001.

Lakhouit, A. (2025). Revolutionizing urban solid waste management with AI and IoT: A review of smart solutions for waste collection, sorting, and recycling. *Results In Engineering*, *25*, 104018. https://doi.org/10.1016/J.Rineng.2025.104018.

Land, M. K., & Aronson, J. D. (2020). Human rights and technology: New challenges for justice and accountability. *Annual Review of Law and Social Science*, *16*(1), 223–240. https://doi.org/10.1146/Annurev-Lawsocsci-060220-081955.

Lifelo, Z., Ding, J., Ning, H., Qurat-Ul-Ain, & Dhelim, S. (2024). Artificial intelligence-enabled metaverse for sustainable smart cities: Technologies, applications, challenges, and future directions. *Electronics*, *13*(24), 4874. https://doi.org/10.3390/Electronics13244874.

Malek, J. A., Lim, S. B., & Yigitcanlar, T. (2021). Social inclusion indicators for building citizen-centric smart cities: A systematic literature review. *Sustainability*, *13*(1), 376. https://doi.org/10.3390/Su13010376.

Marchau, V., Walker, W., & Van Duin, R. (2008). An adaptive approach to implementing innovative urban transport solutions. *Transport Policy*, *15*(6), 405–412. https://doi.org/10.1016/J.Tranpol.2008.12.002.

Meiser, M., & Zinnikus, I. (2024). A survey on the use of synthetic data for enhancing key aspects of trustworthy AI in the energy domain: Challenges and opportunities. *Energies*, *17*(9), 1992. https://doi.org/10.3390/En17091992.

Menezes, J., Hemachandra, N., & Isidro, K. (2024). Role of big data analytics and hyperspectral imaging in waste management for circular economy. *Discover Sustainability*, *5*(1), 298. https://doi.org/10.1007/S43621-024-00483-0.

Muhmad Kamarulzaman, A. M., Wan Mohd Jaafar, W. S., Mohd Said, M. N., Saad, S. N. M., & Mohan, M. (2023). UAV implementations in urban planning and related sectors of rapidly developing nations: A review and future perspectives for Malaysia. *Remote Sensing*, *15*(11), 2845. https://doi.org/10.3390/Rs15112845.

Olugboja, A., & Agbakwuru, E. M. (2024). Bridging healthcare disparities in rural areas of developing countries: Leveraging artificial intelligence for equitable access. In *2024 International Conference on Artificial Intelligence, Computer, Data Sciences and Applications (ACDSA)* (pp. 1–6). https://doi.org/10.1109/ACDSA59508.2024.10467443.

Ortega-Fernández, A., Martín-Rojas, R., & García-Morales, V. J. (2020). Artificial intelligence in the urban environment: Smart cities as models for developing innovation and sustainability. *Sustainability*, *12*(19), 7860. https://doi.org/10.3390/Su12197860.

Pérez-Escolar, M., & Canet, F. (2023). Research on vulnerable people and digital inclusion: Toward a consolidated taxonomical framework. *Universal Access in the Information Society*, *22*(3), 1059–1072. https://doi.org/10.1007/S10209-022-00867-X.

Rashid, A. Bin, & Kausik, M. A. K. (2024). AI revolutionizing industries worldwide: A comprehensive overview of its diverse applications. *Hybrid Advances*, *7*, 100277. https://doi.org/10.1016/J.Hybadv.2024.100277.

Rodriguez-Rey, D., Guevara, M., Linares, M. P., Casanovas, J., Armengol, J. M., Benavides, J., Soret, A., Jorba, O., Tena, C., & García-Pando, C. P. (2022). To what extent the traffic restriction policies applied in Barcelona city can improve its air quality? *Science of the Total Environment*, *807*, 150743. https://doi.org/10.1016/J.Scitotenv.2021.150743.

Sadaf, M., Iqbal, Z., Javed, A. R., Saba, I., Krichen, M., Majeed, S., & Raza, A. (2023). Connected and automated vehicles: Infrastructure, applications, security, critical challenges, and future aspects. *Technologies*, *11*(5), 117. https://doi.org/10.3390/Technologies11050117.

Sakkaravarthy, S., Jano, N. A., & Vijayakumar, A. (2024). Overcoming challenges in traditional waste water treatment through AI-driven innovation. In *Springer Water* (pp. 53–81). https://doi.org/10.1007/978-3-031-67237-8_3.

Saul, J. E., Willis, C. D., Bitz, J., & Best, A. (2013). A time-responsive tool for informing policy making: Rapid realist review. *Implementation Science*, *8*(1), 103. https://doi.org/10.1186/1748-5908-8-103.

Sayed, E. T., Olabi, A. G., Elsaid, K., Al Radi, M., Semeraro, C., Doranehgard, M. H., Eltayeb, M. E., & Abdelkareem, M. A. (2023). Application of artificial intelligence techniques for modeling, optimizing, and controlling desalination systems powered by renewable energy resources. *Journal of Cleaner Production, 413*, 137486. https://doi.org/10.1016/J.Jclepro.2023.137486.

Shaamala, A., Yigitcanlar, T., Nili, A., & Nyandega, D. (2024). Algorithmic green infrastructure optimisation: Review of artificial intelligence driven approaches for tackling climate change. *Sustainable Cities and Society, 101*, 105182. https://doi.org/10.1016/J.Scs.2024.105182.

Stavrev, S., & Ginchev, D. (2024). Reinforcement learning techniques in optimizing energy systems. *Electronics, 13*(8), 1459. https://doi.org/10.3390/Electronics13081459.

Stecuła, K., Wolniak, R., & Grebski, W. W. (2023). AI-driven urban energy solutions—from individuals to society: A review. *Energies, 16*(24), 7988. https://doi.org/10.3390/En16247988.

Suryavanshi, A., Mehta, S., Chattopadhyay, S., & Aeri, M. (2024). Navigating water scarcity with IoT: A smart management system approach. In *2023 4th International Conference on Intelligent Technologies (CONIT)* (pp. 1–5). https://doi.org/10.1109/CONIT61985.2024.10627282.

Susantono, B., & Li, S. H. (2021). Urban water future: What can we learn from the Singapore experience? *CSID Journal of Infrastructure Development, 4*(1), 4. https://doi.org/10.32783/Csid-Jid.V4i1.220.

Timmons, A. C., Duong, J. B., Simo Fiallo, N., Lee, T., Vo, H. P. Q., Ahle, M. W., Comer, J. S., Brewer, L. C., Frazier, S. L., & Chaspari, T. (2023). A call to action on assessing and mitigating bias in artificial intelligence applications for mental health. *Perspectives On Psychological Science, 18*(5), 1062–1096. https://doi.org/10.1177/17456916221134490.

Urban, M. C., Bocedi, G., Hendry, A. P., Mihoub, J.-B., Pe'er, G., Singer, A., Bridle, J. R., Crozier, L. G., De Meester, L., Godsoe, W., Gonzalez, A., Hellmann, J. J., Holt, R. D., Huth, A., Johst, K., Krug, C. B., Leadley, P. W., Palmer, S. C. F., Pantel, J. H., … Travis, J. M. J. (2016). Improving the forecast for biodiversity under climate change. *Science, 353*(6304). https://doi.org/10.1126/Science.Aad8466.

Yan, Z., Jiang, L., Huang, X., Zhang, L., & Zhou, X. (2023). Intelligent urbanism with artificial intelligence in shaping tomorrow's smart cities: Current developments, trends, and future directions. *Journal Of Cloud Computing, 12*(1), 179. https://doi.org/10.1186/S13677-023-00569-6.

York, N. D. L., Pritchard, R., Sauls, L. A., Enns, C., & Foster, T. (2023). Justice and ethics in conservation remote sensing: Current discourses and research needs. *Biological Conservation, 287*, 110319. https://doi.org/10.1016/J.Biocon.2023.110319.

2

Ethical Implications of AI in Urban Governance

Mazida Ahmad, Amirulikhsan Zolkafli,
Huda Ibrahim, and Omar Al-Jamili

2.1 Introduction

AI has extended its impact on urban management, where it has changed how resources are deployed, how public services are improved, and how societal problems are solved. They extend from managing traffic flows to improving public security, providing ultimate efficiency and unexampled innovations. However, there is a significant ethical dilemma in integrating the AI system since some are privacy violators, big data discriminators, or abusers of surveillance technologies. This chapter analyzes these two faces of AI and why it is crucial to regulate them in a way that makes technology the catalyst of more social good and protects the rights of citizens.

2.1.1 An Overview of AI in Urban Governance

AI technologies are incorporated in almost all urban authorities and their management domains, such as traffic control and public security. For instance, the AI system developed by Kumar in 2024 for traffic management in Singapore and Los Angeles makes an efficient traffic plan based on data from the sensors and cameras. These technologies assist city administrators in collecting a lot of information from which they can predict some possibilities of what is to happen in the future and hence come up with the best decisions. Certainly, the use of AI presents many advantages, but privacy big data protection, and the influence of Prejudiced outcomes are recorded as ethical issues. Transparency of these patterns and protection of citizens' information should be taken as measures against these challenges. Figure 2.1 illustrates the dual role of AI in urban governance, highlighting its benefits, such as efficiency, resource optimization, and innovative solutions, alongside challenges, including privacy concerns, bias in algorithms, and ethical dilemmas.

DOI: 10.1201/9781003630371-2

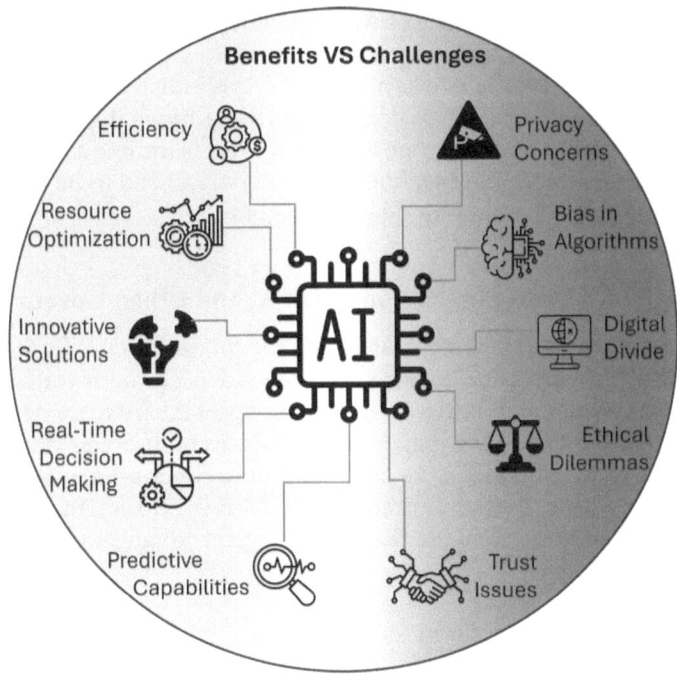

FIGURE 2.1
Dual role of AI in urban governance: benefits and challenges.

2.1.2 The Role of AI in Urban Governance and Its Potential

Artificial intelligence (AI) is now a key part of the management and growth of cities. Its incorporation into urban administration seeks to increase the effectiveness and the quality of services offered while at the same time supporting sustainable development. The everyday use of technologies such as AI can help decrease the amount of work done on administrative tasks, efficiently allocate resources, and offer real-time data analysis. Nevertheless, they present several important ethical issues regarding its use in this field which deserve further consideration about the applications and consequences of AI. Questions such as what may happen to the data, what may happen to algorithms, and concerns that arose from AI as a form of surveillance also need to be addressed if AI is to be a booster for all the people in society.

The need for ethical considerations in artificial intelligence is becoming increasingly important due to the following factors: The world is rapidly becoming urbanized. Due to the COVID-19 pandemic that embarked on digitization of many areas' cities have come to rely on AI for handling health risks and sharing resources. Innovations of smart city projects across the globe, ranging from Singapore to Smart Nation and from Barcelona to

Digital Democracy, are evidence of AI's capability to redesign the cityscapes. However, they remain a topic of controversy as they present certain fundamental issues such as data privacy, misuse or prejudice in algorithms, and the ethical application of AI in surveillance. This surge in dependency on AI across the globe supports the proposition that even as individuals design and implement these systems and technologies, there is a need to do so based on principles that protect and uphold human rights.

2.1.3 Why Ethics Matter in the Context of AI and Urban Governance

Over the years, AI has been integrated into the management of urban areas; hence, whenever aspects of governance are evidenced, be it traffic flow or public safety and policymaking, advanced forms of AI are in evidence. Such technologies show one of the biggest potentials in daily usage, but their use has several ethical concerns. This argument underlines ethical implications to mitigate the harm that enhanced use of AI has on societies' disadvantaged groups, and how to ensure that technological advancement is suited in capacities for society.

a. *Minimizing Unintended Negative Impact*

  Ethics is important due to factors such as algorithmic bias being a massive issue lately. Data input is another significant issue, as AI systems based on historical data can reflect societal prejudices. For instance, predictive policing algorithms have been accused of bias through their preferences for minority groups. This has been seen in the US, where the historical crime data acted like biases and gave preference to African Americans (Noble, 2018). Such risks can be reduced through ethical scrutiny by insisting on proper ways of designing the algorithm and verifying the samples used in the development of datasets to be reasonable and ethically sound.

b. *Justice: Protecting Privacy and Personal Data*:

  Ethical perspectives are instrumental in solving the dilemma of managing big data on urban governance and citizens' privacy rights. In cities where surveillance is already present, facial recognition systems are common as seen in Shenzhen, with critics arguing those can lead to authoritarianism (Wiesenthal, 2022). Using strong ethical systems assists in managing the relative advantages of data-oriented governance while protecting citizens' right to privacy.

c. *Ensuring Accountability in Decision-Making*:

  AI systems can be integrated with strategic and high-stakes processes of urban life, including the assignment of housing or disaster response operations. Two drawbacks of AI are crucial, yet they are still under investigation. The model's 'black box' nature means it is challenging to know how decisions are made (Burrell, 2016). Ethical governance frameworks require exculpation of the various processes that take place in AI systems so that public administrators are held responsible for various intelligent decisions that may be issued.

d. *Techniques of Developing and Maintaining Public Trust and Its Social Relevance*:

Therefore, public trust is a crucial element to enhance the effectiveness of urban governance initiatives. Research has also revealed that the self-serving application of AI, or the absence of consumer permission when compiling data, undermines public trust in government projects (Shin, 2021). Such ethical standards play the role of nurturing and sustaining this trust because they encourage transparency, participation, and accountability which on their part swings the citizens toward accepting the use of AI solutions.

e. *Sustainable and Inclusive Urbanization*:

Ethics are core for the common good in the realization of its impact on serving the entire society including minor groups. If not for ethical considerations, there is the possibility that the developed AI systems of the urbanized society may only aim at optimizing efficient means while reinforcing the social injustice of the society (Eubanks, 2018). Ethical imperatives make urbanists and policymakers develop AI solutions to support the vision of sustainability and accessibility of progressive urbanism.

2.2 Objectives and Scope of the Chapter

This chapter aims to provide a comprehensive analysis of the ethical implications of AI in urban governance, focusing on key issues such as privacy, bias, transparency, and accountability. The objectives include:

1. Identifying and analyzing the ethical challenges posed by AI in urban governance, with practical examples and case studies to ground theoretical discussions.

2. Exploring global trends and specific instances of AI applications in urban settings, highlighting both successes and failures.

3. Proposing actionable recommendations for policymakers, technologists, and urban planners to embed ethical principles in AI system design and implementation.

4. Contributing to the literature by offering a multidisciplinary perspective that bridges ethical theory, practical applications, and policy considerations in AI-driven urban governance.

The following sections of this chapter are devoted to the systematic fulfill-ment of these objectives. The rationale for the current technological discussion regarding AI and its application in urban systems is laid down here. Specific ethical dilemmas are designated and discussed concerning actual material as well as theoretical models of ethical decision-making. Recommendations and conclusions provide suggestions for addressing the challenges of AI eth-ics in urban governance.

This chapter is novel in the following ways: The chapter provides a global perspective on the problem with localized contexts and is grounded in ethi-cal theories that are meaningful and usable in practice. It also points out the trends that exist in the dynamics and prospects of development for AI and urban management and fills gaps in comprehending such a connection.

2.3 Understanding AI in Urban Governance

AI thus has a broad range of governance tasks in cities that range from resource management to citizen participation. Therefore, this section intends to demystify the complexity and opportunity of AI in addressing urban issues by scrutinizing its incorporation into public systems.

2.3.1 Overviews and Distinctive Characteristics of AI Technologies in Urban Systems

AI is an application of computing technology that enables machines to perform tasks in a manner that simulates human intelligence. But when associated with the context of urban systems, AI can be defined as an ensemble of intelligent technologies that involve syntactic and semantic analysis, pattern recognition, knowledge acquisition, decision-making, and natural language processing. These technologies derive from analytical tools to come up with intelligent, efficient, and sustainably applicable solutions for the dynamic and evolving character of cities (Nikitas et al., 2020). Subsystems found in urban systems include transportation services, security services, infrastructure services, and shelter services or housing facilities that define urban settings. The AI interface in these systems is about handling large data streams in real time, enhancing business processes, and improving the delivery of citizen services.

2.3.1.1 Key Features of AI Technology in Urban Systems

a. *Data-Driven Insights*: AI technologies are all using the concept of big data to define patterns and trends that are occurring in city-states to make informed decisions regarding policy and service refinements. For instance, AI-based systems can look at traffic information as a means of minimizing traffic jams (Musa et al., 2023).

b. *Automation and Efficiency*: AI eliminates repetitive work since it manages all simple tasks, ensuring better administrative work and organizational productivity. On the same note, applications include automatic control of waste and monitoring of public facilities in real time.

c. *Predictive Capabilities*: Most AI technologies are advanced in predicting future situations with the help of historical and real-time data. This feature is critically relevant to disaster response, city design, and budgeting since predictive scenarios give an idea of what might go wrong in the aspect of disaster or infrastructure planning (Jha et al., 2021).

d. *Personalization and Adaptability*: The AI systems that are already implemented in urban management are developed in such a way that they can address the various segments of the population. For instance, smart utilities in this context change the consumption habits of electricity based on individual or communal consumers.

e. *Interconnectivity and Integration*: AI technologies may be integrated components of systems that make up the smart city solution systems. The use of IoT means that through AI the different parts of a city like transport systems, safety, and health sectors, are connected to work cohesively and respond to changes.

f. *Real-Time Decision-Making*: AI allows city administrators to make sound, accurate decisions in an emergency when decisions need to be made instantly. For example, intelligent systems can help to find evacuation ways during natural disasters relying on the current density of people and cars (Sun et al., 2020).

g. *Scalability*: AI systems lack growth limitations and can be employed for the increased need presented by growing urban centers. This capability makes it easier for urban centers and their structures of management to adapt in line with the advances of the physical attribute that defines the urban region in question.

AI technologies demonstrate a sociotechnical transition in the working of urban systems and the management of their complexes and problems. Employing techniques like data analytics, predictive modeling, automation, and control, AI reforms urban governance and the anticipation of a progressive future city. Similarly, these benefits raise questions about possible ethical issues, which makes it important to tackle the potential of ethical AI.

2.3.2 AI Applications in Urban Governance

a. *Use of Intelligent Artificial Smart Cities*

In the smart cities, AI is steadily changing how cities function. From smart grid systems to intelligent waste management, AI is at the heart of what is now being done. For instance, San Francisco

TABLE 2.1

Comparative Overview of Global AI Adoption in Urban Governance

Region	Smart City Initiatives	AI Projects in Governance	Budget Allocation (% GDP)
North America	25	131	2.9%
Europe	21	151	3.3%
Asia	41	251	4.1%
Africa	12	51	1.6%

employs the use of AI in improving the function of waste management by providing proper garbage collection at appropriate intervals depending on the routes drawn by AI (Masoumi & van Genderen, 2024). These applications are meant to build better, smarter, and more efficient urban environments. However, to embrace the use of AI in smart cities, it has to be done with morality to ensure that all people are captured in the technology. This involves concerns over the digital divide, where some groups lack access to technology, and the risk of AI systems compounding societal prejudices and inequalities.

AI adoption in urban governance varies significantly across regions, influenced by economic resources, technological capabilities, and governance priorities. Table 2.1 provides a comparative overview of AI initiatives globally, showcasing differences in implementation and investment. This data sets the stage for examining applications in specific urban systems.

The data highlights Asia's leadership in AI adoption for urban governance, reflecting substantial investments in smart city projects and a higher number of AI initiatives compared to other regions. Conversely, regions like Africa exhibit fewer initiatives, raising concerns about a growing digital divide. This disparity underscores the importance of ethical frameworks to ensure equitable access to AI benefits globally.

b. *AI Applications in Transportation Policing and Healthcare Sector*

AI's influence on transport, policing, and healthcare is noteworthy. In transportation, AI recommends ways of improving traffic flow and minimizing congestion, such as the case of the Finnish capital Helsinki, where statistics are collected so that the best schedule for bus routes is implemented depending on the loads and traffic patterns (Merugu & Hemachandran, 2023). In policing, AI helps in crime prediction and crime prevention, New York City through AI has improved its policing strategies and has better ways of improving efficiency regarding crime fighting by expanding area coverage and providing efficient ways of distributing resources. In healthcare, AI enhances diagnosis as well as patient and staff experience; Toronto employs AI to anticipate admission rates of its patients and better allocate the availability of its hospitals. However, these applications have to be inspected for their efficiency in terms of the general ethical rules such as the preeminence of surveillance, discriminative measures, and exclusion of human intelligence. AI systems should always be applied and deployed responsibly and ethically to uphold citizens' rights, as the public is the most important stakeholder.

These subsections reveal that while theoretical approximation seems to suggest a productive future for AI for urban governance, ethical policies should be weighed to improve AI governance to the detriment of human rights and principles. Solving such ethical issues presents a collective task for policymakers, technologists, and society to develop accurate, transparent, and fair AI systems.

The majority of ambitious, mid-sized businesses across the world see artificial intelligence, or AI, as a growth opportunity despite the ongoing debate about the technology's impact on humanity.

A study of boardrooms across 12 major economies revealed that AI adoption is widespread across all geographies and industries. Notably, 77% of respondents reported increasing their investment in or use of AI over the last four years. (see Figure 2.2).

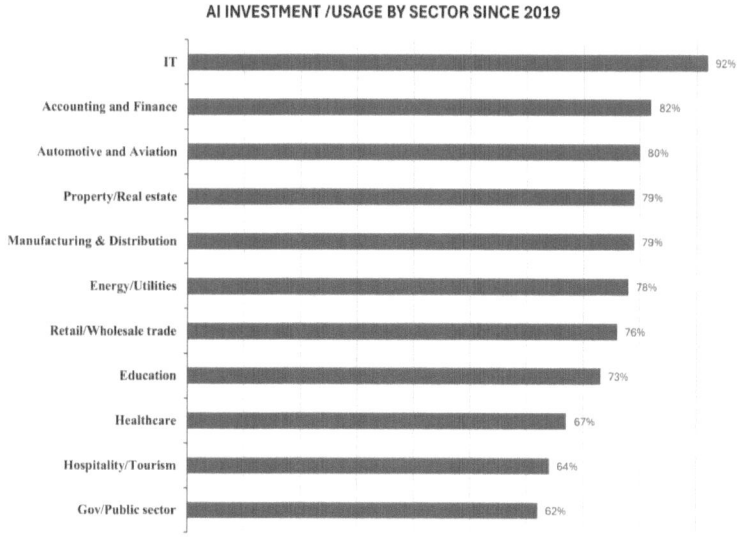

AI INVESTMENT /USAGE BY SECTOR SINCE 2019

Sector	%
IT	92%
Accounting and Finance	82%
Automotive and Aviation	80%
Property/Real estate	79%
Manufacturing & Distribution	79%
Energy/Utilities	78%
Retail/Wholesale trade	76%
Education	73%
Healthcare	67%
Hospitality/Tourism	64%
Gov/Public sector	62%

FIGURE 2.2
AI investment/usage by sector since 2019.

The majority of businesses are actively engaging with AI and exploring how the technology could enhance their operations. Only 4% believe AI will not play a significant role in their business shortly. According to research by the Centre for Business and Economics Research (Cebr), 56% of business leaders view AI as an opportunity for their organizations, while 23% see it as a potential threat. Large companies with at least 250 employees, which have adopted AI at the fastest rate, experienced an average revenue growth of 15% since 2019, more than twice the growth seen in companies that have slowed or halted AI investment over the past four years. To achieve these positive outcomes, businesses have invested an average of $1.5 million in AI technology over the past year, with spending rising to $3.2 million in industries like automotive and aviation.

2.4 Trends and Future Development of AI Employment in Urban Governance

The use of AI in urban administration is continuously evolving due to technological advancements, massive urbanization, and the need for better city management. Key trends include:

2.4.1 AI in IoT and Smart City Platforms

Smart cities leverage AI systems as part of the IoT network to monitor urban spatial functionality intermittently. For instance, through AI and the Internet of Things, Barcelona through smart city solutions improves energy consumption and accessibility of public transport (Ortega-Fernández et al., 2020).

2.4.2 Predictive Governance Models

Governments are figuring out how to harness the power of AI, whose most important prospect is in predicting the future of cities. Singapore's Urban Redevelopment Authority uses AI for proactively predicting population density and development of sustainable infrastructures for future cities (Gad & Aithal, 2021).

2.4.3 AI-Powered Participatory Governance

The use of AI in enhancing the public's participation in decision-making is becoming increasingly popular. There are over 3,000 public attitudes established currently, and they are using chatbots and natural language processing tools to analyze the citizen's feedback and include the public opinion with the policies of urbanization, as seen in the Helsinki participatory budgeting projects (Heyik et al., 2024).

2.4.4 Improvement of the Emergency Management Systems

Advanced technologies are being embraced by organizations to manage disasters namely, through machine algorithms for flood prediction and evacuation, as used in Jakarta Indonesia (Abid et al., 2023).

2.4.5 Future Directions

AI in urban governance is poised to evolve further through:

a. *Decentralized Governance Using Blockchain-AI Integration*: To improve transparency and trust in urban operations.
b. *Ethical AI Frameworks*: A growing emphasis on embedding ethical considerations into AI system design to address fairness, privacy, and accountability.
c. *AI for Climate-Resilient Urban Planning*: Focused on addressing climate change challenges, such as urban heat islands and rising sea levels.

All of these trends indicate a shift to better, more efficient, and responsible governance despite the need to undertake cross-cultural evaluation of potential ethics issues.

2.5 Emerging Trends in AI for Urban Governance

In this context, the rapid development of new AI technologies remains one of the defining processes that transform urban governance. Two key advancements stand out for their transformative potential, mostly generative AI and blockchain integration.

2.5.1 Generative AI and Urban Governance

Applied to urban governance, generative AI is used for language processing, communication, and designing, for instance, large language models and image synthesis tools. For instance, generative AI can be useful to build realistic avatars and virtual environments and, applied to city planning, can help in visualizing how further developments may look like and identify the best location for homes, jobs, stores, schools, and other facilities and buildings taking into consideration sustainability and accessibility.

Potential Ethical Implications:

- *Misinformation*: The ease of generating content raises concerns about the spread of false information in public forums.
- *Bias Amplification*: Generative AI models trained on biased data can perpetuate stereotypes or create exclusionary designs.

Example of Application:

- In Amsterdam, generative AI is used to visualize flood mitigation strategies, allowing policymakers to assess the impact of proposed solutions in real time while incorporating community feedback.

2.5.2 AI and Blockchain Integration

Integrating AI and blockchain provides a strong foundation for improving trust in managing complex urban systems. Blockchain fixes this issue as the records are unalterable, thereby making full and transparent records of the decision-making algorithms used by AI systems.

Potential Ethical Implications:

- *Data Sovereignty*: Combining AI with decentralized systems can empower citizens with greater control over their data but raises questions about governance structures.
- *Resource Intensity*: Blockchain systems require significant computational power, which may conflict with sustainability goals.

Example of Application:

- In Dubai, the integration of AI and blockchain has been implemented in public service delivery, streamlining processes like property registration while ensuring secure, verifiable transactions.

Future Directions:

- Expanding the use of generative AI to improve participatory urban planning through realistic simulations.
- Exploring AI-blockchain synergies to enhance citizen engagement and regulatory compliance in smart cities.

2.6 Ethical Challenges in AI-Driven Urban Governance

2.6.1 Privacy and Data Protection Concerns

The most important points about the application of AI in urban governance are privacy and data protection (Alhitmi et al., 2024). Many AI systems require significant quantities of personal data to operate optimally, and therefore, there are questions concerning the process of data acquisition, etc. The legal requirement set to uphold the privacy of Malaysian citizens and to ensure that data is not used in the wrong way is the PDPA. The principle of data protection and the right of citizens to control their data must be strong enough to ensure that data collected from EU citizens are done following some legal requirement and that citizens are aware of this information is being collected.

2.6.2 Bias and Fairness in AI Algorithms

Algorithms' bias and fairness in AI learning are important ethical issues. AI systems may deepen existing social biases if they are trained on skewed data or if fairness is not a core design principle. In Malaysia, for instance, the Government Transformation Programme (GTP) with wide-ranging goals of enhancing the delivery of service delivery in the country seeks to employ these technologies while being relevant, fair, and more importantly, unbiased. Effective monitoring of AI tools and software as well as conducting periodic evaluations of such systems can go a long way in managing bias and unfairness in urban administration (González-Sendino et al., 2023).

2.6.3 Transparency and Accountability

Transparency and accountability are crucial when it comes to the adoption of AI in the administration of cities. In Malaysia, an example of a big data project is the Malaysia Urban Observatory which utilizes big data for analysis to inform urban development and administration. People quite literally have to know how these AI systems come to some of the decisions that they make regarding our lives, and there have to be means to punish those systems. This entails effective communication of the AI and the mechanisms of the decision-making through codes and reasons governing these decisions (Cheong, 2024). Making certain the interpretation of AI systems is clear assists in creating trust, from which mistakes or prejudices may be spotted and fixed.

2.6.4 Surveillance and Social Control

The practical implications of AI in scrutiny relate to issues of ethical concerns with regard to surveillance and control in society. For increasing public safety and security, AI can do it at the cost of violating individual rights and privacy. The AI technologies in Malaysia include traffic controls and public security in the consumption context of cities. AI surveillance technologies must be monitored properly to avoid misuse and used where necessary under an appropriate level of measure (Data, 2022). Promoting the use of AI in surveillance while respecting the inhabitants' civil liberties is a noble cause in ethical city management.

2.6.5 Impact on Public Trust

Issues of AI having ethical effects on human societal behavior and public trust are core to this foresight narrative. Over-reliance on these technologies requires trust, especially when deploying them in urban administrations. Specifically, if citizens see AI systems as opaque, or even biased in their decision-making, if these systems violate personal privacy, then people lose their confidence in the state institutions. In essence, the elements of trust include trustworthiness, truthfulness, integrity, the principle of right and wrong, and responsible handling of people's data. Responding to public concerns and interacting with the public on issues concerning AI could go a long way toward building the citizens' rapport with the AI-governed city (Chen & Wen, 2021).

These are some of the ethical considerations that, if dealt with, the usage of AI in urban governance will benefit Malaysia without violating any human worth or ethical value. This balance is required to develop 'smart' city systems that are intelligent, sustainable, and fair.

2.6.6 Social and Economic Impact

AI has great opportunities to improve and innovate through efficiency. However, the uses of AI technologies come with challenges, with equal impacts on development (Hagerty & Rubinov, 2019). This chapter aims to ensure that the people who make these decisions are aware of the positive effects that can be expected and, conversely, the potential negative effects that may arise from the deployment of advanced technologies such as AI.

2.6.7 Displacement of Jobs and Automation Risks

Automation is one of the most significant issues today, as it can lead to job displacement. AI technology causes unemployment since it can do what humans can in many fields (Plikas et al., 2023). For example, fewer people are employed when monitoring and controlling traffic with the help of technological systems or AI delivery of public services. This dislocation threatens to hinder growth and needs intervention measures like retraining and welfare measures to enable the displaced workers to find other suitable employment.

2.6.8 Inequality and Digital Divide

The findings include exposing and even widening preexisting gaps and disparities when information technology is unequally distributed. This can be expressed in urban contexts in terms of equity of public services and access to resources between different communities. The equity and equal usage of AI technology among citizens irrespective of their group position is very important (Kitsara, 2022). In general, there is a need to design adequate policies to bridge the digital divide and ensure that every resident of a member state is equipped to harness the potential of AI.

2.6.9 Sustainability and Resource Allocation

In this context, AI has a significant role in influencing urban sustainability and checks and balances in allocating scarce resources. These technologies help cities optimize using resources such as energy, water, and waste as they are based on data analytics and predictive modeling.

- *Energy Management*: Smart grid systems employing aspects of AI manage energy consumers and producers within the grid to minimize energy supply wastage and ultimately cut down on greenhouse gas emissions. For instance, the smart grid system implemented in Barcelona has positively affected energy management in different sectors (Siano, 2014).
- *Water Distribution*: AI systems reduce the chances of leakage and provide equal quantities of clean water by efficiently recognizing the poor efficiency of water supply networks in urban areas (Xiang et al., 2021).
- *Waste Management*: Bins contain smart sensors, which help determine the ideal route for collection. This approach, as adopted in Stockholm, has led to a 35% cut in operational costs and pollution from garbage pickup trucks (Englund et al., 2021).

Although such applications demonstrate how AI will revolutionize several fields, including healthcare, their use also presents new problems, such as how to share resources fairly. For instance, algorithms recommending privileged districts for investment while neglecting more in-need districts aggravate existing inequalities. Equity-oriented algorithms and community decision-making engagement are needed to address these concerns.

AI technologies greatly improve sustainability by increasing the efficiency of energy, water, and waste. However, the increased effectiveness of the methods raises the problem of control over how these technologies are used so that they remain just as much a tool for the poor and marginalized as for the rich and powerful.

To conclude with the above, AI advances for sustainability measures for energy efficiency, water, and waste enhancement have remarkable advantages in efficiently administering cities. However, their use is sensitive to the fact that they must be implemented in such a manner that does not reproduce unfair structures when applied in organizations. At present, technological advancement can complement ethics to enhance the sustainability policies of a city and at the same time, promote fair usage of resources.

2.7 Ethical Frameworks and Applications

To ground the discussion of ethics, this chapter employs three foundational ethical theories:

2.7.1 Utilitarianism

This perspective emphasizes maximizing overall societal benefits (Mill, 1863). For instance, using AI technologies within traffic systems to improve car access and decrease pollution falls under utilitarianism. However, if a high monitoring rate is used, it also raises concerns for low-income areas because resources are unequally divided among different communities.

2.7.2 Deontology

Rooted in duty and adherence to ethical rules, deontology mandates strict adherence to principles such as data privacy and fairness (Kant, 1785). For instance, it includes integrating transparent data policies in artificially intelligent governed tools to protect citizen rights regardless of the results.

2.7.3 Virtue Ethics

Focusing on the character and moral responsibility of decision-makers, virtue ethics stresses the need for transparency and accountability in AI systems (Pakaluk, 2005). For instance, when urban planners embrace AI, they need to show that the decisions they make are 'fair' in a way, say, in the allocation of resources.

These frameworks are applied across case studies and practical examples, ensuring a consistent lens to evaluate ethical challenges and opportunities in AI-driven urban governance. By integrating theoretical insights with real-world applications, the chapter provides a structured approach to addressing the moral complexities of AI.

2.7.4 Application of These Theories to Urban Governance Scenarios

a. *Smart Surveillance Systems*: Moral system utilitarianism may approve using technologies such as AI surveillance technology to boost security as practiced in Singapore with public safety. Nevertheless, a deontological approach requires protection measures to guarantee that such systems erode no one's right to privacy.

b. *Resource Allocation:* For instance, when applied in urban planning, the AI system may include predictive models in disaster response planning, and these fit the type when they encourage greater efficiency. However, meeting needs by output legitimacy relies on deontological-based fairness to avoid discriminating against the worse-off groups.

2.7.5 The Intersection of Public Sector Ethics and AI

In the context of public sector values and professionalism, including integrity, accountability, and equity, the principles of AI governance are intertwined in that technology applications benefit the public. For instance, using XAI in managing urban systems serves the public sector's objectives since it guarantees the explanation of the processed data decisions (Burrell, 2016). In addition, ethical governance involving AI in the urban context should include concerns of stakeholder engagement because the public sector generally has a social responsibility unlike the corporate business sector, which may lean toward efficiency.

2.8 Case Studies of Ethical Dilemmas in AI-Driven Urban Governance

The deployment of AI in urban governance presents both opportunities and ethical dilemmas, offering valuable lessons for navigating the complexities of ethical implementation. This section examines real-world examples from different regions, detailing positive outcomes, ethical failures, and their implications.

2.8.1 Case Study 1: Smart Traffic Management in Singapore (Asia)

Singapore has long been recognized as a global leader in urban innovation and smart city development. One of its most notable achievements is the implementation of the Intelligent Transport System (ITS), spearheaded by the Land Transport Authority (LTA). This system leverages AI to optimize traffic flow, reduce congestion, and enhance the overall efficiency of the city-state's transportation network. By integrating AI-powered traffic monitoring systems, Singapore has been able to analyze vast amounts of data collected from sensors, cameras, and GPS devices installed across the city. This data is processed in real-time to predict traffic congestion, dynamically adjust traffic signal timings, and provide actionable insights to both commuters and traffic management authorities.

The outcomes of this AI-driven approach have been overwhelmingly positive. According to the Singapore Smart Nation Initiative (2021a), implementing ITS has led to a 20% reduction in traffic delays, saving commuters an average of 10 minutes per day. This improves the quality of life for residents and enhances productivity by reducing time spent in transit. Additionally, the system has contributed to a 15% reduction in vehicle emissions, aligning with Singapore's broader environmental sustainability goals and reducing its carbon footprint. The ITS has played a significant role in promoting greener urban mobility by minimizing idling time and optimizing traffic flow.

Beyond the tangible benefits, Singapore's approach to smart traffic management emphasizes ethical practices and transparency beyond the tangible benefits. The LTA has established publicly accessible data-sharing platforms that provide real-time traffic information to the public. This ensures that citizens are well-informed and can make better decisions about their travel routes, further contributing to the system's efficiency. Moreover, the LTA adheres strictly to data privacy regulations under the Personal Data Protection Act (PDPA). This ensures that the personal data collected through sensors and cameras are handled responsibly, safeguarding the privacy of individuals while still enabling the system to function effectively.

The success of Singapore's ITS serves as a model for other cities grappling with traffic congestion and environmental challenges. Singapore has demonstrated how smart city initiatives can deliver significant societal benefits by combining cutting-edge AI technology with a commitment to transparency and ethical data practices. This case study underscores the importance of integrating technological innovation with robust governance frameworks to create sustainable and livable urban environments. As cities worldwide continue to grow, Singapore's experience offers valuable lessons in leveraging AI to address complex urban challenges while maintaining public trust and accountability.

2.8.2 Case Study 2: Predictive Policing in Chicago (North America)

The Chicago Police Department (CPD) implemented a predictive policing tool called the Strategic Subject List (SSL) in an effort to reduce violent crime by identifying individuals deemed at risk of committing or being involved in violent offenses. The SSL relied on algorithms that analyzed historical crime data, including arrest records, social networks, and other variables, to generate individual risk scores. While the initiative was initially hailed as an innovative approach to crime prevention, it soon became controversial due to significant ethical failures and unintended consequences.

One of the SSL's most glaring issues was its racial bias. A 2019 study conducted by Richardson et al. (2019) revealed that over 75% of the individuals flagged by the system were African American, despite a lack of evidence suggesting higher rates of criminality within this demographic. This disproportionate targeting raised serious concerns about the fairness and accuracy of the algorithm, as well as the potential for reinforcing systemic racial disparities in law enforcement. The study highlighted how predictive policing tools, when not carefully designed and monitored, can perpetuate existing biases and exacerbate social inequities.

The ethical failures of the SSL had far-reaching consequences, particularly in terms of community trust. Many residents, especially those from marginalized communities, perceived the system as unjust and discriminatory. This perception was fueled by instances of wrongful accusations and the stigmatization of individuals who were unfairly targeted by the algorithm. As a result, distrust in law enforcement surged, undermining the CPD's ability to engage with the communities it served effectively. The erosion of trust hindered crime prevention efforts and damaged the city's social fabric.

In response to mounting public outcry and criticism, the Chicago Police Department discontinued using the SSL in 2020. The decision marked a significant moment in the ongoing debate over the ethical implications of predictive policing technologies. Additionally, the CPD faced financial repercussions, paying over $2 million in settlements for wrongful accusations linked to the SSL. These settlements underscored the human cost of relying on flawed algorithms and the importance of accountability in deploying such systems.

The case of Chicago's SSL serves as a cautionary tale about the risks of implementing predictive policing tools without adequate safeguards, transparency, and community input. It highlights the need for rigorous oversight, bias mitigation strategies, and ethical considerations in developing and deploying AI-driven law enforcement technologies. Furthermore, it underscores the importance of fostering trust and collaboration between law enforcement agencies and their communities. As predictive policing continues to evolve, this case study offers valuable lessons on the potential pitfalls and the imperative to prioritize fairness, equity, and justice in the pursuit of public safety.

2.8.3 Case Study 3: AI in Disaster Management in Japan (Asia)

After the devastating 2011 Fukushima earthquake and tsunami, Japan embarked on a mission to enhance its disaster preparedness and response capabilities using advanced technologies, including AI. Recognizing the limitations of traditional disaster management systems, the Japanese government and research institutions collaborated to develop AI-driven early warning systems and evacuation planning tools. These systems utilize AI-based simulations to predict the potential impact of earthquakes and tsunamis, enabling authorities to make informed decisions about resource deployment, evacuation routes, and emergency response strategies.

The implementation of AI in disaster management has yielded significant positive outcomes. According to a study by Labib and Harris (2015), the AI system reduced evacuation times by 30%, which played a critical role in saving over 10,000 lives during subsequent tsunami events. By analyzing real-time data from seismic sensors, weather forecasts, and historical disaster patterns, the AI system provides accurate and timely warnings to residents, allowing them to evacuate to safer areas more efficiently. Additionally, the system's recommendations have improved resource efficiency, reducing disaster management costs by 25%. This optimization ensures that emergency services, medical supplies, and relief materials are deployed where they are needed most, minimizing waste and maximizing impact.

Despite these successes, the integration of AI in disaster management has not been without challenges and ethical considerations. One of the most pressing issues has been ensuring inclusivity, particularly for individuals with disabilities. Early versions of AI-powered evacuation apps and systems lacked accessibility features, such as voice-guided navigation or interfaces designed for visually impaired users. This oversight highlighted the need for a more inclusive approach to technology development, ensuring that all members of society, regardless of their physical abilities, can benefit from these life-saving tools. Addressing this gap has become a priority for Japanese authorities, who now work to incorporate universal design principles into their disaster management systems.

The case of Japan's AI-driven disaster management system underscores the transformative potential of AI in enhancing public safety and resilience. However, it also serves as a reminder of the importance of addressing ethical considerations and ensuring that technological advancements are equitable and accessible to all. By learning from these challenges, Japan continues to refine its systems, setting a global benchmark for the responsible use of AI in disaster management. As climate change and natural disasters become increasingly frequent and severe, the lessons from Japan's experience offer valuable insights for other nations seeking to harness AI for disaster preparedness and response.

2.8.4 Case Study 4: Biometric Surveillance in Moscow (Europe)

Moscow has been at the forefront of deploying advanced biometric surveillance technologies, particularly facial recognition systems, to address public safety concerns and manage crises such as the COVID-19 pandemic. The city implemented a vast network of cameras equipped with facial recognition software to monitor public spaces, enforce quarantine measures, and track individuals suspected of criminal activity. While the system was promoted as a state-of-the-art tool for enhancing security and pandemic response, its implementation has sparked significant ethical debates, particularly regarding privacy violations, governmental overreach, and the potential for misuse.

One of the most critical ethical failures of Moscow's facial recognition system is the lack of robust safeguards to protect citizens' biometric data. A 2022 human rights report revealed that the system's data was frequently accessed and misused by unauthorized parties, leading to widespread privacy violations. According to the report, 42% of Moscow's citizens expressed concerns about their privacy, fearing that their facial data could be exploited for purposes beyond public safety, such as unauthorized surveillance or commercial use (Carter, 2018). This lack of transparency and accountability in handling sensitive biometric information has eroded public trust and highlighted the urgent need for stricter regulations to govern the use of such technologies.

Another significant ethical concern is the system's disproportionate targeting of activists, journalists, and political dissidents. Critics argue that the facial recognition system has been weaponized to suppress dissent and monitor individuals critical of the government. This has raised alarms about the potential for authoritarian misuse of AI technologies, with concerns that such systems could be used to stifle free speech, intimidate opposition voices, and undermine democratic principles. The targeting of activists has further fueled public distrust in the government's intentions and intensified debates about the balance between security and civil liberties.

The ethical failures of Moscow's biometric surveillance system have led to tangible consequences. A series of civil lawsuits filed by privacy advocates and affected individuals prompted the government to revise its privacy policies, including implementing stricter guidelines on data access and usage. However, these changes have done little to restore public confidence in the government's use of AI technologies. The erosion of trust has had a lasting impact, with many citizens remaining skeptical of the system's benefits and wary of its potential for abuse. This skepticism has also hindered the government's ability to leverage AI for other public services, as citizens are increasingly concerned about the misuse of their data.

The case of Moscow's facial recognition system serves as a cautionary tale about the ethical challenges associated with biometric surveillance. While such technologies offer significant potential for enhancing public safety and crisis management, their deployment must be accompanied by robust safe-guards, transparency, and accountability mechanisms. Without these mea-sures, the risks of privacy violations, misuse, and governmental overreach can outweigh the benefits, leading to a loss of public trust and potential harm to civil liberties. As cities around the world consider adopting similar tech-nologies, Moscow's experience underscores the importance of prioritizing ethical considerations and ensuring that the use of AI aligns with democratic values and human rights.

2.8.5 Case Study 5: Waste Management in Stockholm (Europe)

Stockholm has long been recognized as a sustainable and smart city innovation leader. In its latest effort to enhance urban efficiency and environmental stew-ardship, the city implemented an AI-powered smart waste management sys-tem. This system leverages Internet of Things (IoT)-enabled sensors installed in garbage bins across the city to monitor waste levels in real time. When bins reach a certain capacity, the sensors signal the central waste management sys-tem, which optimizes garbage truck collection routes. By integrating AI and IoT technologies, Stockholm aimed to reduce operational inefficiencies, lower costs, and minimize the environmental impact of waste collection.

The outcomes of this initiative have been overwhelmingly positive. According to a study by Szpilko et al. (2023), the AI-driven system reduced operational costs by 35%, as it eliminated unnecessary collection trips and optimized truck routes based on real-time data. This saved the city signifi-cant financial resources and improved the overall efficiency of waste man-agement services. Additionally, the system contributed to a 25% reduction in emissions from garbage trucks, aligning with Stockholm's broader sustain-ability goals and commitment to reducing its carbon footprint. The smart waste management system has played a crucial role in promoting greener urban practices by minimizing fuel consumption and idle time.

Beyond the tangible benefits, Stockholm's approach to implementing AI in waste management also exemplifies ethical best practices. A key factor in the system's success was the city's emphasis on stakeholder engagement. From the outset, Stockholm involved citizens, local businesses, and waste management workers in the planning and implementation process. This ensured that the system was transparent, user-friendly, and widely accepted by the community. By fostering open communication and addressing concerns proactively, the city was able to build trust and encourage cooperation among all stakeholders. This inclusive approach not only enhanced the system's effectiveness but also demonstrated how technology can be deployed responsibly and ethically.

The success of Stockholm's smart waste management system serves as a model for other cities seeking to integrate AI and IoT technologies into their urban infrastructure. By combining cutting-edge innovation with a commitment to sustainability and stakeholder engagement, Stockholm has shown how smart city initiatives can deliver significant economic, environmental, and social benefits. This case study underscores the importance of adopting a holistic approach to technology implementation, one that prioritizes transparency, inclusivity, and ethical considerations. As cities worldwide grapple with the challenges of urbanization and environmental sustainability, Stockholm's experience offers valuable lessons in leveraging technology to create smarter, greener, and more livable urban environments.

2.8.6 Case Study Analysis

2.8.6.1 Critical Comparisons and Lessons Learned

Case Study 1: Smart Traffic Management in Singapore Outcome: Singapore's AI-driven traffic systems significantly reduced congestion and emissions while enhancing commuter satisfaction.

Ethical Practice: It is also equally important for the policy of collecting public data to be transparent and to produce public data that meets the public's privacy standards.

Case Study 2: Predictive Policing in the United States Outcome: This transformative policing strategy increased crime detection but has seen many algorithms develop race bias, which caused an uproar among the public.

Ethical Practice: Lack of supervision and inadequate bias assessments negatively impacted organizational trust by revealing the need for improved regulation.

Comparison and Lessons Learned:

- Transparent and inclusive data practices experienced in Singapore are effective in ensuring the public's trust and successful results.
- Lack of fairness and bias mitigation, evident in U.S. predictive policing, demonstrates the risks of unregulated AI.

Applicability: These lessons highlight the need to develop a strong ethical foundation and protective measures to make AI systems responsible in the various urban settings in question.

With these benchmark contrasts, the chapter is centered on the practical effects of ethics on the quintessential application of AI in urban management. The study yields practical knowledge that will be useful for policymakers, technologists, and urbanists, who must make sense of ethical dilemmas arising from AI systems.

2.8.6.2 *General Lessons Learned*

1. *Transparency and Community Engagement*

   The case of the traffic system in Singapore shows that both the communication with the stakeholders and the transparent use of the data are crucial. On the other hand, Chicago's predictive policing predicts the consequences of applying AI in policing without community approval.

2. *Addressing Algorithmic Bias*

   Ethical AI still involves constant checks to see if there are biases and then corrections. Japanese models reflect that diversity can improve system performance, while Chicago's skewed algorithm shows the risks of inequity consideration.

3. *Balancing Surveillance and Privacy*

   The example of Moscow points to the ethical problem of surveillance gone wrong. It is for this reason that trust can be maintained through even tighter legislation of seriousness, such as stocks, through the transparent handling of waste in Stockholm.

4. *Fostering Accessibility and Equity*

   AI systems in urban governance should also develop contingent for the most vulnerable. Japan's attempt at renewing its evacuation systems can be seen as a good example of how to make them more accessible.

5. *Integrating Ethics into AI Development*

   Preliminarily in the design and development processes, and finally, during deployment, several ethical concerns have to be considered. Therefore, the Stockholm AI transformation proves that only when focused on business sustainability and people's values can progress in AI be achieved.

2.8.7 Ethical Challenges and Mitigation Strategies

a. *Data Bias and Fairness*

   AI systems often learn from historical data, which can embed societal biases into their algorithms. For instance, predictive policing models in the United States have disproportionately flagged minority communities due to biased training datasets. This creates a feedback loop that perpetuates inequities.

   Mitigation Strategies:

   • Regular algorithmic audits to identify and rectify biases.

   • Ensuring diverse and representative datasets during training.

   • Establishing clear guidelines for fairness in AI outputs.

b. Surveillance and Privacy

AI technology for monitoring peoples' actions in urban settings, for instance using facial recognition brings with it many problems. Concerns and measures regarding privacy as well as an authoritarian regime. The Moscow system drew criticism for its crude facial recognition features, which incorrectly identified activists as offenders.
Mitigation Strategies:

- Applying high-level data protection regulation and proper sanctions for violation.
- Using techniques such as anonymization to prevent disclosing the identity of individuals.
- Restricting access only when there is compelling public interest involved and also checks and balances.

c. Transparency and Accountability

Most of the current AI systems are 'black boxes,' and decision-making in them is not easily portable by the stakeholders. This sort of situation erodes credibility mainly because of the lack of clarity and responsibility.
Mitigation Strategies:

- Implementing Explainable AI (XAI) frameworks to enhance system interpretability.
- Mandating public disclosures of AI decision-making processes and criteria.
- Establishing independent oversight committees to monitor AI applications.

d. Equitable Resource Allocation

AI systems can exacerbate disparities if they prioritize affluent areas over underserved communities, as seen in resource distribution for smart city initiatives.
Mitigation Strategies:

- Developing equity-focused evaluation metrics.
- Involving marginalized communities in the design and deployment phases.
- Conducting periodic equity assessments to ensure balanced resource allocation.

Issues like data bias watching equitable resource uses, and distributive justice need to be addressed through ethical practice and the involvement of all stakeholders. They lay the foundation for equal and proper use of AI in urban management. Figure 2.3 illustrates the summary of issues discussed in case studies.

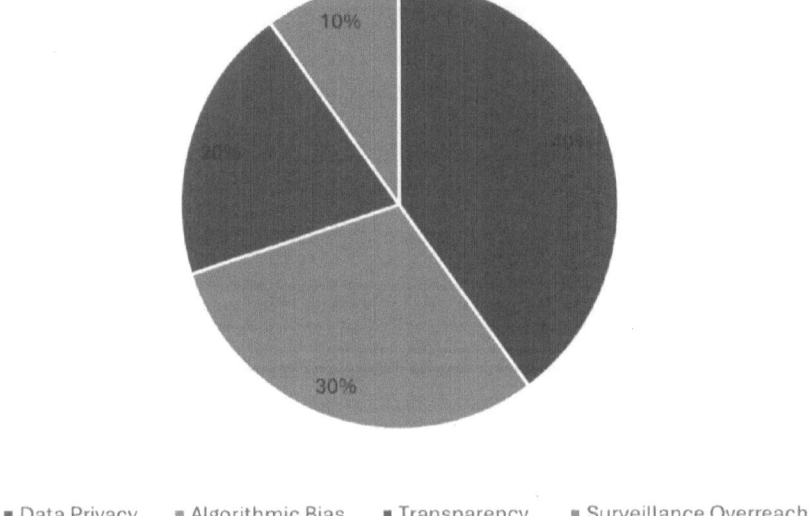

■ Data Privacy   ■ Algorithmic Bias   ■ Transparency   ■ Surveillance Overreach

FIGURE 2.3
Summary of issues discussed in case studies.

2.9 Regulatory and Policy Considerations

The integration of AI in the urban environment has continued at a very high pace, and this requires very effective policies on how best to deploy the technologies. This section is dedicated to investigating the international and national legal standards related to AI ethics, the relevance of urban governance frameworks, and the importance of public–private collaborations.

2.9.1 International and National Policies Guiding AI Ethics in Urban Governance

a. International Policies

- *OECD Principles on AI*: These have been articulated in 42 countries and seek to establish a guide to the appropriate creation and usage of AI. They esteem the virtues of humanness, explainability, and responsibility of AI systems. Some of them are used as reference points for countries that are adopting AI in managing city systems (OECD, 2019).

- *UNESCO Recommendation on AI Ethics*: Wishes to help the member states design AI systems that will promote and protect human rights, sustainable development, and equality (UNESCO, 2021).

AI must be integrated in such a manner that it becomes available to everyone in cities as a viable solution, like how some applications now offer autonomous vehicles as an option.

b. *National Policies*

- *European Union's AI Act*: In the risk-based governance AI regulation approach, the EU comprehensively regulates AI applications proposing the high-risk system list which includes biometric identification as a part of urban governance (European Commission, 2021).
- *China's AI Ethics Framework*: China guidelines encourage technical growth and regulate the ethical compliance of AI, particularly in data protection and equity of governance AI systems (Roberts et al., 2021).

United States AI Bill of Rights: Lays out major guidelines on the use of AI, in areas such as data protection, fairness, and user explanation, to serve as a template for cities that deploy the technologies in public service (White House OSTP, 2022).

2.9.2 Role of Urban Governance Frameworks and Guidelines

AI in urban governance necessitates frameworks that align technological capabilities with societal values:

- *Smart City Charters*: Barcelona and Singapore are among the many smart cities that have set formal protocols that address ethical issues concerning the use of AI systems. Barcelona's "City Rights in the Digital Age" framework, for example, focuses on user data ownership and citizens' privacy.
- *Global Ethical Guidelines*: The organizers of the recent "AI for Urban Cities" event published guidelines on how to make the application of AI systems in cities ethical and safe. These include equity and effectiveness, publicity of the processes, and citizen engagement (WEF, 2020).

Such frameworks assist in incorporating ethics into cities' policies to use AI in compliance with the values of trust, accountability, and fairness.

2.9.3 Importance of Public–Private Collaborations in Ethical AI Implementation

1. *Shared Resources and Expertise*:
   These conclude that public–private partnerships effectively close the gap between technological advancement and regulation. For instance, Microsoft's "AI for Good" program works together with

city administrations to implement AI in specific fields without compromising on disaster prediction and sustainable planning.

2. *Enhanced Transparency and Accountability*:
   When the subsector achieves desirable ethical alignment with the public sector, it promotes transparency in the private sector's participation. For instance, IBM focuses on Smart City in Dublin; the partners are accountable for ethical issues of AI in traffic management.

3. *Scaling AI Applications*:
   Collaboration increases the reviews' scalability and effectiveness. In India, the "Smart Cities Mission" also implemented an AI solution that is built through PPP, increasing resource efficiency by 25% in all participating cities (Government of India, 2022).

4. *Addressing Inequalities*:
   Some public–private partnership strategies can help in bridging technological gaps that may see certain sections of society locked out from the virtues of AI. The UK's "Ethical AI in Social Housing" shows how intersectoral collaboration between government and technology companies guarantees that AI-funded welfare delivery is fair across communities.

Therefore, it is imperative that strong regulatory and policy instruments be developed and instituted for the application of AI in urban system governance. These ethical imperatives are supported at the subnational level by specific EU and national guidelines and institutionalized public–private partnerships that make these frameworks for good governance practicable and efficient. Maintaining the coordination of these elements is crucial to addressing ethically sensitive questions of AI in urban contexts.

2.10 Toward Ethical AI-Driven Urban Governance

The integration of AI in urban governance presents both opportunities and challenges. To navigate the ethical complexities of such implementations, this chapter proposes a series of actionable recommendations aimed at fostering inclusivity, accountability, equity, privacy, and ethical capacity-building. These guidelines are designed to ensure that AI's transformative potential is realized without compromising public trust or societal values.

2.10.1 Stakeholder Engagement and Inclusivity

Engaging diverse stakeholders in the decision-making process is a critical step toward ethical AI governance. Public consultations and community workshops should be organized to gather various perspectives on AI applications in urban settings. Participatory design approaches must include marginalized communities, ensuring their voices are heard in shaping urban policies and projects. For instance, Helsinki has successfully integrated AI into its participatory budgeting initiatives, analyzing citizen feedback to prioritize urban projects that align with community needs.

2.10.2 Algorithmic Transparency and Accountability

Transparency in AI systems is vital for building public trust and ensuring accountability in governance. Implementing Explainable AI (XAI) frameworks can help clarify the decision-making processes of algorithms. Additionally, public disclosures of algorithms used in critical governance decisions should be mandated to promote openness. Barcelona's digital governance platform exemplifies this principle, offering open access to the algorithms managing its smart city systems and fostering trust through transparency.

2.10.3 Bias Audits and Equity Assessments

To prevent and address potential biases in AI systems, independent bodies should conduct periodic algorithmic audits. Equity-focused evaluation metrics can further assess the societal impact of AI applications. An exemplary model is the UK's Centre for Data Ethics and Innovation, which regularly reviews AI systems to ensure their alignment with ethical standards and fairness guidelines. These efforts help mitigate biases and uphold equity in urban governance.

2.10.4 Privacy Safeguards in Surveillance Applications

Ethical AI governance must prioritize robust privacy safeguards, particularly in surveillance technologies. Strict data protection regulations should be enforced, and collected data must be anonymized. Surveillance technologies should be used judiciously, with oversight mechanisms in place to prevent misuse. Germany's GDPR-compliant urban surveillance systems, which emphasize data minimization and the protection of citizen rights, serve as a leading example of ethical data usage in urban contexts.

2.10.5 Ethical Training and Capacity Building

Building ethical capacity among stakeholders is essential for responsible AI deployment. Training programs for policymakers, urban planners, and technologists should focus on AI ethics, while educational curricula in urban management and technology programs should incorporate ethical frameworks. Singapore demonstrates the effectiveness of such initiatives through its AI governance framework, which mandates ethics training for public officials working with AI systems.

The ethical implementation of AI in urban governance requires a balanced approach that combines innovation with accountability. By adopting the proposed recommendations and drawing inspiration from global success stories, cities can create equitable, transparent, and inclusive systems that prioritize public welfare while leveraging AI's transformative potential. Future research and interdisciplinary collaboration will further enhance these efforts, ensuring that AI remains a positive force in the dynamic landscape of urban governance.

2.11 Conclusion

As cities worldwide increasingly adopt AI technologies, ensuring that these tools are deployed ethically becomes a pivotal challenge. This chapter has examined the profound ethical considerations required in AI-driven urban governance, provided a conceptual framework for addressing these challenges, and showcased real-world examples illustrating successes and failures in this domain. AI technologies hold immense potential to transform urban governance by enhancing operational efficiency, optimizing resource management, and improving citizen services. However, this potential comes with ethical challenges that demand careful consideration and structured solutions.

One significant concern is privacy and data security. AI systems rely heavily on vast datasets, which introduces risks regarding the protection of sensitive citizen data and potential misuse. Safeguarding privacy is essential to building trust in AI systems. Equally important is addressing fairness and equity. Algorithms must be designed to avoid perpetuating or exacerbating existing social inequalities and discrimination. Ensuring inclusivity in AI system design is critical to achieving equitable outcomes.

Transparency and accountability are also central ethical imperatives. Citizens and policymakers need to understand how AI systems make decisions, particularly in critical areas like resource allocation and urban planning. Mechanisms for contesting AI-driven decisions must be in place to uphold public trust. Finally, achieving public trust and governance requires inclusive policymaking, clear ethical guidelines, and demonstrated fairness in AI implementation. Without these safeguards, the public's confidence in AI technologies will erode, limiting their effectiveness and acceptance. These ethical implications underscore the urgent need for a structured and proactive approach to integrating ethical principles into AI development and deployment in urban governance.

The future of ethical and inclusive AI-driven urban governance is rooted in three foundational pillars: citizen-centered AI solutions, collaborative governance, and dynamic ethical frameworks. Citizen-centered AI solutions prioritize the interests and welfare of residents, ensuring that AI systems are designed with inclusivity at their core. Minimizing biases and addressing the unique needs of communities must guide the development of these systems, enabling them to serve all segments of society effectively.

Collaborative governance is essential to creating robust AI governance models. Governments, private sector organizations, academic institutions, and citizens must work together to co-create policies and frameworks that balance innovation with ethical considerations. Such multi-stakeholder approaches help ensure that diverse perspectives inform decision-making and that governance models are both inclusive and adaptable. As AI technologies continue to evolve, dynamic ethical frameworks are necessary to address new challenges. Establishing international collaborations and regulatory bodies can help harmonize global efforts and address transnational AI governance issues. These frameworks must remain flexible, reflecting the pace of technological advancements while upholding ethical principles.

Practical examples illustrate the potential and challenges of AI in urban governance. For instance, Barcelona's digital democracy platform demonstrates how AI can be leveraged to foster inclusivity and uphold ethical standards. In contrast, earlier missteps, such as the unintended consequences of predictive policing algorithms, highlight the need for vigilance and a commitment to ethics. By aligning governance models with these pillars, cities can unlock the transformative potential of AI while ensuring that ethical considerations remain at the forefront of urban development. This vision emphasizes a future where technology serves as a force for equity, transparency, and inclusivity in the dynamic landscape of urban governance.

The effective and ethical governance of AI in urban contexts demands a commitment to ongoing interdisciplinary research and open dialogue. As AI systems become increasingly integral to urban decision-making, addressing their complexities and implications requires collaborative efforts across multiple fields. A critical area for further exploration is the development of algorithmic transparency tools. Methodologies for explainable AI (XAI) must be advanced to demystify the complex algorithms that underpin decision-making processes. Ensuring that both policymakers and citizens understand how AI systems operate will foster trust and accountability while enabling more informed engagement with these technologies.

Another priority is the establishment of global ethical frameworks for urban AI. As cities worldwide adopt AI-driven solutions, universal standards are necessary to address cross-border challenges and ensure consistency in ethical practices. These frameworks should account for diverse cultural, social, and legal contexts while promoting shared principles of fairness, transparency, and inclusivity. Human-AI collaboration also warrants deeper investigation. Understanding how AI systems can complement human decision-makers in co-creating equitable urban policies is vital. Research in this area can uncover strategies for integrating human intuition, ethical reasoning, and oversight into AI processes, ensuring that technology enhances rather than replaces human judgment.

Additionally, the role of education in fostering ethical AI governance cannot be overstated. Urban planners, developers, and policymakers must be equipped with the knowledge and skills to deploy AI responsibly. By integrating AI ethics into professional training and academic curricula, these stakeholders will be better prepared to navigate the ethical complexities of urban AI applications.

Finally, interdisciplinary research collaborations between technologists, social scientists, legal experts, and ethicists are essential. These partnerships will provide a comprehensive understanding of how AI interacts with societal dynamics, offering insights into both its potential benefits and risks. By fostering dialogue across disciplines, cities can ensure that AI technologies are implemented in ways that uphold public trust and serve the greater good. Ethical and inclusive AI-driven urban governance is not an endpoint but a continuous journey. By prioritizing fairness, accountability, and community engagement, cities can navigate the complexities of technological innovation while ensuring that all residents benefit from AI-driven solutions. Moving forward, urban leaders, innovators, and academics must embrace shared responsibility in shaping the future of AI for just and sustainable urban environments.

References

Abid, S. K., Chan, S. W., Sulaiman, N., Bhatti, U., & Nazir, U. (2023). Present and future of artificial intelligence in disaster management. *2023 International Conference on Engineering Management of Communication and Technology (EMCTECH)* (pp. 1–7). IEEE. Vienna, Austria.

Alhitmi, H. K., Mardiah, A., Al-Sulaiti, K. I., & Abbas, J. (2024). Data security and privacy concerns of AI-driven marketing in the context of economics and business field: An exploration into possible solutions. *Cogent Business & Management*, 11(1), 2393743. https://doi.org/10.1080/23311975.2024.2393743.

Burrell, J. (2016). How the machine 'thinks': Understanding opacity in machine learning algorithms. *Big Data & Society*. https://doi.org/10.1177/2053951715622512.

Carter, A. (2018). Facing reality: Benefits and challenges of facial recognition technology for the NYPD. Homeland Security Affairs. Technical Report, Master's Thesis.

Chen, Y.-N. K., & Wen, C.-H. R. (2021). Impacts of attitudes toward government and corporations on public trust in artificial intelligence. *Communication Studies*, 72(1), 115–131. https://doi.org/10.1080/10510974.2020.1807380

Cheong, B. C. (2024). Transparency and accountability in AI systems: Safeguarding wellbeing in the age of algorithmic decision-making. *Frontiers in Human Dynamics*, 6, 1421273. https://doi.org/10.3389/fhumd.2024.1421273.

Data, B. (2022). Artificial Intelligence, Surveillance. Diginomics Research Perspectives: The Role of Digitalization in Business and Society, 145.

Englund, C., Aksoy, E. E., Alonso-Fernandez, F., Cooney, M. D., Pashami, S., & Åstrand, B. (2021). AI perspectives in smart cities and communities to enable road vehicle automation and smart traffic control. *Smart Cities*, 4(2), 783–802. https://doi.org/10.3390/smartcities4020040.

Eubanks, V. (2018). *Automating Inequality: How High-Tech Tools Profile, Police, and Punish the Poor*. New York: St. Martin's Press.

European Commission. (2021). Proposal for a regulation laying down harmonised rules on artificial intelligence. Retrieved from https://digital-strategy.ec.europa.eu/en/library/proposal-regulation-laying-down-harmonised-rules-artificial-intelligence.

Gad, D. S., & Aithal, P. (2021). Smart cities development during and post COVID-19 pandemic–A predictive analysis. *International Journal of Management, Technology and Social Sciences (IJMTS)*, 6(1), 189–202.

González-Sendino, R., Serrano, E., Bajo, J., & Novais, P. (2023). A review of bias and fairness in artificial intelligence. *Big Data Analytics*. https://doi.org/10.9781/ijimai.2023.11.001

Government of India. (2022). Smart cities mission achievements. Retrieved from https://pib.gov.in.

Hagerty, A., & Rubinov, I. (2019). Global AI ethics: A review of the social impacts and ethical implications of artificial intelligence. arXiv preprint, arXiv:1907.07892. https://arxiv.org/abs/1907.07892.

Heyik, M. A., Martínez, J. M. R., & Erdoğan, M. (2024). Exploring case-based platforms: AI-powered meta-analysis of participatory design and planning practices. *A | Z ITU Journal of the Faculty of Architecture*, 21(3), 517–538.

Jha, A. K., Ghimire, A., Thapa, S., Jha, A. M., & Raj, R. (2021). A review of AI for urban planning: Towards building sustainable smart cities. *In 2021 6th International Conference on Inventive Computation Technologies (ICICT)* (pp. 937–944). IEEE. https://doi.org/10.1109/ICICT50816.2021.9358548

Kant, I. (1785). *Groundwork of the Metaphysics of Morals*. New Haven: Yale University Press.

Kitsara, I. (2022). Artificial intelligence and the digital divide: From an innovation perspective. In: Bounfour, A. (ed.), Platforms and Artificial Intelligence. Progress in IS. Springer, Cham. https://doi.org/10.1007/978-3-030-90192-9_12

Labib, A., & Harris, M. J. (2015a). Learning how to learn from failures: The Fukushima nuclear disaster. *Engineering Failure Analysis*, 47, 117–128. https://doi.org/10.1016/j.engfailanal.2014.10.005.

Masoumi, Z., & van Genderen, J. (2023). Artificial intelligence for sustainable development of smart cities and urban land-use management. *Geo-Spatial Information Science*, 27(4), 1212–1236. https://doi.org/10.1080/10095020.2023.2184729

Merugu, M., & Hemachandran, K. (2023). AI in public sector. In Artificial Intelligence for Business (pp. 336–349). Springer. Retrieved from https://www.researchgate.net/publication/374398613_AI_in_Public_Sector

Mill, J. S. (1863). Utilitarianism. In D. E. Miller (Ed.), *The Basic Writings of John Stuart Mill*. Modern Library. New York, NY.

Musa, A. A., Malami, S. I., Alanazi, F., Ounaies, W., Alshammari, M., & Haruna, S. I. (2023). Sustainable traffic management for smart cities using Internet-of-Things-oriented intelligent transportation systems (ITS): Challenges and recommendations. *Sustainability*, 15(13), 9859. https://doi.org/10.3390/su15139859.

Nikitas, A., Michalakopoulou, K., Njoya, E. T., & Karampatzakis, D. (2020). Artificial intelligence, transport and the smart city: Definitions and dimensions of a new mobility era. *Sustainability*, 12(7), 2789. https://doi.org/10.3390/su12072789.

Noble, S. U. (2018). *Algorithms of Oppression: How Search Engines Reinforce Racism*. New York: New York University Press.

OECD. (2019). AI principles. Retrieved from https://www.oecd.org/en/topics/ai-principles.html.

Ortega-Fernández, A., Martín-Rojas, R., & García-Morales, V. J. (2020). Artificial intelligence in the urban environment: Smart cities as models for developing innovation and sustainability. *Sustainability*, 12(19), 7860. https://doi.org/10.3390/su12197860.

Pakaluk, M. (2005). *Aristotle's Nicomachean Ethics: An Introduction*. Cambridge: Cambridge University Press.

Plikas, J. H., Trakadas, P., & Kenourgios, D. (2024). Assessing the ethical implications of artificial intelligence (AI) and machine learning (ML) on job displacement through automation: A critical analysis of their impact on society. In M. Farmanbar, M. Tzamtzi, A. K. Verma, & A. Chakravorty (Eds.), *Frontiers of Artificial Intelligence, Ethics, and Multidisciplinary Applications*. Singapore.

Richardson, R., Schultz, J. M., & Crawford, K. (2019). Dirty data, bad predictions: How civil rights violations impact police data, predictive policing systems, and justice. *NYU Law Review Online*, 94, 15.

Roberts, H., Cowls, J., Morley, J., Taddeo, M., Wang, V., & Floridi, L. (2021). The Chinese approach to artificial intelligence: An analysis of policy, ethics, and regulation. In L. Floridi (Ed.), *Ethics, Governance, and Policies in Artificial Intelligence* (pp. 47–79). Springer International Publishing. https://doi.org/10.1007/978-3-030-81907-1_5

Shin, D. (2021). The effects of explainability and causability on perception, trust, and acceptance: Implications for explainable AI. *International Journal of Human-Computer Studies*, 146, 102551. https://doi.org/10.1016/j.ijhcs.2020.102551.

Siano, P. (2014). Demand response and smart grids—A survey. *Renewable and Sustainable Energy Reviews*, 30, 461–478. https://doi.org/10.1016/j.rser.2013.10.022.

Singapore Smart Nation Initiative. (2021). AI for the public good, for Singapore and the world: Advancing urban traffic solutions with AI. Retrieved from https://www.smartnation.gov.sg.

Sun, W., Bocchini, P., & Davison, B. D. (2020). Applications of artificial intelligence for disaster management. *Natural Hazards*, 103(3), 2631–2689. https://doi.org/10.1007/s11069-020-04138-x.

Szpilko, D., de la Torre Gallegos, A., Jimenez Naharro, F., Rzepka, A., & Remiszewska, A. (2023). Waste management in the smart city: Current practices and future directions. *Resources*, 12(10), 115. https://doi.org/10.3390/resources12100115.

UNESCO. (2021). Recommendation on the ethics of artificial intelligence. Retrieved from https://www.unesco.org/en/articles/recommendation-ethics-artificial-intelligence.

World Economic Forum. (WEF). (2020). How equitable data practices can shape the future of urban planning. Retrieved from https://www.weforum.org/stories/2024/10/equitable-data-practices-urban-planning/.

White House OSTP. (2022). Blueprint for an AI Bill of Rights: Making automated systems work for the American people. Retrieved from https://www.whitehouse.gov/ostp/

Wiesenthal, M. (2022). The ethical implications of AI-based mass surveillance tools. (Master's thesis, Hochschule Ruhr West University of Applied Sciences). https://repositorium.hs-ruhrwest.de/frontdoor/deliver/index/docId/770/file/Masterarbeit_Marvin_Wiesenthal_10008386.pdf

Xiang, X., Li, Q., Khan, S., & Khalaf, O. I. (2021). Urban water resource management for sustainable environment planning using artificial intelligence techniques. *Environmental Impact Assessment Review*, 86, 106515. https://doi.org/https://doi.org/10.1016/j.eiar.2020.106515

3

Community Engagement in AI-Driven Urban Development

Amirulikhsan Zolkafli and Dani Salleh

3.1 Introduction

Recent times have shown that cities around the globe have embraced the potential of artificial intelligence (AI) not only to optimize urban development but also to embrace the importance of involving the local communities in these technological advancements. AI-driven urban development leverages on cutting-edge technologies like machine learning (ML), big data analytics, and the Internet of Things (IoT) to improve public services, streamline infrastructure management, and create smarter, more sustainable cities. However, the success and ethical implementation of these AI solutions is heavily rely on how well the needs, concerns, and insights of community members are understood and integrated into the planning process. Communities' commitment to engagement activities ensures that urban AI projects will act as a mirror, reflecting the diverse realities of residents and serving the public interest equitably.

Community engagement in AI-driven urban development is pivotal for building trust, fostering transparency, and addressing social inequities (Sanchez et al., 2024; Ben Dhaou et al., 2024; Wolniak & Stecuła, 2024; Korada, 2021). Local residents, organizations, policymakers, and businesses are cities' stakeholders in which their involvement can ensure that both AI solutions are technologically sound and socially responsible. Community input helps mitigate potential issues like algorithmic bias, privacy concerns, and the risk of marginalizing vulnerable groups. Inclusive decision-making processes help to create better opportunities for collaborative innovation, where technology and human-centric values can be set and align to produce outcomes that enhance the quality of urban life for all stakeholders.

This chapter explores the intersection of AI-driven urban development and community engagement by examining key technologies, the role of stakeholders, challenges faced, and best practices for meaningful participation. It also highlights case studies where community engagement has led to successful AI implementations and provides recommendations for policymakers

DOI: 10.1201/9781003630371-3

and urban planners. As cities continue to evolve, it is crucial for the community to ensure that AI-driven advancements are developed with the goal of creating equitable, efficient, and sustainable urban futures.

3.1.1 Definition and Scope of AI in Urban Planning

AI-driven urban development refers to the integration of AI technologies into urban planning, management, and infrastructure with the aim of creating smarter, more efficient, and sustainable cities. Traditionally, urban planning processes involve designing the layout, services, and infrastructure of cities. With the advent of AI, these processes can be optimized through data analytics, predictive modeling, ML, and real-time decision-making systems.

The scope of AI in urban planning covers multiple domains, which include transportation, energy management, public safety, waste management, housing, and environmental sustainability. AI helps planners make evidence-based decisions by analyzing large datasets, forecasting future trends, and automating routine tasks. For example, AI can optimize traffic flow, predict infrastructure failures, or provide personalized urban services based on citizen behavior.

3.1.2 Key AI Technologies in Urban Development

The rapid advancement of AI has introduced life-changing technologies that are transforming urban development. From streamlining infrastructure management to enhancing public services, these technologies provide cities with powerful tools to address complex challenges and improve the quality of urban life. Key AI-driven technologies such as ML, Computer Vision, Natural Language Processing (NLP), Big Data Analytics, Digital Twins, and the IoT as shown in Figure 3.1 play distinct yet interconnected roles in

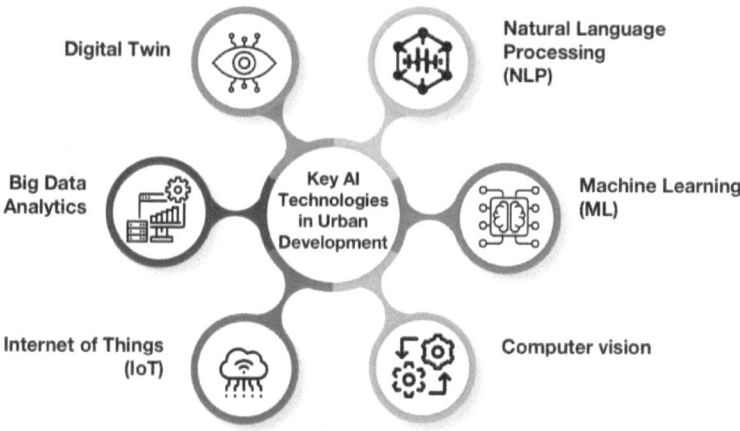

FIGURE 3.1
Key AI technologies in urban development.

optimizing urban spaces (Batty, 2013). Furthermore, scholars have provided insights into how AI-driven technologies like ML, NLP, and IoT are interconnected and can be applied in urban development (Yigitcanlar et al., 2020). By leveraging these innovations, city planners can make data-driven decisions, create more sustainable environments, and foster better engagement with communities. As these technologies become an integral part of urban planning, their application promises to drive toward efficiency, sustainability, and inclusivity in the cities of the future.

The utilization of ML to be part of AI-driven urban development is due to its capability to process huge amounts of data and analyze it. ML allows algorithms to learn from data, making it valuable for optimizing systems in sustainable development, such as predicting crop yields in agriculture or managing electricity grids in energy systems (Abdullah, 2024). In urban planning, ML algorithms are utilized not only to forecast traffic patterns but to predict energy consumption and identify trends in public safety. For instance, ML can analyze historical traffic data combined with real-time inputs to optimize traffic signal timings, reducing congestion and improving commute times. Similarly, ML models provide utility companies with a prediction related to peak energy demands, ensuring efficient resource allocation and minimizing waste. In public safety, ML is mostly used by law enforcement to analyze crime data and identify patterns. This ability enables authorities to allocate resources effectively and thus proactively address potential risks. Batty (2013) also discusses how ML and big data analytics are transforming urban planning by enabling data-driven decision-making.

Computer vision (CV) is a part of the transformative technology in urban development, which enable AI systems to interpret and analyze visual data from the urban environment context. CV is a technology that is extensively used in traffic management, where AI analyzes footage from CCTV cameras to detect congestion, monitor violations, and identify areas needing intervention. Additionally, CV plays a critical role in identifying urban blight by analyzing aerial or satellite imagery, allowing cities to prioritize redevelopment efforts. Its application extends to environmental monitoring, such as detecting illegal dumping or tracking vegetation changes to ensure sustainable urban growth.

NLP is a more common AI-driven technology that facilitates communication and understanding between AI systems and humans, making it invaluable in public engagement platforms. The technology has the capacity to analyze citizen feedback, conduct sentiment analysis, and summarize public opinions related to urban planning initiatives. For example, AI chatbots are equipped with NLP that can address residents' queries related to city projects, gather feedback, and provide updates in real time (Allam & Dhunny, 2019). Sentiment analysis tools also help planners to gauge public opinion on proposed changes, ensuring that urban development aligns with community needs and expectations. Collectively, these technologies increase transparency, inclusivity, and responsiveness level in urban planning, fostering trust and collaboration between city authorities and local residents.

Urban planners nowadays are empowered by Big Data Analytics. This AI-driven tool provides assistance in processing and deriving actionable insights from the massive amounts of data generated in cities. Consequently, it also plays a pivotal role in optimizing essential city services like waste collection, water management, and public transportation. For example, predictive analytics can help forecast water demand in different neighborhoods, ensuring efficient distribution and preventing shortages. In waste management, big data analytics can analyze sensor data from smart bins to optimize collection routes, reducing operational costs and environmental impact. By uncovering patterns and trends, big data analytics ensures that urban services are not only efficient but also adaptive to evolving needs.

Digital twins are virtual replicas of physical cities or infrastructure that allow urban planners to simulate various scenarios and assess their impact before implementation. These digital models incorporate real-time data and historical records, enabling planners to test the effects of policy changes, infrastructure upgrades, or disaster scenarios. For example, a city can simulate the impact of a new transportation policy on traffic flow through the use of digital twin technology, allowing planners to optimize routes before making physical changes. Tao et al. (2019) further explain that digital twins can simulate and optimize urban systems, such as energy grids and transportation networks. This technology enhances decision-making, minimizes risks, and ensures that urban development initiatives are both effective and sustainable.

The IoT is the backbone of real-time data collection in AI-driven urban environments (Zanella et al., 2014). IoT devices, such as smart sensors for traffic lights, air quality monitors, and waste bins provide continuous streams of data that AI systems can analyze to improve and optimize urban management. For instance, IoT-enabled traffic lights can adjust timings dynamically based on real-time traffic conditions, reducing delays and emissions. Air quality monitors equipped with IoT sensors allow cities to identify pollution hotspots and implement targeted interventions. By integrating IoT with AI, urban planners can create adaptive, efficient, and responsive cities that prioritize sustainability and livability.

3.1.3 Current Trends and Innovations in AI-Driven Urban Development

The integration of AI into urban development has given rise to innovative solutions that address long-standing challenges while shaping the future of cities. From revolutionizing transportation to enhancing sustainability and resilience, these trends demonstrate how AI can create smarter, more livable urban environments. Key innovations include smart mobility solutions, sustainable city initiatives, predictive maintenance, resilient urban infrastructure, and smart governance systems. Together, these advancements highlight the potential of AI to not only improve efficiency but also prioritize equity, inclusivity, and adaptability in urban planning.

3.1.3.1 *Smart Mobility Solutions*

AI is fundamentally transforming urban transportation and traffic management, with autonomous vehicles (AVs) leading this revolution. AVs are able to navigate roads with unprecedented safety and efficiency through the integration of advanced AI technologies such as computer vision, sensor fusion, and deep learning. These systems process real-time data from cameras, LiDAR, and radar to make split-second decisions, reducing the likelihood of accidents caused by human error. Companies like Tesla and Waymo are at the forefront of this innovation, deploying AVs that promise to alleviate traffic congestion and lowering the emissions by optimizing driving patterns and minimizing inefficiencies (Garikapati & Shetiya, 2024). For instance, AVs can communicate with each other and traffic infrastructure to maintain optimal speeds and reduce stop-and-go traffic, which is a major contributor to fuel consumption and pollution. As these technologies mature, they hold the potential to revolutionize urban mobility, making transportation systems safer, greener, and more efficient. The widespread adoption of AVs could also lead to reduced reliance on private car ownership, promoting shared mobility solutions and further easing urban congestion (Garikapati & Shetiya, 2024).

Figure 3.2 illustrates the trends identified by scholars, revealing a notable trend in AI algorithm usage for AVs (Garikapati & Shetiya, 2024). In 2013, the number of algorithms in deep neural networks (DNNs) exceeded those in generic AI and ML, highlighting the growing emphasis on DNN research

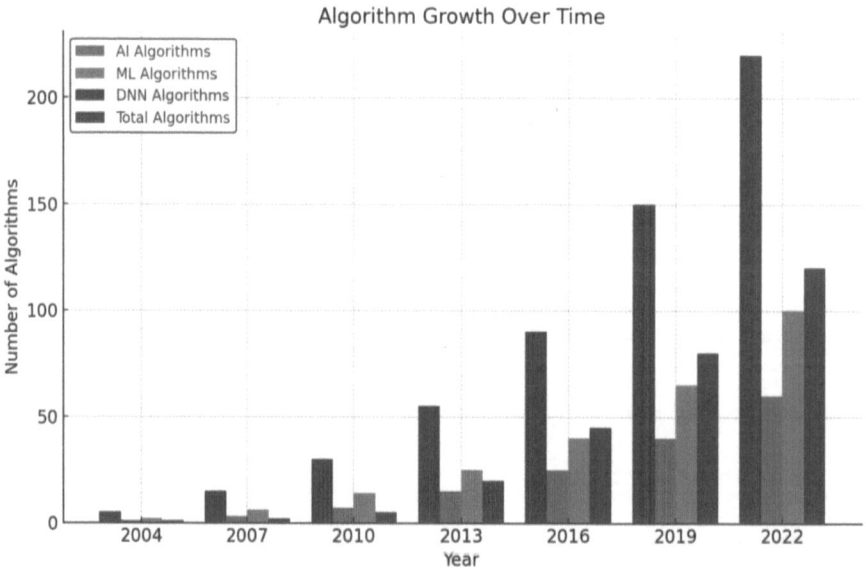

FIGURE 3.2
Trends in AI algorithm usage in autonomous vehicles.

and its increasing prominence within the AI community. The most significant insight from the graph, however, is the exponential rise in the number of algorithms developed over the years for AI applications, underscoring the rapid advancement and expanding scope of AI technologies.

3.1.3.2 Sustainable Cities

AI technologies play a pivotal role in helping cities achieve their sustainability goals. Through advanced analytics, AI optimizes energy consumption by monitoring and managing electricity usage in buildings, reducing waste, and promoting renewable energy integration. For example, smart grids powered by AI can balance energy supply and demand in real time, ensuring efficiency and reliability.

Waste management is another area where AI drives innovation. AI-enabled systems use IoT sensors in waste bins to monitor fill levels and optimize collection routes, reducing operational costs and environmental impact. Additionally, AI supports the development of green infrastructure by analyzing environmental data to identify areas for urban greening, water conservation, and pollution control. These solutions not only address immediate environmental challenges but also promote long-term ecological balance.

3.1.3.3 Predictive Maintenance

Predictive maintenance is a ground breaking application of AI-driven models that is revolutionizing urban infrastructure management. By leveraging sensor data and historical trends, these models can forecast potential failures in critical infrastructure such as bridges, roads, and utility lines. This capability allows cities to transition from reactive maintenance—addressing issues after they occur—to a proactive approach that anticipates problems before they escalate. Early detection not only reduces repair costs but also minimizes disruptions to public services, ensuring smoother operations and improved quality of life for residents. For example, water utilities are increasingly adopting AI to monitor pipeline systems, identifying leaks or pressure anomalies before they develop into costly or hazardous failures. This shift toward predictive maintenance represents a significant advancement in urban resilience and resource management (Tselentis et al., 2023).

In the transportation sector, AI-driven predictive maintenance is proving equally transformative. Tools equipped with ML algorithms analyze huge numbers of data from road and railway networks to assess their condition and predict areas at the highest risk of degradation. This enables city planners and maintenance teams to prioritize repairs and allocate resources more efficiently, ensuring that critical infrastructure remains safe and functional. For instance, AI can identify subtle signs of wear and tear on road surfaces or railway tracks that might otherwise go unnoticed until they cause significant damage or accidents. By addressing these issues early, cities can extend the lifespan of their infrastructure assets, reduce long-term maintenance costs, and enhance public safety. This approach helps in improving operational efficiency and contributes toward sustainable urban development by minimizing unnecessary resource consumption (Tselentis et al., 2023).

The broader implications of predictive maintenance extend beyond cost savings and operational efficiency. By preventing infrastructure failures, cities can avoid the social and economic disruptions that often accompany such events, such as traffic delays, service outages, or even public safety hazards. Furthermore, the data collected through these AI-driven systems can inform future infrastructure planning, enabling cities to design more resilient and adaptive systems. For example, insights gained from monitoring utility lines or transportation networks can guide the development of smarter, more durable materials and construction methods. As urban populations continue to grow, the ability to maintain and optimize infrastructure through predictive maintenance will become increasingly critical. By integrating AI into these processes, cities can address current challenges and build a foundation for sustainable, future-ready urban environments (Tselentis et al., 2023).

3.1.3.4 Resilient Urban Infrastructure

As cities face increasing risks from climate change and natural disasters, AI is becoming a key tool in designing resilient infrastructure. Flood prediction systems powered by AI analyze weather data, topography, and historical flooding patterns to provide accurate forecasts, enabling cities to take preventive measures and protect vulnerable areas. For example, Jakarta has adopted AI-based flood monitoring systems that issue early warnings and help authorities allocate resources effectively during heavy rains.

AI also supports disaster response by enabling real-time analysis of data from drones, satellites, and IoT devices. This information helps emergency services plan evacuations, allocate resources, and prioritize rescue efforts. By incorporating AI into resilience planning, cities can adapt to evolving threats and recover more quickly from disruptions.

3.1.3.5 Smart Governance

AI-driven platforms are transforming governance by enabling cities to engage with citizens more effectively and deliver transparent decision-making processes. Digital participation tools powered by AI, such as Barcelona's Decidim platform, allow residents to voice opinions, propose initiatives, and vote on policies. These platforms use NLP to analyze feedback and ensure that community input is considered in urban planning.

AI also enhances public service delivery by streamlining administrative processes and improving accessibility. For instance, chatbots powered by AI assist citizens with tasks like filing complaints, accessing information, and paying bills, reducing the burden on government offices and improving user experience. By embracing AI in governance, cities can foster greater trust, efficiency, and inclusivity in their operations.

In summary, the current trends and innovations in AI-driven urban development underscore the technology's potential to revolutionize how cities are planned, managed, and experienced. By prioritizing smart mobility, sustainability, predictive maintenance, resilience, and governance, cities can leverage AI to create more efficient, equitable, and adaptive urban spaces that meet the demands of a rapidly changing world.

3.1.4 Benefits of AI Integration in Urban Spaces

The integration of AI into urban spaces offers benefits that enhance the functionality, sustainability, and livability of cities. By leveraging AI-driven technologies, urban areas can address complex challenges, optimize resource use, and improve the quality of life for their residents. Key benefits include efficiency and optimization, advancements in sustainability, enhanced public services, data-driven decision-making, and improved overall quality of life. These benefits highlight AI's potential to create smarter and more equitable urban environments.

3.1.4.1 Efficiency and Optimization

AI enables cities to achieve remarkable levels of efficiency by optimizing resource allocation, reducing waste, and improving the functionality of urban services. Evidently, this can be seen from an AI-powered traffic management system that can analyze real-time data from sensors and cameras to adjust signal timings, reducing congestion and commute times. Ride-sharing platforms, using ML algorithms, optimize routes and passenger matches to ensure efficient utilization of vehicles, contributing to reduced energy consumption and emissions.

In waste management, AI integrates with IoT sensors to monitor bin fill levels and plan collection routes dynamically, cutting down operational costs and environmental impact. Similarly, in energy management, AI tools can predict energy demand patterns and distribute resources more effectively, ensuring reliable supply while minimizing waste. This capacity to optimize multiple facets of urban life helps cities function more effectively while conserving resources.

3.1.4.2 Sustainability

AI plays a pivotal role in supporting sustainable urban development by reducing carbon footprints, optimizing energy usage, and promoting green infrastructure. Smart grids powered by AI help to create a balance between energy supply and demand, through synergizing renewable energy sources like solar and wind into urban power systems. By analyzing weather patterns and energy consumption trends, these systems maximize efficiency and reduce reliance on fossil fuels.

AI also contributes to sustainable waste management by identifying patterns in waste generation and suggesting strategies for reduction and recycling. Furthermore, AI technologies are instrumental in promoting urban greening initiatives. By analyzing environmental data, AI identifies areas suitable for tree planting, urban farming, or green roofs, enhancing air quality and mitigating urban heat island effects. These measures not only address environmental challenges but also foster resilience against climate change.

3.1.4.3 Enhanced Public Services

One of the most significant benefits of AI integration in urban spaces is the enhancement of public services such as healthcare, education, and public safety. In healthcare, AI-powered systems enable early diagnosis of diseases through predictive analytics, while telemedicine platforms ensure accessibility to medical care, particularly in underserved areas. Similarly, in education, AI tools personalize learning experiences by tailoring content to individual student needs, improving outcomes for learners of all ages.

Another area where AI can deliver improvements is in public safety. AI-driven surveillance systems equipped with computer vision analyze live feeds to detect and respond to incidents such as accidents, crimes, or emergencies in real time. Predictive policing tools, while requiring careful ethical oversight, use historical data to allocate resources more effectively, reducing response times and improving community safety (Sanchez et al., 2024). These advancements make public services more responsive, efficient, and tailored to the needs of urban populations.

3.1.4.4 Data-Driven Decision-Making

AI empowers urban planners and policymakers with the ability to make data-driven decisions based on accurate, real-time insights. Through big data analytics, AI processes vast amounts of information from sensors, social media, and other sources, identifying trends and patterns that guide urban planning. For instance, by analyzing traffic data, planners can identify bottlenecks and implement targeted solutions to improve mobility.

In disaster management, AI tools use predictive modeling to assess risks and prepare cities for natural disasters such as floods, earthquakes, or storms (Zolkafli et al., 2024). These insights enable authorities to allocate resources strategically and mitigate potential damage. By grounding decisions in comprehensive data analysis, cities can address challenges proactively and achieve better long-term outcomes.

3.1.4.5 Improved Quality of Life

Ultimately, AI-driven urban development enhances the quality of life for residents by creating safer, cleaner, and more livable cities. Traffic congestion, a persistent urban challenge, is mitigated through AI-powered transportation systems that optimize routes and manage traffic flow. Pollution levels are reduced as AI supports the transition to sustainable energy sources and efficient waste management practices.

AI also fosters safer communities by improving emergency response systems and ensuring equitable access to essential services. Smart city initiatives, such as intelligent lighting systems and real-time public transit updates, enhance convenience and safety for residents. Additionally, the integration of community feedback through AI-driven platforms ensures that urban planning reflects the needs and priorities of residents, fostering a sense of inclusion and empowerment.

In conclusion, the benefits of AI integration in urban spaces extend beyond technological advancements to encompass sustainability, equity, and enhanced quality of life. By leveraging AI's capabilities, cities can address pressing urban challenges, optimize their operations, and create environments where residents can thrive.

3.2 The Significance of Community Engagement

Community engagement serves as a cornerstone for the success of AI-driven urban development projects, ensuring that technological advancements align with the needs and aspirations of the people they are designed to serve. By involving residents, local organizations, policymakers, and businesses in the decision-making process, cities can foster transparency, trust, and inclusivity. This section delves into the definition and principles of community engagement, the importance of community involvement in AI-driven projects, the role of stakeholders, and the case for inclusive decision-making (Zolkafli et al., 2024).

Community engagement refers to the collaborative process of involving individuals, groups, and organizations in the planning, implementation, and evaluation of initiatives that affect their lives. In the context of urban development, it emphasizes active participation, dialogue, and shared decision-making between residents and authorities. The goal is to ensure that all voices, especially those of marginalized communities, are heard and considered in the creation of policies and projects.

The principles of community engagement include transparency, inclusivity, and mutual respect. Transparency ensures that stakeholders are informed about the goals, methods, and potential impacts of a project. Inclusivity focuses on engaging diverse community members, including underrepresented groups, to address systemic inequities. Mutual respect fosters trust and collaboration, recognizing the unique insights and lived experiences that each stakeholder brings to the table. These principles are critical for building strong partnerships and ensuring the success of urban development initiatives.

3.2.1 The Importance of Community Involvement in AI-Driven Projects

Community involvement is particularly crucial in AI-driven urban development due to the potential for these projects to significantly impact everyday life. AI technologies often operate on complex algorithms and datasets that may not be easily understood by the general public. Involving the community helps bridge this knowledge gap, ensuring that AI systems are designed and implemented in ways that reflect the needs and values of the population.

Moreover, community engagement mitigates risks such as algorithmic bias, privacy concerns, and ethical dilemmas. For instance, by including residents in discussions about data collection and usage, cities can address fears about surveillance and ensure that privacy is protected. Engagement also builds trust, which is essential for the successful adoption of AI technologies. When residents feel that their input is valued and their concerns are addressed, they are more likely to support and participate in AI-driven initiatives.

3.2.2 Role of Stakeholders in Urban Development

Diversity is expected among stakeholders in urban development, which includes a diverse group of participants such as government officials, urban planners, community organizations, businesses, and residents. Each group plays a unique role in shaping the direction and outcomes of AI-driven projects.

Governments and urban planners are responsible for setting the vision, policies, and frameworks that guide development. Their role includes ensuring that AI technologies are deployed ethically and equitably (Sanchez et al., 2024). Scholars have argued that government-backed organizations are crucial in ensuring AI technologies are used ethically to serve the public good (Floridi et al., 2018). Community organizations act as intermediaries, amplifying the voices of marginalized groups and facilitating dialogue between residents and authorities.

Conversely, private enterprises stimulate innovation by creating and using AI solutions that are customized to address urban problems (Almirall et al., 2016). These businesses often work with governments to test new technologies in a practical environment. Businesses, particularly those in the tech sector, provide the tools and expertise needed to implement AI solutions, while residents offer invaluable local knowledge and lived experiences that ground projects in real-world contexts.

Academic institutions also contribute by teaching the next generation of data scientists and urban planners and undertaking research that helps build AI models (Batty, 2018). Finally, the community is becoming increasingly acknowledged as an important stakeholder, offering insightful feedback on the social effects of AI, and guaranteeing that urban planning projects are in line with the requirements and values of the people they will influence. Collaboration among stakeholders ensures that multiple perspectives are considered, leading to more comprehensive and effective solutions. It also helps distribute responsibility and accountability, fostering a sense of collective ownership over urban development projects.

3.2.3 Case for Inclusive Decision-Making

Inclusive decision-making is not only a moral imperative but also a practical necessity in AI-driven urban development. Cities are diverse entities, and their success depends on addressing the needs and aspirations of all residents, including those from underrepresented or vulnerable groups. Excluding certain populations from decision-making can lead to outcomes that exacerbate inequalities, erode trust, and spark resistance.

Inclusive decision-making involves creating platforms and mechanisms that enable all community members to participate meaningfully. For example, participatory design workshops, public forums, and digital engagement tools allow residents to voice their opinions and collaborate on solutions. AI can enhance these efforts by analyzing feedback and identifying trends, ensuring that all input is considered.

Ultimately, inclusive decision-making leads to urban AI projects that are more equitable, effective, and sustainable. When residents feel a sense of ownership and empowerment, they are more likely to support initiatives, fostering long-term success and resilience. Engaging the community is not merely a step in the planning process but a vital component of building smarter, more inclusive cities.

3.3 Challenges in Community Engagement for AI-Driven Urban Projects

Community engagement in AI-driven urban development, while essential, is fraught with challenges that stem from the complexity of the technology, ethical concerns, and systemic inequities (Sanchez et al., 2024). These challenges can hinder meaningful participation and undermine trust, ultimately impacting the success of AI initiatives. This section explores the major obstacles to effective community engagement, including technological complexity and public understanding, trust and ethical concerns, power imbalances and marginalization, and data privacy and surveillance concerns.

3.3.1 Technological Complexity and Public Understanding

AI systems often rely on advanced algorithms, ML models, and vast datasets, making them difficult for nonexperts to understand. One of the most significant barriers to community engagement in AI-driven urban projects is the inherent complexity of the technology. This knowledge gap can create a sense of exclusion among community members, as they may feel ill-equipped to contribute meaningfully to discussions about AI implementation.

Moreover, the technical jargon associated with AI can be alienating, leading to disengagement or skepticism. For instance, residents might struggle to comprehend how predictive models optimize traffic flow or why certain data is collected for urban planning purposes. To bridge this gap, urban planners must invest in educational initiatives, such as workshops, informational campaigns, and interactive tools that demystify AI concepts and explain their relevance to everyday life.

Failing to address technological complexity risks creating a divide between those who understand AI and those who do not, further marginalizing vulnerable populations. Simplifying technical concepts and fostering open dialogue can empower communities to participate in shaping AI-driven urban projects.

3.3.2   Trust and Ethical Concerns

Trust is a cornerstone of successful community engagement, but it is often challenged in the context of AI-driven projects. Residents may harbor doubts about the motives of governments or private companies involved in these initiatives, especially if past experiences have eroded confidence in public institutions. Ethical concerns, such as algorithmic bias, lack of transparency, and potential misuse of AI, further compound these issues (Sanchez et al., 2024).

For example, if an AI system used for housing allocation is perceived as unfair or biased, it can lead to public backlash and resistance. Similarly, opaque decision-making processes—where residents are unaware of how AI-generated insights influence urban planning—can breed suspicion. To address these concerns, it is essential to prioritize transparency, explain how AI decisions are made, and involve communities in ethical evaluations of AI systems.

Engaging independent auditors and ethical committees to assess AI projects can also help build trust. By demonstrating a commitment to fairness, accountability, and community welfare, urban planners can create an environment where residents feel confident in the integrity of AI-driven initiatives.

3.3.3   Power Imbalances and Marginalization

Power imbalances present another challenge in community engagement for AI-driven urban projects. Marginalized groups, such as low-income residents, ethnic minorities, and people with disabilities, often lack the resources, representation, or platforms needed to influence decision-making processes. This can result in urban AI projects that cater to privileged populations while neglecting the needs of vulnerable communities. For instance, the deployment of smart technologies in affluent neighborhoods might improve services like transportation or waste management, while underserved areas continue to face systemic challenges. Such disparities can exacerbate existing inequalities and undermine the inclusivity of urban development efforts.

To counteract power imbalances, urban planners must actively seek out and prioritize the participation of underrepresented groups. Strategies include forming partnerships with community organizations, conducting outreach programs, and providing resources such as translation services or stipends for participation. Ensuring that all voices are heard and valued is critical to creating equitable AI-driven urban projects.

3.3.4 Data Privacy and Surveillance Concerns

Data privacy and surveillance are among the most contentious issues in AI-driven urban development. Many AI applications rely on collecting and analyzing data from residents, such as location information, spending habits, or social behavior. While this data is essential for optimizing urban services, it raises concerns about privacy infringement and potential misuse. For example, the use of facial recognition technology for public safety might deter criminal activity, but it also risks creating a surveillance state where residents feel constantly monitored. Similarly, data breaches or unauthorized access to personal information can erode trust and lead to public opposition.

To address these concerns, urban planners must implement robust data protection measures and adhere to ethical guidelines for data collection and usage (Sanchez et al., 2024). Transparent communication about what data is being collected, how it is used, and who has access to it is essential. Engaging communities in discussions about data governance can also help ensure that privacy concerns are addressed and that residents have a say in how their information is handled.

Overcoming the challenges of community engagement in AI-driven urban projects requires a multifaceted approach that prioritizes education, transparency, inclusivity, and ethical accountability (Sanchez et al., 2024). By addressing technological complexity, building trust, balancing power dynamics, and safeguarding data privacy, urban planners can foster meaningful participation and create AI solutions that benefit all residents equitably.

3.4 Case Studies in AI-Driven Urban Development with Strong Community Engagement

AI-driven urban development with strong community engagement demonstrates the transformative potential of integrating advanced technology with inclusive participatory processes. Numerous cities like Barcelona, Boston, and Amsterdam have implemented AI-powered systems for optimizing traffic management, energy consumption, and waste collection highlighting how effective community engagement can enhance AI-driven urban projects.

3.4.1 Case Study 1: Smart Cities and Local Governance (Barcelona, Spain)

Barcelona has emerged as a global leader in leveraging AI to enhance urban governance and foster community engagement through its innovative "Smart City" program. At the heart of this initiative is the Decidim Platform, an open-source participatory democracy tool that empowers residents to actively shape urban development. Decidim enables citizens to propose, debate, and vote on local initiatives, ensuring that urban projects align with community preferences and priorities. The platform integrates AI to analyze large volumes of citizen feedback, allowing local authorities to prioritize proposals and make data-driven decisions that reflect the collective needs of the population. This approach not only enhances transparency but also strengthens trust between the government and its citizens, making Decidim a benchmark for participatory governance worldwide (Barcelona City Council, 2023).

Beyond participatory democracy, Barcelona's Smart City program incorporates AI technologies to address critical urban challenges, including transportation, energy efficiency, and public service delivery. For instance, the city has implemented an AI-driven traffic management system that optimizes traffic flow and reduces congestion. This system integrates real-time data from sensors and citizen feedback collected through digital surveys. AI algorithms analyze this data to identify patterns, predict traffic bottlenecks, and design more efficient routes. By involving residents in the decision-making process, Barcelona ensures that its traffic solutions are not only technologically advanced but also responsive to the lived experiences of its citizens (Bakici et al., 2020).

Moreover, Barcelona's commitment to transparency and community involvement extends to other areas of urban development. For example, the city uses AI to enhance energy efficiency in public buildings and street lighting, reducing its carbon footprint while improving service quality. These initiatives are often co-designed with residents, ensuring that technological advancements are aligned with local needs and values. The success of Barcelona's AI-driven governance model lies in its ability to balance technological innovation with inclusive decision-making, fostering a sense of ownership and collaboration among its citizens (March & Ribera-Fumaz, 2016).

In summary, Barcelona exemplifies how smart cities can harness AI to improve urban governance while prioritizing community engagement. By integrating tools like Decidim and AI-driven traffic management systems, the city demonstrates that technology can be a powerful enabler of participatory democracy and sustainable urban development. Barcelona's approach underscores the importance of transparency, inclusivity, and data-driven decision-making in building trust and ensuring the successful implementation of AI solutions in urban contexts.

3.4.2 Case Study 2: AI in Transportation and Public Input (Boston, USA)

Boston's Go Boston 2030 initiative is a pioneering example of how cities can leverage AI to enhance transportation systems while actively involving residents in the planning process. This initiative highlights the importance of combining technological innovation with robust public engagement to create transportation solutions that are both efficient and equitable. Through a series of workshops, surveys, and digital engagement campaigns, Boston gathered extensive input from its residents, identifying key priorities such as improving bike lanes, enhancing pedestrian safety, and reducing traffic congestion. AI tools were then employed to analyze this feedback, enabling the city to design and implement infrastructure changes that directly address community needs (City of Boston, 2023).

At the core of Go Boston 2030 is the use of AI-powered analytics to process and interpret large volumes of public input. Sentiment analysis tools, a subset of AI, were utilized to identify common themes and concerns expressed by residents. For instance, AI analysis revealed a strong demand for safer and more accessible bike lanes, as well as improved pedestrian pathways. These insights informed the city's decision-making process, leading to targeted infrastructure projects such as the expansion of protected bike lanes, the installation of pedestrian-friendly crosswalks, and the optimization of traffic signal timings to prioritize safety and efficiency (Zhang et al., 2021).

In addition to addressing specific community concerns, Boston's AI-driven transportation system also focuses on broader urban mobility challenges. The city has implemented AI algorithms to optimize public transit schedules, reduce traffic congestion, and improve the overall reliability of its transportation network. Similarly, predictive analytics are used to anticipate and mitigate potential bottlenecks, ensuring smoother commutes for residents and visitors alike (Chen et al., 2020).

The success of Go Boston 2030 lies in its commitment to transparency and inclusivity. The active involvement of residents in the city planning process has fostered a sense of ownership and collaboration among its citizens. Public workshops and digital engagement platforms provided residents with opportunities to voice their opinions and contribute to the development of transportation policies. This participatory approach not only ensures that solutions are aligned with community needs but also builds trust between the government and its constituents (Goodspeed, 2020).

In summary, Boston's Go Boston 2030 initiative demonstrates how AI can be effectively integrated with public input to create smarter, more responsive transportation systems. By combining advanced AI analytics with extensive community engagement, the city has developed infrastructure solutions that prioritize safety, efficiency, and equity. This case study highlights the transformative potential of AI in urban transportation planning, particularly when paired with a commitment to inclusivity and transparency.

3.4.3 Case Study 3: Urban Sustainability Projects and Public Collaboration (Amsterdam, Netherlands)

Amsterdam's Buiksloterham Project is a ground breaking example of how cities can integrate AI and participatory design to co-create sustainable urban solutions. As part of the broader Amsterdam Smart City initiative, this circular economy pilot project emphasizes the importance of community collaboration in shaping environmentally conscious neighborhoods. By leveraging AI-driven tools to simulate the environmental impacts of proposed changes and engaging residents through workshops and digital platforms, Amsterdam has established a model for inclusive and sustainable urban development (City of Amsterdam, 2023).

The Buiksloterham project focuses on transforming a former industrial area into a sustainable, circular neighborhood where resources are reused, and waste is minimized. Central to this initiative is the use of AI-powered simulations to model the environmental and economic impacts of various design proposals. These tools enable planners and residents to visualize the potential outcomes of different sustainability measures, such as energy-efficient building designs, renewable energy systems, and waste management solutions. By providing data-driven insights, AI helps stakeholders make informed decisions that balance environmental goals with practical feasibility (Bibri & Krogstie, 2020).

Residents play a critical role in the Buiksloterham project, actively participating in the co-design process through workshops, community meetings, and interactive digital platforms. These engagement mechanisms ensure that the neighborhood's development reflects the values and priorities of its inhabitants. For example, residents have contributed ideas for green spaces, shared energy systems, and circular waste management practices. AI tools are then used to analyze this input, identify common themes, and refine proposals to align with community aspirations (van Bueren et al., 2021).

Amsterdam's commitment to sustainability extends beyond Buiksloterham, as evidenced by its broader Smart City initiatives. The city employs AI technologies to optimize energy use, manage waste, and promote sustainable living across its urban landscape. For instance, AI systems analyze data from smart meters and Internet of IoT sensors to monitor and improve energy efficiency in homes and public buildings. These systems enable real-time adjustments to energy consumption, reducing carbon emissions and lowering costs for residents (Amsterdam Smart City, 2023).

The success of Amsterdam's approach lies in its ability to combine technological innovation with meaningful public participation. Involving resident's involvement in the planning and implementation of sustainability projects ensures that the initiatives taken by the city are technologically advanced and socially inclusive. This collaborative model fosters a sense of owner-ship and accountability among citizens, enhancing the long-term viability of urban sustainability efforts (Caprotti et al., 2022).

In summary, Amsterdam's Buiksloterham project and its broader Smart City initiatives demonstrate how AI can be harnessed to drive sustainable urban development while fostering community collaboration. By integrat-ing AI-driven simulations with participatory design processes, the city has created a replicable framework for building neighborhoods that are both environmentally sustainable and socially inclusive. This case study high-lights the transformative potential of combining advanced technologies with grassroots engagement to achieve urban sustainability goals.

3.5 Recommendations for Policy Makers and Urban Planners

As AI-driven urban development advances, policymakers, and urban plan-ners play a pivotal role in ensuring these projects align with societal values and address community needs. Effective governance and planning require frameworks and policies that prioritize inclusivity, equity, and long-term benefits for communities. This section provides detailed recommendations for integrating community feedback into AI projects, promoting equitable urban AI development, and ensuring sustainable outcomes.

3.5.1 Framework for Integrating Community Feedback in AI Projects

Integrating community feedback into AI-driven urban projects is essential to ensure that these initiatives align with the needs, aspirations, and concerns of the people they are designed to serve. A structured and comprehensive framework ensures that community input is gathered, analyzed, and imple-mented effectively throughout the project lifecycle (Figure 3.3).

Below is an elaborated version of the framework, broken into five key stages:

> *a. Pre-Project Assessment: Building a Foundation of Understanding*
>   Before launching any AI-driven urban project, it is crucial to con-duct a thorough pre-project assessment to understand the communi-ty's needs, priorities, and expectations. This stage involves engaging residents through various methods such as surveys, focus groups, and town hall meetings. Surveys can quantitatively capture data based on community preferences, while focus groups and town halls provide qualitative insights into residents' concerns and aspirations. This initial engagement helps to establish a ground work for under-standing local priorities, ensuring that the project is grounded in the

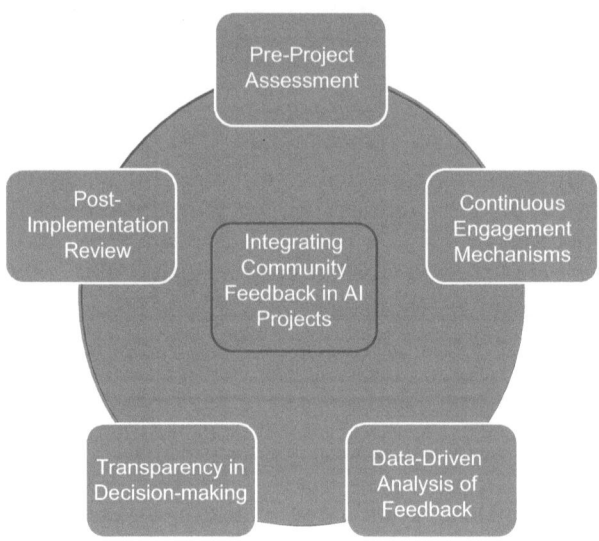

FIGURE 3.3
Framework for integrating community feedback in AI-driven urban projects.

realities of the community it aims to serve. By identifying potential challenges and opportunities early on, planners can design solutions that are both relevant and impactful.

b. *Continuous Engagement Mechanisms: Fostering Ongoing Dialogue*
      Community engagement should be an ongoing process that evolves together with the project development. Establishing continuous feedback loops is essential to maintain an open dialogue with residents throughout the project life cycle. Digital platforms, mobile apps, and online portals can facilitate real-time communication, making it easier for community members to share their thoughts and concerns as the project progresses. However, it is equally important to ensure inclusivity by organizing in-person workshops, forums, and meetings for those with limited digital access. These mechanisms ensure that all voices are heard, regardless of socioeconomic status or technological literacy, encouraging collaboration among the locals and building their sense of ownership.

c. *Data-Driven Analysis of Feedback: Turning Input into Action*
      As community feedback is collected, it often comes in large volumes and diverse formats, making it challenging to process manually. This is where AI tools in the form of NLP and sentiment analysis become invaluable. NLP can analyze text-based feedback to identify recurring themes, emerging concerns, and areas of improvement, while sentiment analysis gauges the overall tone of the feedback—whether

it is positive, negative, or neutral. These tools enable planners to distill complex and varied input into actionable insights, ensuring that community feedback directly informs decision-making. By leveraging AI, planners can efficiently prioritize issues and tailor solutions to address the most pressing needs.

d. *Transparency in Decision-Making: Building Trust and Accountability*

Transparency is a cornerstone of effective community engagement. Residents need to see how their feedback is being used to shape the project. Clearly communicating the role of community input in decision-making helps build trust and accountability. This can be achieved by regularly publishing progress updates, sharing how specific concerns have been addressed, and explaining the rationale behind certain decisions. Transparency not only demonstrates responsiveness but also reinforces the value of community participation. When residents feel heard and see tangible results, they are more likely to remain engaged and supportive of the project.

e. *Post-Implementation Review: Learning and Improving for the Future*

The engagement process does not end with the completion of the project. A post-implementation review is essential to evaluate the outcomes and gather feedback on the initiative's effectiveness. This stage involves engaging the community in assessing whether the project has met its goals and addressing any unintended consequences. The outcomes obtained from this review are invaluable for refining future projects and ensuring continuous improvement. By involving residents in the evaluation process, planners can assist in cultivating a culture of learning and adaptation that can ultimately lead to more successful and community-driven urban initiatives.

This framework emphasizes the importance of community feedback at every stage of an AI-driven urban project. From the initial assessment to the post-implementation review, each step is designed to ensure that the project remains aligned with the community's needs and aspirations. By fostering continuous engagement, leveraging data-driven tools, maintaining transparency, and learning from each initiative, planners can build trust, inclusivity, and long-term success in their urban development efforts. This approach not only enhances the effectiveness of AI-driven projects but also strengthens the relationship between communities and the institutions that serve them.

3.5.2 Policies for Inclusive and Equitable Urban AI Development

Policies for Inclusive and Equitable Urban AI Development are essential to ensure that the benefits of AI-driven urban projects are distributed fairly and do not exacerbate existing inequalities. Equity and inclusivity must be at the core of urban AI development, as these technologies have the potential to either empower or marginalize communities, depending on how they are implemented. Policymakers have an important role to play in designing and enforcing frameworks that protect vulnerable populations, promote fairness, and ensure that all residents have a voice in shaping the future of their cities. Without such measures, AI risks perpetuating systemic biases and deepening social divides, undermining its potential to create smarter, more equitable urban environments.

Anti-bias and fairness policies are foundational steps in addressing the risks of AI systems inadvertently reinforcing discrimination. Algorithms used in urban planning, such as those for resource allocation, housing, or transportation, must conduct a rigorous testing to identify and mitigate biases. For example, an AI system designed to optimize public transit routes might inadvertently neglect underserved neighborhoods if historical data reflects past inequities. By mandating fairness audits and requiring transparency in algorithmic decision-making, policymakers can ensure that AI systems prioritize equitable outcomes. This approach helps to build trust in AI technologies and aligns it with broader social justice goals, ensuring that marginalized communities are not neglected (Smith & Brown, 2023).

Digital Inclusion Programs are critical to bridging the digital divide and ensuring that all residents can participate in the AI-driven transformation of their cities. Many communities, particularly those in low-income or rural areas, lack access to the digital tools and skills needed to engage with AI technologies. Initiatives such as providing affordable internet access, offering technical training, and creating multilingual resources can empower residents to contribute meaningfully to AI-related discussions. For instance, digital literacy programs can help community members understand how AI impacts their lives and enable them to advocate for their needs. By addressing these barriers, cities can foster a more inclusive dialogue around AI development, ensuring that diverse voices are heard and valued (Johnson et al., 2023).

Community representation in decision-making is vital to ensure that AI-driven projects reflect the needs and aspirations of all residents. Establishing advisory boards or committees composed of diverse community representatives can provide a platform for marginalized groups to influence urban planning processes. These bodies should have a meaningful role in shaping AI initiatives, from identifying priorities to evaluating outcomes. For example, a community advisory board could provide input on the deployment of AI-powered surveillance systems, balancing security concerns with privacy rights. By institutionalizing participatory practices, cities can create a more democratic and inclusive approach to AI development, ensuring that decisions are not dominated by technocrats or private interests (Martinez & Lee, 2023).

Privacy and data protection laws are essential to addressing growing concerns about surveillance and data misuse in AI-driven urban projects. As cities collect huge numbers of data to power AI-based systems, residents must assured that their information is handled responsibly. Policymakers should implement strict regulations governing data collection, usage, and storage, ensuring transparency and accountability. For instance, clear guidelines on how data from smart city sensors is used can help build public trust and prevent misuse. Additionally, residents should have the right to access, correct, or delete their data and empowering them to maintain control over their personal information. These measures are critical to protecting individual rights while enabling the responsible use of AI in urban development (Green & Patel, 2023).

Funding for Grassroots Engagement is a key strategy for ensuring that AI-driven urban development is rooted in the needs and priorities of local communities. Allocating resources to support grassroots organizations and community-led initiatives can empower residents to take an active role in shaping AI projects. For example, funding could be used to organize workshops, create educational materials, or develop platforms for community feedback. This bottom-up approach complements top-down governance, ensuring that AI initiatives are not imposed on communities but developed in collaboration with them. By investing in grassroots engagement, cities can build stronger partnerships with residents, fostering a sense of ownership and shared responsibility for the success of AI-driven urban projects (Taylor & Nguyen, 2023).

In conclusion, the success of AI-driven urban development hinges on the implementation of policies that prioritize equity, inclusivity, and community participation. Cities can harness the potential of AI in ways that benefit all residents by addressing biases, bridging the digital divide, ensuring representation, protecting privacy, and supporting grassroots engagement. These measures not only enhance the fairness and effectiveness of urban projects but also build trust and foster collaboration, charting the path for a more inclusive and equitable urban future.

3.5.3 Ensuring Long-Term Community Benefits

The integration of AI into urban development holds immense potential to transform cities, but its success hinges on ensuring that these advancements deliver long-term benefits to communities. To achieve this, policymakers and urban planners must adopt a forward-thinking approach that prioritizes sustainability, equity, and inclusivity. The strategies outlined—capacity-building programs, long-term monitoring and evaluation, equitable economic opportunities, environmental sustainability, and institutionalizing community engagement—provide a comprehensive framework for creating AI-driven urban projects that are innovative but also deeply rooted in the needs and aspirations of the communities.

Capacity-building programs are a cornerstone of ensuring that communities are not passive recipients of AI-driven initiatives but active participants in their development. By investing in education and skill development, cities can empower residents to understand and engage with AI technologies. This not only encourages a sense of ownership but also provides individuals with the tools to adapt to a rapidly evolving technological landscape. For instance, training programs that teach coding, data analysis, or AI ethics can open up new career pathways and enable residents to contribute meaningfully to future urban projects. Moreover, an informed community is better positioned to hold policymakers accountable, ensuring that AI solutions align with local values and priorities.

Long-term monitoring and evaluation is critical to maintaining the relevance and effectiveness of AI-driven projects over time. Urban challenges and community needs are dynamic, and what works today may not be sufficient tomorrow. By establishing robust mechanisms for ongoing assessment, cities can identify areas for improvement, adapt to changing circumstances, and ensure that projects continue to deliver value. For example, regular evaluations might reveal that an AI-powered traffic management system needs updates to address new patterns of urban mobility or that a smart energy grid requires adjustments to better serve underserved neighborhoods. This iterative approach ensures that AI solutions remain responsive and resilient in the face of evolving urban realities.

Equitable economic opportunities are essential to ensuring that the benefits of AI-driven urban development are shared broadly across communities. AI projects should be designed to create jobs, support local businesses, and provide training programs that prepare residents for the demands of a digital economy. For instance, an AI initiative aimed at optimizing public transportation could include partnerships with local vocational schools to train mechanics and technicians in maintaining smart infrastructure. By prioritizing economic inclusivity, cities can prevent the widening of socio-economic disparities and ensure that technological progress translates into tangible improvements in the quality of life for all residents.

Environmental sustainability must be a central consideration in AI-driven urban projects. As cities grapple with the urgent challenges of climate change, AI can play a pivotal role in promoting sustainable practices. However, these benefits must be carefully balanced with the environmental costs of deploying AI technologies, such as the energy consumption of data centers. By aligning AI projects with long-term environmental goals, cities can create solutions that not only address immediate urban challenges but also contribute to a healthier, more sustainable future.

Institutionalizing community engagement ensures that the voices of residents remain at the heart of urban planning processes. Too often, community input is treated as an afterthought rather than a fundamental component of decision-making. By embedding participatory practices into the fabric of urban development, policymakers can create a culture of collaboration and trust. This might involve establishing permanent advisory boards, hosting regular town halls, or leveraging digital platforms to gather feedback from diverse stakeholders. When communities feel heard and valued, they are more likely to support and sustain AI-driven initiatives, fostering a sense of shared ownership and collective responsibility.

The successful integration of AI into urban development requires more than just technological innovation—it demands a commitment to equity, sustainability, and community empowerment. By prioritizing capacity-building, long-term monitoring, economic inclusivity, environmental stewardship, and participatory decision-making, cities can harness the transformative potential of AI in ways that benefit all residents. These strategies not only enhance the effectiveness of urban projects but also build trust, foster collaboration, and pave the way for a shared urban future. In doing so, they ensure that AI-driven solutions are not just smart, but also just and inclusive, reflecting the diverse needs and aspirations of the communities they serve.

3.6 Future Directions for Community Engagement in AI-Driven Urban Development

The rapid evolution of AI and urban development opens up new possibilities for community engagement. As cities become smarter and more data-driven, the role of residents in shaping urban landscapes must also evolve. Future directions for community engagement will be defined by emerging technologies, innovative participatory models, and collaborative opportunities that prioritize inclusivity and equity. This section explores trends in AI and community engagement, discusses the potential of new technologies to enhance participation, and highlights opportunities for fostering collaborative urban innovation.

3.6.1 Trends in AI and Community Engagement

AI-driven urban development is increasingly focusing on participatory approaches that actively involve communities in decision-making processes. One key trend is the use of AI-enhanced citizen feedback systems, which analyze public input to inform urban planning. For instance, NLP tools can process mass numbers of citizen feedback, identifying recurring themes and pinpointing specific concerns. This trend ensures that community voices are heard and acted upon more effectively.

Another emerging trend is the integration of AI-driven predictive modeling in public consultations. These tools allow planners to present data-backed projections of how proposed projects might impact communities, enabling more informed discussions. For example, AI can simulate traffic patterns, environmental changes, or housing market trends, giving residents a clearer understanding of potential outcomes.

Additionally, there is a growing emphasis on ethical AI governance, where communities participate in shaping guidelines and policies for AI applications in urban development. Residents are being invited to contribute to discussions in relation to the ethical implications of AI technologies, fostering greater transparency and trust (Sanchez et al., 2024).

3.6.2 Emerging Technologies for Enhanced Participation

Technological advancements are revolutionizing how communities engage with urban planning and AI projects. Augmented reality and virtual reality tools are becoming increasingly popular for visualizing urban development projects. These technologies allow residents to explore proposed changes to their neighborhoods in immersive, interactive environments, making abstract concepts more tangible and accessible.

Blockchain technology is another innovation poised to enhance community participation. Blockchain's decentralized and transparent nature ensures that community feedback, voting results, or resource allocation decisions are recorded securely and cannot be altered. This builds trust and accountability in participatory processes (Singh et al., 2020). Effective communication between residents and planners is expected to be the new norm with the help of AI-powered chatbots. These tools ensure immediate responses to any concern raised by the community, gather their feedback, and guide residents through complex planning documents. Similarly, interactive platforms with built-in AI-driven sentiment analysis tools are able to help planners gauge public opinion in real time, enabling more responsive decision-making. Emerging technologies are also addressing the digital divide. For instance, mobile-based platforms with multilingual support and offline functionality are empowering underrepresented communities to engage with urban planning processes, ensuring that technology serves everyone, not just the tech-savvy elite.

3.7 Conclusion

This chapter highlights the critical role of community engagement in the successful implementation of AI-driven urban development. AI-driven technologies have the potential to contribute to city transformation by improving urban efficiency, sustainability, and quality of life. However, this positive transformation is thwarted by the ethical and equitable deployment of these technologies which relies heavily on involving local communities' participation in decision-making processes. The integration of community feedback allows cities to ensure AI solutions address the actual needs and concerns of residents.

Key findings highlight that challenges such as technological complexity, trust issues, and data privacy concerns must be addressed through transparent communication, ethical policies, and inclusive practices (Sanchez et al., 2024). Best practices like participatory design, leveraging digital platforms for engagement, and ensuring equitable access to technology help mitigate these challenges. Case studies from cities like Barcelona, Boston, and Amsterdam illustrate the tangible benefits of collaborative approaches, where AI innovation and community involvement work hand in hand.

The future of AI-driven urban development depends on the continued commitment to inclusive and ethical practices. As AI technologies advance, the need for strong community engagement will only grow. Cities that prioritize transparency, equity, and collaboration are more likely to be experiencing the most success in building smart, resilient, and livable urban spaces. Additionally, all stakeholders in the form of policymakers, urban planners, and technologists must sit down and work in tandem to create AI frameworks that serve the public good and enhance the lives of all residents. Fostering a culture of participation and innovation will instigate better urban environments that are technologically advanced, socially just, and sustainable.

References

Abdullah, W. (2024). Artificial intelligence for achieving sustainable development goals: Applications, techniques and progress. *International Journal of Computers and Informatics (Zagazig University)*, 5, 117–128.

Allam, Z., & Dhunny, Z. A. (2019). On big data, artificial intelligence, and smart cities. *Cities*, 89, 80–91.

Almirall, E., Wareham, J., & Ratti, C. (2016). Smart cities at the crossroads: New tensions in city transformation. *California Management Review*, 59(1), 141–152.

Amsterdam Smart City. (2023). Energy Efficiency and AI in Amsterdam. Retrieved from https://www.amsterdamsmartcity.com/projects.

Bakici, T., Almirall, E., & Wareham, J. (2020). The role of public open innovation and smart city platforms in urban transformation. *Journal of Urban Technology*, 27(1), 1–20.

Barcelona City Council. (2023). Decidim Barcelona: Participatory Democracy Platform. Retrieved from https://www.decidim.barcelona.

Ben Dhaou, S., Isagah, T., Distor, C., Ruas, I.C. (2024). Global Assessment of Responsible Artificial Intelligence in Cities: Research and Recommendations to Leverage AI for People-Centred Smart Cities; United Nations Human Settlements Programme (UN-Habitat): Nairobi, Kenya, 2024. Retrieved from https://www.unhabitat.org

Batty, M. (2013). Big data, smart cities and city planning. *Dialogues in Human Geography*, 3(3), 274–279.

Batty, M. (2018). Artificial intelligence and smart cities. *Environment and Planning B: Urban Analytics and City Science*, 45(1), 3–6.

Bibri, S. E., & Krogstie, J. (2020). Smart sustainable cities of the future: The role of AI and citizen participation in urban planning. *Sustainable Cities and Society*, 52, 101–115.

Caprotti, F., Cowley, R., & Flynn, A. (2022). Smart cities and urban sustainability: Lessons from Amsterdam*. *Urban Studies*, 59(5), 987–1005.

Chen, M., Liu, W., & Wang, Y. (2020). AI applications in urban traffic management: Lessons from Boston. *Transportation Research Part C: Emerging Technologies*, 115, 102–120.

City of Amsterdam. (2023). Amsterdam Smart City: Buiksloterham Circular Economy Project. Retrieved from https://www.amsterdamsmartcity.com.

City of Boston. (2023). Go Boston 2030: Transportation Plan. Retrieved from https://www.boston.gov/transportation/go-boston-2030.

Floridi, L., Cowls, J., Beltrametti, M., Chatila, R., Chazerand, P., Dignum, V., ... & Vayena, E. (2018). AI4People—an ethical framework for a good AI society: opportunities, risks, principles, and recommendations. *Minds and Machines*, 28, 689–707.

Garikapati, D., & Shetiya, S. S. (2024). Autonomous vehicles: Evolution of artificial intelligence and the current industry landscape. *Big Data and Cognitive Computing*, 8(42). https://doi.org/10.3390/bdcc8040042.

Goodspeed, R. (2020). Participatory urban planning and AI: Enhancing public engagement in smart cities. *Journal of the American Planning Association*, 86(3), 321–335.

Green, T., & Patel, S. (2023). Privacy and data protection in smart cities: Balancing innovation and rights. *International Journal of Urban AI*, 7(3), 200–215.

Johnson, L., et al. (2023). Bridging the digital divide: Strategies for inclusive AI development. *Urban Studies Quarterly*, 18(4), 112–130.

Korada, L. (2021). Unlocking urban futures: The role of big data analytics and AI in urban planning–A systematic literature review and bibliometric insight. *Migration Letters*, 18(6), 775–795.

March, H., & Ribera-Fumaz, R. (2016). Smart contradictions: The politics of making Barcelona a self-sufficient city*. *European Urban and Regional Studies*, 23(4), 816–830.

Martinez, R., & Lee, K. (2023). Community representation in AI governance: A framework for inclusive decision-making. *Journal of Public Policy and Technology*, 12(1), 75–90.

Sanchez, T. W., Brenman, M., & Ye, X. (2024). The ethical concerns of artificial intelligence in urban planning. *Journal of the American Planning Association*. https://doi.org/10.1080/01944363.2024.2355305.

Singh, S., Sharma, P. K., Yoon, B., Shojafar, M., Cho, G. H., & Ra, I. H. (2020). Convergence of blockchain and artificial intelligence in IoT network for the sustainable smart city. *Sustainable Cities and Society*, 63, 102364.

Smith, J., & Brown, A. (2023). Ensuring fairness in AI-driven urban planning: Policies and practices. *Journal of Urban Technology*, 30(2), 45–60.

Tao, F., Qi, Q., Wang, L., & Nee, A. Y. C. (2019). Digital twins and cyber–physical systems toward smart manufacturing and industry 4.0: Correlation and comparison. *Engineering*, 5(4), 653–661.

Taylor, M., & Nguyen, H. (2023). Grassroots engagement in AI-driven urban development: Lessons from global case studies. *Urban Innovation Review*, 25(2), 88–102.

Tselentis, D. I., Papadimitriou, E., & van Gelder, P. (2023). The usefulness of artificial intelligence for safety assessment of different transport modes. *Accident Analysis & Prevention*, 186, 107034.

van Bueren, E., van Bohemen, H., & Itard, L. (2021). Sustainable urban environments: The role of AI and community engagement in the Netherlands. *Journal of Urban Planning and Development*, 147(3), 1–12.

Wolniak, R., & Stecuła, K. (2024). Artificial intelligence in smart cities—Applications, barriers, and future directions: A review. *Smart Cities*, 7(3), 1346–1389. https://doi.org/10.3390/smartcities7030057.

Yigitcanlar, T., Kankanamge, N., Regona, M., Ruiz Maldonado, A., Rowan, B., Ryu, A., … & Li, R. Y. M. (2020). Artificial intelligence technologies and related urban planning and development concepts: How are they perceived and utilized in Australia? *Journal of Open Innovation: Technology, Market, and Complexity*, 6(4), 187.

Zanella, A., Bui, N., Castellani, A., Vangelista, L., & Zorzi, M. (2014). Internet of things for smart cities. *IEEE Internet of Things Journal*, 1(1), 22–32.

Zhang, Y., Li, X., & Wang, Q. (2021). AI-driven sentiment analysis for urban planning: A case study of Boston's transportation initiatives. *Journal of Urban Technology*, 28(2), 45–62.

Zolkafli, A., Mansor, N. S., Omar, M., Ahmad, M., Ibrahim, H., & Yasin, A. (2024). AI for smart disaster resilience among communities. In *Intelligent Systems Modeling and Simulation III: Artificial Intelligent, Machine Learning, Intelligent Functions and Cyber Security* (pp. 369–395). Cham: Springer Nature Switzerland. https://doi.org/10.1007/978-3-031-67317-7_22.

4

AI for Environmental Sustainability in Urban Areas

Ilyas Ahmad Huqqani, Mohd Amirul Mahamud,
Mohd Azmeer Abu Bakar, Muhammad Wafiy Adli Ramli,
Tan Mou Leong, and Narimah Samat

4.1 Introduction

Urbanization has a great positive impact on economic growth and has enhanced the living standards of people all over the globe. Over half of the global population resides in urban areas, which are the hubs of lively human activities and make considerable contributions to economic growth, but, in turn, contribute to environmental concerns such as greenhouse gas emissions, pollution, and waste management as cities grow and expand (United Nation, 2022). Achieving a balance for the future is a challenge, and it is essential as sustainability becomes a prime issue for urban centers around the world. To overcome every issue at hand, the latest advances that bring together technology and eco-friendly practices in order to make a well-balanced ecosystem, need to be implemented.

Aiding the world in this transition, artificial intelligence (AI) has emerged as a very strong tool that provides clinical real-time solutions. AI combined with predictive analytics, machine learning, and neural networks provides a one-of-a-kind tool for resource and asset management in both public and private areas. AI also has the ability to help with urban places as it can analyze, monitor, and optimize systems for an enhanced eco-friendly system. Applying the latest technologies of AI into urban planning and management opens up plenty of opportunities for potent responses to such challenges. Cities can move toward more sustainable and ecologically conscious behaviors by leveraging AI's strengths in data analysis, forecasting, and automation, as illustrated in Figure 4.1 (Yigitcanlar and Cugurullo, 2020).

AI plays a significant role in energy management. AI-powered smart grids minimize energy waste, increase energy distribution efficiency, and include renewable energy sources (Yussuf and Asfour, 2024). AI-based solutions in the transportation sector, such as driverless cars and intelligent

DOI: 10.1201/9781003630371-4

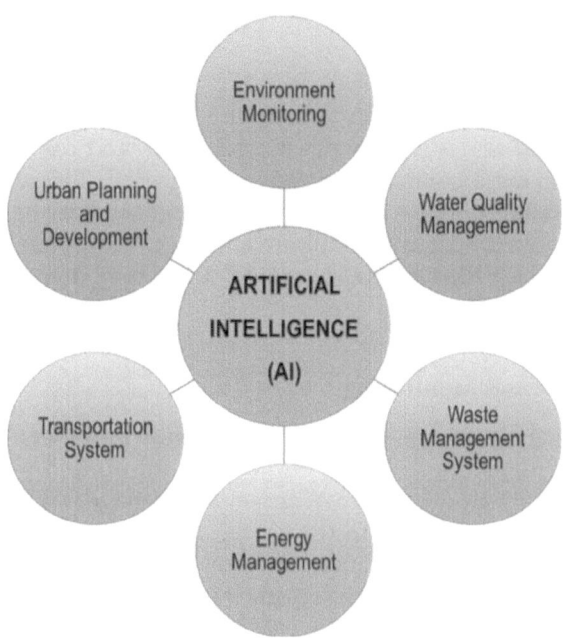

FIGURE 4.1
Artificial intelligence utilization in urban area.

traffic control, lower pollutants, and fuel consumption (Elassy et al., 2024; Lakshumiah et al., 2025). In addition, by improving recycling, forecasting waste creation, and optimizing waste collection routes, AI helps to improve waste management systems (Fang et al., 2023).

In this aspect, AI aids urban planning by simulating the environmental implications of construction projects and encouraging sustainable growth. It also helps to monitor air and water quality using sensors and AI algorithms that detect pollutants and offer solutions (Subramaniam et al., 2022; Alotaibi and Nassif, 2024). Furthermore, AI-powered disaster management systems improve natural catastrophe preparedness and response, minimizing environmental damage, and saving lives (Xu and Xue, 2024).

Despite the enormous potential of AI for environmental sustainability, there are challenges to overcome in its implementation. These are the concerns about the massive investment necessary, the potential of privacy data breaches, and uneven access to AI technologies across geographies. To mitigate these risks, governments, corporations, and communities must collaborate to provide safe, inclusive, and equitable AI-based solutions for sustainability.

This chapter highlights the role of AI technologies to enhance environmental sustainability in urban regions. It analyzes applications, advantages, and challenges, showcasing AI in sustainable urban growth and how it moves toward a greener planet.

4.2 Utilization of AI

While urban regions are rapidly expanding, they are also facing mounting environmental issues such as waste, pollution, and resource shortages. Therefore, achieving a balance between urban growth and sustainability is essential. AI provides innovative data-driven approaches to these challenges, as well as promoting sustainable urban activities. It presented the applications of AI in a multitude of environmental and urban areas are addressed as follows:

4.2.1 Environmental Monitoring

Sustainability requires real-time environmental parameter monitoring. AI sensors and algorithms detect pollutants in the air and water, enabling prompt intervention to lessen environmental damage. AI is also capable of analyzing satellite pictures to track urbanization, water quality issues, and deforestation, providing crucial information for environmental management. One particularly notable negative consequence of urbanization is air pollution. AI technologies use machine learning models and sensor networks to provide real-time monitoring and predictive analytics for air quality. For instance, using data processed by AI algorithms, Internet of Things (IoT) sensors are able to detect hotspots and predict trends. This enables policymakers to pursue specific solutions, such as regulating industrial emissions and reducing transportation congestion.

4.2.2 Water Quality Management

Water in cities must be clean and safe for it to be a public health imperative as well as an ecological imperative. AI tools analyze data from water monitoring systems to detect contaminants and predict water quality problems. This highlights the need for Adaptive Intelligent Dynamic Water Resource Planning (AIDWRP) for the water environment sustainability of urban regions. For instance, in AIDWRP, Markov Decision Process (MDP) is introduced as a strategy for managing dynamic water resources, by carrying out environmental planning through sensitivity-driven methods and locational constraints on annual usage and release (Xiang et al., 2021). AI simulations can give many key points and insights about the role of urban activities in water quality, and this will lead the way to mitigation strategies.

4.2.3 Waste Management Systems

Sustainable urban development depends on the efficiency of the management of waste. Waste management is a highly complex operation in urban areas, comprising trash collection, transportation, recycling, and disposal.

AI enhances waste collection by developing optimal routes and schedules, resulting in decreased fuel consumption and expenditure. An AI image recognition system does a better job of sorting recyclables, leading to higher recycling rates and less trash diverted to landfills (Ponis et al., 2023). Predictive models help cities to get ahead of waste trends, which can inform planning and improvement of resource streams. This has also led startups to innovate in the general waste management sector, where Italian Startup ReLearn has developed NANDO, an advanced AI solution that makes it easier to manage waste in a more sustainable way, thanks to its process optimization, waste production monitoring, and insights in one dashboard. Through gamified awareness campaigns on waste reduction, reuse, and recycling, it decreases environmental impact and also, in return, it leads to a greater engagement of individuals and local communities (Mulè, 2024).

4.2.4 Energy Management

AI powered technologies are vastly improving energy efficiency, which is essential for environmental sustainability. Smart grids driven by AI enhance energy distribution, balancing supply and demand, and integrating renewable sources such as solar and wind (Ijala et al., 2024). Through predictive analysis, AI can predict energy consumption, reduce wastage, and add reliability to the grid. Moreover, AI systems also assist in microgrid management with the goal of promoting local energy production and reducing dependency on nonrenewable sources (Bassiliades and Chalkiadakis, 2018). Ultimately, these are the applications that would render AI an indispensable tool in the quest for energy efficiency, sustainability, and resilience in the cities of tomorrow.

4.2.5 Transportation Systems

Transportation creates a lot of urban emissions. AI helps make this sector more sustainable by improving traffic management, optimizing public transit, and creating autonomous electric vehicles (Elbroumi et al., 2025). Machine learning looks at real-time traffic to optimize signal timings, reduce congestion, and improve traffic flow, ultimately reducing fuel consumption (Louati, 2025). AI also aids delivery companies with route planning and promotes shared mobility to reduce vehicles on the road (Tao et al., 2024). AI optimizes the operations by analyzing data to plan routes, predict delivery times, and enhance fuel efficiency, which enables dynamic routing and reducing costs and environmental impact.

4.2.6 Urban Planning and Development

AI-driven tools are changing urban planning by helping with data-informed decisions. Predictive modeling helps planners assess environmental impacts of developments, promoting green infrastructure and sustainable land use.

Geographical Information System (GIS) combined with AI offers insights into heat islands, water management, and renewable energy placement. Green infrastructure in urban areas, like parks, urban forests, and green roofs, has several key functions to help improve air quality, mitigate urban heat, and enhance biodiversity (Shaamala et al., 2024). AI helps in planning and maintenance of green infrastructures by enabling spatial data analyses and ecological impact modeling. For example, AI can identify the most favorable locations to plant trees based on environmental factors. Furthermore, AI-driven remote-sensing technologies can monitor health conditions of any green areas and detect any signs of decline or stress in them (Ma et al., 2022).

4.2.7 Climate Resilience and Disaster Management

Natural disasters are major threats to cities, worsened by climate change. AI improves readiness and reaction by predicting events such as floods, wildfires, and earthquakes. AI predictive models forecast extreme weather conditions like heatwaves and floods, helping with preparation and response. In addition, AI analyzes historical data and simulates future scenarios to assist urban planners in creating resilient infrastructure and policies. Projects like EnviroAtlas offer insights into the impacts of climate change on societies, ecosystems, and healthcare (Pickard et al., 2015).

4.2.8 Summary

Based on the above discussion, it can be summarized as in Table 4.1.

TABLE 4.1

Overview of Utilization of Artificial Intelligence in Urban Area

Theme	Utilization of Artificial Intelligence
Environmental monitoring	• Monitors air and water pollutants in real time, leveraging machine learning models and IoT devices to provide predictive analytics. • Identifies environmental concerns like deforestation, urban expansion, and water quality issues using satellite imagery.
Water quality management	• Analyze water monitoring data to detect contaminants and predict water quality issues. • AIDWRP uses Markov decision processes for dynamic water resource management, aiding in mitigation strategies for urban water environments.
Waste management systems	• Optimizes waste collection routes and schedules, sorts of recyclables using image recognition, and predicts waste trends for better planning. • Solutions like NANDO improve sustainability by monitoring waste production and engaging communities through gamified awareness campaigns.

(Continued)

TABLE 4.1 (*Continued*)

Overview of Utilization of Artificial Intelligence in Urban Area

Theme	Utilization of Artificial Intelligence
Energy management	• Enhances energy efficiency via smart grids that optimize energy distribution and incorporate renewables. • Promote local energy production and reduce dependency on nonrenewables, fostering sustainability and resilience.
Transportation systems	• Improves traffic management through real-time optimization of signals and traffic flow. • Optimizes public transit schedules, route planning for delivery services, and promotes shared mobility. • Contributes to autonomous electric vehicle development, reducing emissions and fuel consumption.
Urban planning and development	• AI-driven tools like GIS assist in sustainable land use and green infrastructure development. • Assesses environmental impacts, and AI recommends optimal locations for planting trees, monitors green spaces, and ensures effective maintenance of urban greenery.
Climate resilience and disaster management	• Forecasts natural disasters such as floods, wildfires, and earthquakes, enabling cities to prepare better. • Analyze historical data to simulate future scenarios and guide resilient infrastructure planning, ensuring readiness against climate change impacts.

4.3 Challenges and Ethical Considerations

AI has immense potential to improve a city's sustainability, efficiency, and quality of life within society. AI adoption in urban sustainability has potential but faces challenges and ethical concerns. High costs for implementation and maintenance are major issues, especially in developing regions (Elbroumi et al., 2025). The vast majority of developing nations deal with a number of possible limitations in terms of digital connectivity, obsolete systems, and other infrastructural elements within their lands that make it difficult if not impossible to use AI technologies. Furthermore, they require a large financial investment in both skilled staff and technology to implement AI systems, which is a challenge for many smaller cities.

Moreover, massive data collection in urban regions also creates challenges in regard to privacy and security, which necessitate proper management of sensitive data. However, ensuring individual's privacy requires ensuring sensitive information is handled ethically (Mirindi et al., 2024). Discussion about AI issue circumstantially raises concern about unequal access to technology and potentially exacerbating the digital divide, marginalizing some communities. Another significant difficulty is unpredictability and complexity in urban systems, which results in inaccurate predictions if AI oversimplifies urban settings, particularly in the context of human movement, policy interventions, or climate change (Sanchez et al., 2024).

Algorithmic bias and fairness lead to ethical issues, as AI systems can unintentionally reinforce the biases present in their training data, leading to unfair results. In addition, privacy concerns like the mishandling of private data and monitoring arise from the extensive data harvesting essential for AI (Mirindi et al., 2024). The most worrisome, by far, is algorithmic bias based on AI trained on substandard datasets that prop up discrimination and other problems for previously marginalized communities. This calls for AI algorithms to be designed in a transparent and equitable manner (Ferrara, 2024). Communities that see their needs addressed and elevated within AI boundaries are likely to give trust to the public (Xu and Xue, 2024). The importance of transparency and accountability in AI decision-making cannot be overstated; trust must be earned. Responsible use of AI requires stakeholders to understand how such systems make decisions.

In summary, cooperation among governments, businesses, and research institutes is required to overcome these challenges. They should address the importance of ethical foundations for AI, transparency, equality, equitableness, and accessibility to the technology. Public–private partnerships can diversify the financial risk associated with AI adoption, making it less costly. If these issues are solved, AI can be shaped and executed in an ethical way, such that even urban spaces can get a bit more influenced and become more sustainable.

4.4 Conclusion

AI can help to make them more sustainable, and it plays an important role and is a prerequisite for environmental sustainability within urban regions by offering new solutions in a multitude of contexts. It allows to increase in efficiency of energy consumption, optimize waste management, and improve the operation of transport. AI enables real-time monitoring of environmental conditions, supports urban planning, and enhances disaster management, all of which help lower emissions and increase the efficient use of resources.

However, key barriers to successfully leveraging AI in urban sustainability include the high costs of these technologies, data privacy concerns, and equitable access to the technology. These challenges are surmountable through collaboration among governments, industries, and communities, combined with policies for responsible AI usage. Together, AI can support sustainable and healthy urban development. In short, AI is a powerful solution for urban sustainability, empowering cities to be greener and smarter as they prepare for the future environmental challenges.

Acknowledgment

The authors would like to thank the Ministry of Higher Education, Malaysia, for funding this research through the Fundamental Research Grant Scheme, Project No: 203.PHUMANITI.6712162.

References

Alotaibi, E. and Nassif, N., (2024), Artificial intelligence in environmental monitoring: In-depth analysis, *Discover Artificial Intelligence*, **4**, 84.

Bassiliades, N. and Chalkiadakis, G., (2018), Artificial intelligence techniques for the smart grid, *Advances in Building Energy Research*, **12**, 1–2.

Elassy, M., Al-Hattab, M., Takruri, M. and Badawi, S., (2024), Intelligent transportation systems for sustainable smart cities, *Transportation Engineering*, **16**, 100252.

Elbroumi, S., Idrissi, M.A., Chaaouan, M. and Eddahmouny, H., (2025), Exploring trends, perspectives, and challenges of artificial intelligence in sustainable mobility: A systematic review, in *Utilizing Technology to Manage Territories*, 207–238. https://doi.org/10.4018/979-8-3693-6854-1.ch007.

Fang, B., Yu, J., Chen, Z., Osman, A.I., Farghali, M., Ihara, I., Hamza, E.H., Rooney, D.W. and Yap, P.-S., (2023), Artificial intelligence for waste management in smart cities: A review, *Environmental Chemistry Letters*, **21**, 1959–1989.

Ferrara, E., (2024), Fairness and bias in artificial intelligence: A brief survey of sources, impacts, and mitigation strategies, *Science*, **6**, 3.

Ijala, A., Idowu-Bismark, B., Jemitola, P., Obadiah, A. and Wikiman, O., (2024), Artificial neural network-based home energy management system for smart homes, *Computer and Telecommunication Engineering*, **2**, 2372.

Lakshumiah, A., Malaiarasan, A., Packianathan, R., Natarajan, S.K. and Arumugam, G., (2025), Application of artificial intelligence (AI) techniques for green transportation in smart city, in A. Khang (ed.) Driving Green *Transportation System Through Artificial Intelligence and Automation*. Cham: Springer Nature Switzerland, 335–358.

Louati, A., (2025), Machine learning framework for sustainable traffic management and safety in AlKharj city, *Sustainable Futures*, **9**, 100407.

Ma, Y., Zheng, X., Liu, M., Liu, D., Ai, G. and Chen, X., (2022), Spatio-temporal evolution characteristics analysis and optimization prediction of urban green infrastructure: A case study of Beijing, China, *Scientific Reports*, **12**, 10702.

Mirindi, D., Sinkhonde, D. and Mirindi, F., (2024), An advance review of urban-AI and ethical considerations, in *Proceedings of the 2nd ACM SIGSPATIAL International Workshop on Advances in Urban-AI*. New York, NY: Association for Computing Machinery, 24–33.

Mulè, L., (2024), *Revolutionizing Waste Management: The Role of AI in Building Sustainable Practices, AI for Good Stories*, International Telecommunication Union (ITU), Geneva, Switzerland.

Pickard, B.R., Daniel, J., Mehaffey, M., Jackson, L.E. and Neale, A., (2015), EnviroAtlas: A new geospatial tool to foster ecosystem services science and resource management, *Ecosystem Services*, **14**, 45–55.

Ponis, S., Plakas, G., Aretoulaki, E., Tzanetou, D. and Maroutas, T.N., (2023), LoRaWAN for tracking inland routes of plastic waste: Introducing the smart TRACKPLAST bottle, *Cleaner Waste Systems*, **4**, 100068.

Sanchez, T.W., Brenman, M. and Ye, X., (2024), The ethical concerns of artificial intelligence in urban planning, *Journal of the American Planning Association*, **91**, 1–14.

Shaamala, A., Yigitcanlar, T., Nili, A. and Nyandega, D., (2024), Algorithmic green infrastructure optimisation: Review of artificial intelligence driven approaches for tackling climate change, *Sustainable Cities and Society*, **101**, 105182.

Subramaniam, S., Raju, N., Ganesan, A., Rajavel, N., Chenniappan, M., Prakash, C., Pramanik, A., Basak, A.K. and Dixit, S., (2022), Artificial intelligence technologies for forecasting air pollution and human health: A narrative review, *Sustainability*, **14**, 9951.

Tao, X., Cheng, L., Zhang, R., Chan, W.K., Chao, H. and Qin, J., (2024), Towards green innovation in smart cities: Leveraging traffic flow prediction with machine learning algorithms for sustainable transportation systems, *Sustainability*, **16**, 251.

United Nation, (2022), *World Population Prospects 2022*, Department of Economic and Social Affairs, New York, USA.

Xiang, X., Li, Q., Khan, S. and Khalaf, O.I., (2021), Urban water resource management for sustainable environment planning using artificial intelligence techniques, *Environmental Impact Assessment Review*, **86**, 106515.

Xu, C. and Xue, Z., (2024), Applications and challenges of artificial intelligence in the field of disaster prevention, reduction, and relief, *Natural Hazards Research*, **4**, 169–172.

Yigitcanlar, T. and Cugurullo, F., (2020), The sustainability of artificial intelligence: An urbanistic viewpoint from the lens of smart and sustainable cities, *Sustainability*, **12**, 8548.

Yussuf, R.O. and Asfour, O.S., (2024), Applications of artificial intelligence for energy efficiency throughout the building lifecycle: An overview, *Energy and Buildings*, **305**, 113903.

5

Digital Inclusion and Accessible Technologies in Smart Cities

Mazni Omar, Kamal Imran Mohd Sharif, Abdullah Almogahed, and Hamzah Alaidaros

5.1 Introduction to Digital Inclusion of Smart Cities

Nowadays, smart cities are the ultimate achievement of urban advancement because of the use of Internet of Things (IoT), Artificial Intelligence (AI), and big data to enhance the living standards of people (Dwivedi et al., 2021). Smart cities can fundamentally change the way people live, work, and communicate with the incorporation of these technologies. The main aim of smart cities is to increase the effectiveness, sustainability, and livability of urban centers. One of the ways to accomplish it is by augmenting public system services and increasing energy efficiency with smart grids. Nonetheless, as urban areas implement these sophisticated systems, these cities face the challenge of narrowing the gap between the privileged and underprivileged groups of citizens. These benefits should no longer be limited to people from specific socioeconomic classes, age groups, or physical ability (Makkonen & Inkinen, 2024).

Digital inclusion is a concept that when applied in the context of smart cities, becomes a concerted effort to ensure individuals from disadvantaged communities have access to and can make effective use of information and communications technologies (Kempin Reuter, 2019). Conversely, accessibility is geared toward the development of technologies, services, and environments that will be usable by people with different levels of ability (Khanlou et al., 2021). The two concepts work together to create a smart city that is inclusive by narrowing the digital gap and enabling everyone to have access to the information they need.

Despite the notion of smart cities depicting greater prospects, many obstacles inhibit people from distinct backgrounds to completely embrace this digital shift (Mhlongo et al., 2023). A case in point is that many older adults lack the digital literacy that would help them operate advanced technologies, while people with disabilities meet barriers when it comes to accessing infrastructure or devices. Likewise, some underprivileged groups are economically disadvantaged and unable to access digital services. Such factors work together to maintain the digital divide that leads to a large segment of the population being unable to reap the benefits associated with smart city initiatives.

These issues need to be solved not only on moral grounds, but also on economic and social ones. There is an opportunity for inclusive smart cities to enhance economic growth, develop social unity, and better the standard of living within an urban area (Robinson et al., 2015). Effective city planners and policymakers ensure that all residents, regardless of their specific circumstances, have the opportunity to succeed using accessible and inclusive technology.

The digital inclusion and the smart city technology phenomenon, as well as the ease of obtaining them, will be studied and explored in this chapter. The concepts like assistive technology and engagement of the community in building an inclusive system of a digital society will be highlighted. In addition, this chapter will also address the gaps to be filled by policymakers, technology designers, and urban engineers to ensure inclusiveness is achieved. Some exemplary studies will be reviewed that focus on accessibility and inclusion, as well as provide advanced planning for smart cities in the future. Digital transformation of cities worldwide must take into account the risk of exclusion. It is possible to achieve advanced technological development in smart cities while ensuring equity by focusing on providing digital accessibility and inclusion.

5.2 Digital Inclusion in Smart Cities

Wolniak and Stecuła (2024) argue that the simultaneous use of digital technologies is possible across all communal units and socioeconomic levels, which is why inclusion is a core aspect in building a smart city. Digital inclusion can be divided into three pillars: accessibility, affordability, and digital literacy. Accessibility ensures that people with disabilities and elderly individuals can use technological tools and digital platforms. Affordability refers to access to a functional device, the Internet, and assistive technologies (AT) that are economically priced. Digital literacy means having the skills to use digital instruments cost-effectively, which is crucial for functioning in a smart city.

The integration of technology helps to foster inclusiveness in smart cities as it is a key factor during the planning and implementation stage. Using technology such as the Internet of Things (IoT), artificial intelligence (AI), and urban informatics, smart cities can improve the quality of public service delivery, resource allocation, and even civic engagement (Farahani et al., 2018).

For example, smart public transport systems with real-time locating services or other forms of access control can assist mobility-impaired people. In addition, AI applications can help people with very low digital literacy learn how to use computers. If these technologies are implemented with an inclusive approach in mind, they can greatly reduce the existing disparity in access and opportunity in the digital urban ecosystem for the marginalized communities.

Underserved areas are still greatly hindered in terms of using technology and its capabilities. The "digital divide," concerning the gap between those who have access to digital tools and those who don't have it, remains persistent. Rural areas lack appropriate infrastructure, while urban areas do not have enough broadband access. Further, the overall expense of technology poses additional hurdles (Perera et al., 2015). In addition, most marginalized groups face low levels of digital literacy coupled with lack of proper training programs which systemically act as roadblocks in resource availability. Furthermore, language barriers, differing cultures, and lack of trust in technology add to the challenge, putting vulnerable groups in a smothering position in the smart cities.

A variety of these global efforts have included programs if not all, which have demonstrated some promise (Smith et al., 2022). For instance, in Barcelona, Spain, the city has a goal called "Barcelona Digital City Plan," which intends to open the accessibility of technology via open source software, free public Wi-Fi, and participatory technology workshops. Also in India, the Digital India initiative attention toward developing the internet infrastructure for rural areas and encouraging literacy training. In the United States, there are programs like "ConnectHomeUSA," which targets low-income families by giving them easy access to the internet and training them on the basics of computers. These programs illustrate how civil societies, governments, and some corporations work together to make "smart cities" work and be accessible to as many people as possible.

Along with guaranteeing equality, the inclusion of digital technologies in the strategies for smart city developments helps to improve the economy and social relations. Making it possible for all citizens to access and utilize technology enables cities to harness the power of their diverse abilities and viewpoints (Kaiser, 2024). Private companies gain broader markets, and public agencies can attend to the requirements of all citizens most efficiently. Furthermore, people from different communities can engage in civic matters and help transform their city, which enhances the feeling of community and inclusivity.

In the coming years, it will be critical to provide digital inclusion in a more integrated manner that covers all three components: infrastructure, cost, and education. Governments must approach the expansion of affordable, quality broadband services in rural and economically disadvantaged areas (Benedicta et al., 2024). There should be outreach and instructional materials that cater to older citizens, disabled people, and other disadvantaged audiences. On the other hand, every effort that enables digital inclusion has to be done within the context of urban planning; so, all smart city facilities and services are created with the principle of inclusivity.

In the end, the digital inclusion concept given to the smart city is greater than simple technology accessibility. It is a dedication to fostering urban settings in which each and every citizen, no matter their standing, can flourish. By adopting inclusion as a primary concern, smart cities can reach their actual goals as centers for creativity, ecological balance, and social justice. This vision promises to unite a range of players but needs regular changes to match new barriers and determination toward inclusion.

5.3 Universal Design Principles and Accessibility

Universal design principles serve as a foundation for creating environments, products, and technologies that are inherently accessible and usable by everyone, regardless of their abilities or circumstances (Iwarsson & Stahl, 2003). This concept emphasizes inclusivity from the initial stages of development, ensuring that no one is excluded or disadvantaged. Architect Ronald Mace, a key advocate for universal design, popularized the term by promoting the "design for all" philosophy, which encourages the creation of goods and services that do not require adaptations or modifications to accommodate specific groups. This approach highlights the importance of considering diverse needs during the design process to foster equal access and usability.

When applied to smart cities, universal design principles become even more important. These cities are frequently distinguished by sophisticated public transportation networks, digital services, and creative urban amenities. Universal design guarantees that these elements are accessible to all individuals, including those with disabilities, seniors, and other disadvantaged groups (Borowczyk, 2018). Smart cities may better serve their varied populations and improve urban living quality by making these advancements more inclusive. This strategy not only addresses accessibility concerns but also coincides with the overall objective of building equal urban settings.

Adopting universal design principles in smart city construction does more than improve accessibility; it promotes social justice by removing obstacles that hinder vulnerable groups from fully participating in society. Inclusive technology and services reduce barriers that frequently marginalize specific communities, allowing for increased participation and interaction. As a result, universal design not only improves the operation of smart cities but it also develops a sense of community and equality. Smart cities that prioritize inclusion may become examples of development, reflecting the principles of justice and accessible to everyone.

5.3.1 Relevance to Smart Cities

Smart cities strive to enhance urban living standards through the integration of advanced technologies such as the Internet of Things (IoT), AI, and big data. These technologies enable cities to become more efficient, sustainable, and responsive to the needs of their inhabitants (Rashid & Kausik, 2024). A key aspect of this transformation is inclusivity, ensuring that all citizens, regardless of age, ability, or socioeconomic status, can benefit from the advancements. The development of smart cities emphasizes the importance of creating environments where technology is accessible and usable for everyone, fostering equitable opportunities for participation and engagement within the urban ecosystem.

Smart city aims are strongly aligned with universal design principles, which emphasize the creation of adaptable, user-friendly, and equitable solutions for all persons. Universal design aims to meet various demands by ensuring that physical environments and technology are accessible to individuals of varying abilities (Lifelo et al., 2024). In the context of smart cities, this idea assures that technical breakthroughs are available to everybody, rather than just a chosen few. For example, a public transit application that includes text-to-speech features might substantially help visually challenged users, as well as people with inadequate reading skills or those who struggle with utilizing sophisticated digital interfaces.

By incorporating accessibility into the design and deployment of smart city technology, communities can satisfy the demands of all populations while not leaving any inhabitants behind. As technology advances at a rapid speed, the issue is to ensure that all people, regardless of circumstance, can access and use these technologies. A creative, inclusive approach to the integration of technology in urban planning can help build smart cities that are intelligent in their ability to serve all citizens, fostering a more inclusive and sustainable urban future.

5.3.2 Designing Urban Technologies for Accessibility and Usability

Designing urban technologies for accessibility and usability involves ensuring that all technological solutions are inclusive and functional for a wide range of users, including those with disabilities. One of the key factors in achieving this is prioritizing user experience, which ensures that technology is intuitive, easy to use, and adaptable for diverse needs (Paiva et al., 2021). When designing smart kiosks, mobile applications, or transportation-related technologies, it is crucial to consider the varying abilities of users. For instance, integrating features such as adjustable font sizes, voice commands, and tactile feedback on digital buttons can enhance usability for people with visual, auditory, or motor impairments.

To boost accessibility even further, urban technology should focus on the physical components of the environment. One example is the use of sensor-equipped crosswalks that detect pedestrians and modify signals appropriately, resulting in safer crossings for those with mobility issues. Furthermore, making public places such as parks, transit hubs, and retail malls wheelchair accessible ensures that everyone can easily navigate the urban environment. These adaptations not only benefit those with physical impairments, but they also improve the general usability of public areas for elders, parents with strollers, and others who may need additional help.

Incorporating these accessibility measures into urban infrastructure design saves money in the long run. Rather than retrofitting spaces or technology later, including these elements in the design process guarantees that they are both cost-effective and easily incorporated into the community. When accessibility is incorporated into the base of urban technology, it creates a fair and inclusive environment for all citizens, regardless of physical or cognitive ability. This innovative technique helps develop cities that are accessible and functional for everyone.

5.3.3 The Role of Policy Frameworks and Standards

Smart city construction is underpinned by policies and strategies that set out criteria for the integration of universal design principles. Legislative provisions such as the Americans with Disabilities Act in the United States and the United Nations' Convention on the Rights of Persons with Disabilities ensure that access is provided legally. In the context of the internet, people with disabilities are provided comprehensive standards through the Web Content Accessibility Guidelines (WCAG) (Burzagli et al., 2022). In addition, these frameworks and policies make sure that all design efforts are properly aligned and that there is responsibility on the part of developers so that appropriate technologies are created. For example, in complying with WCAG, smart cities' websites and applications should be usable through screen readers, keyboard-only use, and other assistive devices.

Policies and standards not only assure compliance with accessibility regulations, but they also encourage the development of inclusive technology (Kolotouchkina et al., 2024). Furthermore, governments and regulatory agencies often change these regulations to reflect technological improvements and changing societal demands. This enables ongoing development in accessibility, ensuring that both physical and virtual settings inside smart cities are inclusive of all. These adaptable policy frameworks serve as a guide for city planners, technology developers, and service providers, ensuring that accessibility is included throughout all stages of smart city design and implementation.

The incorporation of universal design principles into smart city frameworks is critical to creating an environment in which all inhabitants may benefit from technology improvements. Smart communities may prioritize accessibility from the start by including diversity into their core laws and standards, rather than retrofitting solutions after the fact. Furthermore, these frameworks contribute to the establishment of performance benchmarks, allowing cities to evaluate the efficacy of their accessibility efforts. Standards such as the European Union's Accessibility Act and the International Telecommunication Union's accessibility guidelines provide additional guidance for ensuring that smart city infrastructures meet the needs of people with disabilities, particularly in transportation, healthcare, and public services. Through continuous collaboration among policymakers, technology developers, and disability advocacy groups, smart cities can evolve into truly inclusive environments for all individuals, regardless of their abilities or limitations.

5.3.4 Examples of Case Studies of Universally Designed Urban Technologies

Principles of universal design have shown their value in practice by deploying them in smart cities across the globe. These designs are augmenting even a disabled person's access to technologies, which has made it effortless for them to engage in the social life of the city. Table 5.1 outlines examples of cities and describes how universal design facilitates better access and use of the technology.

5.3.5 The Impact of Universally Designed Technologies

These studies shown in Table 5.1, demonstrate that universal design increases accessibility for targeted groups, but also improves the usability of urban technologies. These projects make people feel more valued and self-sufficient, enabling them to engage utterly with urban life. They are also good examples for other cities that want to be more inclusive, demonstrating that these cities can be and are transformed by incorporating universal design into smart city policies.

5.4 AT in Smart Cities

The incorporation of AT increases the attractiveness of smart cities for diverse populations. AT is targeted toward disabled persons, elderly individuals, and other disadvantaged groups to assist them in navigating conventional urban settings (Fotteler et al., 2022). As previously stated, some of the common assistive devices used in urban areas include mobility aids, screen readers, hearing aids, and communications devices. For example, GPS-enabled smart wheelchairs or scooters allow individuals to get around complex urban areas with greater freedom. Visually impaired people can access digital information via screen readers or braille displays, while people with

TABLE 5.1

Examples of City Applying Universal Design Features

City	Universal Design Features	Impact and Benefits	References
Barcelona	Smart bus stops with tactile paving, audio announcements, and real-time updates via accessible apps. Accessible apps provide personalized journey planning with features for wheelchair users.	Enhances mobility for the visually impaired and wheelchair users by integrating physical infrastructure with digital tools, making public transport more accessible and efficient.	Padrón Nápoles et al. (2020)
Singapore	Cashless payment systems with voice-guided functionality, wheelchair-accessible digital kiosks, smart home technologies for aging populations, remote monitoring systems, and voice-activated devices.	Ensures inclusive access to urban services, promoting independence for individuals with disabilities and enhancing the quality of life for the elderly through accessible technologies.	Sha and Taeihagh (2024)
London	Step-free access retrofits for Tube stations, elevators, ramps, and an accessible journey planner app that provides step-free routes, live updates, and accessible boarding areas for buses and trains.	Improves public transport accessibility for individuals with mobility impairments, making it easier to travel around the city while offering a user-friendly digital tool for planning accessible routes.	Harding (2024)
New York City	Accessible pedestrian signals (APS) with auditory cues and tactile push buttons at intersections. Integration of apps such as Aira and Be My Eyes, which connect visually impaired users with sighted volunteers or professionals.	Enhances independent navigation for visually impaired users, contributing to a safer and more inclusive city environment.	Xu et al. (2024)
Tokyo	Tactile guidance paths, audible announcements, priority seating areas in public transportation, multilingual and accessible mobile apps for tourists with wheelchair-accessible routes and accommodations.	Promotes inclusivity for residents and visitors with disabilities, particularly during international events, by integrating accessibility into public transport and tourism infrastructure.	Bian (2021)
Toronto	Smart traffic management systems with audio-enabled crosswalk signals, adaptive traffic lights, accessible public Wi-Fi networks, and digital kiosks with voice-to-text and text-to-speech capabilities.	Prioritizes pedestrian safety and accessibility, ensuring that public spaces and transportation networks are usable by people with disabilities. This integration of accessibility into urban infrastructure fosters a more inclusive and user-friendly environment for all.	Zhuang (2018)

hearing problems can use hearing aids linked to public systems to receive audio information instantaneously.

The combination of these technologies and the wider smart city framework is important for enhancing the usability of the environments (Salha et al., 2020). For example, devices within the IoT ecosystem can be utilized for environmental surveillance and implementing adaptive functionalities. Smart traffic lights, for example, can extend their green lights to pedestrians as needed, especially those who require mobility aids. Moreover, AI can further enhance AT by anticipating and addressing needs. For instance, AI can facilitate navigation by issuing spoken directions as they are needed or proposing more accessible alternatives. This is highly relevant for people with restricted movement or eyesight.

The synergistic effect of IoT and AI adds to the autonomy of the users and ensures that they remain integrated to the complex urban environment, hence ensuring their social participation.

AT are crucial to people with disabilities, the elderly, and other marginalized demographics. Such devices foster greater participation in routine activities through improved autonomy (Rosa, 2025). Fall detection sensors, health monitoring devices, and virtual assistants enable the elderly to stay connected to healthcare services while enhancing their independence. The disabled can utilize smart city technologies such as voice-activated elevators, automated kiosks with text-to-speech functionality, and automated street systems, which help make day-to-day errands easier and more efficient. These technologies also enable the previously marginalized to partake and engage more actively in urban life, including improving their access to healthcare, education, and job opportunities. Furthermore, smart city AT remove traditional social and physical barriers that these previously isolated people face, allowing everyone to actively partake in the development of the city and fully benefit from its resources.

Nevertheless, there are a number of challenges that hinder the full integration of AT. To begin with, the lack of interoperability between urban infrastructure and the latest assistive devices poses a challenge. Sometimes, it is the case that the AT have digital systems or platforms that are not compatible with the smart city services (Hariri et al., 2019). Moreover, the pricing for designing and executing AT is much too high for less economically developed regions. In this way, a city is not able or willing to pay for the infrastructure, thus deselecting it, and subsequently misses out on its benefits. Lastly, lack of information regarding the use and advantages of AT leads to underutilization (Hoppestad, 2007). These obstacles can be overcome if more affordable, flexible, and interoperable AT are designed and developed. Awareness campaigns can be sponsored by a collaboration among the government, technology firms, and civil organizations to provide funding and increase the utilization of these systems.

5.5 Challenges in Achieving Digital Inclusion and Accessibility

Maintaining digital accessibility and inclusion in the context of smart cities presents a difficult problem because it requires addressing multiple challenges on the technical, economic, social, and policy fronts. Figure 5.1 demonstrates issues and challenges in achieving digital inclusion and accessibility in smart cities.

The foremost technical problem is the absence of sufficient infrastructure that can enable individuals to make use of digital devices and services. In a lot of cities, particularly in developing areas (Aruleba & Jere, 2022), there tends to be a deficit of essential digital infrastructure required for smart technologies such as high-speed broadband, Wi-Fi networks, and mobile data coverage. This widening gap in infrastructure can pose serious challenges even to the most basic of services being offered such as telemedicine, online educational opportunities, and for those who are handicapped (Radu, 2020), including government services. In addition, differing technologies and platforms not being able to work together can also serve as a barrier to access. For instance, smart city interventions may not be fully assistive technology-friendly.

In terms of economic barriers, device cost and internet accessibility are economic barriers that restrict digital inclusion from being attained. For marginalized groups and low-socioeconomic individuals, the price of such readily available technology can be overly burdensome. Even though smartphones and other devices are relatively cheaper than they used to be, most of the

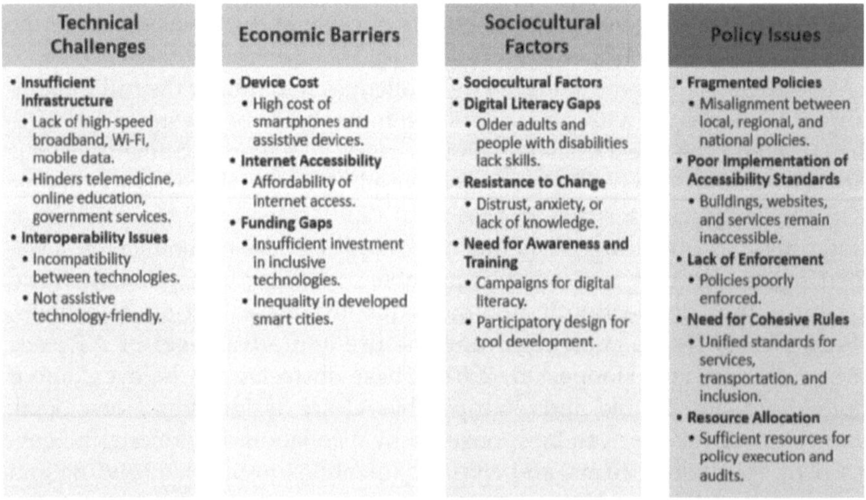

Technical Challenges	Economic Barriers	Sociocultural Factors	Policy Issues

• **Insufficient Infrastructure**
  • Lack of high-speed broadband, Wi-Fi, mobile data.
  • Hinders telemedicine, online education, government services.
• **Interoperability Issues**
  • Incompatibility between technologies.
  • Not assistive technology-friendly.
	• **Device Cost**
	  • High cost of smartphones and assistive devices.
	• **Internet Accessibility**
	  • Affordability of internet access.
	• **Funding Gaps**
	  • Insufficient investment in inclusive technologies.
	  • Inequality in developed smart cities.
		• **Sociocultural Factors**
		• **Digital Literacy Gaps**
		  • Older adults and people with disabilities lack skills.
		• **Resistance to Change**
		  • Distrust, anxiety, or lack of knowledge.
		• **Need for Awareness and Training**
		  • Campaigns for digital literacy.
		  • Participatory design for tool development.
			• **Fragmented Policies**
			  • Misalignment between local, regional, and national policies.
			• **Poor Implementation of Accessibility Standards**
			  • Buildings, websites, and services remain inaccessible.
			• **Lack of Enforcement**
			  • Policies poorly enforced.
			• **Need for Cohesive Rules**
			  • Unified standards for services, transportation, and inclusion.
			• **Resource Allocation**
			  • Sufficient resources for policy execution and audits.

FIGURE 5.1
Issues and challenges of digital inclusion and accessibility in smart cities.

population still struggles with purchasing assistive devices, maintaining internet access, and using a plethora of digital services (Marikyan et al., 2019). Furthermore, the lack of proportional funding in endeavors of the public and private sectors will restrain the deployment of such inclusive technologies in densely populated regions. Even the most developed smart cities face issues of greater inequality that stem from insufficient investment in initiatives related to digital inclusion. Private and governmental bodies should unify in the face of these obstacles and provide affordable solution and incentives to alleviate financial hardships on groups and individuals.

Achieving digital inclusion is complicated further due to several sociocultural factors. Many people, including older adults and people with disabilities, may not have the requisite skills to use smart city technologies (Agboola & Tunay, 2023). Even when these individuals have access to assistive devices, they may not possess the requisite skills to fully utilize them, rendering them unable to operate within the digital sphere. Additionally, there could be a reluctance to embrace newer technologies owing to distrust, anxiety about the change, or simply a lack of knowledge about the gadgets. As an illustration, elderly citizens may be apprehensive about using digital health technologies because of issues related to privacy and security. The MIS in these studies has also pointed out the need to focus on removing these social barriers through specific campaigns to promote digital literacy, more awareness about inclusion, and providing training to enhance the skills of the population (Colding et al., 2024). Targeting the needed social acceptance can also be helped via participatory design, where the affected populations are involved to ensure that their needs and preferences govern the construction of the required tools.

Governmental policy issues drastically impede the advancement toward digital inclusion (Raihan et al., 2024). Different fragmenting policies at the local, regional, and even national levels can create barriers in the execution procedures of the inclusion policies. There are several cases where such local or even regional policies do not coincide with national policies, causing confusion, which is certainly counterproductive. Furthermore, the failure to implement accessibility standards often leaves buildings, websites, and digital services as an illusion of accessibility for the person with disabilities (Slayi et al., 2024). Often, policies are designed for inclusivity but are implemented in poorly enforced and nonsatisfactory manners. These gaps are most evident in the attempt to utilize a more inclusive technology. One approach is the development of a defined cohesive set of rules for all sectors including services, transportation, and areas that prioritize digital inclusion. Equally important is the need for the assistance of the governments in assuring that the set standards are met and regularly audited for compliance. These technologies must be suitable for every resident within the country. Furthermore, the assertion that policy changes lead to a successful inclusionary initiative rests on receiving sufficient resources for its execution.

5.6 Strategies for Enhancing Digital Inclusion Within Smart Cities

There are several strategies that can be recommended to promote digital inclusion within smart cities, including the following:

5.6.1 Public and Private Collaborations in Increasing Digital Reach

One of the best steps to eliminating the digital gap in smart cities is done through public–private partnership (Patrick & Wenjing, 2017; Putri et al., 2024). Unfortunately, government authorities might not possess the optimal skill set or sufficient funds to further develop the digital infrastructure of a city, specifically in the underserved areas of a city. Partnerships with the private sector do possess some form of financial and technical know-how. Companies in the technology, electronics, and telecommunications industries can make a profit while further expanding digital infrastructure by building high-speed internet networks and other services. For instance, New York and London have teamed up with private technology organizations to provided free Wi-Fi and subsidized broadband to the public. These initiatives, alongside improving access to digital tools, increase civic innovation that comprehensively considers the entire city.

5.6.2 Community Engagement through Participatory Design Methods

Achieving a digital economy in smart cities is only possible when there is engagement from the targeted communities (Gooch et al., 2018). Community engagement is critical for identifying the needs, preferences, and challenges posed by different people for technological interventions. Such an approach ensures that citizens, especially from marginalized communities, actively participate in formulating smart city solutions that affect them (Kangana et al., 2024). The community is educated on ways to participate in the decision-making process so that technologies that are not relevant or accessible are not mandated upon them. For example, Barcelona has undertaken projects to improve digital inclusivity through the use of community consultations in the co-design of accessible technologies for the elderly and people with disabilities. Also, as with other local governments, they can work with civil society organizations to better understand the needs of at-risk groups so that relevant digital services can be designed and provided.

5.6.3 Educational and Training Approaches on Improving Digital Literacy

In order to participate in the benefits presented by a smart city, one must possess the skills to utilize and navigate through the digital tools. Therefore, digital literacy is crucial in the aspect of "inclusion," which makes it a prerequisite.

However, there is a need to focus on equipping these skills in all demographic niches, especially the elderly, people with disabilities, and other marginalized groups. These types of educational and training programs can be provided through schools, community centers, libraries, and even online. Further, these basic programs should also cover more advanced topics, for example, digital security and privacy. Examples of some of these programs include government nonprofit programs that provide basic computer skills training for senior citizens or comprehensive digital training programs. Such initiatives are fundamental for closing the gap that exists in the possibilities of utilizing a smart city.

5.6.4 Synergy of Policy Makers, Governments, and City Planners

It is evident that governments and city planners have a significant responsibility in determining how a city will change in the future (Mazzetto, 2024). To achieve greater digital inclusion, policymakers need to facilitate greater accessibility to digital resources. These policies should cut across all levels of urban planning, ensuring that all spaces, including public and civic amenities, transport infrastructural features, and even services like healthcare, are purposely designed to be more inclusive (Dingil, 2025). Moreover, government policies have to establish minimum standards around accessibility considerations such as disabilities and other vulnerable populations (Sze & Christensen, 2017). This might include stipulating requirements that social services' portable websites and other digital public services are functional and usable for the referred categories of people. In addition, these policies should also require and encourage corporate responsibility targeted toward supporting digital inclusion. In addition, city municipalities are required to allocate budgetary resources for the construction of buildings and facilities that support digital infrastructure in problem regions, and for social scientific research and creation of tools for accessible technology.

5.7 Future Directions and Emerging Trends

The following are potential future directions for utilizing AI to ensure inclusivity in smart cities.

5.7.1 The Use of AI and ML Technologies in New Cities and Their Impact on Accessibility

AI and ML as tools could change the scope of digital inclusion in smart cities to better cater to people with disabilities (PwD) differently. For example, AI-based boom technologies like voice recognition systems and computer vision can assist the visually or mobility impaired people to comprehend and interact with the digital world far better (Isazade, 2023). A glance at AI-powered voice assistants, such as Amazon Alexa or Google Assistant, shows how these devices allow people with disabilities to control smart devices and gather information without using interfaces. The algorithms of machine learning (ML) can also be applied to devise systems that can predict the needs of the users and respond in real-time (Botelho, 2021). For instance, AI could assist in efficiently designing public transport systems by changing the routes for the able-bodied and disabled passengers separately. The incorporation of AI and ML with smart city technologies improves not only the basic needs of accessibility but also provides intelligent, tailored services to varying groups of users.

5.7.2 Utilization of Big Data and Urban Analytics within Urban Planning

The application of big data and urban analytics seeks to enhance the planning and governance of smart cities (Gómez-Carmona et al., 2023). With the use of sensors, mobile devices, social media, and more, city sociologists are able to collect and dissect an abundance of data to determine the requirements and habits of residents. This data helps cities understand how various residents access and engage with public services, and which obstacles are present. For instance, mobility application data can reveal geographic areas where people with disabilities or elderly persons experiencing difficulty accessing public transportation live. This means that services can be provided precisely where people need them, and policies can be crafted that ensure maximum participation from all members of society. Furthermore, these data can also be used to gauge what aid is needed the most, and more resources can be allocated toward that field to achieve better and more inclusive urbanization.

Emerging technologies such as virtual reality (VR) and augmented reality (AR) hold great promise in improving the accessibility of smart cities (Wang et al., 2021). These technologies can transform the interactions of people with disabilities with their external environment by providing them with immersive and interactive experiences. For example, AR can assist people with visual impairment to navigate through public areas by providing audio or text descriptions overlaid on the physical world. VR can create a simulation of the environment to be used as a training tool or to assist people with disabilities in navigating real-life situations. For example, VR training could help people with mobility impairment learn to use public transportation systems. As AR and VR technologies continue to grow, the possibilities and opportunities to enrich the urban spaces grow as well.

The notion of "smart inclusion" is the most recent concept incited by Urban Innovation, which involves the seamless integration of Artificial Inclusion Technologies within already existing smart city technologies for effective utilization. In broader scope, Harb and Sidani (2022) explain it as an inclusion in society's digital ecosystem wherein everybody, regardless of their socio-economic or personal background, is able to engage with and make use of the system. It is not just access to technology; the notion outlines a design of a city which works fully, meaning that all facets, from transportation, healthcare, education, and even public service are catered in a matter which makes it feasible for every citizen to use (Bercaru & Popescu, 2024; Malek et al., 2021). Smart inclusion relies on technologies such as AI, IoT, and Data Science to provision tailored experiences aimed at addressing the particular needs of individuals. The purpose goes beyond just being smart in the employment of technologies but being smart in equity, inclusivity, and caring for the people.

5.8 Conclusion

As highlighted before, the combination of digital inclusion with accessible technologies within smart cities goes beyond a mere technology focus to encompass a social need that has to be attended to. Cities are now becoming more urbanized than ever before, and there is increasing dependence on smart technologies for improving the quality of life. It is paramount that such innovations remain universal and accessible to all, especially the vulnerable and marginalized sectors of society. The strategies presented in this chapter, including public and private cooperation, community participation, digital skills training, and comprehensible policy initiatives, are the key ingredients required to advance the inclusive development of cities so that no one is left behind.

The impact of new technologies on the achievement of the accessibility goal, especially AI, ML, big data, or AR and VR, cannot be understated. These technologies not only promise better accessibility but also have the capability to provide empowerment to disabled persons, the elderly, and other marginalized groups through an assisted and immersive experience. The notion of "smart inclusion" embodies this desirable futuristic perspective of cities where technology is advanced and socially inclusive, meaning tools are developed for all users, and not just a selected few.

The obstacles that impede achieving digital inclusion in cities that use smart technology are not straightforward. City governments and planners have to deal with issues related to the affordability of services, digital skills, and the existing infrastructure, while making sure that any new developments put forward can cater to everyone. These challenges can be overcome by working together with the business community and nonprofit organizations to develop all-inclusive cities. The dedication to inclusivity as the cornerstone of smart city design must permeate all spheres, including infrastructure, services, governance, and policies.

A smart, inclusive, and equitable urban future can be constructed through the effort of policymakers, businesses, and people toward the efficient and sustainable use of the towns' resources while using digital technology. The changing face of metropolitan areas as more and more people acquire the skills needed for the digital age stems from the construction of spaces and policies concerned with the citizens' different conditions.

Finally, society needs to comprehend the applicability of smart cities and their technology in its true sense. This means that resources and benefit opportunities available in the digital environment should be accessible to all, irrespective of their social class, disability, and even age. Smart, technologically enabled cities should not only be enhanced with sophisticated technology but also have policies that promote equity and social willingness to enable every citizen to actively participate in socioeconomic gesture, which should become a norm rather than the exception.

AI and ML have the potential to revolutionize digital inclusion in smart cities by providing new ways to support accessibility for individuals with disabilities. AI-powered tools, such as voice recognition systems and computer vision, can help individuals with visual or mobility impairments interact with the digital world more effectively (Isazade, 2023). For example, AI-powered voice assistants like Amazon Alexa or Google Assistant provide people with disabilities a way to control smart devices and access information without using traditional interfaces. In addition, ML algorithms can be used to develop predictive systems that anticipate and respond to the specific needs of users in real time (Botelho, 2021). For instance, AI could help to optimize transportation systems by adjusting routes based on the needs of disabled passengers. The integration of AI and ML into smart city technologies not only enhances accessibility but also offers personalized, adaptive services for a diverse range of users.

References

Agboola, O. P., & Tunay, M. (2023). Urban resilience in the digital age: The influence of information-communication technology for sustainability. *Journal of Cleaner Production, 428,* 139304. https://doi.org/10.1016/j.jclepro.2023.139304.

Aruleba, K., & Jere, N. (2022). Exploring digital transforming challenges in rural areas of South Africa through a systematic review of empirical studies. *Scientific African, 16,* e01190. https://doi.org/10.1016/j.sciaf.2022.e01190.

Benedicta, E., Anthony, A., Temidayo, O., Odunayo, J. A., Temitayo, O. A., & Oluwatosin, R. (2024). Digital inclusion initiatives: Bridging the connectivity gap in Africa and the USA – A review. *International Journal of Science and Research Archive, 11*(1), 488–501. https://doi.org/10.30574/ijsra.2024.11.1.0061.

Bercaru, V., & Popescu, N. (2024). A systematic review of accessibility techniques for online platforms: Current trends and challenges. *Applied Sciences, 14*(22), 10337. https://doi.org/10.3390/app142210337.

Bian, M. (2021). Analysis on the development of Tokyo rail transit and its enlightenment to Chengdu. *OALib, 08*(07), 1–15. https://doi.org/10.4236/oalib.1107631.

Borowczyk, J. (2018). Sustainable urban development: Spatial analyses as novel tools for planning a universally designed city. *Sustainability*, 10(5), 1407. https://doi.org/10.3390/su10051407.

Botelho, F. H. F. (2021). Accessibility to digital technology: Virtual barriers, real opportunities. *Assistive Technology, 33*(sup1), 27–34. https://doi.org/10.1080/10400435.2021.1945705.

Burzagli, L., Emiliani, P. L., Antona, M., & Stephanidis, C. (2022). Intelligent environments for all: A path towards technology-enhanced human well-being. *Universal Access in the Information Society*, *21*(2), 437–456. https://doi.org/10.1007/s10209-021-00797-0.

Colding, J., Nilsson, C., & Sjöberg, S. (2024). Smart cities for all? Bridging digital divides for socially sustainable and inclusive cities. *Smart Cities*, 7(3), 1044–1059. https://doi.org/10.3390/smartcities7030044.

Dingil, A. E. (2025). Fostering inclusive urban transportation in planning and policy-making: An umbrella review using ALARM methodology. *Sustainable Futures*, 9, 100420. https://doi.org/10.1016/j.sftr.2024.100420.

Dwivedi, Y. K., Hughes, L., Ismagilova, E., Aarts, G., Coombs, C., Crick, T., Duan, Y., Dwivedi, R., Edwards, J., Eirug, A., Galanos, V., Ilavarasan, P. V., Janssen, M., Jones, P., Kar, A. K., Kizgin, H., Kronemann, B., Lal, B., Lucini, B., … Williams, M. D. (2021). Artificial Intelligence (AI): Multidisciplinary perspectives on emerging challenges, opportunities, and agenda for research, practice and policy. *International Journal of Information Management*, 57, 101994. https://doi.org/10.1016/j.ijinfomgt.2019.08.002.

Farahani, B., Firouzi, F., Chang, V., Badaroglu, M., Constant, N., & Mankodiya, K. (2018). Towards fog-driven IoT eHealth: Promises and challenges of IoT in medicine and healthcare. *Future Generation Computer Systems*, 78, 659–676. https://doi.org/10.1016/j.future.2017.04.036.

Fotteler, M. L., Mühlbauer, V., Brefka, S., Mayer, S., Kohn, B., Holl, F., Swoboda, W., Gaugisch, P., Risch, B., Denkinger, M., & Dallmeier, D. (2022). The effectiveness of assistive technologies for older adults and the influence of frailty: Systematic literature review of randomized controlled trials. *JMIR Aging*, 5(2), e31916. https://doi.org/10.2196/31916.

Gómez-Carmona, O., Buján-Carballal, D., Casado-Mansilla, D., López-de-Ipiña, D., Cano-Benito, J., Cimmino, A., Poveda-Villalón, M., García-Castro, R., Almela-Miralles, J., Apostolidis, D., Drosou, A., Tzovaras, D., Wagner, M., Guadalupe-Rodriguez, M., Salinas, D., Esteller, D., Riera-Rovira, M., González, A., Clavijo-Ágreda, J., … Bujalkova, N. (2023). Mind the gap: The AURORAL ecosystem for the digital transformation of smart communities and rural areas. *Technology in Society*, 74, 102304. https://doi.org/10.1016/j.techsoc.2023.102304.

Gooch, D., Barker, M., Hudson, L., Kelly, R., Kortuem, G., Linden, J. Van Der, Petre, M., Brown, R., Klis-Davies, A., Forbes, H., Mackinnon, J., Macpherson, R., & Walton, C. (2018). Amplifying quiet voices: Challenges and opportunities for participatory design at an urban scale. *ACM Transactions on Computer-Human Interaction*, 25(1), 1–34. https://doi.org/10.1145/3139398.

Harb, B., & Sidani, D. (2022). Smart technologies challenges and issues in social inclusion – case of disabled youth in a developing country. *Journal of Asia Business Studies*, 16(2), 308–323. https://doi.org/10.1108/JABS-10-2020-0389.

Harding, J. (2024). How service design improves inclusivity within a new underground station. *Proceedings of the Institution of Civil Engineers - Municipal Engineer*, 1–21. https://doi.org/10.1680/jmuen.23.00061.

Hariri, R. H., Fredericks, E. M., & Bowers, K. M. (2019). Uncertainty in big data analytics: Survey, opportunities, and challenges. *Journal of Big Data*, 6(1), 44. https://doi.org/10.1186/s40537-019-0206-3.

Hoppestad, B. S. (2007). Inadequacies in computer access using assistive technology devices in profoundly disabled individuals: An overview of the current literature. *Disability and Rehabilitation: Assistive Technology*, 2(4), 189–199. https://doi.org/10.1080/17483100701249540.

Isazade, V. (2023). Advancement in navigation technologies and their potential for the visually impaired: A comprehensive review. *Spatial Information Research*, 31(5), 547–558. https://doi.org/10.1007/s41324-023-00522-4.

Iwarsson, S., & Stahl, A. (2003). Accessibility, usability and universal design—Positioning and definition of concepts describing person-environment relationships. *Disability and Rehabilitation*, 25(2), 57–66. https://doi.org/10.1080/dre.25.2.57.66.

Kaiser, Z. R. M. A. (2024). Smart governance for smart cities and nations. *Journal of Economy and Technology*, 2, 216–234. https://doi.org/10.1016/j.ject.2024.07.003.

Kangana, N., Kankanamge, N., De Silva, C., Goonetilleke, A., Mahamood, R., & Ranasinghe, D. (2024). Bridging community engagement and technological innovation for creating smart and resilient cities: A systematic literature review. *Smart Cities*, 7(6), 3823–3852. https://doi.org/10.3390/smartcities7060147.

Kempin Reuter, T. (2019). Human rights and the city: Including marginalized communities in urban development and smart cities. *Journal of Human Rights*, 18(4), 382–402. https://doi.org/10.1080/14754835.2019.1629887.

Khanlou, N., Khan, A., Vazquez, L. M., & Zangeneh, M. (2021). Digital literacy, access to technology and inclusion for young adults with developmental disabilities. *Journal of Developmental and Physical Disabilities*, 33(1), 1–25. https://doi.org/10.1007/s10882-020-09738-w.

Kolotouchkina, O., Ripoll González, L., & Belabas, W. (2024). Smart cities, digital inequalities, and the challenge of inclusion. *Smart Cities*, 7(6), 3355–3370. https://doi.org/10.3390/smartcities7060130.

Lifelo, Z., Ding, J., Ning, H., Qurat-Ul-Ain, & Dhelim, S. (2024). Artificial intelligence-enabled metaverse for sustainable smart cities: Technologies, applications, challenges, and future directions. *Electronics*, 13(24), 4874. https://doi.org/10.3390/electronics13244874.

Makkonen, T., & Inkinen, T. (2024). Inclusive smart cities? Technology-driven urban development and disabilities. *Cities*, 154, 105334. https://doi.org/10.1016/j.cities.2024.105334.

Malek, J. A., Lim, S. B., & Yigitcanlar, T. (2021). Social inclusion indicators for building citizen-centric smart cities: A systematic literature review. *Sustainability*, 13(1), 376. https://doi.org/10.3390/su13010376.

Marikyan, D., Papagiannidis, S., & Alamanos, E. (2019). A systematic review of the smart home literature: A user perspective. *Technological Forecasting and Social Change*, 138, 139–154. https://doi.org/10.1016/j.techfore.2018.08.015.

Mazzetto, S. (2024). A review of urban digital twins integration, challenges, and future directions in smart city development. *Sustainability*, 16(19), 8337. https://doi.org/10.3390/su16198337.

Mhlongo, S., Mbatha, K., Ramatsetse, B., & Dlamini, R. (2023). Challenges, opportunities, and prospects of adopting and using smart digital technologies in learning environments: An iterative review. *Heliyon, 9*(6), e16348. https://doi. org/10.1016/j.heliyon.2023.e16348.

Padrón Nápoles, V. M., Gachet Páez, D., Esteban Penelas, J. L., García Pérez, O., García Santacruz, M. J., & Martín de Pablos, F. (2020). Smart bus stops as interconnected public spaces for increasing social inclusiveness and quality of life of elder users. *Smart Cities, 3*(2), 430–443. https://doi.org/10.3390/smartcities3020023.

Paiva, S., Ahad, M., Tripathi, G., Feroz, N., & Casalino, G. (2021). Enabling technologies for urban smart mobility: Recent trends, opportunities and challenges. *Sensors, 21*(6), 2143. https://doi.org/10.3390/s21062143.

Patrick, T. I. L., & Wenjing, Y. (2017). A study of the costs and benefits of smart city projects including the scenario of public-private partnerships. *International Journal of Urban and Civil Engineering, 11*, 1–6.

Perera, C., Liu, C. H., & Jayawardena, S. (2015). The emerging internet of things marketplace from an industrial perspective: A survey. *IEEE Transactions on Emerging Topics in Computing, 3*(4), 585–598. https://doi.org/10.1109/TETC.2015.2390034.

Putri, C. R., Berawi, M. A., Rahman, H. Z., Saroji, G., & Sari, M. (2024). Development of public private partnership scheme in the development of intelligent transportation system in Nusantara Capital City (IKN) to support mobility and connectivity: A literature review. *AIP Conference Proceeding*, 020010. https://doi. org/10.1063/5.0235745.

Radu, L.-D. (2020). Disruptive technologies in smart cities: A survey on current trends and challenges. *Smart Cities, 3*(3), 1022–1038. https://doi.org/10.3390/ smartcities3030051.

Raihan, M. M. H., Subroto, S., Chowdhury, N., Koch, K., Ruttan, E., & Turin, T. C. (2024). Dimensions and barriers for digital (in)equity and digital divide: A systematic integrative review. *Digital Transformation and Society*. https://doi. org/10.1108/DTS-04-2024-0054.

Rashid, A. B., & Kausik, M. A. K. (2024). AI revolutionizing industries worldwide: A comprehensive overview of its diverse applications. *Hybrid Advances, 7*, 100277. https://doi.org/10.1016/j.hybadv.2024.100277.

Robinson, L., Cotten, S. R., Ono, H., Quan-Haase, A., Mesch, G., Chen, W., Schulz, J., Hale, T. M., & Stern, M. J. (2015). Digital inequalities and why they matter. *Information, Communication & Society, 18*(5), 569–582. https://doi.org/10.1080/1 369118X.2015.1012532.

Rosa, J. P. P. (2025). The potential role of artificial intelligence to promote the participation and inclusion in physical exercise and sports for people with disabilities: A narrative review. *Journal of Bodywork and Movement Therapies, 42*, 127–131. https://doi.org/10.1016/j.jbmt.2024.12.024.

Salha, R. A., Jawabrah, M. Q., Badawy, U. I., Jarada, A., & Alastal, A. I. (2020). Towards smart, sustainable, accessible and inclusive city for persons with disability by taking into account checklists tools. *Journal of Geographic Information System, 12*(04), 348–371. https://doi.org/10.4236/jgis.2020.124022.

Sha, K., & Taeihagh, A. (2024). Designing adaptive policy packages for inclusive smart cities: Lessons from Singapore's smart nation program. *Sustainable Cities and Society, 115*, 105868. https://doi.org/10.1016/j.scs.2024.105868.

Slayi, M., Zhou, L., Thamaga, K. H., & Nyambo, P. (2024). The role of social inclusion in restoring communal rangelands in Southern Africa: A systematic review of approaches, challenges, and outcomes. *Land, 13*(9), 1521. https://doi.org/10.3390/land13091521.

Smith, H., Medero, G. M., Crane De Narváez, S., & Castro Mera, W. (2022). Exploring the relevance of 'smart city' approaches to low-income communities in Medellín, Colombia. *GeoJournal, 88*(1), 17–38. https://doi.org/10.1007/s10708-022-10574-y.

Sze, N. N., & Christensen, K. M. (2017). Access to urban transportation system for individuals with disabilities. *IATSS Research, 41*(2), 66–73. https://doi.org/10.1016/j.iatssr.2017.05.002.

Wang, C. (Herbert), Steinfeld, E., Maisel, J. L., & Kang, B. (2021). Is your smart city inclusive? Evaluating proposals from the U.S. Department of Transportation's Smart City Challenge. *Sustainable Cities and Society, 74*, 103148. https://doi.org/10.1016/j.scs.2021.103148.

Wolniak, R., & Stecuła, K. (2024). Artificial intelligence in smart cities—applications, barriers, and future directions: A review. *Smart Cities, 7*(3), 1346–1389. https://doi.org/10.3390/smartcities7030057.

Xu, T., Bika, Y., & Levin, M. W. (2024). Ped-MP: A pedestrian-friendly max-pressure signal control policy for city networks. *Journal of Transportation Engineering, Part A: Systems, 150*(7). https://doi.org/10.1061/JTEPBS.TEENG-7956.

Zhuang, Z. C. (2018). *Toronto: Planning for Diversity, Inclusion and Urban Resilience*. Toronto: Cities of Migration.

6

Civic Technology and Open Data: Transforming Urban Governance for Participatory Democracy

Abdul Rehman Gilal, Mazni Omar, Ruqaya Gilal,
Kamal Imran Mohd Sharif, and Haythem Nakkas

6.1 Introduction

Urban governance has undergone a transformative shift in recent years, driven by the emergence of civic technology and open data initiatives. Civic technology encompasses a wide range of digital tools and platforms that empower citizens, improve communication with government entities, and facilitate participatory governance (Meijer et al., 2012). On the contrary, open data initiatives give free access to government data to the general public for innovation, transparency, and accountability (Zuiderwijk & Janssen, 2014). Both concepts have recently been regarded as cornerstones in fostering participatory democracy and good governance in cities. It allows access to real-time information and interactive platforms for engagement. Therefore, civic technologies and open data create avenues through which governments can become more inclusive, responsive, and effective in addressing urban challenges around resource management, environmental sustainability, and equity in service delivery (Janssen et al., 2012; Fung et al., 2013). As noted by Chatfield and Reddick (2018), integrating Internet of Things (IoT) with open data platforms can significantly enhance urban governance by enabling real-time data-driven decision-making, as demonstrated by London's smart city initiatives.

As urbanization accelerates globally, cities are becoming more complex ecosystems requiring innovative approaches to governance. Civic technology and open data initiatives offer the tools to navigate these complexities by fostering collaboration between governments and citizens. From participatory budgeting platforms to real-time monitoring of urban infrastructure, these tools are reshaping governance models to be more citizen-centric. Case studies from cities such as Barcelona, London, and New York demonstrate

DOI: 10.1201/9781003630371-6

the transformative potential of these initiatives, providing valuable lessons on how technology can drive participatory democracy, and enhance trust in government institutions (Zuiderwijk et al., 2014; Heeks, 2017). The focus of this chapter is on the cities of Barcelona, New York City, and London because they are leading globally in implementing civic technology and open data projects. Each city is a representative of a different approach to using these tools: Barcelona to capture decentralized, individual ownership of data through blockchain, New York City for exceptional large-scale openness to open data, and London for integrating open data into smart city technologies with IoT. These cases are an asset in lessons of various applications and challenges stemming from different urban contexts.

However, while these examples are becoming increasingly prevalent, there are still some formidable barriers to overcome in the broader dissemination and successful operation of civic technology and open data initiatives. The first is a digital divide, in terms of access and use. The disparities in digital infrastructure, internet access, and technological literacy affect many developing countries and disproportionately harm their marginalized groups with limited accessibility toward civic technologies; Heeks (2017), Davies and Bawa (2012). Though open data would increase government openness, too much data leads governments to wrestle with standardization and proper presentation in service delivery, affecting its usage (Zuiderwijk & Janssen, 2014). Poor-quality and inaccessible data cannot generate trust among citizens toward meaningful insights and thus are a significant barrier to civic engagement in the formulation of policies (Janssen et al., 2012).

Another problem revolves around the governance of data itself. Issues related to data privacy, security, and ownership have been growing since cities started to collect huge volumes of personal and public data. The issues will be partly overcome by initiatives such as the DECODE project of Barcelona, which aims to enable citizens to take control of their data. Yet, such initiatives remain isolated and hardly scalable across various urban contexts, as evidenced by Harrison et al. (2012). Secondly, research on the effectiveness of civic technology and open data in promoting participatory governance is still in its early stages. While case studies present success stories, there is a lack of comparative research to identify general best practices that can be applied across diverse urban contexts (Fung et al., 2013; Meijer et al., 2012). It is also difficult for policymakers to sustain such initiatives in the longer term. Partial funding, political obstruction, and organizational silos may hinder integration of civic technologies into larger governing institutions Davies and Bawa (2012). Without strong institutional support and any clear vision about how these tools align with urban governance objectives, these could remain futile in paving the path to transparency and accountability. Research updated by Janssen et al. (2012) points out that perceived lack of usability is one of the causes that has generated myths impeding the progress of transparency-driven initiatives in open data adoption.

This chapter discusses the transformative potential of civic technology and open data to promote participatory democracy and good governance in urban contexts. Through an analysis of case studies of successful initiatives, such as the DECODE project in Barcelona and the open data portal in New York City, it identifies best practices, critical success factors, and barriers to implementation. It also investigates the interrelationships between civic technology, open data, and a set of critical challenges such as privacy, scalability, and digital inequality. These contributions build upon the increasing literature about digital innovation within urban governance, but also point to practical pathways forward for policymakers and practitioners.

The chapter is organized as follows: First, a review of the existing related literature on civic technology and open data underlines their role for urban governance. Then, this is followed by a detailed analysis of selected case studies with the purpose of illustrating their practical applications and impacts. Finally, this chapter synthesizes findings into recommendations for leveraging these tools to enhance participatory democracy, transparency, and accountability in cities worldwide.

6.2 Related Work

The integration of civic technology and open data into urban governance has been a growing area of interest, given its potential to transform how cities operate and interact with citizens. Civic technology, according to Meijer et al. (2012), is a form of digital tool designed to enhance citizen participation, transparency, and accountability. On the other hand, open data is defined as publicly accessible datasets that enable innovation, collaboration, and more transparency in decision-making processes. In this respect, Zuiderwijk and Janssen (2014) state that together, these tools provide a backbone for participatory governance that enables cities to respond to such modern challenges as rapid urbanization, resource management, and environmental sustainability. This review explores key contributions from the literature, highlighting both the potential and the challenges of leveraging these tools.

According to Fung et al. (2013), "Civic technology is really about making participatory governance more viable." They outline six models of internet-enabled governance, ranging from participatory budgeting to public feedback systems and collaborative policymaking. For instance, participatory budgeting involves direct engagement with citizens in the allocation of municipal resources through methods such as digital voting. This allows for transparency and coownership by the people. However, Fung et al. sound a note of caution in that these tools, as empowering as they may be for citizens, require robust institutional support to make them legitimate and sustainable.

Without governmental commitment, civic technology is at risk of becoming tokenistic rather than transformational.

The link between open data and accountability within government has been discussed extensively within the literature. Zuiderwijk and Janssen (2014) argue that open data platforms can allow citizens to monitor government activities, hence promoting transparency and accountability. For example, when budgetary data is made available to the public, it enables citizens to monitor municipal expenditures, ensuring that they are well allocated. The authors further emphasize that open data drives innovation, since several examples can be found where the development of applications by developers based on public datasets enables the improvement of services in cities. However, they do show that the success of open data depends on the quality, usability, and accessibility of such data, as poorly maintained datasets can undermine citizen trust.

Heeks (2017) identifies the issue of digital inequality, a significant barrier to civic technology and open data initiatives. He brings out disparities in internet access, technological literacy, and digital infrastructure in marginalized communities. For instance, while open data initiatives have proved to be successful in developed cities such as New York and London, most cities in developing countries lack the resources and expertise to replicate such successes. According to Heeks, this digital divide can only be addressed through strategic interventions, which include investing in digital literacy programs and expanding the internet infrastructure to areas that have not been covered.

Specifically, Janssen et al. (2012) talk about how open data can lead to privacy risk. They said that the increasing availability of public datasets led to growing criticism about the risk of data misuse. Their findings pointed out that re-identification after anonymization is a case and thus compromised individuals' privacy. They concluded that balancing openness and the protection of individual privacy requires stringent frameworks of data governance for open data platforms. These include data anonymization, controls on access, and transparent information on how data is used. The authors also argue that educating citizens about the risks and benefits of sharing data will lead to trust in these systems.

Meijer et al. (2012) go further and suggest that civic technology enables citizen engagement but does so in a manner that is collaborative with government in solving urban challenges. It is already happening, as in the case of Barcelona, where through Decidim, citizens are proposing and voting on municipal policies. In this respect, not only does such a step strengthen public confidence but also secures decision-making in governance as per the needs and aspirations of citizens. However, the authors note that such initiatives do require a change to full collaboration and openness in organic culture on the part of governments. Davies and Bawa (2012) go on to discuss issues regarding the scaling of civic technologies and open data initiatives across different urban contexts. Their work highlights political resistance, lack of funding, and bureaucratic inertia as major obstacles. Whereas some cities have been able to successfully implement open data portals, for instance, other cities are resisting such implementation because government agencies are refusing to release data due to scrutiny or loss of control. Davies and Bawa said that this, in practice, requires massive political leadership, multisectoral collaboration, and binding policy frameworks that place transparency and accountability as core. While the literature highlights the potential transformative power of civic technology and open data, there are gaps in the literature on the subject that call for further research. It is here that scholars such as Harrison et al. (2012) warn that what are required now are more comparative studies that evaluate the effectiveness of these projects in different cultural and socioeconomic environments. Lastly, research on civic technology projects should be conducted with a view to their long-term viability, specifically regarding funding and support by institutions. As their use within cities proliferates, the impact of this class of applications on urban governance is going to be a function of. Future research is needed that focuses on the critical gaps in the implementation and scalability of civic technologies and open data. First, one of the most important questions concerns how different governance models influence the scalability of civic technologies in varied urban contexts. There might be a comparison between centralized and decentralized governance through comparative studies that could explore how this influences the adoption and sustainability of these tools. As cities become more imbued with artificial intelligence (AI), research is needed on what contribution the technology could make to increasing open data usability: for example, through automated cleaning, standardization, and visualization provided by AI-driven tools, making open data platforms more usable and accessible both for citizens and policymakers. By addressing such questions, further studies can present recommendations that would improve the sustainability of civic technology and open data initiatives.

6.3 Case Studies

The case studies of Barcelona, New York City, and London present the transformative potential of civic technology and open data in the context of urban governance challenges. Each city offers unique insights: Barcelona focuses on decentralized data governance for empowering citizens, New York City presents the societal and economic impact of open data accessibility, and London showcases the integration of open data with smart technologies for sustainable urban solutions. Taken together, these cases reflect the flexibility of the tools in very different urban contexts. The chapter identifies key factors of success, challenges, and best practices from these cases, synthesizing them in the following sections to provide actionable recommendations for policymakers and practitioners.

6.3.1 Barcelona: The DECODE Project

Barcelona has become one of the leading cities in using civic technology to advance participatory governance, especially with the DECODE project. The DECODE project was launched in 2017 and allows citizens to obtain full control over their data while contributing to public decision-making processes. The project utilizes blockchain technology to enable secure and transparent data transactions, allowing citizens to determine who can access their data and for what purposes (Barcelona City Council, 2019). By aligning with the city's broader goals of digital sovereignty and data transparency, DECODE has created a robust ecosystem for participatory democracy.

Empirical evidence is very clear about how the project has impacted active citizenry participation and public trust. More than 15,000 citizens have been actively involved in the decision-making process through DECODE-enabled platforms, up from less than 5,000 participants before the introduction of the technology in 2017. The project also supported 12 public policy initiatives on issues such as urban planning to social welfare, integrating citizen-generated data into the governance process (Harrison et al., 2012). Surveys show that 90% of users believe that municipal governance is more trustworthy because of the emphasis DECODE has placed on data security and citizen control. The dramatic rise in both citizen participation and public trust outlined in Table 6.1 underlines the project's measurable success in fostering participatory governance.

Figure 6.1 shows the continued increase in the number of citizen engagement since DECODE was implemented. In this way, the project showcases how technology can shift attitudes to civic engagement, even as scalability remains the biggest challenge since it is wholly dependent on blockchain infrastructure and the communities' digital skill level. Barcelona's DECODE project represents an innovative take on civic technology through the emphasis on the digital sovereignty of its citizens' personal data. What makes this project so unique is the use of blockchain to ensure that every dealing of data is secure, transparent, and controlled by users themselves. This will help dispel the growing concerns about the misuse of data by tech giants and government entities. In giving citizens the power over their data—to whom and for what purpose—DECODE offers a governance model based on trust and citizen participation.

TABLE 6.1

Impact of the DECODE Project in Barcelona

Metric	Pre-DECODE (2016)	Post-DECODE (2023)
Citizen participation (no.)	5,000	15,000
Policy projects influenced	3	12
Public trust in governance (%)	62	90

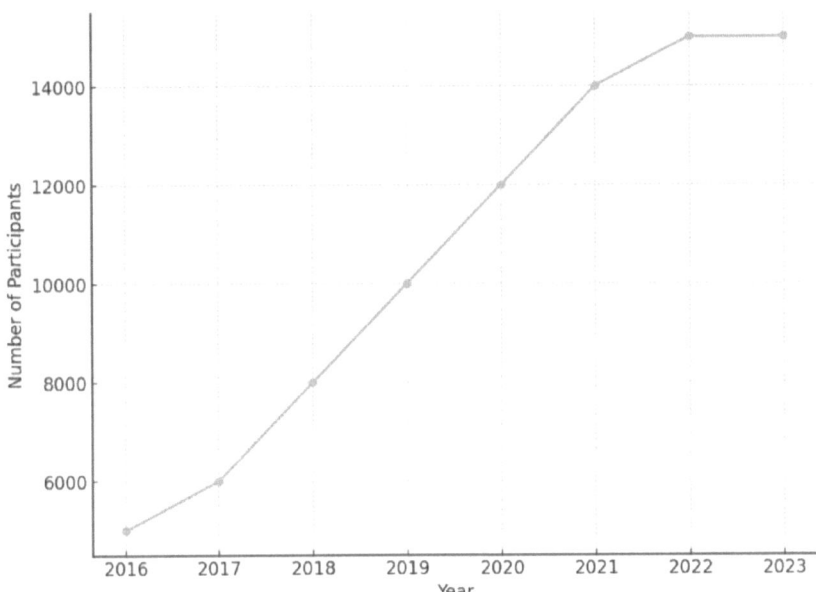

FIGURE 6.1
Growth of citizen participation via DECODE (2016–2023).

More than a technological prototype, DECODE sets the scene for a new approach that civic technology can play for socioeconomic purposes. The aggregation of citizen contributions is being fed, for example, directly to urbanistic policy decisions such as the conversion and reallocation of public areas toward neighborhoods that needed additional services and funding. Yet scaling up is a problem. That would be tough, considering this requires more blockchain solutions throughout cities. This underlines the need for adaptable frameworks to take into consideration local technological capabilities and levels of digital literacy.

Scaling the project to other urban contexts still faces many challenges. DECODE is highly dependent on blockchain technology, which requires huge amounts of technical expertise and infrastructure that may be unrealistic in certain cities. Low digital literacy also inhibits effective participation by almost 30% of the underserved communities in Barcelona, and hence, targeted educational programs should be delivered. The project has underlined a series of issues related to infrastructure and inclusivity as key factors to better realize the potential of civic technologies.

6.3.2 New York City: Open Data Portal

The Open Data Portal in New York City, launched in 2012, exemplifies how open data initiatives can enhance urban governance. By providing public access to over 3,000 datasets, the portal has fostered transparency,

TABLE 6.2

Growth of New York City's Open Data Portal Usage

Year	Total Datasets	Annual Downloads (millions)	Applications Developed
2014	1,200	1.2	100
2020	2,800	7.5	400
2023	3,000	10.0	500

accountability, and innovation. Citizens, developers, and businesses leverage these datasets to create solutions for urban challenges, such as public safety, transportation, and waste management (NYC Open Data, 2023).

Empirical evidence underlines the transformative impact of the portal. For example, from 1.2 million downloads annually in 2014 to more than 10 million downloads in 2023, the use of the portal by citizens demonstrates the increased interest in government data. According to Janssen et al. (2012), Table 6.2 gives the details of the growth of the portal, from the increase in datasets, annual downloads, and applications developed over the years. The platform has enabled the development of more than 500 civic applications, such as the "SafeNYC" app, which uses crime data to inform residents about safer neighborhoods. Another notable application, "TransitNow," leverages transit data to provide real-time updates on bus and subway schedules, significantly reducing commuter delays. Efficiency in waste management has also improved, with the city saving an estimated $3 million annually through data-driven optimizations (Harrison et al., 2012).

Figure 6.2 shows an exponential growth in the number of dataset downloads from 2014 to 2023, which basically elaborates the increasing dependence on open data for civic and economic development. While this portal has been quite successful, challenges are still evident concerning data quality and privacy issues since about 17% of the datasets hold incomplete or outdated information. In fact, Martin (2014) asserts that poor data quality and a lack of usability are common barriers for open data platforms to overcome. Indeed, these challenges still exist in the Open Data Portal initiative in New York City. The New York City Open Data Portal stands out for its scale and scope, with over 3,000 datasets available to the public. These datasets create opportunities for new applications that solve urban problems in areas such as public safety and transportation. For example, the "Vision Zero View" tool visualizes traffic accident data to help policymakers and the public identify high-risk areas where safety measures can be implemented.

It underlines that open data acts as an impetus to economic development through the portal. Small businesses and startups have also utilized the portal in creating products and services, such as real-time navigation apps and neighborhood guides. This economic impact complements the civic impact of this portal in fostering improved civic engagement since citizens use the data in holding municipal agencies accountable.

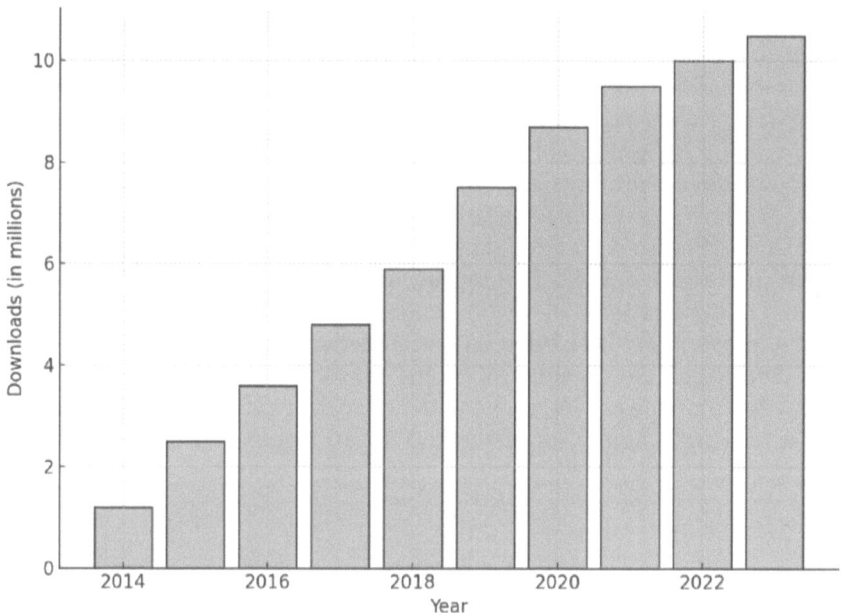

FIGURE 6.2
Annual growth in dataset downloads on the NYC open data portal (2014–2023).

Nevertheless, several challenges related to data completeness and quality still need to be overcome. A recent audit found that 17% of all datasets available on the site were incomplete or outdated which undermines the utility of datasets. Solving such issues requires stronger governance and maintenance for continuous data to maintain trust and public engagement.

6.3.3 London: Smart Governance and Open Data Applications

London's Greater London Authority (GLA) has effectively integrated open data and smart governance to address critical urban challenges. Since launching its open data platform in 2010, the city has prioritized transparency and innovation to improve transportation, housing, and environmental sustainability. London's approach combines open data with IoT technology, providing a blueprint for other cities aspiring to leverage smart city tools (Greater London Authority, 2022).

The data-driven initiatives of the city have quantifiable benefits. For example, the "Citymapper" app uses GLA's transportation data to optimize travel routes, reducing average commute times for each commuter by 15 minutes. Besides this, air quality monitoring tools, developed using IoT sensors and open data, resulted in a reduction in health complaints related to air pollution by 10%. This is the "Open Planning Database, which has made housing development more transparent, and over 20,000 applications can be followed by citizens" (Zuiderwijk & Janssen, 2014; Harrison et al., 2012).

Figure 6.3 and Table 6.3 illustrate the public use of London's major open data applications. Great as these applications are, a number of obstacles remain in bringing together datasets across different agencies, and in balancing open transparency with individual privacy, especially around sensitive health and housing data. Integration of London open data into smart city technologies as shown above represents just one of many ways that cities can put technology to work in solving difficult urban challenges. Citymapper, among other applications powered by open data on transportation, has helped minimize delays in traveling while making several journeys wheelchair accessible through its applications.

Other examples of how open data acts include air quality monitoring systems within London. By integrating IoT sensors with openly available data, the city has managed to intervene with activities such as low-emission zones, thus achieving tangible improvements in air quality. The Open Planning

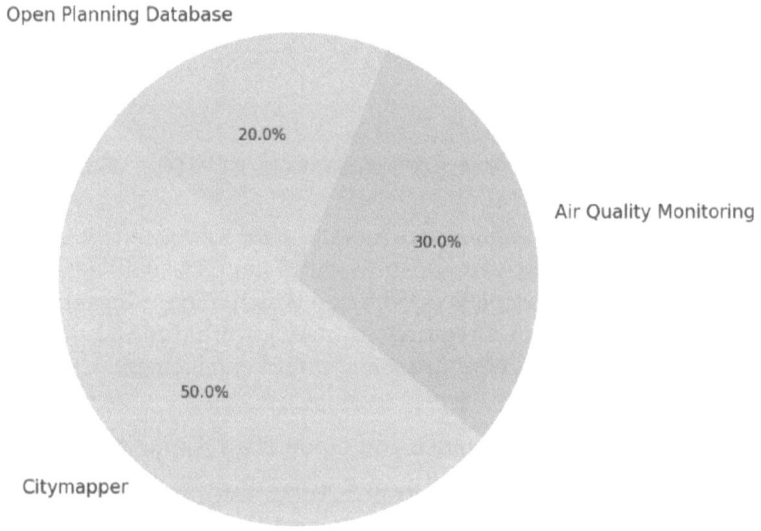

FIGURE 6.3
Public engagement with London's open data applications (2010–2023).

TABLE 6.3

Impact of Open Data Applications in London

Application	Key Metric	Measured Impact
Citymapper	Average commute time reduction	15 minutes per commuter
Air quality monitoring	Reduction in health complaints (%)	10%
Open planning database	Planning applications publicly tracked	20,000

Database lets the housing development process become more transparent; citizens can track ongoing projects and raise questions about possible problematic situations.

However, London's open data initiatives face challenges related to data integration and the privacy of that data. With diverse data coming from various agencies, consistency and interoperability are still a big challenge. The city also has to balance transparency with privacy, particularly in sectors relating to health and housing, which involve sensitive information. This shows the many complexities involved in implementing smart governance in big urban contexts.

6.4 Conclusion and Key Findings

Case studies in Barcelona, New York City, and London show the transformative potential of civic technologies and open data in urban governance. In each of these examples, the practice of civic technology and open data bears tremendous potential for improvement with regard to transparency, accountability, and engagement of citizens under appropriate conditions. Each case study provides a set of insights into the opportunities and challenges associated with these tools. The DECODE project in Barcelona is a perfect example of how the decentralization of data ownership can be empowering for citizens while engendering trust in governance. Integration of blockchain technology into this model provides security and transparency, hence a greater degree of participation and confidence from the public (Al-Ashmori et al., 2022). Yet, such advanced infrastructures also introduce challenges related to scalability. While DECODE is already successful, scaling up to more varied urban contexts may involve modifications according to the level of technological readiness and digital literacy. New York City's Open Data Portal shows economic and civic benefits that emanate from the wide availability of municipal datasets. It has brought innovation in public safety, transportation, and waste management and engendered confidence in government institutions. This is a sign of the high extensiveness of the platform, reflected in the exponential growth of the use of datasets and the more than 500 civic applications that have been created. However, issues of data quality and completeness persist, and stringent data governance frameworks need to be in place with periodic auditing. In addition, London provides an example of how smart city technologies and open data can be integrated to address pressing urban challenges, such as transportation inefficiencies, housing transparency, and environmental sustainability. The Citymapper app, air quality monitoring systems, and the Open Planning Database demonstrate how data-driven solutions can improve urban living standards. Yet, London's case also illustrates more effectively the challenges with regard to the integration of disparate data from a multitude of agencies and balancing transparency with concerns about privacy.

The most important conclusion from these case studies is that civic technology and open data need to be situated within their local contexts. While the principles of guiding transparency, inclusivity, and innovation may remain the same, their design and implementation must take into consideration the socioeconomic, political, and technological context of each city. For instance, less digitally developed cities may have to first invest in connectivity and digital literacy before more advanced solutions, such as blockchain or IoT systems, can be implemented (Sredhar et al., 2024). Besides, the success of these initiatives will depend on strong institutional support, collaboration across sectors, and sustained funding. Public–private partnerships have catalyzed innovation and scaling of meaningful solutions from New York City to London. In addition, other important areas such as programs focused on ensuring digital equity, data protection, and that systems are sustainable for the long term will be essential in terms of long-term relevance and viability given evolving urban pressures.

Finally, the cases underscore a final imperative: the ongoing need for research and knowledge sharing. A comparative study like this chapter can, therefore, be instructive in best practices and lessons learned that could be used by cities around the world in better leveraging civic technology and open data for improved governance. These findings provide practical insights not only into the implementation of civic technology and open data initiatives but also contribute to the broader discourse on urban governance. These case studies, through different challenges of rapid urbanization, a digital divide, and data privacy concerns, identify how innovative models of governance would contribute to enhancing transparency, accountability, and public participation. They underscore that technological developments need to go hand in hand with inclusive policies in order to make systems of urban governance fair and sustainable against the background of increasing global challenges.

References

Al-Ashmori, A., Basri, S. B., Dominic, P. D. D., Capretz, L. F., Muneer, A., Balogun, A. O., Gilal, A. R., & Ali, R. F. (2022). Classifications of sustainable factors in blockchain adoption: A literature review and bibliometric analysis. *Sustainability, 14*(9), 5176.

Barcelona City Council. (2019). *DECODE Project: Giving People Back Control over their Data*. Barcelona: DECODE. Retrieved from https://decodeproject.eu at Jan-01-2025.

Chatfield, A. T., & Reddick, C. G. (2018). A framework for Internet of Things-enabled smart government: Case of open data-centric smart cities. *Government Information Quarterly, 35*(4), 703–713. https://doi.org/10.1016/j.giq.2018.07.001.

Davies, T., & Bawa, Z. A. (2012). The promises and perils of open government data. *Journal of Community Informatics, 8*(2), 1–16.

Fung, A., Gilman, H. R., & Shkabatur, J. (2013). Six models for the Internet+politics. *International Studies Review, 15*(1), 30–47. https://doi.org/10.1111/misr.12028.

Greater London Authority. (2022). *London's Smart City Initiatives: Open Data and Innovation*. London.gov.uk. Retrieved from https://data.london.gov.uk at Jan-01-2025.

Harrison, T. M., Pardo, T. A., & Cook, M. (2012). Creating open government ecosystems: A research and development agenda. *Future Internet, 4*(4), 900–928. https://doi.org/10.3390/fi4040900.

Heeks, R. (2017). *Information and Communication Technology for Development (ICT4D)*. Abingdon: Routledge.

Janssen, M., Charalabidis, Y., & Zuiderwijk, A. (2012). Benefits, adoption barriers and myths of open data and open government. *Information Systems Management, 29*(4), 258–268. https://doi.org/10.1080/10580530.2012.716740.

Martin, C. J. (2014). Barriers to the open government data agenda: Taking a multi-level perspective. *Policy & Internet, 6*(3), 217–240. https://doi.org/10.1002/1944-2866. POI367.

Meijer, A., Curtin, D., & Hillebrandt, M. (2012). Open government: Connecting vision and voice. *International Review of Administrative Sciences, 78*(1), 10–29. https://doi.org/10.1177/0020852311429533.

NYC Open Data. (2023). *NYC Open Data Portal: An Overview*. NYC.gov. Retrieved from https://opendata.cityofnewyork.us.

Sredhar, A., Khan, A., Gilal, A. R., Alsughayyir, A., Alshanqiti, A., & Talpur, B. A. (2024). Assessing and mitigating network vulnerabilities in Philips Hue and Nest Protect smart home devices. *International Journal of Advanced Computer Science and Applications, 15*(2). https://doi.org/10.14569/IJACSA.2024.0150202.

Zuiderwijk, A., & Janssen, M. (2014). Open data policies, their implementation and impact: A framework for comparison. *Government Information Quarterly, 31*(1), 17–29. https://doi.org/10.1016/j.giq.2013.04.003.

Zuiderwijk, A., Janssen, M., Choenni, S., Meijer, R., & Alibaks, R. S. (2014). Sociotechnical impediments of open data. *Government Information Quarterly, 31*(1), 10–17. https://academic-publishing.org/index.php/ejeg/article/view/571/534

7

Adaptive Cities: AI-Based Climate Resilience Strategies from Sensor Networks

Salmah Fattah, Siti Hasnah Tanalol, Asni Tahir, and Samsul Ariffin Abdul Karim

7.1 Introduction: Background and Driving Forces

Climate change is one of the biggest challenges of this century, and it affects our ecosystems, economies, and people all over the world. Moreover, with these changes, some advanced tools that allow the monitoring and anticipatory capabilities of these changes in a real-time manner with a response before the climatic disaster happened can help in mitigating these impacts. In this context, sensor networks, particularly those with enhanced artificial intelligence (AI) capabilities, are critical. These networks provide live data on important environmental parameters (temperature, humidity, pressure, and water quality), promoting exact tracking and prediction of climate events (Akyildiz et al., 2005).

There are a couple of traditional types of sensor networks: static or fixed sensor networks; the most established networks with a programmed system controlled by a few standard equipment are hybrid suspendable. The data-generating process remains static for an extended period, yet the constraints of static networks make it complex to collect data. Mobile networks offer the advantages of flexibility and coverage, making them ideal for tracking broad or inaccessible regions (Mohamed et al., 2017). Hybrid systems utilize the strengths of both system types, providing an appropriate solution in more complex population density environments (Felemban et al., 2015). The early detection of disasters and optimizing the movement/conservation efforts of people and resources are essential components to enhance climate resilience using such networked systems (Jain & Virmani, 2017). Deployment and operation of a smart platform require certain consideration of energy resources, communication ranges, data management issues, and mobility of vessels that are subject to environmental conditions.

The integration of AI with sensor networks improved the operations more efficiently, adapting to real-time scenarios and providing a decision-making

DOI: 10.1201/9781003630371-7

process. AI strategies such as machine learning (ML), fuzzy systems, and multi-objective optimization methods have been highly effective in extreme environments such as underwater ecosystems (Ullah et al., 2019). The MOGA-AMPazy heuristic solutions (Fattah et al., 2022) are employed to solve the problem of optimizing the placement and operation of sensors in underwater wireless sensor networks (UWSNs) regarding energy efficiency and coverage. This case study highlights how AI-enabled sensor networks can transform climate monitoring and resilience.

This chapter addresses the possibilities of the sensor network for climate trend monitoring, its constraints, and significance with the integration of AI. This paper then presents a case study on the MOGA-AMPazy algorithm and how complex AI can be applied to create more intelligent sensors that can assist in solving climate challenges. The last subsection elaborates on the implications for the future and how these could greatly align with emerging technologies (i.e., the integration of edge computing, Internet of Things (IoT), quantum computing Gankotiya et al., 2023), and inter/cross-disciplinary convergence (Periasamy et al., 2025) to address the sustainable management of the environment.

7.2 The Role of Sensor Networks in Climate Monitoring

7.2.1 Types of Sensor Networks

Monitoring of climate is heavily reliant on sensor networks. It provides real-time data on temperature, humidity, pressure, and water quality. Based on deployment and operational characteristics, there are three types of static networks which are static systems, mobile systems, and hybrid systems.

Static Sensor Networks: In a more practical sense, however, these are actually networks of stationary sensor nodes strategically deployed to predetermined points for continuous and real-time monitoring of environmental parameters at higher time scales. As a result, such networks are typically found in applications such as weather stations, ocean buoys, or forest monitoring. Static networks also provide a stable pedestal for long-term data capture. However, they are constrained in their ability to adapt themselves as environmental conditions change.

Mobile Sensor Networks: These are networks of nodes that can move through the environment itself or be moved by some driving force. Drones and autonomous underwater vehicles are both examples. They are suitable for large-area monitoring with poor accessibility. However, they pose their unique set of problems: limited energy reserves in comparison to stationary sensors. Mobile communication protocols can become unstable when they begin moving about randomly on some unpredictable course (Mohamed et al., 2017).

Hybrid Sensor Networks: Hybrid methods are combination of both static and mobile nodes, allowing designers to utilize the respective strengths of each. Static nodes can provide continuous monitoring, whilst mobile nodes can be deployed where necessary to target area to gather data. As a result, in a complex or dynamic environment that requires adaptability and node system scalability beyond anything else, such hybrid networks become highly useful (Felemban et al., 2015).

7.2.2 Applications in Climate Resilience

Through early disaster detection, optimal resource management, and decision-making support, sensor networks will help improve resilience to climate challenges. Key applications include:

Disaster Detection and Early Warning: The sensor networks play a vital role in detecting natural calamities such as tsunami, flood, hurricane, and so on. For instance, underwater sensors can provide seismic activity and oceanographic observations which can identify early warnings for coastal communities (Jain & Virmani, 2017). Likewise, terrestrial sensors can pick up changes in soil moisture and precipitation patterns that can help predict landslides and floods.

Resource Optimization: Sensor networks are used to manage natural resources such as water, energy, and agricultural land efficiently. For example, gathered sensor data may be used to optimize irrigation in precision agriculture, minimize water wastage, and increase yield (Majid et al., 2022). In cities, energy consumption and air quality can be monitored using sensor networks, which can assist in managing resources sustainably.

Environmental Monitoring and Protection: Ecosystem and biodiversity sensor networks are pervasive. In fact, there are even underwater sensors that track coral reef health, along with terrestrial sensors to monitor deforestation and wildlife habitats. This was due in no small part to its application to conservation and climate change mitigation (Sempere-Valverde et al., 2023).

7.2.3 Challenges in Deployment and Operation of Sensor Networks

Nevertheless, sensor networks are still encountering numerous challenges during deployment and operation, especially in complex and dynamic environments:

Energy Constraints: Such sensor nodes are typically battery-powered, and therefore, energy efficiency is a significant concern. To extend their operational lifetime, novel solutions such as energy harvesting, 5AA protocols, and adaptive algorithms to further lower energy consumption are needed.

Communication Limitations: Radio frequency communication (Akyildiz et al., 2005) is slower and less reliable (due to obstacles such as underwater noise, etc.) and is therefore widely used in underwater networks.

Deployment and Maintenance: Designing and deploying sensor networks over remote or hazardous environments, such as deep oceans or disaster zones, is logistics-intensive and expensive. Moreover, such environments can make it challenging to maintain and repair the nodes which would demand a strong and self-sustaining designs (Felemban et al., 2015).

Data Management and Processing: Sensor networks generate tremendous amounts of data which must be stored, processed, and analyzed efficiently. Numerous ML and AI methods have been used to analyze and derive meaningful information from sensor data but such systems are costly in terms of computational power (Ullah et al., 2019).

Scalability and Adaptability: As the needs for climate monitoring grow, sensor networks must scale to cover larger areas and adjust to changing environmental conditions. Novel hybrid systems and MOGA-AMPazy-based solutions can help in such cases by optimizing the positioning and the working of sensors (Fattah et al., 2022).

7.3 Integration of AI in Sensor Networks for Climate Resilience

AI in designated sensor networks for climate monitoring and resilience strategies can be a driving force. Through AI algorithms and technology, more features are added to the sensor web, an integrated system of hardware and software that can monitor ecological conditions efficiently and send data directly to a station for responding on global warming. In this section, the key AI-based methodologies for sensor networks optimization are introduced along with the advantages of integrating AI.

7.3.1 Artificial Intelligence Approaches for Sensor Network Optimization

Machine Learning for Predictive Modeling:
    Environmental monitoring data are frequently used by ML algorithms to predict environmental changes. For example, ML models

are used to predict floods and hurricanes (extreme weather events) based on both historical and real-time data sources collected from sensor networks (Lin et al., 2018). Regression, a supervised learning technique for predicting continuous values, and classification, for predicting categorical values, is able to build relationships between environmental variables, while unsupervised learning clustering allows patterns to be identified in greater depth across a dataset. It is also gaining traction in the optimization of operations of sensor networks, including adaptive routing and energy management (Ullah et al., 2019).

Decision-Making in Uncertain Environments: Fuzzy Systems for Decision-Making:

Fuzzy logic is a powerful tool to deal with uncertainty and imprecision, which is widely found in environmental parameters. As an example of a fuzzy application, it is hard to find useful data from green robots (e.g., water quality that fluctuates without having a utility value); so, fuzzy systems can treat this data and be used for making decisions regarding the management of the resources or disaster response. Fuzzy systems strengthen sensor networks in unstructured environments by incorporating human-like reasoning.

Multi-Objective Optimization Approaches:

Hence, multi-objective optimization techniques such as MOGA-AMPazy algorithm useful for conflicting objectives in sensor network deployment (Fattah et al., 2022), which cater to two conflicting objectives such as coverage maximization and energy consumption minimization. The approach employed utilizes multi-objective optimization techniques based on evolutionary algorithms such as genetic algorithms to identify ideal trade-off solutions for conflicting objectives. For instance, in the case of underwater sensor networks, multi-objective optimization can be employed to identify the optimal locations of sensor nodes to provide adequate coverage while also minimizing energy consumption.

7.3.2 Benefits of AI Integration

1. *Energy Efficiency:* With AI-powered optimization techniques, sensor network energy efficiency has greatly improved. However, adaptive algorithms are able to change the working mode of nodes—when entering sleep, and their power consumption rates to save energy while still ensuring data integrity (Mohamed et al., 2017). This is particularly valuable in environments remote or underwater where it is difficult to change a battery pack.

2. *Scalability:* AI allows sensor networks to efficiently scale to monitor more extensive regions and to process higher volumes of data. In this way, it is possible to train ML algorithms on the data from thousands of sensors and come up with insights that would have taken cumbersome effort for manual analysis. As noted in Felemban et al. (2015), while AI helps balance the need for additional node deployment due to the expanding network, it can ensure the same functioning performance.

3. *Real-Time Adaptability:* Integrating ML algorithms improves the sensor network's adaptation to real-time environmental change. Predictive models, for example, can predict environmental changes, such as a sudden temperature drop or rising water levels. In addition, the solution can initiate appropriate responses, such as activating additional sensors or sending alerts (Jain & Virmani, 2017). Adapting the strategy in real time is a key to both effective disaster management and resource allocation.

4. *Improved Decision-Making:* AI can combine with sensor networks to bring decision-makers the most actionable insights. AI algorithms can analyze information from sensors to come up with optimized irrigation schedules for agriculture and pinpoint areas that are at risk of flooding. Such insights can be used for taking proactive actions to prevent climate-related risks and improve resilience (Majid et al., 2022).

5. *Improved Accuracy and Reliability of Data:* Using techniques such as anomaly detection and data fusion, AI can help ensure that sensor data is as accurate and reliable as possible. Algorithmic techniques have also been developed to screen data for sensor malfunctions or environmental noise, achieving better input for high-quality data analyses through anomaly detection (Ullah et al., 2019). Data fusion methods are used to merge data from a set of sensors in order to obtain a clearer and better understanding of environmental conditions.

7.4 Case Study: MOGA-AMPazy Algorithm in Underwater Wireless Sensor Networks (UWSNs)

7.4.1 Overview of UWSNs: Unique Challenges and Relevance to Climate Resilience

UWSNs are characterized by their unique features and restrictions and have become an invaluable tool for exploring marine environments that are vital to global climate systems. UWSNs are used to monitor several factors that influence climate conditions (such as ocean temperature, salinity, and pressure). However, UWSNs also create obstacles, for example:

Harsh Environmental Conditions: The sensor nodes are required to work in high-pressure corrosive saltwater where the harsh environmental conditions may damage these sensor nodes and the communication follows unpredictable current (Akyildiz et al., 2005).

Energy Constraints: Energy in UWSNs sensor nodes is usually associated with batteries and replacing or re-charging batteries is difficult and expensive in under-dynamics (Felemban et al., 2015).

Communication Constraints: Underwater data is primarily transmitted using acoustic communication, which has long delays with limited bandwidth and signal fading (Mohamed et al., 2017).

Dynamic Topology: The movement of water currents and marine animals can temporarily change the positions of sensor nodes, which can lead to coverage holes and network connectivity.

These challenges make UWSNs particularly relevant to climate resilience, as they require innovative solutions to ensure reliable and efficient monitoring of marine environments.

7.4.2 Methodology

In this case study, an organized methodology (as shown in Figure 7.1) is employed, which involves four broad phases in the context of solving the deployment problem of mobile UWSNs, focusing on energy consumption and coverage maximization.

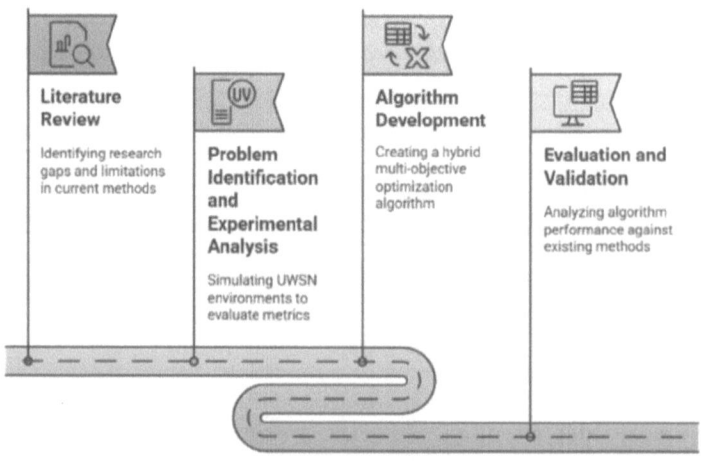

FIGURE 7.1
Methodology of MOGA-AMPazy solution.

1. *Literature Review*:

   To identify research gaps and limitations, a critical review was performed on the current state-of-the-art methods for mobile underwater sensor node deployment. These methods were logically categorized and analyzed by devising a thematic taxonomy. The study highlighted the difficulty of establishing a uniform deployment of mobile nodes, the challenge of unpredictable underwater environments, and the need for a balance between energy consumption and coverage.

2. *Problem Identification and Experimental Analysis*:

   In this phase, a simulation of UWSN environments was done using a deployment application. Coverage rate, deployment time, and energy consumption were key metrics used in evaluating performance. It showed the importance of decentralized systems, which can exploit local information for making intelligent decisions regarding moving sensor node positions and optimizing coverage.

3. *Algorithm Development*:

   A hybrid multi-objective optimization algorithm, MOGA-AMPazy, was designed to address conflicting deployment objectives. It employs an adaptive multi-parent crossover (AMP) in conjunction with a fuzzy dominance-based decomposition approach for balancing exploration and exploitation. We considered the concept of fuzzy Pareto dominance and prospect theory to design the fitness function to handle the stochastic underwater problem.

4. *Evaluation and Validation*:

   We evaluated the performance of MOGA-AMPazy with alternative performance metrics including coverage rate, energy consumption, Pareto optimal metrics (inverted generation distance (IGD), hypervolume (HV), diversity), and execution time. To verify the effectiveness of this algorithm, it was compared with existing methods on ZDT test functions and so on.

Thus, this methodology implemented a systematic approach to solving the deployment issues of mobile UWSNs, thus serves as a robust solution for energy-efficient and coverage-optimized deployment.

7.4.3 The MOGA-AMPazy Algorithm

MoGA-AMPazy (Multi-Objective Genetic algorithm based on Adaptive Multi-Parent Crossover and fuzzy Dominance) is a multi-objective hybrid optimization algorithm focused on UWSN. A fuzzy dominance-based algorithm capable of AMP crossover operators and applied to such a problem is utilized in this work to optimize the deployment and operation of the sensor in the network (see Figure 7.2).

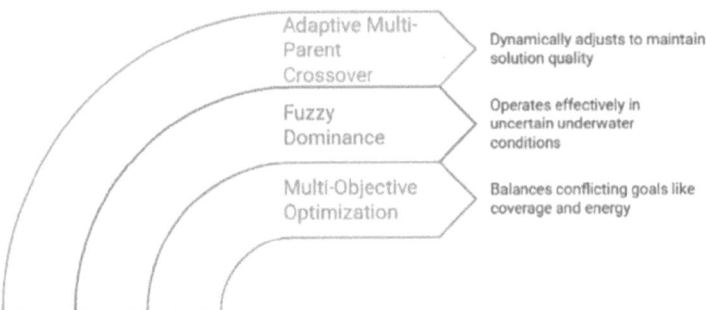

FIGURE 7.2
Components of MOGA-AMPazy algorithm.

The hybrid multi-objective optimization aids the algorithm in optimizing multiple conflicting objectives, such as maximizing coverage and minimizing energy consumption. This not only executes a smooth operation of the sensor network but also supports a more in-depth monitoring of the environment. To overcome both these challenges, the second integration uses fuzzy dominance to operate in uncertainty and imprecision common in underwater environments. It relies on fuzzy logic, which can enable strong and guaranteed decisions even in situations where sensor data is unclear or absent. Finally, this dynamic multi-parent crossover approach within limits maintains a balance for exploration and exploitation of the algorithm. This mechanism maintains a diverse, high-quality population of solution as it adjusts the number of parents used in crossover.

7.4.4 Results and Insights from the Case Study

The proposed MOGA-AMPazy algorithm is outperforming the existing algorithms in terms of several integral performance metrics demonstrating the usefulness of the proposed algorithm for UWSNs.

1. *Performance Metrics*:
   The algorithm greatly improves the values of execution time, energy consumption, and coverage rates. It reduces the consumption of energy (and extends the lifetime of the entire sensor network) and minimizes maintenance by optimally performing various sensor node operations, such as movement and data transmission. In addition, increased coverage due to optimum placement of sensors with arrangement of data distance model; monitoring wider areas is equally important in climate monitoring, with respect to disaster detection. Moreover, the optimized process requires fewer runs to compute the data, leading to shorter execution time, and enabling real-time decision making and adaptability in dynamic underwater environments.

2. Comparison with Existing Algorithms:

The MOGA-AMPazy algorithm outperforms the traditional algorithms (as shown in Figures 7.3 and 7.4) in terms of energy efficiency, coverage rates, and execution time. It records a 40.93% energy

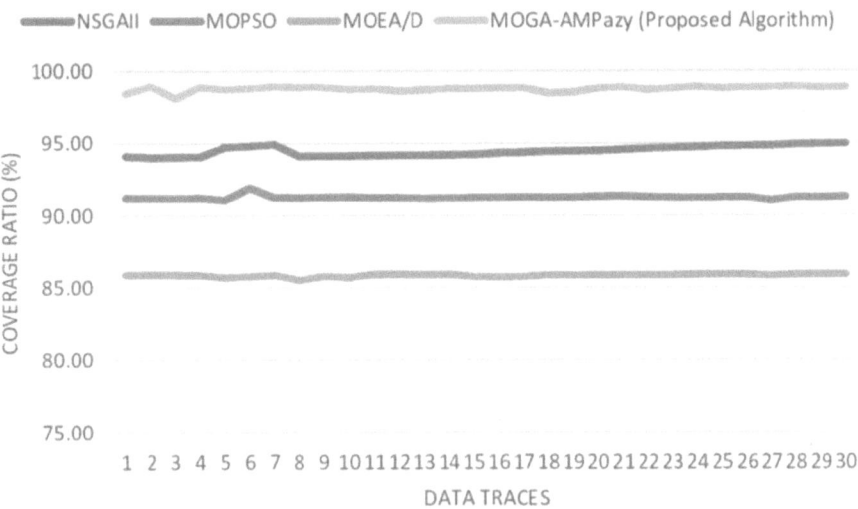

FIGURE 7.3
Comparison of coverage rates between existing and MOGA-AMPazy algorithm.

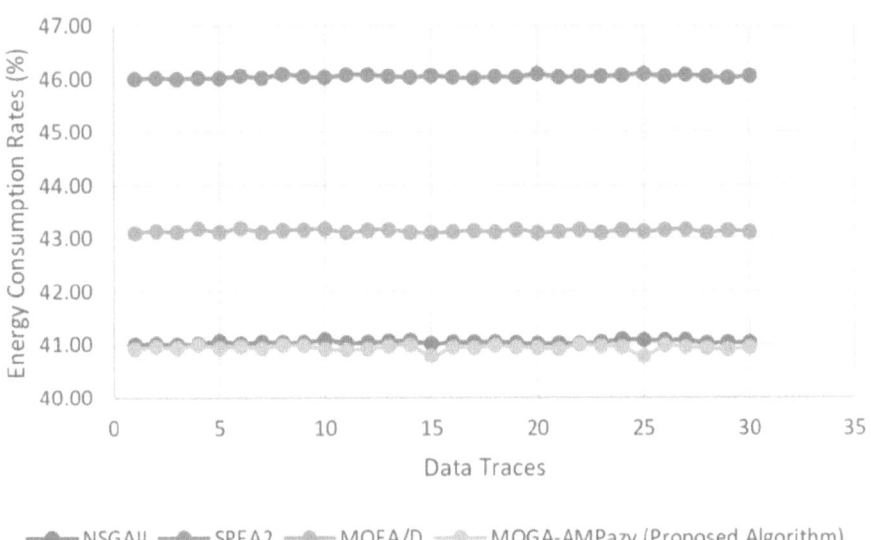

FIGURE 7.4
Comparison of energy consumption rates between existing and MOGA-AMPazy algorithm.

consumption rate, lower than NSGA-II (41.04%), SPEA2 (46.04%), and MOEA/D (43.13%). Likewise, its coverage rate (98.75%) is higher than NSGA-II (94.46%), SPEA2 (91.25%), and MOEA/D (85.87%). Besides, the average of the execution time of the algorithm is 0.4101 hours, which is shorter than NSGA-II (0.4235 hours) and MOEA/D (0.4634 hours).

The success of the MOGA-AMPazy algorithm in UWSNs has important consequences for applications pertaining to climate resilience. Because of its scalability, it can be used to optimize large-scale sensor networks used to monitor oceanic, forested, and urban regions. Conducting fuzzy dominance-based adaptive methods allows the algorithm to respond to uncertainties and dynamic situations for multiple climate monitoring scenarios. Moreover, its effectiveness and quickness facilitate real-time analysis of data and decision-making, which are crucial for disaster response and resource management.

7.5 Applications Beyond UWSNs

The ability of AI-enabled sensor networks, such as those in UWSNs can be applied in other areas. Here are a few examples of potential use cases:

Smart Agriculture: Advancements in technology, such as AI-enabled sensor networks, are revolutionizing agriculture, particularly by solving the problem of drought and water scarcity. These networks monitor soil moisture, temperature, humidity, and crop health in real time, giving farmers important data to streamline irrigation and reduce water waste. These systems also improved the efficiency of crop yield through precision agriculture technology. The goal of maximizing productivity is supported through data-driven decision making that aids in the optimal allocation of resources leading to higher productivity on the farm. Through ML, these algorithms aggregate and analyze data that enable farmers to make data-driven decisions.

Flood Prediction and Early Warning Systems: AI-enabled sensor networks can assist with flood prediction and early warning systems. These systems operate by deploying sensors to monitor key parameters such as rainfall, river water levels, and soil saturation in areas susceptible to flooding, with real-time data. These systems are an extremely important aspect of disaster management as they reduce the threat to human life and damage to property. Moreover, the ability to tie these networks into emergency response systems further facilitates the rapid implementation of evacuation and aid deployment plans (Periasamy et al., 2025). With time, using historical data and real-time inputs, AI algorithms enable prediction accuracy to consistently develop, making these systems more accurate and perfect to protect our most vulnerable areas (Wu et al., 2022).

Forest Fire Detection and Management: AI-enabled sensor networks have the potential to transform forest fire detection and management through next-generation solutions such as early wildfire detection and urgent response methods. These systems incorporate sensors and devices that can identify real-time environmental changes such as temperature, smoke, humidity, and so on, in the forest. AI models can process this data on real-time basis, identifying the early signs of a wildfire, enabling more efficient action to combat fire outbreaks, and minimize damages (Agrawal, 2025). Furthermore, the integration of AI-controlled sensor networks with unmanned aerial vehicles (UAVs)/drone/satellite systems allows for integrated fire combating, thus providing a multi-tiered approach to monitoring and action (Buchelt et al., 2024). The algorithms learn patterns and predict fire propagation, which are based on historical and real-time information, making these systems more reliable (Von Nonn et al., 2024).

7.6 Challenges and Limitations

The prospect of transforming agriculture with AI-enabled sensor networks is significant, but it is not without its challenges. At a formal level, data quality and noise in sensor readings are common issues that can undermine insight reliability (Liakos et al., 2018). Furthermore, the use of these architectures in larger and more complex agricultural ecosystems has challenges associated with infrastructure and the computational cost.

Farmers' data security and privacy concerns would consider ethical and social issues of AI monitoring systems (Wolfert et al., 2017). Moreover, access and affordability are major concerns, particularly for low-resource farmers. They may lack funds to purchase the technology or sufficient technical assistance to incorporate it into their operation. If the economic and technical challenges are addressed, the application of AI-enabled sensor networks in agriculture can be equitable and sustainable.

7.7 Future Directions

With emerging technologies and innovative approaches, the future of AI-enabled climate monitoring systems seems to be promising and transformative. Introducing edge computing, IoT, and quantum computing will actually take these systems to another level. IoT has made the groundwork for real-time analytics and rapid data processing with minimum latency, with the support of the existing technologies such as Edge computing. The probability and faster throughput would enable us to change the way we process complex, multi-domain climate modeling problems with any prior technology (Alahi et al., 2023). In addition to publicizing global partnerships, AI algorithms could be trained to combat interconnected climate issues such as drought, floods, and wildfires, giving an even stronger base for predicting and preventing environmental risks. However, proper deployment would require an effective policy infrastructure to address ethical issues, protect data privacy, and ensure equitable access to AI-led climate solutions (Periasamy et al., 2025). By leveraging cutting-edge technologies and novel policy approaches, AI-powered climate monitoring systems can play a pivotal role in steering the world toward a more sustainable, climate-resilient future.

7.8 Conclusion

In summary, AI-enabled sensor networks have become a game changer in meeting the rising challenges of climate change and improving global climate resilience. Through the utilization of cutting-edge technologies, including ML, edge computing, and IoT, these networks facilitate real-time monitoring, precise forecasts, and preemptive action toward environmental dangers such as floods, wildfires, and droughts. The MOGA-AMPazy case study illustrates just how powerful an AI-enabled system can be, as an optimal algorithm alongside an adaptive and dynamic established sensor network, can improve environmental monitoring of natural disasters. This research spotlights where a lot of the innovation is happening in AI—but also reminds us that for real-world applications to make a difference, they need to be scalable and adaptable to a wide variety of climate conditions. In the future, we open the interdisciplinary cooperation among researchers, policy makers, and industrial sectors to expand AI solutions toward ecosystem sustainable management. Through the promotion of innovation and the adoption of ethical governance frameworks, we can unlock the full potential of AI to create a more resilient and sustainable future for all generations.

References

Agrawal, U. (2025). Role of UAV-IoT networks in future wildfire detection. In *Machine Learning and Internet of Things in Fire Ecology* (pp. 273–300). IGI Global Scientific Publishing. https://doi.org/10.4018/979-8-3693-7565-5.ch013.

Akyildiz, I. F., Pompili, D., & Melodia, T. (2005). Underwater acoustic sensor networks: Research challenges. *Ad Hoc Networks*, 3(3), 257–279.

Alahi, M. E. E., Sukkuea, A., Tina, F. W., Nag, A., Kurdthongmee, W., Suwannarat, K., & Mukhopadhyay, S. C. (2023). Integration of IoT-enabled technologies and artificial intelligence (AI) for smart city scenario: Recent advancements and future trends. *Sensors*, 23(11), 5206.

Buchelt, A., Adrowitzer, A., Kieseberg, P., Gollob, C., Nothdurft, A., Eresheim, S., ... & Holzinger, A. (2024). Exploring artificial intelligence for applications of drones in forest ecology and management. *Forest Ecology and Management*, 551, 121530.

Fattah, S., Ahmedy, I., Idris, M. Y. I., & Gani, A. (2022). Hybrid multi-objective node deployment for energy-coverage problem in mobile underwater wireless sensor networks. *International Journal of Distributed Sensor Networks*, 18(9). https://doi.org/10.1177/15501329221123533.

Felemban, E., Shaikh, F. K., Qureshi, U. M., Sheikh, A. A., & Qaisar, S. B. (2015). Underwater sensor network applications: A comprehensive survey. *International Journal of Distributed Sensor Networks*, 11(11), 896832.

Gankotiya, A., Agarwal, S. K., Prasad, D., & Kumar, S. (2023, April). Cloud computing and IoT integration: Issues, challenges and opportunities. In *2023 International Conference on Power, Instrumentation, Control and Computing (PICC)* (pp. 1–8). IEEE.

Jain, N., & Virmani, D. (2017). Feature classification for underwater seismic prediction using wireless sensor nodes. In *Proceedings of the International MultiConference of Engineers and Computer Scientists* (Vol. 1). Hong Kong.

Liakos, K. G., Busato, P., Moshou, D., Pearson, S., & Bochtis, D. (2018). Machine learning in agriculture: A review. *Sensors*, 18(8), 2674.

Lin, Q., Zhang, F., Jiang, W., & Wu, H. (2018). Environmental monitoring of ancient buildings based on a wireless sensor network. *Sensors*, 18(12), 4234.

Majid, M., Habib, S., Javed, A. R., Rizwan, M., Srivastava, G., Gadekallu, T. R., & Lin, J. C. W. (2022). Applications of wireless sensor networks and internet of things frameworks in the industry revolution 4.0: A systematic literature review. *Sensors*, 22(6), 2087.

Mohamed, S. M., Hamza, H. S., & Saroit, I. A. (2017). Coverage in mobile wireless sensor networks (M-WSN): A survey. *Computer Communications*, 110, 133–150.

Periasamy, J. K., Reddy, K. S., Salve, P. R., Ushasukhanya, S., & Malleswari, T. N. (2025). AI-driven disaster forecasting by integrating smart technology. In *Edible Electronics for Smart Technology Solutions* (pp. 383–414). IGI Global. https://doi.org/10.4018/979-8-3693-5573-2.ch016.

Sempere-Valverde, J., Guerra-García, J. M., García-Gómez, J. C., & Espinosa, F. (2023). Coastal urbanization, an issue for marine conservation. In *Coastal Habitat Conservation* (pp. 41–79). Academic Press. https://doi.org/10.1016/B978-0-323-85613-3.00007-4.

Ullah, I., Liu, Y., Su, X., & Kim, P. (2019). Efficient and accurate target localization in underwater environment. *IEEE Access*, 7, 101415–101426.

Von Nonn, J., Villarreal, M. L., Blesius, L., Davis, J., & Corbett, S. (2024). An open-source workflow for scaling burn severity metrics from drone to satellite to support post-fire watershed management. *Environmental Modelling & Software*, 172, 105903.

Wolfert, S., Ge, L., Verdouw, C., & Bogaardt, M. J. (2017). Big data in smart farming–a review. *Agricultural Systems*, 153, 69–80.

Wu, C. J., Raghavendra, R., Gupta, U., Acun, B., Ardalani, N., Maeng, K., ... & Hazelwood, K. (2022). Sustainable AI: Environmental implications, challenges and opportunities. *Proceedings of Machine Learning and Systems*, 4, 795–813.

8

AI Strategies for Effective Text Summarization in Urban Contexts: Insights and Developments

Afrodite Papagiannopoulou and Chrissanthi Angeli

8.1 Introduction: Background on Urban Contexts and Social Summarization

Urban environments present challenges for summarizing texts due to the variety of topics, stakeholders, and data sources. Typical examples include city council proceedings, urban planning documents, social media, and metropolitan news. Effective summarization must address a variety of areas, from multilingualism to technical terminology.

The main difficulty in summarizing social media content is generating structured reports from its unstructured and rapidly changing nature. Social platforms, encompassing text, audio, images, and video, have reshaped the way social data is shared and analyzed, driving decisions in business, politics, and economics.

Textual content is emerging as a particularly important aspect of social expression. Over the past 25 years, Natural Language Processing (NLP) has emerged as an interdisciplinary field of processing and interpreting human language. However, applying NLP to informal, unstructured social media text poses unique challenges that require innovative approaches. One of the most important areas of NLP is text summarization, due to the overwhelming volume of user-generated content. Automated Text Summarization (ATS) (Gupta & Gupta, 2019) condenses large amounts of text into concise forms using AI and machine learning methods, saving time while preserving critical information.

In the field of text summarization, research initially is focused on summarizing formal documents such as books, journals, and reports using heuristic and statistical methods. Summarizing was considered primarily a linguistic task. With the rise of the Internet, the volume of information in circulation increased exponentially, and the focus shifted to summarizing web content,

DOI: 10.1201/9781003630371-8

including posts and social media. Accordingly, research shifted to methods capable of handling huge amounts of data, such as AI, neural networks, and deep learning. Thus, summarization algorithms fall into two main categories: preneural methods and deep learning techniques.

8.1.1 Preneural Systems

Preneural generation models various operations based on three input categories: Text-to-Text, Data-to-Text, and Meaning Representations-to-Text. Summarization involves three main steps: content selection, aggregation, and generalization—mimicking how humans extract key information, combine it, and discard unnecessary details to create abstractive summaries. Automated systems, particularly preneural ones, have difficulty with this, which often forces them to use extractive summaries.

In the early stages of research on summarizing social networks, websites, and microblogs, researchers used probability and optimization techniques to generate summaries from various data sources, such as text, images, videos, and hashtags. Some models provide multimedia representations. The models proposed by Amato et al. (2018, 2019) process real-time user interactions from social media streams. They do not generate text summaries but multimedia summaries that combine photographs, videos, and text. In order to determine the most significant topics, they employ an optimization method based on graph modeling and influence analysis. The framework proposed by Bian et al. (2015) generates visual summaries derived from various media microblogs. This approach separates events into sub-events and generates clear, concise summaries for each. The process includes steps such as noise removal, secondary event extraction using Cross-Media-LDA (CMLDA), and summary generation. The algorithm assesses microblogs for ambiguity, relevance, and diversity, utilizing both text and visual summarization mechanisms.

Several research papers focus on summarizing social media content (Sharifi, Hutton, & Kalita, 2010), (Sharifi, Inouye, & Kalita, 2014) by producing text summaries. These approaches generate summaries from Twitter posts, using the Twitter API to search for trending topics. A Phrase Reinforcement (PR) algorithm is used in conjunction with TF-IDF to filter and select relevant tweets. The process involves segmenting tweets into phrases, filtering posts based on relevance, and constructing a graph with word nodes to generate a summary through iterative refinement.

Similarly, a model for summarizing sports-related tweets is developed (Chakrabarti & Punera, 2011), focusing on real-time event detection. This model segments timelines into sub-events based on word distributions and then selects the most relevant tweets to capture key information. Furthermore, in Chong, Chua, and Assur (2021), a framework for organizing Twitter discussions and generating summaries using the Decomposition Topic Model (DTM) and the Gaussian Topic Model (GDTM) focuses on temporal correlations to produce concise and informative event summaries.

8.1.2 Deep Learning Systems

Deep learning has seen significant expansion, fueled by its ability to access large datasets and powerful computing resources. It has made significant inroads into areas such as image recognition and text processing. Various deep learning architectures, including Convolutional Neural Networks (CNN), Recurrent Neural Networks (RNN), and Long Short-Term Memory Networks (LSTM), have been used, alongside newer methods based on Transformers. Transformers, first proposed in the groundbreaking paper "Attention is All You Need" (Vaswani et al., 2017), leverage an attention mechanism, distinguishing them from traditional recurrent or convolutional approaches. The realm of social media summarization, in particular, remains an evolving field. Current research highlights several key considerations in this domain:

> *Non-Transformer-Based Social Media Summarization Systems*: In the study conducted by Gao et al. (2019), a social media summarization project is introduced, which incorporates user comments to better align with the reader's focus. The model, called Reader-Aware Summary Generator (RASG), uses a sequence-to-sequence (seq2seq) framework. RASG consists of four main components: (1) a seq2seq summary generator, (2) an attention module that focuses on capturing the reader's attention, (3) a supervisor module designed to minimize semantic gaps between the generated summary and the reader's focus, and (4) a goal detector that guides the generation process. This seq2seq architecture, combined with an attention mechanism, facilitates the generation of summaries by associating user comments with document content. Attention weights guide the decoder's focus, while the supervisor unit ensures that differences between the reader-centred and decoder-centred perspectives are reduced. Text summarization for social media and customer reviews has made progress using several models. A seq2seq model with attention (Bhandarkar & Thomas, 2023) uses bidirectional RNNs, LSTM-based encoders and decoders, and an attention mechanism to generate summaries, allowing the decoder to focus on relevant input. The summary-aware attention model (Wang & Ren, 2021) improves abstractive summarization by addressing challenges such as unstructured text and lack of comprehensive summary information. It uses a "summary-aware attention" mechanism to incorporate context from previous layers, enhancing consistency. For Turkish social media data, Varol (2019) uses the Word2Vec model for semantic preservation, GRU neural networks for sentiment classification, and latent semantic analysis (LSA) to extract meaningful summaries from tweets. Finally, an Attentional Encoder–Decoder model (Liang, Du & Li, 2020) improves on traditional architectures by adding a

hidden layer to filter out irrelevant data. With reinforcement learning, it excels in multi-sentence abstract summarization tasks.

Transformers for Social Media Summarization: The framework for abstractive event summarization on Twitter, as developed by Li & Zhang (2020), integrates a pretrained BERT encoder with a transformer decoder. To improve the decoding process, a topic prediction component allows the decoder to focus on specific aspects of posts, while the most liked comments help improve the coherence of the generated summaries. The framework incorporates: (1) A mechanism for selecting the most relevant tweets for the decoder, arranging them in ascending order based on timestamps, followed by comparison to evaluate the importance of the tweets based on representativeness and informativeness. (2) A topic category prediction mechanism, which allows the decoder to create custom summary styles for specific topics. (3) A BERT encoder combined with a transformer decoder, supported by two optimizers to ensure seamless integration of the pre-trained BERT model.

Several studies highlight advancements in summarizing social media content using transformer-based models. A combination of BERT and reinforcement learning is adopted in (Kerui, Haichao & Yxia, 2020) in order to generate summaries from texts on the Chinese platform Sina Weibo. Similarly, a multi-document summarization approach for user feedback on news discussions is introduced in Tampe, Mendoza, and Milios (2021), using BERT as an encoder and a transformer-based decoder. Their model includes an attention encoding layer to prioritize socially impactful comments and a data-driven strategy to reflect user preferences. Expanding further, another approach (Blekanov, Tarasov & Bodrunova, 2022) creates a multilingual abstractive summarization system using fine-tuned models such as T5, LongFormer, and BART for Reddit and Twitter data, demonstrating the potential of transformer models in processing multilingual social media content effectively.

While prior research predominantly emphasizes abstractive summarization, an alternative system utilizes an extractive summarization approach to generate summaries of social networks using transformers (Nguyen et al., 2020). This framework strategically integrates relevant social media posts to augment web document summarization. By employing a Convolutional Neural Network (CNN) layered atop BERT, the system enhances both classification precision and summarization effectiveness, showcasing a novel synergy between extractive techniques and transformer architectures.

Transformer Models applied to Non-Summarization Tasks: A range of transformer-based approaches has advanced abstractive summarization across various domains. For Chinese articles, a two-stage system employs BERT and bidirectional LSTM for text segmentation, followed by the extractive BERTSUM model to identify key information, culminating in collaborative training with a document transformer to generate summaries (Su, Wu & Cheng, 2020). In meeting conversations, the classic Transformer model underpins an abstractive summarization system (Singhal et al., 2020). Comparisons of PTM—BART, PEGASUS, and T5—revealed T5 as the most effective for news article summarization after fine-tuning, based on ROUGE scores (Gupta, Gupta & Katarya, 2022). Similarly, using the WikiHow knowledge base, BERT and T5 models were evaluated for abstractive summarization, with performance assessed through ROUGE metrics (Pal, Fan & Igodifo, 2021).

Prompt Engineering Systems: In the domain of NLP, prompt engineering has proven to be a disruptive and transformative technique, enhancing the performance and versatility of large language models (LLMs) like GPT (Radford & Narasimhan, 2018) and BERT (Devlin et al., 2019), which leverage extensive data and complex algorithms to understand language. By designing task-specific prompts, researchers streamline NLP tasks such as summarization, question answering, and text classification. OpenPrompt (Ding et al., 2022) introduces a modular framework for prompt-learning over pre-trained language models, while Narayan et al. (2021) propose generating abstractive summaries using entity chains to improve semantic coherence.

To address the high costs of fine-tuning massive models (Li & Liang, 2021), approaches like prefix-tuning and prompt-tuning selectively modify small, task-specific parameters, enabling efficient customization without altering core model weights (Lester, Al-Rfou & Constant, 2021). Prompt engineering has also demonstrated success in domains such as healthcare, overcoming traditional NLP challenges (Wang et al., 2024), and continues to be a pivotal strategy in advancing natural language understanding (Liu et al., 2021).

8.2 Evolution of Urban Context Summarization

Urban environments through social networks play a crucial role in shaping public opinion, influencing political, economic, and social debates. Social media data offers valuable insights into emotions and behaviors, supporting decision-making, business strategies, and policy-making. The openness of online conversations - enabled by anonymity, privacy, and reduced bias—allows for authentic expression, making urban data a primary source of understanding societal trends. Social interactions, particularly during major events, generate a huge amount of data. While statistical methods excel at identifying trends, text summaries provide deeper insights and concepts for decision-making.

Recent advances in Automatic Text Summarization (ATS), driven by deep learning, neural networks, and transfer learning, have enabled the creation of concise and meaningful summaries. Automated summarization, which has been evolving since its first appearance in 1958 (Luhn, 1958), is now transforming time-consuming manual processes into simplified, yet cognitively powerful processes. Tools that adopt it manage to reduce cognitive load, detect trends, and lead to informed decision-making, empowering businesses and governments. AI and deep learning have significantly advanced ATS. Deep learning improves its effectiveness by using AI systems alongside large datasets and advanced computational power. Transformer models lead NLP tasks such as sentiment analysis, translation, and summarization for several reasons:

1. *High-Level Performance*: They outperform other models in processing sequential input for NLP tasks.
2. *Parallel Computation*: Unlike RNNs, Transformers utilize attention mechanisms, enabling efficient parallel processing.
3. *Handling Long-Distance Dependencies*: Their architecture effectively manages lengthy sequences, addressing limitations of RNNs and CNNs without compromising data.

Transformers dominate NLP due to these advantages, including their exceptional capabilities in unsupervised text processing. Using the attention mechanism found in encoder–decoder structures, Transformers are well-suited for sequential tasks while avoiding the need for sequential processing required by RNNs. This allows them to operate in parallel, significantly accelerating training and improving efficiency. They have the ability to transform social media content beyond its specificities due to their cognitive and lexical richness. Their ability to analyze and generate language and graphics at scale makes them a dominant tool in modern business and urban environments. As the Internet replaces traditional modes of information—especially in areas such as news, politics, advertising, and opinion—research has shifted toward summarization systems designed for web content, microblogs, and social media. These systems address the unique challenges of summarizing dynamic, diverse, and informal social media content, offering new opportunities for research and application.

8.2.1 Text Summarization

The Internet nowadays is the main resource of information through websites, blogs, social media, news, and a variety of legal documents and scientific papers. With the huge volume of text content growing exponentially, finding relevant information has become time-consuming and inefficient, often with repetitive and irrelevant content. The huge volume of data makes manual summarization impossible, making ATS necessary. ATS, leveraging AI techniques, creates concise, coherent summaries that preserve the original meaning while eliminating redundancy (Vilca & Cabezudo, 2017; Nenkova & McKeown, 2012; Varma, Kurisinkel & Radhakrishnan, 2017). This kind of summary aims to present the main points of a discussion or text, allowing users to understand the important information quickly (Radev, Hovy & McKeown, 2002; Nazari & Mahdavi, 2019). As emphasized by Gambhir and Gupta (2017), an effective summary should keep the main content of a document, while maintaining clarity and brevity.

ATS faces the following challenges (El-Kassas et al., 2020):

1. Selecting relevant and essential information from the main document.
2. Presenting the summary in a clear, concise, and reader-friendly manner.
3. Evaluating the computer-generated summary independently, without relying on comparisons to human-created summaries.
4. Ensuring the generated summary closely resembles a human-written one.

ATS systems can be classified in various ways (Tandel, Mistree & Shah, 2019):

a. Based on the collection of documents →
   - *Single-document summarization* produces a summary from a single document focused on a particular topic.
   - *Multi-document summarization* creates a summary by synthesizing information from multiple documents related to the same topic.
b. Based on types of details →
   - *Indicative*: Offers a brief overview, highlighting the primary subject of the document without delving into specific details.
   - *Informative*: Delivers a thorough summary, encompassing key information from the entire document in a concise manner (El-Kassas et al., 2020).
c. Based on the output →
   - Extractive summarization
   - Abstractive summarization
   - Hybrid summarization
d. Based on the type of content→
   - *Generic*: Displays information directly linked to the original search query.
   - *Query-Based*: Offers a comprehensive overview of the document's content (Gong & Liu, 2001).

e. Based on language→

- *Monolingual*: Produces a summary in the same language as the source document (e.g., English to English).
- *Multilingual*: Identifies the language of the source document and generates the summary in that same language, utilizing multilingual capabilities.
- *Cross-Lingual*: Generates a summary in a language different from the original document (e.g., English to Greek).

Research on ATS has advanced significantly, transitioning from extractive methods to more sophisticated abstractive techniques. Early extractive approaches leveraged fuzzy logic (Kirmani et al., 2019), swarm intelligence optimization for concise text summarization (Mosa, Anwar & Hamouda, 2019), and deep learning methods tailored to extract salient information from texts (Suleiman & Awajan, 2019; 2020). Deep learning has become a crucial framework when the researchers move their interest toward abstractive summarization, as seen by the approaches put out in (Gupta & Gupta, 2019) and (Lin & Ng, 2019). RNNs and CNNs are particularly successful at catching complicated text relationships (Gupta & Lehal, 2010), and their extensive use in NLP applications has produced noticeable performance gains (Suleiman & Awajan, 2019). The subject has recently been dominated by transformer-based models and transfer learning, which have improved performance in a variety of NLP applications and produced good results (Chakrabarti & Punera, 2011; Vaswani et al., 2017).

8.2.2 Text Summarization Methods

The main goal of text summarization is to convert a large text into a shorter one, by keeping the meaning and critical information unchanged. In a discussion, such as the exchange of opinions on social platforms, the volume of user comments is huge that is almost impossible to read all of them. ATS, especially when is performed by AI systems, can highlight critical content and preserving the overall meaning of the text (Wang et al., 2017), keeping the audience informed. Three primary categories can be used to classify text summarization (El-Kassas et al., 2020):

Extractive Summarization: In the extractive summarization, the summarizer extracts phrases and keywords directly from the original text and combines them to create a summary (Figure 8.1). These selected words and phrases remain unchanged from the original document and with small rearrangement create a coherent and structured sentence (Shi et al., 2020).

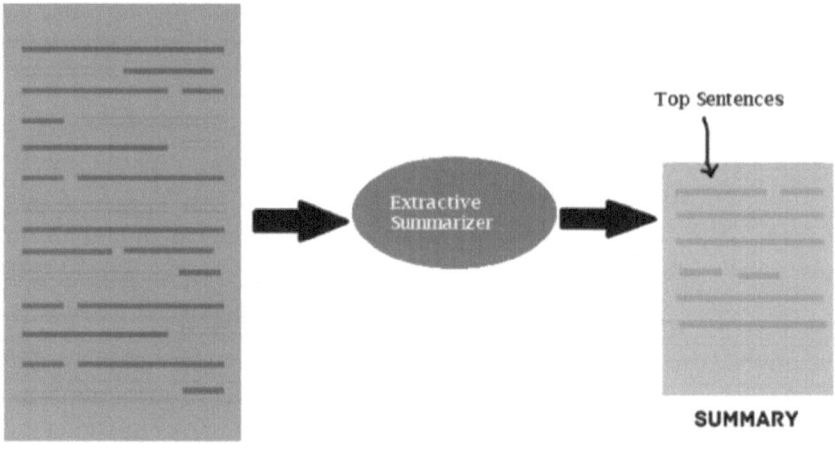

FIGURE 8.1
Extractive text summarization.

The process typically involves the following steps:

- Create a representation of sentences from the input text using topic-based and indexing approaches. Techniques for deriving topic-based representations include using word frequency and the log-likelihood ratio (Conroy, Schlesinger & O'Leary, 2006) to identify statistically significant words. Previous methods have used tf.idf ratios and word probabilities (Nenkova, & Vanderwende, 2005). Others have applied LSA (Dumais et al., 1988), Bayesian topic models (Daume III & Marcu, 2006), and lexical chains (Galley et al., 2003). The indexing approach relies on factors such as sentence position or similarity to the document title. They use either graph-based or vector-based methods. In the graph-based approach, the input text is represented as a graph with sentences as vertices and their relationships as edges. In the vector-based method, sentences are represented as vectors, and classifiers determine their inclusion in the final summary based on features such as sentence position, type, similarity to the title, and length.

- Scoring these sentences based on the representation. Each sentence is assigned a score that indicates the weight of the sentence's existence in the final text. The way in which the score is calculated depends on each system. The main decision-making methods are either machine learning algorithms or stochastic techniques, especially when it comes to summarizing multiple texts.

- Selection of the most relevant sentences. This stage involves selecting the appropriate sentences to create the summary. A key challenge in this step is determining the desired length of the summary. Length control mechanisms, such as thresholding or truncation, are used to adjust the size of the summary, while maintaining the original sequence of sentences as in the input text (Wang et al., 2017).

Abstractive Summarization: Abstractive summarization produces summaries that resemble human writing, in opposed to extractive summarization, which relies on directly gathering data from the source. This method builds on the meaning of the original text and uses new words and phrases to create a shorter version that differs in form but retains the essence of the original (Varma, Kurisinkel & Radhakrishnan, 2017). This method is highly sophisticated and complex, focusing on NLP to understand the fundamental ideas of the input text and generate new sentences from them (Figure 8.2). Abstract summarization involves two fundamental steps: (1) forming an internal semantic model of the input by extracting words and phrases that indicate the meaning of that input and (2) applying natural language generation methods to generate the final human-like summaries (El-Kassas et al., 2020).

Abstractive summaries have traditionally been developed using linguistic and semantic methodologies. However, recent developments have been largely driven by deep learning and neural network approaches. In particular, encoder–decoder architectures and

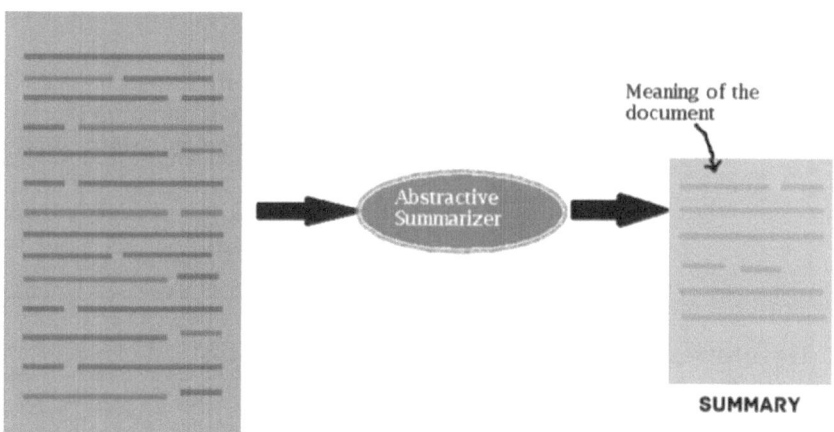

LONG FORM TEXT

FIGURE 8.2
Abstractive text summarization.

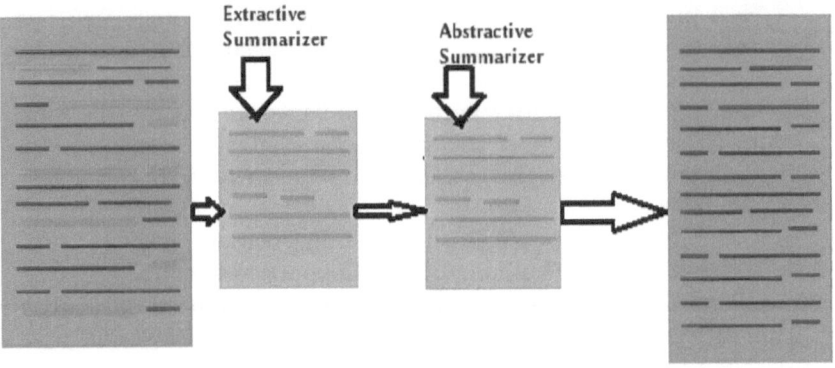

FIGURE 8.3
Hybrid text summarization.

Transformer models have become dominant due to their efficiency and ability to automatically tune parameters, offering a more seamless and adaptive solution.

Hybrid Summarization: This method combines the strengths of both the extractive and abstract summarization approaches (Figure 8.3). The process unfolds in two distinct stages:

a. Identifying and selecting the most important sentences from the input text, similar to the extractive summarization approach. A first fixed-length summary is created which then becomes input to the abstractive model.

b. Abstractive summarization techniques to the input text in order to rewrite and create the final summary. This combination leverages the strengths of both methodologies to create summaries that are both concise and contextually rich.

8.3 Revolutionizing Abstractive Summarization with Transformer Models

8.3.1 Practical Insights into Abstractive Summarization

Abstractive summarization aims to distil the essence of a text by restating its main ideas rather than simply extracting and repeating phrases. This approach creates concise summaries that retain the main concepts, eliminate redundant information, and provide a more effective means of conveying the main points of the text or discussion. These summaries tend to mirror human summarization because they paraphrase the source material, producing results that are more natural and understandable. Abstractive methods excel at synthesizing multiple ideas from different sections of a text into a single, coherent sentence, yielding summaries with greater information density. This is a particular advantage for summarizing complex or lengthy documents, where conveying a series of ideas in a compact form is essential. Furthermore, abstractive summarization allows flexibility in emphasizing the most relevant details, tailoring the summary to specific user needs or contexts, such as focusing on key issues or key topics.

Unlike extractive summaries, abstractive techniques eliminate redundancy and improving the quality and readability of the produced text. The flexibility of the abstract makes it applicable to a variety of fields, including news, legal, medical, and scientific fields, where clear, concise, and human-like summaries are invaluable. In specialized contexts, abstract summaries can convey complex ideas in more accessible language, broadening their appeal to a wider audience.

8.3.2 Advancing AI through Transfer Learning

Transfer learning—a machine learning technique—reflects the way humans acquire knowledge. It plays an unconscious but important role in people's everyday behavior, drawing on previously acquired knowledge to enhance abilities in related domains. In machine learning, transfer learning applies a previously trained model to a new domain or task. The basic idea involves applying knowledge gained from a data-rich task to a new task with limited data, thereby saving time and computational resources.

This approach is particularly popular in AI, especially in computer vision and NLP, where significant computational power is required. Transfer learning provides many benefits, such as minimizing the time required for training, improving performance across a variety of neural networks, and minimizing reliance on large datasets. By using PTM, machine learning systems can be built with relatively small amounts of training data—an invaluable advantage, especially in NLP, where generating large labeled datasets often requires expert input. For neural networks, the training process can be extremely time-consuming, spanning days or even weeks. Transfer learning significantly alleviates this burden.

Recently, transfer learning has become essential to address many NLP challenges. Initially, research focused on the application of PTMs, which was followed by the use of LLMs. Pretrained transformer models integrate transfer learning with training on huge and diverse datasets for general language understanding tasks. Instead of building models from scratch, these models can be adapted to specialized tasks. LLMs, a recent innovation, are transformer-based neural language models pretrained on vast amounts of text data. Transformers are a revolution in abstractive summarization, effectively solving persistent challenges such as coherence, fluency, and relevance that previous models faced. Architectures such as T5 (Raffel et al., 2021), BERT (Devlin et al., 2019), and

GPT (Radford & Narasimhan, 2018) have emerged as dominant frameworks, renowned for their remarkable performance, scalability, and ability to produce summaries with a level of quality approaching human standards.

8.3.3 Transformer Encoder–Decoder Model

The Transformer model (Vaswani et al., 2017), as illustrated in Figure 8.4, builds on the traditional encoder–decoder approach used in RNNs for processing seq2seq tasks, incorporating the attention mechanism as a

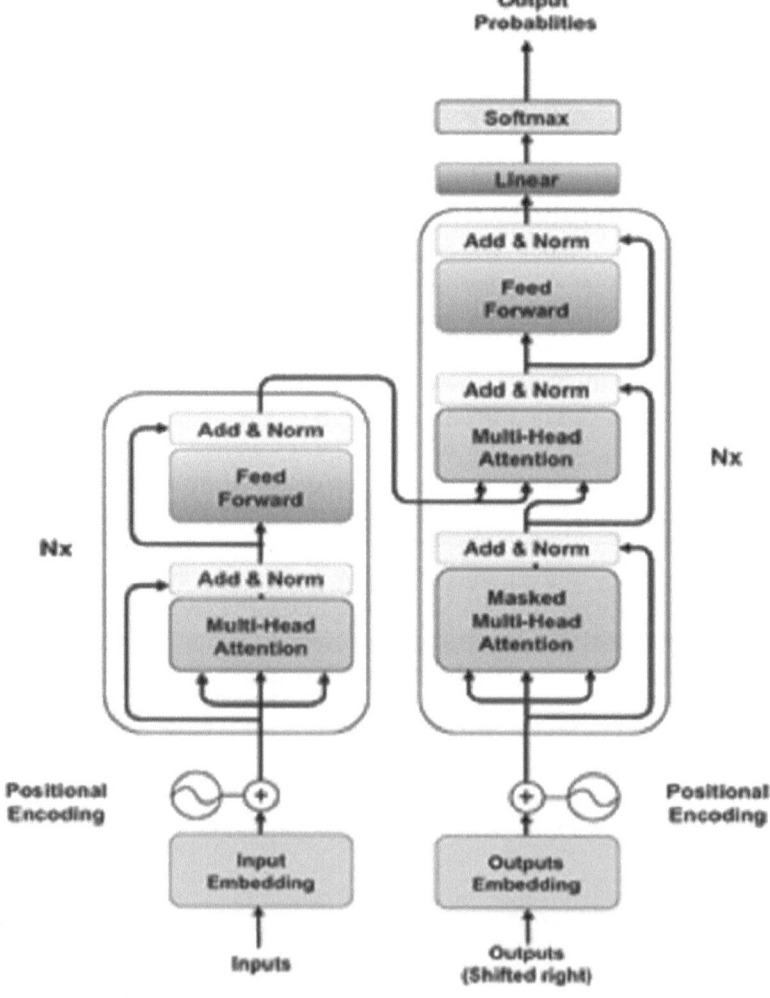

FIGURE 8.4
Transformer model architecture.

fundamental component. A groundbreaking feature of Transformers is their ability to eliminate sequential dependencies, enabling parallel processing and significantly reducing training time. These models efficiently handle variable-length sequences, excelling in natural language domains such as translation and summarization.

Transformer architecture consists of two components: the encoder and the decoder. Each consists of Nx identical layers, where Nx is typically set to 6 in the original basic model. Unlike models that rely on repetition (RNNs) or convolution (CNNs), Transformers introduce positional encoding layers to preserve information about the sequence order. Each layer incorporates two main subcomponents: Multi-Head Attention and feedforward layers.

Abstractive summarization with transformers faces the following challenges: (1) Factual Consistency: Transformers may generate plausible-sounding but factually incorrect information, (2) Coherence: Maintaining coherence, especially in multi-sentence summaries, can be challenging, and (3) Controlling Length and Content: Ensuring that the summary covers essential information while remaining concise is nontrivial. However, the Transformer encoder–decoder architecture offers a robust approach for abstractive summarization, leveraging attention mechanisms to produce fluent, coherent, and informative summaries.

Transformer models excel at generating concise, comprehensive summaries for a variety of reasons:

Attention Mechanism for Contextual Understanding: The core innovation of Transformers is the self-attention mechanism, allowing the model to focus on relevant words by assigning varying levels of importance, irrespective of their position. This helps the model prioritize important content, even if words are far apart, ensuring a coherent and accurate summary. The self-attention mechanism captures both local and global relationships, essential for abstractive summarization, where the model not only extracts key ideas but also creates new summaries by rephrasing and shaping the information.

Encoder–Decoder Architecture: In transformer models such as T5 and BART, the architecture is based on an encoder–decoder framework for generating summaries. The encoder extracts the essential meaning of the input text, while the decoder synthesizes a concise and semantically coherent summary. This architecture enhances abstractive summarization, allowing the model to paraphrase and generate new sentences while preserving the original intent.

Handling Long-Distance Dependencies: Models such as RNNs and LSTMs face limitations in handling long-distance dependencies due to their sequential nature. Transformers, on the other hand, process all tokens simultaneously, allowing them to efficiently capture relationships across the entire input regardless of distance. This capability allows Transformers to handle complex, large documents where key information may be scattered across different parts of the text.

Parallelization and Scalability: Unlike RNNs, which process words sequentially, transformers process the entire input sequence at once. This parallelism enables faster training and inference, allowing transformers to efficiently handle larger data sets and more complex models. This capability is particularly important for abstractive summarization, which requires diverse and extensive data to generate high-quality summaries.

Generative Abilities: Transformers such as GPT (autoregressive) and T5 (sequence-in-sequence) are models for producing new, reconstructed text beyond simple extraction. Transformer models perform exceptionally well in the area of abstractive summarization, which preserves the central meaning while paraphrasing the original text.

Contextual Understanding via Self-attention and Cross-Attention: In encoder–decoder models, self-attention in the encoder allows words to focus on every other word, building deep contextual understanding. In the decoder, cross-attention connects output tokens to relevant parts of the input sequence, ensuring that the produced output remains contextually accurate. This capability is particularly effective in tasks such as machine translation and question answering.

Scalability and Model Expansion: Transformer models can be scaled in levels and parameters, enhancing their ability to handle complex tasks and larger environments. These larger models are suitable for industrial applications and state-of-the-art NLP benchmarks, enabling high-quality outputs for complex language tasks, such as summarizing complex documents or legal texts.

Effective Handling of Noisy or Ambiguous Inputs: Due to their pre-training on large datasets with diverse contexts, transformer models learn to handle noise and ambiguity in language. Techniques such as masking or corruption during pre-training improve their robustness to incomplete or noisy data inputs. This robustness is critical in real-world applications where data quality can vary, such as in social media summarization or user-generated content.

Improved Attention to Input for Task-Specific Summarization: The fine-tuning allows precise control over which parts of the input are emphasized, which is critical for summarization and paraphrasing. Models such as BART and T5 can be fine-tuned to focus on relevant sections, producing concise and high-quality summaries. The use of self-attention and cross-attention mechanisms in the encoder–decoder architecture enhances the extraction and transformation of information for specific task needs.

Pre-training on Large Datasets: Transformers, particularly models like T5 and BERT, are pre-trained on large amounts of text data and can be fine-tuned on specific tasks like summarization. The large-scale pre-training helps transformers develop a deep understanding of language, grammar, facts, and context, which is crucial for generating coherent and accurate summaries.

Flexibility in Task Handling: Transformer models, such as T5, operate within a text-to-text framework, treating all NLP tasks—like translation, question answering, and summarization—as text generation tasks. This single-model solution empowers transformers to address multiple tasks without distinct models. For summarization, the model is fine-tuned on a summarization dataset and can generate summaries directly by using task-specific prompts (e.g., "summarize:").

Fine-Tuning and Transfer Learning: Fine-tuning transformer models on datasets such as CNN/Daily Mail, XSum, or Gigaword enable them to specialize in summarization tasks, building on the general language understanding from pre-training. Transfer learning allows PTM to adapt effectively, significantly enhancing performance on summarization tasks.

Quality of Output Summaries: Transformers deliver well-structured and meaningful summaries, ensuring the original text's key ideas are maintained. With their ability to paraphrase and create new content, summaries are meaningful and fluent. Models such as BART and T5 demonstrate leading-edge results in abstractive summarization, producing more readable and contextually relevant outputs compared to earlier methods.

Use of Specialized Models for Summarization: Models like BART and PEGASUS are specifically designed for summarization, enhancing performance by combining the strengths of encoders and decoders. They consistently deliver superior summaries by skilfully extracting both the form and significance of the input content.

8.3.4 Transformers versus Classical Neural Network Designs

The three fundamental neural network architectures currently employed in AI and deep learning applications are RNNs, CNNs, and Transformers. Recently, Transformers have attracted considerable interest from researchers because of their outstanding performance and cutting-edge results. But what are the features that distinguish Transformers from RNNs and CNNs? A brief comparison of these models is presented to highlight their key differences.

Transformers vs. CNNs: CNNs are tailored to handle structured data, such as images, where spatial arrangements and positional connections are of paramount importance. Their architecture is based on convolutional layers that apply filters to the input, allowing the extraction of local patterns that are essential for image processing. While CNNs are tailored for language processing, their performance falls short of that of transformers. In contrast, transformers, optimized for sequential data, may convert image data into a sequential format, but they fail to surpass CNNs in the discipline of computer vision. CNNs continue to be the most effective architecture for image-related applications.

Transforms vs. RNNs: Sequential data processing is a focus of both Transformer models and RNNs, yet they do so in fundamentally different ways. RNNs approach sequences piece by piece in recurring cycles. At each time step, the first element of the sequence is passed to a hidden layer, where it is processed, and the output is forwarded to the next time step. The output, along with the next input, is then fed back into the hidden layer, updating the hidden state vector and retaining information from previous inputs. In contrast, transformers process entire sequences simultaneously, leveraging parallel processing to handle much larger sequences more efficiently than RNNs. Using the self-attention mechanism, transformers analyze the entire sequence simultaneously, avoiding repeated computations or reliance on hidden states. Information retention is instead managed through positional encoding. Transformers have shown outstanding capabilities, especially in NLP tasks, owing to their ability to manage large datasets and capture long-range dependencies effectively. Meanwhile, RNNs remain valuable in contexts where computational efficiency and model size are prioritized over the need to model long-term dependencies.

8.4 A System for Urban Context Summarization

The challenges posed by urban and social texts to "traditional" NLP include their informal style, the introduction of new language trends, and the prevalence of abbreviations. A social network does not simply provide a dry template text, instead it consists of a set of factors: individuals and groups that have a set of relationships, interactions and connections between them. The goal, therefore, is the modeling of social groups as well as the semantic analysis and processing of posts and text messages, with the aim of creating smart systems incorporating social media information. Social and urban content confronts interesting challenges and limitations. Texts posted on these platforms are unstructured, created by various authors, in a range of languages and writing styles. In addition, the people who write are not authors; so, the posts have typos and slang expressions. The information presented on social platforms is continually shifting and encourages interaction among all participants. Moreover, they struggle with noise interference and limited capabilities in automatic clustering and classification. Detecting sentence boundaries is quite difficult due to the inconsistency (or absence) of punctuation. Making sense of each sentence is also a difficult process, as many words are replaced by symbols and references starting with # or @ followed by user or group names. Using emojis, irregular spelling, and shorthand disrupts tokenization and part-of-speech tagging, among other processing tasks. Language processing tools should be modified to account for variations such as repeating letters ("yeeeeeees" or "Ooooooooh") that differ from common spelling errors. The objective of the proposed system is to automatic summarize user interactions from social platforms, identify key themes, and highlight urgent issues to assist businesses and individuals in making timely and crucial decisions (Papagiannopoulou & Angeli, 2024a).

8.4.1 Utilizing Pretrained Encoder–Decoder Architectures

Transformer encoder–decoder architecture offers a robust approach for abstractive summarization, leveraging attention mechanisms to produce fluent, coherent, and informative summaries. The design of the proposed system leveraged PTM rather than building a transformer model from scratch, motivated by several key advantages. First, PTM yield superior performance when the input data is thoroughly pre-processed. Second, they offer a robust learning foundation, enabling effective adaptation to a wide range of datasets. Lastly, PTM simplify the development of new models, as minor adjustments in training and fine-tuning can lead to quicker and more efficient results (Blekanov, Tarasov & Bodrunova, 2022).

A diverse array of pre-trained transformer models (PTLMs) is now available, delivering outstanding performance across various NLP tasks. These PTLMs differ significantly in both architecture and pre-training methodologies. While many models are based on Transformer architecture, some focus exclusively on training the encoder, such as BERT and UniLM (Dong et al., 2019; Bao et al., 2020), whereas others prioritize training only the decoder, like GPT. Understanding the unique features and strengths of each PTLM is crucial for selecting the most suitable model for a given application. For this project, the following selection criteria have been established (Papagiannopoulou & Angeli, 2024b):

1. The model must take text as its input and generate text as its output.
2. It should be capable of creating abstractive summaries and should utilize an Encoder–Decoder framework (Pipalia, Bhadja & Shukla, 2020).
3. PTM should be adaptable, allowing fine-tuning to align with the specific requirements and limitations of the given datasets.

Three PTM appear to satisfy these criteria:

- BART (Bidirectional and Auto-Regressive Transformer) (Lewis et al., 2019): BART is pre-trained on denoising tasks and fine-tuned for summarization, making it highly effective at generating coherent summaries.
- T5 (Text-To-Text Transfer Transformer) (Raffel et al., 2021): T5 frames all NLP tasks, including summarization, as text-to-text problems, making it versatile and effective.
- PEGASUS (Zhang et al., 2020): Specially designed for summarization by pre-training with a "gap sentence generation" objective, where sentences are masked out and then reconstructed.

A comparison of these models was initially performed, which led to the conclusion that T5 has the best behavior, applied to social media content data (Papagiannopoulou & Angeli, 2023). Furthermore, T5 is an early large language model (LLM) that delivers exceptional performance on natural language tasks. However, applying and testing it in the less-explored domain of social media posed a significant challenge.

8.4.2 T5-Architecture for Summarization

The T5 (Text-to-Text Transfer Transformer) model follows the traditional Transformer architecture. It is an encoder–decoder model with multi-head attention. However, it exhibits certain distinctions from the conventional transformer architecture:

1. *Placement of Layer Normalization*: Layer normalization is applied directly preceding each attention mechanism and feedforward transformation, positioned outside the residual pathway.
2. *Exclusion of Additive Bias in Layer Normalization*: The implementation of LayerNorm utilizes only scaling, omitting the additive bias component.
3. *Position Embedding Strategy*: A straightforward positional embedding technique is employed, wherein a scalar value is added to the corresponding logit utilized in the computation of attention weights.
4. *Application of Dropout*: Dropout regularization is incorporated throughout the network, including attention weights, feedforward layers, and skip connections, among other components.

It works well for summarization tasks due to its seq2seq architecture, pre-training on the span-corruption objective, and flexible task setup. It has an exceptional performance in abstractive summarization due to its powerful architecture and its ability to generate coherent, concise summaries. The main features of T5 are the following:

Text-to-Text Framework for Summarization: T5 encompasses a diverse set of NLP tasks as text-to-text problems, unifying input and output as text sequences. This consistent format simplifies task setup and enables seamless transfer across NLP tasks like translation, question answering, and summarization.

Encoder–Decoder Architecture: T5 follows an encoder–decoder structure well-performed in summarization. The encoder processes the input text, extracting its context and meaning, while the decoder synthesizes a coherent summary by building on the encoder's output and previous generated content.

Pre-training on Span-Corruption Task: T5 is pre-trained using a span-corruption, where masked text spans are predicted based on context. This teaches T5 to generate and rephrase content, making it highly effective for abstractive summarization and creating concise summaries.

Task-Specific Prefixes and Training Data for Summarization: T5 uses the prompts to introduce a particular task. It uses prompt "summarize:" to indicate summarization tasks, training on datasets like CNN/Daily Mail to learn effective summary structures and styles. Fine-tuning enhances its ability to generate high-quality summaries tailored to the domain.

Autoregressive Text Generation for Coherent Summaries: The T5 decoder generates texts autoregressively, producing one word at a time by using previously generated words as context. Sequential production is enhanced by the masked self-attention mechanism ensuring that each token depends only on previous tokens. Techniques such as beam search or top-k sampling enhance summary quality by exploring multiple candidate sequences and selecting the most probable one based on model scores.

Controlling Output Length and Content in Summaries: Output length and content control in summaries: T5 can be configured to produce summaries of different lengths based on the use case, such as concise news summaries or detailed medical/legal summaries. Customizing the datasets and applying length control techniques allows T5 to meet specific length requirements.

Handling Different Summarization Requirements: Handling different summary requirements: T5 can be fine-tuned for both short and long summaries. By training on datasets for a specific domain (e.g. medical or legal), T5 can create summaries tailored to more specialized information in those fields.

8.4.3 Model Structure

The specific nature of urban content discussions, as discussed earlier, presents significant challenges for generating textual summaries. In contrast to formal texts, articles, or documents that adhere to structured grammar and language standards, urban and social media content tends to be short and filled with informal elements such as abbreviations, slang expressions, emoticons, and special characters (hashtags, feeling expressions). Furthermore, the frequent presence of redundancy and repetition in such posts can contribute to reader confusion, further complicating the summarization process.

The present system focuses on creating human summaries of social media discussions, with the aim of distilling and preserving the essential information conveyed to the audience, while preserving the original meaning and key ideas. To achieve this, it leverages the T5 transformer model, an encoder–decoder architecture known for its effectiveness in abstractive summarization. As mentioned earlier, T5 is highly adaptable for supervised or unsupervised tasks. Its flexibility extends to a wide range of NLP tasks, including translation, linguistic inference, information extraction, and summarization. The model's training utilizes teacher forcing, processing input sequences alongside corresponding target sequences.

The choice to adopt a PTM, rather than constructing one from scratch, was guided by several advantages: (1) PTM deliver superior results with thoughtful data pre-processing; (2) they offer a robust foundation for fine-tuning across diverse datasets; and (3) they facilitate the creation of specialized models with minimal adjustments to training and fine-tuning, enabling faster and more efficient outcomes.

The project's core design involves the following steps (Figure 8.5):

Data Collection: Data from social network platforms is downloaded and modified to suit summarization needs. The dataset must align with the specific summarization task, such as news, scientific, or social media summaries, and include high-quality, human-written examples that are coherent, concise, and informative. High-quality datasets help models generate clearer outputs, while poor datasets with noisy or incoherent summaries lead to poor performance. The dataset should also match the intended summary length—short for headlines or longer for detailed summaries—so, the model learns appropriate patterns. A small or narrow dataset risks overfitting, reducing the model's ability to generalize.

Pre-processing: Pre-processing is an important step in converting raw text data into actionable insights, transforming it into a cleaner and more standardized format to improve NLP results. Raw text is often messy and inconsistent, so, pre-processing enhances the accuracy and efficiency of models. Key techniques involve:

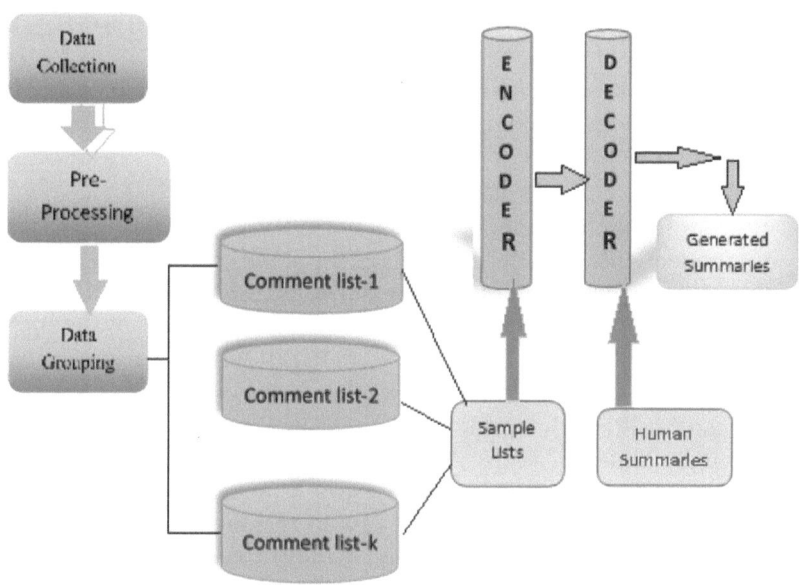

FIGURE 8.5
A transformer-based social media summarization system.

- *Tokenization*: Dividing text into individual tokens such as words or sentences.
- *Lowercasing*: Converting all text to lowercase for consistency.
- *Stemming/Lemmatization*: Reducing words to their base or root forms (e.g. "running" → "run").
- *Removing Punctuation/Special Characters*: Eliminating symbols like "!" and "&" that add little value.
- *Text Normalization*: Standardizing text, for example, expanding contractions ("can't" → "cannot").
- *Handling Numbers*: Removing or replacing numbers to avoid overfitting.
- *Data Grouping*: Comments are categorized by post titles and stored as lists, with each list containing comments specific to a particular post. The input to the model is a dictionary that maps each post ID to its corresponding list of comments, prepared after undergoing a secondary data-cleaning process.

Model Initialization: The model is based on a transformer framework designed to produce abstractive text summaries. It operates with a pre-trained T5 model and tokenizer to convert text into token IDs with attention masks and uniform input lengths. Training data makes up 80% of the dataset, with 20% allocated for validation/testing purposes. The encoder has 6 self-attention layers with 8 heads, feedforward layers (2048 hidden units), and normalization layer. The decoder has 6 cross-attention layers, attending to encoder outputs to generate tokens autoregressively.

Input of Encoder–Decoder: The encoder transforms the input text into meaningful embedding, capturing semantic connections throughout the sequence. The decoder gets as input the output of the encoder along with a dictionary of human-generated reference summaries. It then applies cross-attention to highlight relevant parts of the input during the generation of each token in the summary.

Training and Optimization: The T5 model is fine-tuned for text summarization through tokenization, data loading, optimization, and training/validation loops, saving checkpoints when performance improves. Training involves 11 epochs. It iterates over 16 batches, each containing input tokens, attention masks, target tokens, and output masks. Gradient scaling manages mixed-precision loss adjustments and optimizer updates, followed by clearing gradients to prevent accumulation. The model uses Adam optimization, setting a predefined learning rate.

Validation and Performance: The validation process evaluates a trained model on a validation dataset at each epoch. It calculates the average training, validation, and perplexity loss (PPL) to monitor performance and detect and avoid overfitting. The function prepares the model for validation, initializes the loss, and times the process. With gradients disabled, it reduces memory usage and speeds up evaluation. For each batch, it computes the model outputs, losses, and predictions, and computes the average loss. Finally, it computes the PPL, a key metric for language models, where lower values indicate better performance.

Fine-Tuning and Prediction: The testing process evaluates the trained model against the test dataset. It computes the average test loss, perplexity, and generates predictions, which are compared to reference summaries to evaluate performance. The model is set to evaluation mode, initializing variables to track test loss and store predictions. For each test batch, inputs and masks are moved to the GPU, and calculations are performed without gradient computations to save memory and improve speed. The model predicts outcomes, computes the loss, and computes the average test loss. Finally, the predictions and targets are decoded to text and stored for analysis. This process allows for efficient evaluation of a trained model on a test dataset, providing information on how well the model generalizes to new data and stores predictions for further analysis. The output layer uses a softmax function that normalizes the scores into class probabilities, and the final prediction is made by selecting the class with the highest probability.

8.5 Conclusion

The continued adoption of smart technology in everyday life has resulted in social media interactions playing a central role in shaping discourse and public opinion. The increase in online communication methods and rapid information exchange has led to an exponential increase in the content of social dialogues. Reading all this volume of data every day is becoming impractical and time-consuming. Creating summaries is considered essential to provide timely, valid, and meaningful information. Comments generated from interactions in urban environments, which often reflect public sentiment, are a critical source, but are difficult to process due to their huge volume and informal nature. The evolution of deep learning mechanisms with a dominant Transformer framework has led to excellent results. The performance of these models is an ideal solution for summarizing informal and conversational text, capturing long-range dependencies containing slang expressions, syntactic and grammatical errors, and annotations such as emoticons and hashtags. A transformer-based system offers a convenient way to generate human-like summaries. It can transform chaotic or informal text into coherent summaries while preserving tone, emotion, and key details. Furthermore, it is an indispensable tool for modern applications in conversational AI.

Fine-tuning on domain-specific data enhances transformers' ability to extract insights from unstructured inputs, making them ideal for conversational AI. Abstractive summarization, a key NLP methodology, generates summaries by understanding context, semantics, and linguistic generation. The combination of transformer models with abstractive summarization techniques leads to excellent results, creating texts that are concise and easily readable by the general public. Transfer learning has revolutionized abstractive summarization by enabling pre-trained language models to efficiently handle this task with reduced computational effort. In addition, it minimizes reliance on task-specific labeled data, improving the generation of coherent, contextually rich summaries for applications such as news reporting, academic research, and personalized content creation.

On the other hand, abstractive summarization preserves the essence of a text by creating concise and natural human-like summaries. It can eliminate redundancy and enhance readability. By presenting complex ideas in accessible language, abstract summaries are effectively applicable to different fields such as news, law, medicine, as well as to different readerships.

This chapter presents insights into the implementation of innovative AI solutions to create summary generation systems tailored for urban contexts, with a focus on social media interactions. As the demand for urban dialogue content grows, producing human-like summaries becomes essential. Such a system effectively summarizes social media dialogues, extracts key themes, and identifies urgent issues, enabling informed decision-making for businesses and individuals. By advancing current methodologies generates coherent, meaningful summaries that account for social media's linguistic complexity, related ideas clustering, and evolving discussions.

References

Amato, F., Castiglione, A., Mercorio, F., Mezzanzanica, M., Moscato, V., Picariello, A., & Sperlì, G. (2018). Multimedia story creation on social networks. *Future Generation Computer Systems, 86*, 412–420. https://doi.org/10.1016/j.future.2018.04.006.

Amato, F., Moscato, F., Moscato, V., Picariello, A., & Sperli, G. (2019). Summarizing social media content for multimedia stories creation. *Proceedings of the 27th Italian Symposium on Advanced Database Systems (SEB 2019)*, Castiglione Della Pescaia, Italy.

Bao, H., Dong, L., Wei, F., Wang, W., Yang, N., Liu, X., Wang, Y., Piao, S., Gao, J., Zhou, M., & Hon, H. W. (2020). UniLMv2: Pseudo-masked language models for unified language model pre-training. *arXiv preprint*. Retrieved from https://arxiv.org/abs/2002.12804.

Bhandarkar, P., & Thomas, K. T. (2023). Text summarization using combination of sequence-to-sequence model with attention approach. In *Springer Science and Business Media Deutschland GmbH* (pp. 283–293). https://doi.org/10.1007/978-981-19-3035-5_22.

Bian, J., Yang, Y., Zhang, H., & Chua, T.-S. (2015). Multimedia summarization for social events in microblog stream. *IEEE Transactions on Multimedia, 17*(2), 216–228. https://doi.org/10.1109/TMM.2014.2384912.

Blekanov, I. S., Tarasov, N., & Bodrunova, S. S. (2022). Transformer-based abstractive summarization for reddit and twitter: Single posts vs. comment pools in three languages. *Future Internet, 14*(3), 69. https://doi.org/10.3390/fi14030069.

Chakrabarti, D., & Punera, K. (2011). Event summarization using tweets. *Proceedings of the International AAAI Conference on Web and Social Media, 5*(1), 66–73. https://ojs.aaai.org/index.php/ICWSM/article/view/14138.

Chong, F., Chua, T., & Asur, S. (2021). Automatic summarization of events from social media. *Proceedings of the International AAAI Conference on Web and Social Media, 7*(1), 81–90. https://doi.org/10.1609/icwsm.v7i1.14394.

Conroy, J., Schlesinger, J. D., & O'Leary, D. P. (2006). Topic-focused multi-document summarization using an approximate oracle score. In *Proceedings of the COLING/ACL 2006 Main Conference Poster Sessions* (pp. 152–159). https://aclanthology.org/P06-2020/.

Daume III, H., & Marcu, D. (2006). Domain adaptation for statistical classifiers. *Journal of Artificial Intelligence Research, 26*, 101–126.

Devlin, J., Chang, M., Lee, K., & Toutanova, K. (2019). BERT: Pre-training of deep bidirectional transformers for language understanding. In *Conference Proceedings of the North American Chapter of the Association for Computational Linguistics: Human Language Technologies (NAACL-HLT 2019)*, (Vol. 1, pp. 4171–4186). Minneapolis, MN.

Ding, N., Hu, S., Zhao, W., Chen, Y., Liu, Z., Zheng, H., et al. (2022). OpenPrompt: An open-source framework for prompt-learning. In *Proceedings of the 60th Annual Meeting of the Association for Computational Linguistics: System Demonstrations* (pp. 105–113). https://doi.org/10.18653/v1/2022.acl-demo.15.

Dong, L., Yang, N., Wang, W., Wei, F., Liu, X., Wang, Y., Gao, J., Zhou, M., & Hon, H. W. (2019). Unified language model pre-training for natural language understanding and generation. *Advances in Neural Information Processing Systems, 32*, 13042–13054.

Dumais, S. T., Furnas, G. W., Landauer, T. K., Deerwester, S., & Harshman, R. (1988). Using latent semantic analysis to improve access to textual information. In *CHI'88: Proceedings of the SIGCHI Conference on Human Factors in Computing Systems* (pp. 281–285). https://doi.org/10.1145/57167.57214.

El-Kassas, W., Salama, C., Rafea, A., & Mohamed, H. (2020). Automatic text summarization: A comprehensive survey. *Expert Systems with Applications, 165*, 113679. https://doi.org/10.1016/j.eswa.2020.113679.

Galley, M., McKeown, K. R., Fosler-Lussier, E., & Jing, H. (2003). Discourse segmentation of multi-party conversation. In *Proceedings of the 41st Annual Meeting of the Association for Computational Linguistics* (pp. 562–569). Sapporo, Japan: Association for Computational Linguistics.

Gambhir, M., & Gupta, V. (2017). Recent automatic text summarization techniques: A survey. *Artificial Intelligence Review, 47*(1), 1–66. https://doi.org/10.1007/s10462-016-9475-9.

Gao, S., Chen, X., Li, P., Ren, Z., Bing, L., Zhao, D., & Yan, R. (2019). Abstractive text summarization by incorporating reader comments. *The Thirty-Third AAAI Conference on Artificial Intelligence (AAAI-19), 33*(1), 6399–6406. https://doi.org/10.1609/aaai.v33i01.33016399.

Gong, Y., & Liu, X. (2001). Generic text summarization using relevance measure and latent semantic analysis. In *Proceedings of the 24th Annual International ACM SIGIR Conference on Research and Development in Information Retrieval* (pp. 19–25). https://doi.org/10.1145/383952.38395.

Gupta, A., Chugh, D., & Katarya, R. (2022). Automated news summarization using transformers. In *Sustainable Advanced Computing* (vol. 840). Springer. Retrieved from https://arxiv.org/pdf/2108.01064.

Gupta, S., & Gupta, S. K. (2019). Abstractive summarization: An overview of the state of the art. *Expert Systems with Applications, 121*, 49–65. https://doi.org/10.1016/j.eswa.2018.12.011.

Gupta, V., & Lehal, G. S. (2010). A survey of text summarization extractive techniques. *Journal of Emerging Technologies in Web Intelligence, 2*(3), 258–268. https://doi.org/10.4304/jetwi.2.3.258-268.

Kerui, Z., Haichao, H., & Yuxia, L. (2020). Automatic text summarization on social media. In *ACM International Conference Proceeding Series*. Association for Computing Machinery. https://doi.org/10.1145/3440084.3441182.

Kirmani, M., Manzoor Hakak, N., Mohd, M., & Mohd, M. (2019). Hybrid text summarization: A survey. In *Soft Computing: Theories and Applications*. Singapore. https://doi.org/10.1007/978-981-13-0589-4_7.

Lester, B., Al-Rfou, R., & Constant, N. (2021). The power of scale for parameter-efficient prompt tuning. In *Proceedings of the 2021 Conference on Empirical Methods in Natural Language Processing* (pp. 3045–3059). Association for Computational Linguistics. https://doi.org/10.18653/v1/2021.emnlp-main.243.

Lewis, M., Liu, Y., Goyal, N., Ghazvininejad, M., Mohamed, A., Levy, O., Stoyanov, V., & Zettlemoyer, L. (2019). BART: Denoising sequence-to-sequence pre-training for natural language generation, translation, and comprehension. In *Proceedings of the 58th Annual Meeting of the Association for Computational Linguistics* (pp. 7871–7880). Association for Computational Linguistics. https://aclanthology.org/2020.acl-main.703.

Li, Q., & Zhang, Q. (2020). Abstractive event summarization on Twitter. In *The Web Conference 2020- Companion of the World Wide Web Conference, WWW 2020* (pp. 22–23). Association for Computing Machinery. https://doi.org/10.1145/3366424.3382678.

Li, X. L., & Liang, P. (2021). Prefix-tuning: Optimizing continuous prompts for generation. In *Proceedings of the 59th Annual Meeting of the Association for Computational Linguistics and the 11th International Joint Conference on Natural Language Processing (Volume 1: Long Papers)* (pp. 4582–4597). Association for Computational Linguistics. https://doi.org/10.18653/v1/2021.acl-long.353.

Liang, Z., Du, J., & Li, C. (2020). Abstractive social media text summarization using selective reinforced Seq2Seq attention model. *Neurocomputing, 410*, 432–440. https://doi.org/10.1016/j.neucom.2020.04.137.

Lin, H., & Ng, V. (2019). Abstractive summarization: A survey of the state of the art. *Proceedings of the AAAI Conference on Artificial Intelligence, 33*(1), 9815–9822. https://doi.org/10.1609/aaai.v33i01.33019815.

Liu, P., Yuan, W., Fu, J., Jiang, Z., Hayashi, H., & Neubig, G. (2021). Pre-train, prompt, and predict: A systematic survey of prompting methods in natural language processing. *ACM Computing Surveys, 55*(1), 1–35. https://doi.org/10.1145/3560815.

Luhn, H. P. (1958). The automatic creation of literature abstracts. *IBM Journal of Research and Development, 2*(2), 159–165. https://doi.org/10.1147/rd.22.0159.

Mosa, M. A., Anwar, A. S., & Hamouda, A. (2019). A survey of multiple types of text summarization with their satellite contents based on swarm intelligence optimization algorithms. *Knowledge-Based Systems, 163*, 518–532. https://doi.org/10.1016/j.knosys.2018.09.008.

Narayan, S., Zhao, Y., Maynez, J., Simões, G., Nikolaev, V., & McDonald, R. (2021). Planning with learned entity prompts for abstractive summarization. *Transactions of the Association for Computational Linguistics, 9*, 1475–1492. https://doi.org/10.1162/tacl_a_00438.

Nazari, N., & Mahdavi, M. A. (2019). A survey on automatic text summarization. *Journal of AI and Data Mining, 7*(1), 121–135. https://doi.org/10.22044/jadm.2018.6139.1726.

Nenkova, A., & Vanderwende, L. (2005). The impact of frequency on summarization. *Microsoft Research*, Redmond, WA, Tech. Rep. MSR-TR-2005-101.

Nenkova, A., & McKeown, K. (2012). *A survey of text summarization techniques*. In Springer US (pp. 43–76). https://doi.org/10.1007/978-1-4614-3223-4_3.

Nguyen, M. T., Nguyen, V. C., Vu, H. T., & Nguyen, V. H. (2020). Transformer-based summarization by exploiting social information. In *Proceedings -2020 12th International Conference on Knowledge and Systems Engineering (KSE 2020)* (pp. 25–30). Institute of Electrical and Electronics Engineers Inc. https://doi.org/10.1109/KSE50997.2020.9287388.

Pal, A., Fan, L., & Igodifo, V. (2021). Text summarization using BERT and T5. Retrieved from https://anjali001.github.io/Project_Report.pdf.

Papagiannopoulou, A., & Angeli, C. (2023). Automatic summarization of events from social media. *Proceedings of the International AAAI Conference on Web and Social Media*, 7(1), 81–90. https://ojs.aaai.org/index.php/ICWSM/article/view/14394.

Papagiannopoulou, A., & Angeli, C. (2024a). Encoder-decoder transformers for textual summarization on social media content. *Automation, Controls and Intelligent Systems*, 12(3), 48–59. https://doi.org/10.11648/j.acis.20241203.11.

Papagiannopoulou, A., & Angeli, C. (2024b). Summarizing user comments on social media using transformers. In *Proceedings of the 11th European Conference on Social Media (ECSM-2024)* (pp. 198–205). ACI, Brighton, UK. https://doi.org/10.34190/ecsm.11.1.2046.

Pipalia, K., Bhadja, R., & Shukla, M. (2020). Comparative analysis of different transformer-based architectures used in sentiment analysis. In *Proceedings of the 9th International Conference on System Modeling and Advancement in Research Trends (SMART 2020)* (pp. 411–415). IEEE, Moradabad, India.

Radev, D. R., Hovy, E., & McKeown, K. (2002). Introduction to the special issue on summarization. *Computational Linguistics*, 28(4), 399–408. https://doi.org/10.1162/089120102762671927.

Radford, A., & Narasimhan, K. (2018). Improving language understanding by generative pre-training. *OpenAI Blog*. https://arxiv.org/pdf/2012.11747.

Raffel, C., Shazeer, N., Roberts, A., Lee, K., Narag, S., Matena, M., Zhou, Y., Li, W., & Liu, P. J. (2021). Exploring the limits of transfer learning with a unified text-to-text transformer. *The Journal of Machine Learning Research*, 21(1), 1–67. https://dl.acm.org/doi/abs/10.5555/3455716.3455856.

Sharifi, B., Hutton, M.-A., & Kalita, J. (2010). Summarizing microblogs automatically. In *Human Language Technologies: The 2010 Annual Conference of the North American Chapter of the Association for Computational Linguistics* (pp. 685–688). Los Angeles, California: Association for Computational Linguistics.

Sharifi, B., Inouye, D., & Kalita, J. K. (2014). Summarization of Twitter microblogs. *The Computer Journal*, 57(3), 378–402. https://doi.org/10.1093/comjnl/bxt109.

Shi, T., Keneshloo, Y., Ramakrishnan, N., & Reddy, C. K. (2020). Neural abstractive text summarization with sequence-to-sequence models. *ACM/IMS Transactions on Data Science*, 2(1), 37. https://dl.acm.org/doi/10.1145/3419106.

Singhal, D., Khatter, K., Tejaswini, A., & Jayashree, R. (2020). Abstractive summarization of meeting conversations. In *2020 IEEE International Conference for Innovation in Technology (INOCON 2020)*. Institute of Electrical and Electronics Engineers Inc. https://doi.org/10.1109/INOCON50539.2020.9298305.

Su, M. H., Wu, C. H., & Cheng, H. T. (2020). A two-stage transformer-based approach for variable-length abstractive summarization. *IEEE/ACM Transactions on Audio, Speech, and Language Processing*, 28, 2061–2072. https://doi.org/10.1109/TASLP.2020.3006731.

Suleiman, D., & Awajan, A. A. (2019). Deep learning based extractive text summarization: Approaches, datasets and evaluation measures. In *Proceedings of the 2019 Sixth International Conference on Social Networks Analysis, Management and Security (SNAMS)*. https://doi.org/10.1109/SNAMS.2019.8931813.

Suleiman, D., & Awajan, A. A. (2020). Deep learning based abstractive text summarization: Approaches, datasets, evaluation measures, and challenges. *Mathematical Problems in Engineering, 2020*, 9365340. https://doi.org/10.1155/2020/9365340.

Tandel, J., Mistree, K., & Shah, P. (2019). A review on neural network-based abstractive text summarization models. In *Proceedings of the 2019 IEEE 5th International Conference for Convergence in Technology (I2CT)*. https://doi.org/10.1109/I2CT45611.2019.9033912.

Tampe, I., Mendoza, M., & Milios, E. (2021). Neural abstractive unsupervised summarization of online news discussions. In Arai, K. (Ed.), *Intelligent Systems and Applications. IntelliSys 2021*. Lecture Notes in Networks and Systems (vol. 295). Springer, Cham. Retrieved from https://arxiv.org/abs/2106.03953.

Vaswani, A., Shazeer, N., Parmar, N., Uszkoreit, J., Jones, L., Gomez, A. N., Kaiser, L., & Polosukhin, I. (2017). Attention is all you need. In *31st Conference on Neural Information Processing Systems (NIPS 2017)* (pp. 5998–6008). Long Beach, CA, USA. June 2017.

Varma, V., Kurisinkel, L. J., & Radhakrishnan, P. (2017). Social media summarization. In *A Practical Guide to Sentiment Analysis* (Chapter 7, pp. 135–153). https://doi.org/10.1007/978-3-319-55394-8_7.

Varol, A. (2019). Innovative technologies for digital transformation. In *Proceedings of the 1st International Informatics and Software Engineering Conference (IISEC-2019)* (pp. 6–7). Ankara, Turkey.

Vilca, G. C. V., & Cabezudo, M. A. S. (2017). A study of abstractive summarization using semantic representations and discourse level information. Paper presented at the *20th International Conference on Text, Speech, and Dialogue*, Prague, Czech Republic.

Wang, J., Shi, E., Yu, S., Wu, Z., Ma, C., Dai, H., Yang, Q., Kang, Y., Wu, J., Hu, H., Yue, C., Zhang, H., Liu, Y., Li, X., Ge, B., Zhu, D., Yuan, Y., Shen, D., Liu, T., & Zhang, S. (2024). Prompt engineering for healthcare: Methodologies and applications. Retrieved from https://arxiv.org/html/2304.14670v2.

Wang, Q., & Ren, J. (2021). Summary-aware attention for social media short text abstractive summarization. *Neurocomputing, 425*, 290–299. https://doi.org/10.1016/j.neucom.2020.04.136.

Wang, S., Zhao, X., Li, B., Ge, B., & Tang, D. (2017). Integrating extractive and abstractive models for long text summarization. In *IEEE International Congress on Big Data (Big Data Congress)* (pp. 305–312). https://ieeexplore.ieee.org/document/8029339.

Zhang, J., Zhao, Y., Saleh, M., & Liu, P. J. (2020). PEGASUS: Pre-training with extracted gap-sentences for abstractive summarization. In *Proceedings of the 37th International Conference on Machine Learning (ICML'20)* (pp. 11328–11339). JMLR. org, Vienna.

9

Adopting AI in Local Government Green Infrastructure Procurement

Dani Salleh, Noni Harianti Junaidi, and Amirulikhsan Zolkafli

9.1 Introduction

The rapid pace of urbanization and climate change has heightened the need for sustainable development practices, particularly in the procurement of infrastructure projects by local governments. Green infrastructure offers a nature-based approach to addressing urban environmental challenges, including air pollution, water management, and biodiversity conservation. However, traditional procurement processes in local government often face challenges such as inefficiencies, lack of transparency, and difficulty in assessing sustainability compliance.

AI has emerged as a transformative tool that can enhance the efficiency, transparency, and sustainability of green infrastructure procurement. AI applications in procurement can automate administrative processes, provide data-driven insights, and optimize supplier selection, ultimately reducing costs and improving project outcomes. Furthermore, predictive analytics, machine learning (ML), and blockchain integration are examples of AI technologies that can help local governments implement green procurement strategies effectively.

The role of AI is explored in this chapter, particularly its role in local government green infrastructure procurement, examining both the challenges of traditional procurement methods and the potential of AI-driven solutions. By integrating AI into procurement processes, local governments can advance sustainable urban development while ensuring compliance with environmental regulations and promoting long-term resilience.

9.1.1 Green Infrastructure Definition

Green infrastructure refers to strategically planned networks of natural and semi-natural areas that provide environmental, economic, and social benefits (Benedict & McMahon, 2006). It integrates green spaces such as wetlands,

DOI: 10.1201/9781003630371-9

parks, wetlands, permeable pavements, green roofs, and urban forests to enhance ecological functions and improve urban sustainability. Unlike traditional gray infrastructure, which relies on engineered solutions like concrete drainage systems and roads, green infrastructure leverages nature-oriented solutions that address urban challenges such as stormwater management, air quality improvement, and heat island mitigation (European Commission: Directorate-General for Environment, 2014).

The concept of green infrastructure is rooted in the idea of enhancing ecosystem services that include water filtration, carbon sequestration, and biodiversity conservation (Gill et al., 2007). These solutions provide cost-effective and adaptable alternatives to conventional infrastructure, contributing to long-term environmental and economic resilience. By integrating natural elements into urban planning, cities can promote a healthier, more livable environment while reducing the negative impacts of rapid urbanization.

9.1.2 Role of Green Infrastructure in Sustainable Urban Development and Climate Resilience

Green infrastructure plays a crucial role in advancing sustainable urban development by addressing environmental challenges and promoting resilience against climate change. Urbanization has led to significant environmental degradation, including increased air pollution, water runoff, and loss of biodiversity. Green infrastructure offers solutions to mitigate these challenges by enhancing urban ecosystems and fostering a balance between built and natural environments (Kabisch et al., 2017).

One of the main functions of green infrastructure is **stormwater management**. Traditional drainage systems struggle to manage excessive rainfall, which leads to flooding and water pollution. Green infrastructure solutions such as bioswales, rain gardens, and green roofs help absorb and filter rainwater, reducing the burden on drainage systems, and improving water quality (Fletcher et al., 2015). In addition, **urban heat island (UHI) mitigation** is another critical function. By increasing vegetation cover, green infrastructure helps lower ambient temperatures, thereby reducing energy consumption for cooling and improving urban livability (Zhang et al., 2017).

Moreover, green infrastructure contributes to **carbon sequestration and air quality improvement**. Trees and plants act as natural carbon sinks, capturing carbon dioxide and filtering pollutants, thereby enhancing urban air quality (Nowak et al., 2006). Furthermore, green spaces provide recreational and esthetic benefits, improving mental well-being, and fostering community cohesion (Tzoulas et al., 2007).

In the context of climate resilience, green infrastructure strengthens urban adaptability to extreme weather events such as heat waves, floods, and droughts. By integrating green solutions into urban planning, cities can increase their capacity level to withstand climate-related shocks while ensuring long-term sustainability and environmental justice (Meerow & Newell, 2017).

9.2 The Need for AI in Local Government Procurement

Local government procurement faces mounting challenges, including inefficiencies in manual processes, escalating costs, risks of fraud, and the growing demand for transparency and sustainability. Traditional methods often struggle to manage complex supply chains, optimize budgets, or ensure compliance with evolving regulations. AI addresses these gaps by automating workflows, enhancing decision-making, and mitigating risks. Historical spending patterns to predict future needs, optimize vendor selection, and identify cost-saving opportunities can be analyzed using ML algorithm while natural language processing (NLP) streamlines contract management by flagging discrepancies and ensuring regulatory compliance. AI-driven tools also bolster accountability through real-time fraud detection, scanning transactions for anomalies that suggest corruption or mismanagement. Furthermore, AI supports sustainability goals by evaluating suppliers' environmental impact and prioritizing green procurement strategies. By integrating AI, local governments can transform procurement into a proactive, data-driven function that aligns with fiscal responsibility, operational efficiency, and public trust—critical priorities in an era of constrained budgets and heightened citizen expectations.

9.2.1 Challenges in Traditional Procurement Processes

Local government procurement of green infrastructure is often hindered by inefficiencies, lack of transparency, and resource constraints. Traditional procurement methods involve complex procedures, extensive paperwork, and time-consuming approvals, making it difficult for municipalities to implement sustainable projects efficiently (Uyarra et al., 2020). Several key challenges include:

i. *Bureaucratic Inefficiencies*: Procurement processes in local governments typically involve multiple stakeholders, extensive documentation, and regulatory compliance requirements. This complexity often leads to delays, cost overruns, and project inefficiencies (Celestin, 2020).

ii. *Lack of Data-Driven Decision-Making*: Many local governments still rely on manual evaluations and subjective assessments when selecting suppliers and contractors. This limits their ability to make informed decisions based on real-time data and sustainability metrics (Thai, 2009).

iii. *Transparency and Corruption Risks*: Traditional procurement is vulnerable to fraud, favoritism, and unethical practices. The lack of digital oversight and accountability mechanisms increases the risk of procurement corruption, leading to inefficiencies and public distrust (OECD, 2025).

iv. *Difficulty in Assessing Sustainability Compliance*: Ensuring that projects meet environmental sustainability standards requires advanced monitoring tools. Traditional methods often lack the capacity to assess compliance with green procurement guidelines effectively (Testa et al., 2016).

v. *Resource Limitations*: Municipal governments frequently encounter fiscal limitations and gaps in technical expertise, particularly in procurement and environmental management systems, which hinder effective deployment of innovative green infrastructure (Bulkeley & Betsill, 2013; Meerow & Newell, 2017). These capacity constraints create significant barriers to implementing sustainable solutions at scale, as resource shortages impede both planning and operational efficiency (Flynn & Davis, 2017).

Given these challenges, adopting AI-driven solutions can help streamline procurement, improve transparency, and enhance sustainability compliance in green infrastructure projects.

9.2.2 AI Potentials in Enhancing Efficiency, Transparency, and Sustainability

AI has the potential to revolutionize local government procurement by automating processes, improving decision-making, and promoting sustainable infrastructure development. AI-driven procurement systems can have the capability analyzing vast big data, identifying patterns, and provide predictive insights that enhance efficiency, transparency, and sustainability (Agrawal et al., 2018). Key AI applications in green infrastructure procurement include:

i. *Automating Procurement Processes*: AI-powered tools can automate contract management, bid evaluations, and compliance checks, significantly reducing administrative burdens and procurement cycle times (Gong et al., 2020). This allows local governments to focus on strategic planning and sustainability goals.

ii. *Enhancing Decision-Making with Predictive Analytics*: AI can analyze historical data, supplier performance, and environmental impact metrics to optimize procurement decisions. Predictive analytics help local governments forecast cost fluctuations, identify the most sustainable suppliers, and assess potential risks (Wirtz et al., 2019).

iii. *Improving Transparency and Accountability*: Blockchain-integrated AI systems can enhance transparency by providing immutable records of procurement transactions. This reduces corruption risks and ensures that procurement decisions align with environmental and ethical standards (Wang et al., 2019).

    iv. *Real-Time Monitoring and Compliance Enforcement*: AI-powered sensors and computer vision technologies can monitor green infrastructure projects in real-time. AI-driven monitoring systems enhances compliance with environmental regulations, improve carbon footprint tracking, and identify inefficiencies in infrastructure performance (Rolnick et al., 2022).

9.3 Understanding AI in the Context of Local Government

AI has emerged as a game-changer in the public sector, offering local governments new opportunities to improve procurement efficiency, decision-making, and infrastructure management. AI technologies, including ML, NLP, and computer vision, are revolutionizing procurement by reducing inefficiencies, ensuring compliance, and improving transparency. As cities strive to achieve sustainability goals, AI-driven solutions can support the adoption of green infrastructure by optimizing resource allocation and risk assessment. By leveraging AI, local governments can enhance their ability to select environmentally responsible suppliers, predict project risks, and automate contract management. However, implementing AI in procurement also presents its own challenges. These challenges include ethical considerations, data privacy concerns, and the need for regulatory frameworks to ensure responsible AI use. By understanding AI's relevance in procurement, local governments can harness its potential to drive innovation, sustainability, and efficiency in urban development. This chapter provides insights into AI-driven procurement strategies, emphasizing how AI can be effectively integrated into local government processes to promote greener and smarter urban solutions. By adopting AI in procurement, local governments can enhance efficiency, ensure sustainability, and improve service delivery.

9.3.1 What Is AI?

AI is a part of computer science that enables machines to simulate human intelligence such as learning, reasoning, problem-solving, perception, and language understanding (Russell & Norvig, 2021). AI systems leverage computational models and algorithms, including ML, deep learning, and NLP, to process huge amounts of data, identify patterns, and make autonomous or semi-autonomous decisions (Goodfellow et al., 2016).

    The development of AI is rooted in both symbolic AI, which focuses on rule-based logic, and connectionist AI, which involves neural networks and statistical models (McCarthy, 2007; LeCun et al., 2015). These approaches have enabled significant advancements in areas such as image recognition, speech processing, and decision support systems. AI-driven automation enhances efficiency, reduces human error, and optimizes complex processes across various domains, including healthcare, finance, and supply chain management (Brynjolfsson & McAfee, 2017).

In the context of local government procurement, AI can play a transformative role by automating routine tasks, improving decision-making, and ensuring transparency and sustainability. AI-driven procurement systems utilize predictive analytics and ML models to analyze trends, detect anomalies, and optimize supplier selection (Agrawal et al., 2018). These systems can assess historical purchasing data, predict future demand, and mitigate risks related to fraud, waste, and inefficiency (Mikhaylov et al., 2018).

Moreover, AI-powered tools can enhance compliance with regulatory requirements and sustainability goals by evaluating environmental, social, and economic factors in procurement decisions (Wirtz et al., 2019). For example, NLP algorithms can process and analyze policy documents to ensure adherence to government procurement guidelines. The integration of AI in procurement fosters greater accountability and resilience in public sector operations, ultimately leading to cost savings and improved service delivery (Schwab, 2016).

9.3.2 Types of AI Relevant to Procurement

AI plays a transformative role in enhancing procurement processes, particularly within the context of local government operations. It highlights three key AI technologies—ML and predictive analytics, NLP, and Computer Vision—and their specific applications in procurement. In addition, it explores how AI can assist local governments in making data-driven decisions, emphasizing its potential to optimize budgets, ensure sustainability, detect fraud, and engage citizens. Below is a more detailed elaboration of this section:

   i. ML and Predictive Analytics:
      ML is a subset of AI that enables systems to learn from historical data and improve their performance over time without explicit programming. In procurement, ML algorithms can analyze vast amounts of historical procurement data to identify patterns, trends, and anomalies. This capability is particularly valuable for local governments, which often deal with complex supply chains and budget constraints. Predictive analytics, a key application of ML, can forecast future procurement needs, anticipate supply chain disruptions, and optimize budget allocation. For instance, by analyzing past spending patterns and market trends, predictive analytics can help local authorities identify the most cost-effective suppliers or predict potential delays in the delivery of goods and services. Furthermore, ML can support sustainability goals by identifying suppliers that meet environmental standards, enabling local governments to align procurement practices with broader economic and ecological objectives (Jordan & Mitchell, 2015; Wirtz et al., 2019).

ii. *NLP for Contract Management*:

NLP is another critical AI technology that has significant implications for procurement, particularly in contract management. NLP enables AI systems to interpret, summarize, and analyze large volumes of text-based procurement documents, such as contracts, invoices, and compliance reports. This capability reduces the administrative burden on procurement teams by automating routine tasks like document review and risk assessment. For example, AI-driven contract management tools can scan contracts for compliance with regulatory requirements, flag discrepancies, and identify potential risks, such as unfavorable terms or clauses that could lead to legal disputes. By streamlining these processes, NLP not only enhances efficiency but also minimizes the likelihood of procurement fraud and inefficiencies, which are common challenges in public sector procurement (Chowdhury, 2003; Kushwaha & Kar, 2020).

iii. *Computer Vision for Infrastructure Monitoring*:

Computer vision focuses on enabling machines to interpret visual data, has emerged as a powerful tool for infrastructure monitoring in procurement. By leveraging AI-powered image recognition, computer vision systems can analyze drone and satellite imagery to assess the condition of infrastructure in real-time. This technology is particularly useful for local governments managing green infrastructure projects, such as parks, renewable energy installations, and water management systems. For instance, computer vision can detect maintenance issues like cracks in roads or leaks in pipelines, enabling timely interventions that reduce costs and prevent larger problems. Additionally, it can monitor the progress of sustainability projects, ensuring that they meet environmental targets and comply with regulatory standards. By automating inspections and reducing reliance on manual processes, computer vision significantly lowers inspection costs, and improves response times (Zhang et al., 2021; Goodfellow et al., 2016).

9.3.3 AI in Public Sector Decision-Making

The integration of AI into public sector decision-making has the potential to revolutionize how local governments operate, particularly in procurement. AI enhances decision-making by providing real-time insights, optimizing resource allocation, and improving governance transparency. Below are four key areas where AI can assist local governments:

i. *Budget Optimization*: AI-driven analytics can forecast financial needs and suggest cost-effective procurement strategies. By analyzing historical spending data and market trends, AI can help local governments allocate budgets more efficiently, ensuring that funds are directed toward the most critical areas (Schwalbe, 2022).

ii. *Sustainability Assessments*: AI can evaluate environmental impact metrics, such as carbon footprints and energy consumption, to ensure compliance with green procurement guidelines. This capability is particularly important for local governments committed to achieving sustainability goals and reducing their environmental impact (Gong et al., 2020).

iii. *Fraud Detection*: AI algorithms can detect anomalies in procurement transactions, such as unusual pricing patterns or unauthorized purchases, reducing the risk of corruption and fraud. By identifying suspicious activities in real-time, AI helps local governments maintain the integrity of their procurement processes (Wang et al., 2019).

iv. *Citizen Engagement*: AI-powered platforms can facilitate citizen engagement by allowing residents to provide feedback on green infrastructure projects and other procurement initiatives. This fosters participatory governance, ensuring that procurement decisions align with community needs and preferences (Ting et al., 2021).

In summary, AI technologies like ML, NLP, and computer vision are transforming procurement processes in local governments by enhancing efficiency, reducing costs, and supporting sustainability goals. Moreover, AI's ability to provide real-time insights and optimize decision-making is empowering local authorities to make proactive, data-driven decisions that align with both economic and environmental objectives. As AI continues to evolve, its applications in procurement and public sector governance are likely to expand, offering even greater opportunities for innovation and improvement.

9.4 The Role of AI in Green Infrastructure Procurement

Green infrastructure encompasses not only natural but also semi-natural systems. These systems provide environmental, social, and economic benefits, such as parks, green roofs, and permeable pavements. Procuring these systems involves complex decision-making processes, where AI can serve as a transformative tool. Adopting AI into local government green infrastructure procurement can significantly enhance decision-making, optimize processes, manage costs and risks, and promote transparency. This section will explore these facets, illustrating how AI can revolutionize sustainable urban development.

9.4.1 Enhancing Decision-Making and Planning

Traditional EIAs are often time-consuming and labor-intensive. AI streamlines this process by analyzing large datasets to predict environmental outcomes swiftly. For instance, AI can process satellite imagery and sensor data to assess urban heat islands, informing the placement of green spaces to mitigate heat effects (Suphavarophas et al., 2024). AI employs predictive analytics to forecast environmental changes, aiding in resource allocation. ML models can predict stormwater runoff patterns, guiding the design of green infrastructure like bioswales and retention ponds to manage flooding effectively (Gomes et al., 2019). This proactive approach ensures sustainability and resilience in urban planning.

9.4.2 Optimizing Procurement Processes

Selecting suppliers for green infrastructure projects requires evaluating numerous criteria, including sustainability credentials and cost-effectiveness. AI systems can analyze supplier data, past performance, and compliance records to identify optimal partners. This data-driven approach enhances efficiency and reduces biases in supplier selection (Sievo, 2024). Ensuring compliance with environmental regulations is critical in green infrastructure projects. AI can automate the monitoring of regulatory changes and assess project adherence to these standards. NLP algorithms can review contracts and documentation to ensure all legal and environmental requirements are met, reducing the risk of noncompliance (Precoro, 2024).

9.4.3 Cost and Risk Management

Accurate cost estimation and risk assessment are vital for the success of infrastructure projects. AI analyzes historical data and market trends to forecast costs and identify potential risks. For example, AI can predict price fluctuations in sustainable materials, allowing governments to budget effectively and mitigate financial risks (Focal Point, 2024).

9.4.4 Promoting Transparency and Accountability

Transparency in project implementation fosters public trust and ensures accountability. AI-powered tools can monitor project progress in real-time, comparing actual performance against planned milestones. This continuous oversight enables timely interventions when deviations occur, ensuring projects stay on track and within budget (NIGP, 2024). AI enhances the integrity of procurement processes by detecting fraudulent activities. ML algorithms can identify patterns indicative of bid-rigging or collusion among contractors. For instance, the UK government has trialed AI-backed tools to detect collusive activities in its £300 billion public procurement market, leading to ongoing investigations and promoting fair competition (CMA, 2024).

The integration of AI in local government green infrastructure procurement offers numerous benefits, including improved decision-making, optimized processes, effective cost and risk management, and enhanced transparency. By embracing AI technologies, local governments can advance their sustainability goals and foster resilient urban environments.

9.5 Case Studies and Best Practices

The integration of AI into local government procurement processes for green infrastructure has demonstrated significant potential in enhancing efficiency, transparency, and sustainability. This section explores notable examples of AI adoption, successful AI-driven procurement models, and the lessons learned to guide future implementations.

9.5.1 Case Studies from Smart Cities and Local Governments Using AI

9.5.1.1 *Optimizing Underground Infrastructure Planning in Casablanca, Morocco*

In Casablanca, the rapid urban expansion necessitated the development of an extensive stormwater management system. The local utility company, Lydec, collaborated with Optimatics, an AI-driven solution provider, to design a stormwater network spanning approximately 300 km. By leveraging AI, the project achieved capital expenditure savings between 10% and 35%, optimizing pipe sizing, alignment, and placement to align with existing road networks and projected urban growth (Global Infrastructure Hub, 2020).

9.5.1.2 *Enhancing Procurement Processes in the United Kingdom*

The UK's public sector has embraced AI to streamline procurement activities. AutogenAI, for instance, has developed tools that automate the drafting of bid proposals, significantly reducing the time required for procurement processes. This approach not only accelerates operations but also allows human resources to focus on strategic decision-making (The Times, 2024).

9.5.2 Successful AI-Driven Procurement Models

AI technologies have been instrumental in refining supplier selection and contract evaluation processes. By analyzing vast datasets, AI systems can assess supplier performance, financial stability, and compliance records, ensuring that local governments engage with reliable and sustainable partners. This data-driven approach minimizes risks associated with supplier defaults and enhances the quality of green infrastructure projects (GEP, 2023). Ensuring adherence to environmental regulations is paramount in green infrastructure projects. AI solutions can automate the monitoring of regulatory changes and assess project compliance in real-time. NLP algorithms can review contracts and project documents to identify potential compliance issues, thereby reducing the likelihood of legal challenges and project delays (Precoro, 2024).

9.5.3 Lessons Learned

The adoption of AI in procurement necessitates a focus on ethical considerations. Local governments must ensure that AI systems are transparent, fair, and do not perpetuate existing biases. Collaborative research with stakeholders is essential to operationalize ethical principles in AI procurement, fostering public trust and ensuring equitable outcomes (Ada Lovelace Institute, 2024).

For successful AI integration, local governments should invest in building internal AI expertise. This involves training procurement professionals to understand and manage AI tools effectively. Establishing centers of excellence can provide sustainable expertise and set consistent standards for responsible AI use, ensuring that AI technologies are harnessed to enhance public services while safeguarding public interests (Federation of American Scientists, 2024).

To expedite AI adoption, municipalities can utilize prenegotiated contracts that eliminate procurement hurdles. For example, partnerships with platforms like Civic Marketplace enable local governments to access AI-driven solutions in areas such as traffic management and infrastructure asset tracking, facilitating the swift deployment of technologies that enhance community well-being (Civic Marketplace, 2024).

The implementation of AI in procurement processes must prioritize data privacy and security. Local governments should establish robust data governance frameworks to protect sensitive information and comply with relevant regulations. This includes conducting regular audits and adopting technologies that enhance data security, thereby maintaining public trust in AI-driven procurement systems (Appian, 2024).

Collaboration between various governmental agencies can lead to the sharing of best practices and resources, facilitating more effective AI adoption. Interagency partnerships can help standardize AI procurement processes, reduce costs, and promote the development of innovative solutions tailored to the unique needs of different communities (Bloomberg Cities, 2024). By learning from existing case studies and adopting best practices, municipalities can enhance efficiency, ensure compliance, and promote sustainability in their infrastructure projects. A strategic approach that emphasizes ethical considerations, capacity building, and collaboration will be essential in harnessing the full benefits of AI in public

9.6 Future Directions and Policy Recommendations

The integration of AI into local government procurement processes for green infrastructure presents a transformative opportunity to enhance efficiency, transparency, and sustainability. Local governments must adopt strategic approaches that encompass capacity building, policy development, and collaborative engagement. This section outlines key strategies for AI adoption in procurement, emphasizes the importance of partnerships with the private sector and academia, and explores the future trajectory of AI in sustainable urban development.

9.6.1 Strategies for Local Governments to Adopt AI in Procurement

i. *Building AI Expertise and Training Procurement Officers*:

A foundational step for local governments is to cultivate internal AI expertise. This involves comprehensive training programs aimed at equipping procurement officers with the necessary skills to effectively utilize AI tools. By fostering both intra-agency and inter-agency capacity-building for responsible AI procurement and use, governments can build sustainable expertise, promote equitable AI adoption, and protect public interest. This ensures that AI enhances—rather than harms—the efficiency and quality of public services (Federation of American Scientists, 2024).

Establishing centers of excellence (CoEs) dedicated to AI can serve as hubs for knowledge sharing and continuous learning. These CoEs can provide guidance on best practices, facilitate workshops, and develop resources tailored to the unique challenges of public sector procurement. Such initiatives enhance the technical proficiency of procurement teams and foster a culture of innovation and adaptability within local governments.

ii. *Developing AI-Friendly Procurement Policies and Frameworks*:

To effectively integrate AI into procurement processes, local governments must develop policies and frameworks that are conducive to AI adoption. This includes revising existing procurement guidelines to accommodate AI technologies and ensuring that these policies address ethical considerations, data privacy, and transparency. Local governments can draw from the Office of Management and Budget's (OMB) guidance to establish effective AI acquisition strategies that focus on risk management and performance oversight (Best Best & Krieger LLP, 2024).

Implementing standardized AI procurement checklists can further streamline the acquisition process. These checklists serve as practical tools to ensure that all necessary considerations—such as vendor accountability, system interoperability, and compliance with regulatory standards—are systematically addressed during procurement. By adopting such structured approaches, local governments can mitigate risks associated with AI implementation and promote responsible use of technology.

iii. *Engaging Private Sector and Academia in AI-Driven Procurement*:

Collaboration with the private sector and academic institutions is pivotal in advancing AI-driven procurement. These collaborations can help manage access to AI technologies and not only provide opportunities for joint research but also offer platforms for piloting innovative solutions. Engaging with technology firms allows local governments to leverage external expertise, while academic collaborations can contribute to the development of evidence-based policies and the evaluation of AI applications in real-world settings.

Moreover, such collaborations can aid in the co-creation of AI tools designed to suit the needs of public procurement. By involving diverse stakeholders in the development process, local governments can ensure that AI solutions are contextually relevant, user-friendly, and aligned with public sector values. This inclusive approach fosters a sense of shared ownership and accountability, which is essential for the successful integration of AI into public services.

9.6.2 The Future of AI in Sustainable Urban Development

Looking ahead, AI is poised to become increasingly important in sustainable urban development. Dylan (2024) emphasized that the year 2025 will see that AI is set to support over 30% of smart city functions, especially in transport (Dylan, 2024). Furthermore, AI's role in urban planning is becoming key in boosting power grid efficiency and reshaping city designs, promising safer, more efficient, and flexible city living.

In the realm of green infrastructure, AI can optimize energy consumption, efficiently manage energy grids, and enhance waste management systems (Sandtech Solutions, 2024). For instance, AI-powered platforms can analyze data from various sensors to predict energy demand patterns, enabling the implementation of energy-saving measures and reducing the overall carbon footprint of urban areas.

Furthermore, AI's predictive capabilities can enhance climate resilience by anticipating environmental changes and informing proactive urban planning. ML algorithms can analyze climate data to forecast extreme weather events, allowing cities to implement adaptive measures that mitigate potential impacts on infrastructure and public safety. This proactive approach will act as a safeguard to urban assets and enhance the quality of life for residents.

AI in local government procurement of green infrastructure is a multifaceted endeavor that requires strategic planning, capacity building, and collaborative partnerships. By investing in AI expertise, developing supportive policies, and engaging with external stakeholders, local governments can gain benefits from the transformative potential of AI to foster sustainable and resilient urban environments. As AI continues to evolve, its integration into urban development will be instrumental toward addressing the complex challenges of modern cities and promoting the well-being of their inhabitants.

9.7 Conclusion

Integrating AI into local government green infrastructure procurement sig-nifies a shift toward more efficient, transparent, and sustainable urban devel-opment. This chapter has explored the multifaceted benefits of AI adoption, examined real-world applications, and provided strategic recommendations for policymakers and local governments.

Several critical insights have emerged, underscoring the potential of AI in reshaping local government procurement practices. AI-driven tools sig-nificantly enhance decision-making and strategic planning by enabling comprehensive EIA and predictive analytics. Advanced algorithms analyze vast datasets—from historical spending patterns to climate projections—allowing governments to forecast resource needs, prioritize sustainability initiatives, and allocate budgets with precision. For example, ML models can simulate the long-term effects of green infrastructure projects, ensur-ing investments align with both environmental goals and community needs. This data-driven approach empowers policymakers to move beyond reactive measures and adopt proactive, evidence-based strategies.

The adoption of AI optimizes procurement processes by streamlining tra-ditionally labor-intensive tasks. Automated systems accelerate supplier selec-tion through real-time performance evaluations and bias-free scoring, while NLP tools parse complex contracts to flag noncompliance or inefficiencies. Routine tasks, such as regulatory checks and invoice validation, are executed with unmatched speed and accuracy, freeing staff to prioritize other impor-tant responsibilities. This operational efficiency not only reduces admin-istrative overhead but also minimizes delays, ensuring projects adhere to timelines and budgets. For example, AI-powered platforms can cross-reference vendor certifications with sustainability criteria, ensuring compli-ance without manual oversight.

AI-based systems revolutionize cost and risk management, which are pivotal to the success of public sector projects. Predictive analytics provide granular cost forecasts, identifying potential budget overruns before they occur, while ML algorithms assess risks such as supply chain disruptions or contractor defaults. These capabilities are particularly critical for green infrastructure initiatives, where financial viability and risk mitigation deter-mine long-term sustainability. By integrating real-time data from IoT sensors or market trends, AI models dynamically adjust projections, enabling gov-ernments to allocate contingency funds strategically and safeguard project outcomes.

AI fosters transparency and accountability, which are foundational to public trust in governmental operations. Blockchain-integrated AI platforms create immutable audit trails for procurement transactions, while anomaly detec-tion algorithms monitor spending patterns to flag irregularities indicative of fraud or corruption. Real-time dashboards provide stakeholders—from auditors to citizens—with visibility into project progress, expenditures, and compliance status. This transparency not only deters malfeasance but also strengthens civic engagement, as communities can track how public funds are utilized to achieve sustainability targets.

Successful AI integration hinges on strategic implementation frameworks. Local governments must invest in building internal expertise through targeted training programs and partnerships with tech firms or academic institutions. Simultaneously, procurement policies must evolve to accommodate AI tools, addressing ethical concerns such as algorithmic bias and data privacy. Collaborative ecosystems, involving private sector innovators and research bodies, can accelerate the development of tailored AI solutions that address region-specific challenges. By adopting a holistic approach—combining technological adoption with institutional readiness—governments can unlock AI's full potential to drive efficiency, equity, and environmental stewardship in procurement.

9.7.1 The Potential of AI in Transforming Green Infrastructure Procurement

AI stands at the forefront of revolutionizing green infrastructure procurement by introducing data-driven methodologies that enhance both efficiency and sustainability. By analyzing vast datasets, AI enables precise EIA, ensuring that infrastructure projects align with ecological preservation goals. For instance, AI can process satellite imagery and sensor data to assess urban heat islands, informing the strategic placement of green spaces to mitigate heat effects.

Moreover, AI's predictive analytics facilitate proactive resource allocation, optimizing the design and implementation of green infrastructure. ML models can forecast stormwater runoff patterns, guiding the development of effective flood management systems such as bioswales and retention ponds. This proactive approach not only enhances urban resilience but also contributes to long-term cost savings.

In procurement processes, AI streamlines operations by automating supplier evaluations and contract management. By analyzing supplier performance data and compliance records, AI systems identify optimal partners, ensuring that projects are executed by reliable and environmentally conscious vendors (Sievo, 2024). In addition, AI-driven contract analysis ensures adherence to environmental regulations, reducing the risk of legal complications and project delays (Precoro, 2024).

The financial implications of AI integration are equally significant. Accurate cost forecasting models enable local governments to budget effectively, anticipating price fluctuations in sustainable materials and labor costs (Focal Point, 2024). Furthermore, AI's risk assessment capabilities identify potential project pitfalls, allowing for the implementation of mitigation strategies that safeguard public investments.

AI-powered monitoring systems can help bolster transparency and accountability by providing real-time insights into project progress. These systems detect anomalies and potential fraudulent activities, ensuring that public funds are utilized appropriately and that projects adhere to established timelines and quality standards (NIGP, 2024).

9.7.2 Call to Action for Policymakers and Local Governments

To harness the full potential of AI in green infrastructure procurement, policymakers and local governments are urged to undertake the following actions:

- *Invest in Capacity Building*: Develop comprehensive training programs to equip procurement officers and relevant staff with the skills necessary to effectively implement and manage AI technologies. Establishing centers of excellence can serve as hubs for continuous learning and knowledge sharing (Federation of American Scientists, 2024).

- *Develop Supportive Policies and Frameworks*: Revise existing procurement policies to accommodate AI integration, ensuring that frameworks address ethical considerations, data privacy, and transparency. Utilizing resources such as the Office of Management and Budget's guidance can aid in establishing effective AI acquisition strategies (Best Best & Krieger LLP, 2024).

- *Foster Collaborative Partnerships*: Engage with private sector entities and academic institutions to leverage external expertise, drive innovation, and co-create AI solutions tailored to the specific needs of local communities. Such collaborations can facilitate access to cutting-edge technologies and research (Ada Lovelace Institute, 2024).

- *Prioritize Ethical and Responsible AI Use*: Implement governance mechanisms that ensure AI applications in procurement are transparent and fair and do not perpetuate existing biases. Establishing clear guidelines and conducting regular audits can uphold public trust and ensure equitable outcomes (Precoro, 2024).

- *Promote Interagency Collaboration*: Encourage communication and resource-sharing between various governmental agencies to standardize AI procurement processes, reduce costs, and develop innovative solutions that address the unique challenges of different communities (Bloomberg Cities, 2024).

By embracing these strategies, local governments can effectively integrate AI into their green infrastructure procurement processes, which will lead urban development to become more efficient, transparent, and sustainable. The transformative potential of AI, when harnessed responsibly, can significantly improve the quality of public services and contribute to the well-being of communities in the future.

References

Ada Lovelace Institute. (2024). *Procurement of AI and Data-Driven Systems in Local Government*. Retrieved from https://www.adalovelaceinstitute.org/project/procurement-ai-local-government/.

Agrawal, A., Gans, J., & Goldfarb, A. (2018). *Prediction Machines: The Simple Economics of Artificial Intelligence*. Brighton, MA: Harvard Business Review Press.

Appian. (2024). *Improving Procurement with AI in Government Contracting*. Retrieved from https://appian.com/blog/acp/public-sector/ai-in-government-contracting.

Benedict, M. A., & McMahon, E. T. (2006). *Green Infrastructure: Linking Landscapes and Communities*. Washington, DC: Island Press.

Best Best & Krieger LLP. (2024). *Federal Guidelines for the Responsible Acquisition of AI—What Local Governments Need to Know*. Retrieved from https://bbklaw.com/resources/la-110424-federal-guidelines-for-the-responsible-acquisition-of-ai.

Bloomberg Cities. (2024). *Strategies for Spreading AI Throughout Local Government*. Retrieved from https://bloombergcities.jhu.edu/news/strategies-spreading-ai-throughout-local-government.

Brynjolfsson, E., & McAfee, A. (2017). *Machine, Platform, Crowd: Harnessing Our Digital Future*. New York: W. W. Norton & Company.

Bulkeley, H., & Betsill, M. M. (2013). *Revisiting the urban politics of climate change*. *Environmental Politics*, 22(1), 136–154.

Celestin, M. (2020). Challenges and solutions in procurement processes for local government contracts in Rwanda. *International Journal of Multidisciplinary Research and Modern Education*, 6(2), 63–70. https://ijmrme.crystalpen.in/uploads/68354265cafbd_793.pdf

Chowdhury, G. G. (2003). Natural language processing. *Annual Review of Information Science and Technology*, 37(1), 51–89.

Civic Marketplace. (2024). *Harnessing AI for Local Government Innovation*. Retrieved from https://www.civicmarketplace.com/insights/harnessing-ai-for-local-government-innovation-building-stronger-safer-smarter-communities.

Dylan, S. (2024). *AI Revolution in Smart Cities: Sustainable Urban Futures*. Retrieved from https://scottdylan.com/blog/technology-and-innovation/building-intelligent-urban-spaces-ai-in-smart-city-development/.

European Commission: Directorate-General for Environment. (2014). *Building a Green Infrastructure for Europe*. Publications Office. Retrieved from https://data.europa.eu/doi/10.2779/54125.

Federation of American Scientists. (2024). *Expanding Local Government Capacity for AI Procurement and Use*. Retrieved from https://fas.org/publication/expanding-state-local-capacity-ai-procurement/

Fletcher, T. D., Andrieu, H., & Hamel, P. (2015). Understanding, management and modelling of urban hydrology and its consequences for receiving waters: A state of the art. *Advances in Water Resources*, 51, 261–279.

Flynn, A., & Davis, P. (2017). Exploring the relationship between sustainability and innovation in public procurement. *Journal of Public Procurement*, 17(1), 58–90.

Focal Point. (2024). *AI in Procurement: Transforming Processes with Artificial Intelligence for Unmatched Efficiency*. Retrieved from https://www.getfocalpoint.com/ai-in-procurement-transforming-processes-with-artificial-intelligence-for-unmatched-efficiency/.

GEP. (2023). *Artificial Intelligence in Procurement: Case Studies from GEP*. Retrieved from https://www.gep.com/blog/technology/artificial-intelligence-in-procurement-case-studies.

Gill, S. E., Handley, J. F., Ennos, A. R., & Pauleit, S. (2007). Adapting cities for climate change: The role of the green infrastructure. *Built Environment*, 33(1), 115–133.

Global Infrastructure Hub. (2020). *AI to Optimise Underground Infrastructure Planning*. Retrieved from https://www.gihub.org/infrastructure-technology-use-cases/case-studies/ai-to-optimise-underground-infrastructure-planning/.

Gomes, C., Dietterich, T., Barrett, C., Conrad, J., & Dilkina, B. (2019). Computational sustainability: Computing for a better world and a sustainable future. *Communications of the ACM*, 62(9), 56–65.

Gong, Y., Jia, F., Brown, S., & Koh, L. (2020). Supply chain learning of sustainability in multi-tier supply chains: A resource orchestration perspective. *International Journal of Operations & Production Management*, 40(6), 745–770.

Goodfellow, I., Bengio, Y., & Courville, A. (2016). *Deep Learning*. Cambridge, MA: MIT Press.

Jordan, M. I., & Mitchell, T. M. (2015). Machine learning: Trends, perspectives, and prospects. *Science*, 349(6245), 255–260.

Kabisch, N., Korn, H., Stadler, J., & Bonn, A. (Eds.). (2017). *Nature-Based Solutions to Climate Change Adaptation in Urban Areas*. Berlin: Springer.

Kushwaha, A. K., & Kar, A. K. (2020). Artificial intelligence in contract management: A review and future research agenda. *Journal of Business Research*, 115, 378–393.

LeCun, Y., Bengio, Y., & Hinton, G. (2015). Deep learning. *Nature*, 521(7553), 436–444.

McCarthy, J. (2007). *What is Artificial Intelligence?* Stanford, CA: Stanford University.

Meerow, S., & Newell, J. P. (2017). Spatial planning for multifunctional green infrastructure: Growing resilience in Detroit. *Landscape and Urban Planning*, 159, 62–75.

Mikhaylov, S. J., Esteve, M., & Campion, A. (2018). Artificial intelligence for the public sector: Opportunities and challenges of cross-sector collaboration. *Philosophical Transactions of the Royal Society A*, 376(2128), 20170357.

National Institute of Governmental Purchasing (NIGP). (2024). *Artificial Intelligence: The Impact on Public Procurement*. Retrieved from https://www.nigp.org/blog/ai-and-public-procurement.

Nowak, D. J., Crane, D. E., & Stevens, J. C. (2006). Air pollution removal by urban trees and shrubs in the United States. *Urban Forestry & Urban Greening*, 4(3–4), 115–123.

OECD (2025). Digital transformation of public procurement: Good practice report, OECD Public Governance Policy Papers, No. 77 https://doi.org/10.1787/79651651-en.

Precoro. (2024). *AI in Procurement: Benefits, Risks, and best practices*. Retrieved from https://precoro.com/blog/ai-in-procurement/.

Rolnick, D., Donti, P. L., Kaack, L. H., Kochanski, K., Lacoste, A., Sankaran, K., ... & Bengio, Y. (2022). Tackling climate change with machine learning. *ACM Computing Surveys (CSUR)*, 55(2), 1–96.

Russell, S., & Norvig, P. (2021). *Artificial Intelligence: A Modern Approach* (4th ed.). London: Pearson.

Sandtech Solutions. (2024). *AI in Urban Planning: Using Tech to Redefine City Design*. Retrieved from https://www.sandtech.com/insight/ai-in-urban-planning-using-tech-to-redefine-city-design/.

Schwalbe, K. (2022). *Information Technology Project Management*. Boston, MA: Cengage Learning.

Schwab, K. (2016). *The Fourth Industrial Revolution*. Cologny: World Economic Forum.

Sievo. (2024). The Ultimate Guide for AI in Procurement. Retrieved from https://sievo.com/resources/ai-in-procurement.

Suphavarophas, P., Wongmahasiri, R., Keonil, N., & Bunyarittikit, S. (2024). A systematic review of applications of generative design methods for energy efficiency in buildings. *Buildings*, 14(5), 123–145.

Testa, F., Annunziata, E., Iraldo, F., & Frey, M. (2016). Drawbacks and opportunities of green public procurement: an effective tool for sustainable production. *Journal of Cleaner Production*, 112, 1893–1900. https://doi.org/10.1016/j.jclepro.2014.09.092.

Thai, K. V. (2017). International public procurement: Concepts and practices. In *International Handbook of Public Procurement* (pp. 1–24). Routledge.

The Competition and Markets Authority (CMA). (2024). UK faces 'significant risk' from procurement collusion, CMA warns. *Financial Times*. Retrieved from https://www.ft.com/content/02eebde2-5628-44f3-b0bc-93aee3b3ba0f.

The Times. (2024). *How AI Firms Take On 'Niche and Boring' Work to Free Up Humans*. Retrieved from https://www.thetimes.co.uk/article/how-ai-firms-take-niche-boring-work-free-humans-zfwz87h8b.

Ting, Y., Wang, P., & Alexander, R. (2021). AI-driven public engagement: Opportunities and challenges. *Public Administration Review*, 81(3), 413–426.

Tzoulas, K., Korpela, K., Venn, S., Yli-Pelkonen, V., Kaźmierczak, A., Niemela, J., & James, P. (2007). Promoting ecosystem and human health in urban areas using Green Infrastructure: A literature review. *Landscape and Urban Planning*, 81(3), 167–178.

Uyarra, E., Edler, J., Gee, S., Georghiou, L., & Yeow, J. (2020). Barriers to innovation through public procurement: A supplier perspective. *Technovation*, 94–95, 102–115.

Wang, F. Y., Zeng, D., Zheng, X., & Wang, H. (2019). Blockchain for AI: Review and open research challenges. *IEEE Transactions on Cybernetics*, 50(6), 2478–2491.

Wirtz, B. W., Weyerer, J. C., & Geyer, C. (2019). Artificial intelligence and the public sector—Applications and challenges. *International Journal of Public Administration*, 42(7), 596–615.

Zhang, Y., Murray, A. T., & Turner, B. L. (2017). Optimizing green space locations to reduce daytime and nighttime urban heat island effects in Phoenix, Arizona. *Landscape and Urban Planning*, 165, 162–171.

Zhang, Y., Wu, L., & Zhu, J. (2021). AI-based monitoring for urban infrastructure sustainability. *Journal of Urban Technology*, 28(4), 53–70.

10

AI-Based Water Quality Detection and Monitoring in Urban Environments

Muhamad Danish Saiful Rizal, Fakhitah Ridzuan,
Mohd Hakimi Aiman Ibrahim, and Nurzulaikha Abdullah

10.1 Introduction

Water is essential for public health, environmental sustainability, and economic development. As the world faces increasing challenges from climate change, industrialization, and urbanization, it is important to monitor and manage water resources. Clean and safe water is critical not only for human use but also for agricultural productivity and industrial processes (Siročić et al., 2023). Water quality deterioration is often associated with pollution and poses a major risk to ecosystems and communities.

Water quality refers to the physical, chemical, and biological qualities of water (Water Science School, 2018). It is an important parameter because it has an intrinsic value and it can affect the health of the public, agriculture, and aquatic life forms (Akhlaq et al., 2024). Water quality monitoring has played an important role in ensuring that water resources are safe and sustainable. Although the traditional methods used in the past were effective, the process was very slow and could not always capture the dynamic characteristics of water quality in aquatic environments. To address these limitations, the Water Quality Index (WQI) was developed. WQI shows water quality in terms of index numbers and offers an identification of water quality that is more suitable for open use or any expectation, in addition to pollution remediation programs and quality management in water (Ahmad et al., 2020). Equation 10.1 shows the WQI calculation based on Brown's Water Quality Equation (Brown et al., 1970):

$$WQI = \Sigma q_n W_n / \Sigma W_n \tag{10.1}$$

where Q_n is the quality rating of the nth water quality parameter, and W_n is the unit weight of the nth water quality parameter.

DOI: 10.1201/9781003630371-10

10.1.1 Water Quality Management

Urban refers to areas that have a higher population density and complex infrastructures (Heisler & Brazel, 2015; Srinivasulu, 2024). These areas include cities, towns, and metropolitan regions that are usually busy with economic, social, and cultural activities. The economic activities for urban areas usually focus on industries, commerce, and services. The infrastructure in urban areas is typically equipped with advanced systems for transportation, community services, and water supply, which are crucial for maintaining public health and well-being.

A good water quality management system should be able to monitor, analyze, and improve water quality to meet environmental and regulatory standards for the community. The urban water management approach is important in addressing these challenges (Kotecha et al., 2024). The objectives of water quality management should be specific and measurable, such as to reduce pollutant levels. A recent study by Algaba et al. (2023) discussed the urban water management being used in Sevilla, Spain. The authors highlighted the issues of water infrastructure, solid waste management, and climate adaptation. It was suggested that the infrastructure should be well-maintained so that it will fit the purpose of solving the issues. For solid waste management, the authors emphasized the challenges of high waste generation, low recycling rates, and low energy recovery from waste. Therefore, the integrated approaches of green infrastructure and innovative technological management strategies focusing on sustainability could be the alternative solution.

10.1.2 Challenge in Water Quality Management

Challenges in ensuring urban sustainability are increasingly complex, which leads to an increased need for advanced technology in water quality management. Artificial Intelligence (AI) can play an important role in water quality management by analyzing large, complex datasets to uncover patterns. AI-driven approaches, particularly machine learning (ML) are very effective tools in decision-making based on collected data. ML involves the use of statistical models or algorithms so that machines can learn, and their performance can be improved from time to time. It can predict future water quality conditions in the absence of various natural and anthropogenic factors while analyzing historical and current water quality data (Rajitha et al., 2024). The use of AI in water quality management is a big step forward toward ensuring everyone has access to clean water. ML models can anticipate changes in water quality, identify potential sources of pollution, and provide appropriate management techniques. This can indirectly result in the availability of clean and safe water that is essential for human health, agriculture, and environmental sustainability.

Rivers with increasing pollution levels require effective water quality prediction models for informing policy and management decisions (Nair & Vijaya, 2021). Pollution is a severe risk to public health, aquatic ecosystems, and environmental sustainability. Traditional water quality monitoring can take a long time and does not always provide data in real time. Therefore, water quality issues cannot be addressed efficiently. Besides, this challenge calls for effective water quality prediction models that will support proactive and impactful interventions.

Recently, AI has been progressing rapidly and has the potential to change how water quality issues can be detected and classified (Rajitha et al., 2024). By applying ML algorithms to historical data, WQI can be predicted. Additionally, specific types of water pollution can be tracked to take appropriate measures to safeguard water resources. This chapter explores several ML algorithms used for WQI prediction, highlighting their potential as tools for environmental protection and providing actionable insights to enhance public health.

10.2 Terminologies

This section explains the important terms associated with water quality and water pollution.

10.2.1 Water Quality

Water quality is an important indicator to determine its suitability for different usages. It refers to the chemical, biological, and physical health of the water. Parameters such as dissolved ion concentration, pH, nitrate, and phosphate nutrients are chemical parameters that indicate the suitability of water for consumption by humans and ecological health (George & Ngole-Jeme, 2022). Poor water quality can lead to adverse health outcomes and disrupt aquatic habitats. Furthermore, it can significantly affect industrial and agricultural operations, as these sectors rely heavily on clean and reliable water sources for their processes and productivity.

Identifying the presence of bacteria, viruses, and other pathogens is essential for evaluating the safety of drinking water sources (Mai et al., 2023). Therefore, advanced techniques and models are needed in water quality monitoring and assessment. The water quality models allow researchers to simulate the changes and predict what to expect in the case of water resource management or pollution control. Water must be of high quality for health, ecology, and economic activity. This can be maintained through continuous monitoring and technological innovation, providing safe and sustainable use of water for all purposes.

10.2.2 Water Pollutant

Water pollutants are materials that degrade water quality, adversely affecting human health and the environment. Some of these pollutants are emitted by industrial processes, agricultural activities and urban runoff stormwater systems. This has been one of the biggest challenges that threaten water sources safety in both domestic and international cities for a long time now. This definition of water pollution does not only include conventional sources, including industrial sewage, domestic wastewater, and agricultural nonpoint sources, but also includes the sudden pollution events. Such events consist of acts of terrorism, chemical discharge from vessels, oil slicks, industrial disasters, stormwater pollution, and poisoning (Cao et al., 2022). These various pollution problems are very crucial in protecting water supplies and promoting the health of the environment and people.

Water pollution is categorized into two main types based on sources like Point and Nonpoint (Madhav et al., 2020). Point sources refer to contamination from a single, identifiable origin, such as industrial discharge into water bodies. Nonpoint sources involve pollutants from multiple origins, like runoff from rain passing through various areas. Additionally, water pollution can stem from natural or anthropogenic sources (Madhav et al., 2020). Natural sources include geological factors, shallow groundwater, saltwater intrusion, or geothermal fluids. Anthropogenic sources involve human activities like excessive pesticide use, industrial effluents, mining waste, and improper waste disposal.

10.3 Current Practice in Water Monitoring

Water quality can be assessed by analyzing water samples for chemical indicators, where unsafe levels of constituents indicate contamination (Madhav et al., 2020). Traditional water quality monitoring generally involves manual sampling, where water samples are collected from various locations and analyzed in laboratories. Typically, these procedures are time-consuming as several WQI parameters need to be examined (Rahu et al., 2023). Additionally, laboratory testing often delays results until it is too late for timely decisions on water quality management. World Health Organization (WHO) has set the acceptable limits of WQI, and the traditional methods find it difficult to satisfy those standards consistently because of the limitations inherent in the methods. Currently, there is an increased demand for solutions that provide real-time, or near real-time, monitoring of water quality conditions (Rahu et al., 2023).

One significant incident that occurred due to delayed action in water quality detection was the 2014 Toledo water crisis in Ohio, USA. This crisis affected nearly 400,000 residents when the city's water supply became contaminated with elevated levels of microcystin, a potent toxin produced by harmful algal blooms (HABs) in Lake Erie (Jetoo et al., 2015). These blooms, which were exacerbated by nutrient pollution from agricultural runoff, particularly phosphorus, had been observed by local agencies. However, the detection of microcystin in the water did not occur until the toxin had reached hazardous levels. As a result, the city issued a "do not drink" advisory, and residents were forced to rely on bottled water for several days.

The delayed identification of the contamination was largely due to the absence of continuous, real-time water quality monitoring systems capable of detecting such toxins promptly. Although the algal blooms were visible earlier, the lack of timely data on the presence and concentration of microcystin meant that the full scope of the contamination was not understood until it had already impacted public health. This incident highlights the critical need for more advanced water quality monitoring technologies, including real-time sensors and predictive models, which could enable early detection and timely intervention. Following the crisis, Toledo and surrounding regions made significant investments in improving water quality monitoring infrastructure, incorporating advanced sensor networks and ML algorithms to ensure the early detection of pollutants and to prevent similar public health risks in the future (Jetoo et al., 2015).

10.3.1 Scope of Existing Study

The integration of AI into water quality monitoring is becoming increasingly critical as the complexity and scale of water pollution challenges continue to grow. This section will explore the scope of existing studies on the application of ML for water quality prediction. The use of ML in water quality analysis covers several goals different from normal analysis and helps manage pollution and security in water. Akhlaq et al. (2024) focus on identifying key water quality parameters in Alpine lakes and rivers in three districts in Pakistan. Similarly, Xu et al. (2022) proposed an automated water quality assessment framework to evaluate water quality and pollution levels with a focus on heavy metal contamination.

Shams et al. (2024), Nguyen et al. (2022), and Azrour et al. (2022) focus on predicting WQI using ML. Shams et al. (2024) emphasize model optimization through grid search, Nguyen et al. (2022) explore ML methods for WQI assessment with a case study, and Azrour et al. (2022) propose a minimal-parameter model using only four key water parameters. These studies converge on the goal of improving WQI prediction but differ in parameter selection and optimization approaches.

Rahu et al. (2023, 2024) address water quality from an operational perspective. The 2024 study focuses on maintaining irrigation water quality by monitoring parameters like Total Dissolved Solid (TDS), turbidity, and pH. On the other hand, the 2023 study integrates Internet of Things (IoT) with ML for water quality analysis and prediction. Both studies aim to ensure practical water management but adopt distinct technological frameworks.

Nallakaruppan et al. (2024) and Khaskheli et al. (2024) emphasize explainability and efficiency in ML-based water quality predictions. Nallakaruppan et al. (2024) provide a detailed analysis using explainable AI for classification, while Khaskheli et al. (2024) propose a supervised ML approach for accurate and cost-effective water quality prediction. Both aim to enhance prediction accuracy while ensuring transparency in ML models.

Lastly, Wang et al. (2023) employ advanced techniques like the entropy weight method and Pearson correlation to predict high-precision water quality indicators, such as dissolved oxygen (DO) and nitrogen compounds, focusing on parameter-specific predictions rather than holistic indices. Table 10.1 summarizes the scope of the recent study such as identifying water pollutants, predicting water quality indices, optimizing model performance, and addressing challenges in water quality management.

TABLE 10.1

Overview of Existing Study

Author	Scope
Akhlaq et al. (2024)	To assess water quality and protect human health from contamination by identifying key water quality parameters and heavy metals in the Alpine glacial lakes and rivers of three districts in Pakistan
Shams et al. (2024)	To predict the WQI and WQC by ML with focus on optimization and model parameter's tuning using grid search method to increase prediction accuracy
Azrour et al. (2022)	To propose a new model by ML algorithms for predicting water quality with minimal parameters, focusing on temperature, pH, turbidity, and coliforms
Xu et al. (2022)	To build an ML model that works with heavy metal indices for the automatic evaluation of water and sediment quality while handling data scarcity and missing data
Nguyen et al. (2022)	To survey the application of ML methods in assessing water quality based on the WQI and to discuss perspectives of WQI calculation, then also examine effectiveness for ML algorithm application in prediction
Rahu et al. (2024)	To keep irrigation water free from harmful chemicals, control TDS levels, and maintain turbidity and appropriate pH while monitoring water temperature
Rahu et al. (2023)	To propose an integrated framework of IoT and ML for analysis and prediction of water quality
Nallakaruppan et al. (2024)	To provide an analysis and white-box description of the classification problem for water quality
Khaskheli et al. (2024)	To assess a diverse approach based on supervised ML for accurate, faster, and cheaper solutions for prediction of water quality
Wang et al. (2023)	To propose a comprehensive weight-based approach to identify and select the most critical features for accurate water quality prediction

The integration of ML in water monitoring is not only transforming the way water quality is assessed but also enhancing the decision-making process by providing actionable insights. Furthermore, the ongoing development of IoT-based systems is expanding the potential applications of ML, making it an essential tool for safeguarding water resources in the face of increasing pollution and climate change challenges.

10.3.2 Machine Learning Algorithm Used in Existing Research

Researchers have employed a diverse range of algorithms tailored to specific objectives, such as predicting WQI, assessing contamination levels, and optimizing water management strategies. These algorithms, ranging from traditional statistical methods to advanced ML models, have been applied to address challenges like data scarcity, missing values, and computational efficiency. This section explores the ML algorithms utilized in existing research, highlighting their implementation, strengths, and contributions to advancing water quality monitoring and prediction. Table 10.2 highlights the ML model used in the existing study.

From Table 10.2, it was reported that the Support Vector Machine (SVM) is the most commonly used algorithm as it was employed by all ten listed authors in their studies. SVM is a powerful supervised learning model, particularly in high-dimensional spaces. Awad et al. (2015) suggested that SVM works by finding the optimal hyperplane that separates data points of different classes with the maximum margin. Its ability to handle nonlinear data through kernel functions makes it a versatile tool for water quality monitoring, especially when dealing with complex, and multidimensional datasets. Decision Trees (DT) are the second most popular algorithm used in the existing study as shown in Table 10.2. Dhebar and Deb (2020) defined DT as a nonlinear,

TABLE 10.2

Summary of Algorithm Used

Authors	SVM	DT	RF	MLP	KNN	GB	XGBoost	LSTM
Akhlaq et al. (2024)	√	√	√	√	√			
Shams et al. (2024)	√	√	√	√	√	√	√	
Azrour et al. (2022)	√	√				√		
Xu et al. (2022)	√	√		√	√			
Nguyen et al. (2022)	√	√	√			√		√
Rahu et al. (2024)	√	√	√					
Rahu et al. (2023)	√	√	√	√			√	√
Nallakaruppan et al. (2024)	√	√	√					
Khaskheli et al. (2024)	√	√	√	√	√	√		
Wang et al. (2023)	√		√	√			√	√

interpretable model that splits data into subsets based on feature values. They are easy to visualize, understand, and implement, making them a popular choice for researchers. The strength of DT lies in its simplicity and ability to model complex decision-making processes. However, they can be prone to overfitting, especially with deeper trees, unless regularized or pruned.

Random Forest (RF) is employed by eight out of the total listed authors. RF is built upon DT by using an ensemble approach. RF creates multiple decision trees and aggregates their predictions to improve accuracy and reduce overfitting (Rane et al., 2024). The ensemble learning method can enhance the robustness of the model, making it less sensitive to noise and outliers in the data. RF is particularly effective for handling large datasets with many features. Multilayer Perceptron (MLP) is a type of artificial neural network used by six out of the listed ten authors. MLP is capable of learning complex, non-linear relationships between input features and target variables (Juna et al., 2022). Its strength lies in its flexibility and capacity to model intricate patterns in data. However, MLP requires significant computational resources and large datasets to achieve optimal performance, which might explain its less frequent application in water quality monitoring compared to other algorithms.

Gradient Boosting (GB) is applied by four out of ten authors. GB is an ensemble technique that builds trees sequentially, where each tree corrects the errors of the previous one (Liu et al., 2022b). It has become popular due to its ability to boost predictive results by optimizing the training target while keeping the training objectives unchanged. GB is known for its ability to work with imbalanced datasets and its robustness against overfitting when tuned properly. However, it can be computationally expensive and sensitive to noisy data.

K-Nearest Neighbors (KNN), XGBoost, and Long Short-Term Memory (LSTM) are each used by three out of ten authors, indicating their less frequent application in the reviewed studies. KNN is a simple, instance-based learning algorithm that classifies data points based on the majority class of their nearest neighbors (Jo & Jo, 2021). It is easy to understand but can be computationally intensive, especially with large datasets. XGBoost is an advanced implementation of GB that has gained popularity for its flexibility, strong predictive power, generalization ability, scalability, efficiency in model training, and robustness (Zhang et al., 2022). LSTM is a type of recurrent neural network (RNN). It is designed for sequential data, making it well-suited for time-series analysis, such as predicting water quality over time (Chen et al., 2022). However, LSTM requires large amounts of data and computational resources to perform well, which may explain its less frequent use in water quality studies.

In conclusion, the algorithms used in the studies vary in their popularity and application, with SVM, DT, and RF being the most commonly used due to their robustness, accuracy, and versatility. While less frequently used, algorithms like XGBoost and LSTM offer specialized capabilities for handling specific types of data, such as sequential data or data requiring fine-tuned boosting techniques. The choice of algorithm depends on the specific requirements of the water quality prediction task, such as the size of the dataset, the complexity of the data, and the need for interpretability or predictive accuracy.

10.3.3 Classification and Regression in Water Quality Monitoring

Classification and regression are two fundamental tasks in supervised ML. Each task addresses specific types of problems based on the nature of the output variable. Classification involves assigning input data to predefined categories or classes. The data will be grouped into quality categories such as "good," "moderate," or "poor." This method helps to identify patterns that differentiate between these classes, providing actionable insights for water quality management. Several authors, including Akhlaq et al. (2024), Shams et al. (2024), Azrour et al. (2022), Xu et al. (2022), Rahu et al. (2023,2024), Nallakaruppan et al. (2024), and Khaskheli et al. (2024), have employed classification techniques in their study.

In contrast, regression focuses on predicting continuous numerical values based on input features. This approach is commonly used in water quality studies to estimate specific parameters, such as WQI value or pollutant concentrations. By mapping input features to a continuous output variable, regression enables precise predictions, which are critical for detailed monitoring and analysis. Authors such as Shams et al. (2024), Nguyen et al. (2022), Rahu et al. (2023), Khaskheli et al. (2024), and Wang et al. (2023) have utilized regression techniques in their work.

10.4 Machine Learning Process

10.4.1 Dataset

The dataset, published on January 10, 2025 by Rahman et al. (2025) provides a comprehensive record of daily water quality measurements collected over 15 years (2007–2023) from Cork Harbour, Ireland. Cork Harbour is a natural harbor influenced by both riverine and coastal dynamics. Its strategic environmental importance makes it an ideal site for long-term water quality monitoring and analysis. The dataset contains 7,790 rows of structured data, capturing 11 critical water quality parameters (as shown in Figure 10.1):

1. Alkalinity
2. Ammonia
3. Biochemical Oxygen Demand (BOD)
4. Chloride

Alkalinity-total (as CaCO3)	Ammonia-Total (as N)	BOD - 5 days (Total)	Chloride	Conductivity @25°C	Dissolved Oxygen	ortho-Phosphate (as P) - unspecified	pH	Temperature	Total Hardness (as CaCO3)	True Colour	WQI Value	Label
8	0.066	1.3	13.2	69	54.1	0.005	6.89	8.9	10.8	33	74.28197782	Fair
9	0.068	1.3	14.8	77	54	0.005	6.89	9.7	11.7	28	74.75575566	Fair
15	0.033	1.4	16	106	53.9	0.021	7.18	6.6	17	22	72.03773106	Fair
13	0.04	1.2	15.7	159	53.35	0.005	6.88	6.4	15	22	76.46568923	Fair
12	0.039	1.1	16	144	53.4	0.021	7.23	6.3	16.3	24	71.9755516	Fair
16	0.025	1.3	16.1	98	55.9	0.006	7.23	17.4	21.3	22	74.87034837	Fair
18	0.041	1.3	14.9	92	52.7	0.005	7.08	16.3	19.5	26	75.24174494	Fair
13	0.066	1.3	9.23	68	53.05	0.012	7.08	12.7	16.8	42	73.72264305	Fair
13	0.068	1.3	8.99	61	46.4	0.007	6.71	8.1	12.4	38	75.59652156	Fair
14	0.075	1.3	9.23	63	46.9	0.008	6.69	8.3	13.3	35	75.76429675	Fair
14	0.068	1.3	8.12	60	44.7	0.006	6.79	8.5	11.4	35	76.30068837	Fair
16	0.044	2.3	8.81	69	55.55	0.021	7.51	16.2	17.6	31	70.87654267	Fair
15	0.046	2.4	7.34	57	50.1	0.021	7.05	14.5	14.2	42	71.18422777	Fair
17	0.03	1.7	8.56	68	53.4	0.021	7.19	14.9	17.3	31	71.40423344	Fair
14	0.035	2.7	7.38	62	58.3	0.021	7	16.2	16.5	42	69.62138843	Fair
11	0.025	1.6	6.16	52	58.3	0.021	6.75	15.8	13.7	48	69.01200315	Fair
12	0.04	1.6	6.68	58	56.7	0.021	6.92	15.9	14.8	44	69.76799122	Fair
16	0.048	2.1	8.2	61	44.7	0.021	6.92	13.9	16.9	37	72.71264736	Fair

FIGURE 10.1
Water quality dataset.

5. Conductivity

6. Dissolved Oxygen

7. Orthophosphate

8. pH

9. Temperature

10. Total Hardness

11. True Color

Alkalinity measures the water's ability to neutralize acids, primarily influenced by bicarbonates, carbonates, and hydroxides, which is essential for maintaining a stable pH and protecting aquatic life (Boyd et al., 2016). Ammonia, measured as ammonium ions (NH_4^+) and free ammonia (NH_3), indicates potential pollution from agricultural runoff, sewage, or industrial waste, with high levels posing toxicity risks to aquatic organisms (Peng et al., 2024). Biochemical Oxygen Demand (BOD) measures the level of organic pollution, where high BOD levels indicate more biochemical contaminants, which can increase ammonia production (Nagaraju et al., 2023).

Chloride in water can come from sources like ion exchange, halite dissolution, industrial effluents, sewage, and farming runoff. Since the biological uptake of chloride is minimal, its concentration tends to remain high once released into the water (Madhav et al., 2020). Conductivity measures water's ability to conduct electricity, which is influenced by the concentration of dissolved ions (Avramov et al., 2023). It is influenced by factors such as hardness, salinity, and metal levels. DO measures the oxygen available in water for aquatic organisms. It is a key indicator of water quality, reflecting the balance between oxygen-producing processes and oxygen-consuming activities (Pant et al., 2024).

Orthophosphate, the bioavailable form of phosphorus (PO_4^{3-}), is a key nutrient for aquatic plants and algae, but excessive levels can lead to eutrophication and HABs (Gopi, 2021). The pH of water, which indicates its acidity or alkalinity, is crucial for maintaining chemical balance and supporting aquatic life, with extreme values potentially harming organisms and altering chemical solubility. Temperature plays a vital role in water quality by influencing the metabolic rates of aquatic organisms, DO levels, and the solubility of chemicals. Total Hardness, which measures the concentration of calcium (Ca^{2+}) and magnesium (Mg^{2+}) ions, affects water chemistry and usability for industrial and domestic purposes (Kheira et al., 2024). Finally, True Color reflects the esthetic and chemical characteristics of water after removing suspended particles, often indicating the presence of dissolved organic matter or pollutants (West et al., 2016).

10.4.2 Data Preprocessing

Data preprocessing is a critical step in ensuring valid data analysis. It involves techniques like outlier removal and missing value imputation to improve the quality of data. For this case study, the dataset was first examined for missing values, and none were identified, ensuring that all observations were complete. Duplicate values were also checked, and it was confirmed that there were no duplicate rows in the dataset, which helped maintain the integrity of the data.

Next, outlier detection was performed using the Interquartile RangeIQR method, and it was found that the dataset contained outliers. Further investigation revealed that these outliers were primarily associated with limited data for certain categories of the Label variable, such as "good" "excellent" and "poor." The distribution of Label is shown in Figure 10.2. The under-representation of these categories in the dataset made classification tasks less effective. As a result, it was decided to remove the outliers and shift the focus to a regression approach, aiming to predict the WQI Value instead of classifying the water quality into discrete categories.

Additionally, unnecessary columns were dropped to streamline the dataset and focus on the most relevant features for predicting the WQI. Since the dataset contained parameters with varying ranges of values, normalization was applied to scale the data. This ensured that all features contributed equally to the model, preventing any one parameter with a larger range from dominating the regression analysis. Through these steps, the dataset was refined and prepared for regression modeling, to accurately predict the WQI based on the available water quality parameters.

10.4.3 Model Development

After completing data preprocessing, the next step involves the modeling phase, which is crucial for detecting and classifying water quality. In this case, regression was chosen as the predictive approach, as it is a statistical method used to model the relationship between a dependent variable and independent variables. In the context of water quality prediction, regression

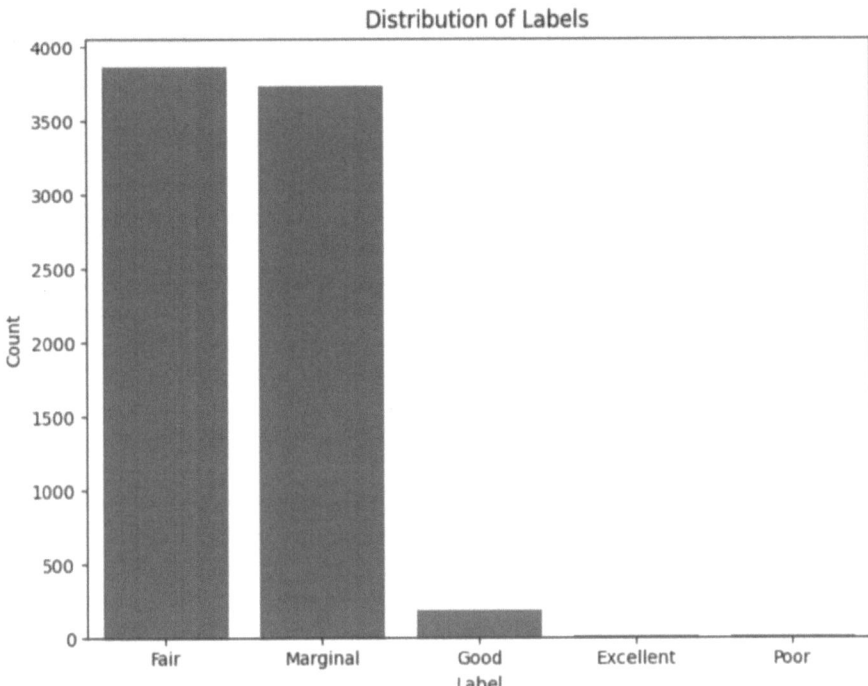

FIGURE 10.2
Distribution of label in the dataset.

aims to predict continuous outcomes, such as the WQI value based on various input parameters. Unlike classification, which categorizes data into distinct classes, regression produces a numerical value that reflects the expected outcome. These methods help identify patterns and trends in the data, allowing for accurate predictions of water quality levels based on historical measurements and other environmental factors. This phase aims to identify the best algorithm for predicting the WQI value. The selection of algorithms directly affects the precision and effectiveness of the ML models. Based on the literature review, six algorithms, including SVM, DT, RF, MLP, GB, and XGBoost, were chosen for the modeling.

10.4.4 Model Evaluation

Model evaluation is a critical step in assessing the performance and reliability of ML models. It involves the use of various metrics to quantify how well the model predicts or fits the data. For this case study, three metrics will be used, which are Mean Squared Error (MSE), R-squared (R^2), and Normalized Percentage Error (NPE). MSE is a widely used metric for regression tasks that measures the average squared difference between the predicted and actual values. A lower MSE is better as it indicates that the model's predictions are more accurate. MSE is sensitive to large errors due to the squaring of differences, making it useful for identifying models that perform poorly on outliers.

R^2 is a statistical measure that represents the proportion of the variance in the dependent variable (WQI) that is predictable from the independent variables (water quality parameters). An R^2 value closer to 1 indicates that the model explains a high proportion of the variance in the data, suggesting a strong fit. Conversely, an R^2 value closer to 0 indicates that the model does not explain much of the variance. NPE measures the percentage error between the predicted and actual values, normalized by the range of the data. It is used to evaluate the relative error of the model's predictions. A lower NPE indicates that the model's predictions are more accurate to the scale of the data, making it a useful metric for comparing models with different ranges of output. Table 10.3 shows the MSE, R^2 and NPE for all algorithms.

The performance of six ML models was evaluated to assess their suitability for water quality forecasting. Among these models, XGBoost demonstrated the best performance, achieving the lowest MSE (0.0546), the highest R^2 (0.9986), and the smallest NPE (0.17%). The R^2 reveals that 99.9% of the variability of the WQI is explained by the regression model. These results indicate that XGBoost provides highly accurate predictions with minimal error, effectively capturing the variance in the dataset. Its consistently outperforming other models makes it the most reliable choice for this task.

RF also performed exceptionally well, with an R^2 of 0.9955, a low MSE of 0.1798, and an NPE of 0.30%. It shows that 99.6% of the regression model explains the variability of the data. While slightly less accurate than XGBoost, it remains a robust alternative, particularly for datasets with complex patterns and nonlinear relationships. GB followed closely, with an R^2 of 0.9935, an MSE of 0.2592, and an NPE of 0.58%, making it a dependable model, though not as precise as XGBoost or Random Forest. Other models, such as SVM and MLP, showed moderate performance. SVM achieved an R^2

TABLE 10.3

Performance Metrics for Each Algorithm

Model	Mean Squared Error (MSE)	R-Squared (R^2)	Normalized Percentage Error (NPE) (%)
SVM	0.9180	0.9771	0.87
DT	0.4014	0.9923	0.22
RF	0.1798	0.9955	0.30
MLP	0.9709	0.9758	1.17
GB	0.2592	0.9935	0.58
XGBoost	0.0546	0.9986	0.17

of 0.9771 and an NPE of 0.87%, while MLP obtained an R^2 of 0.9758 and an NPE of 1.17%. However, both models had higher MSE values compared to the top-performing ensemble methods, indicating that they are less effective at capturing the dataset's complexity. AdaBoost had the weakest performance, with the highest MSE (3.0188), the lowest R^2 (0.9247), and the largest NPE (2.23%), suggesting it is not well-suited for this application.

10.5 Limitation of Automatic Water Quality Monitoring and Detection

The application of ML in automatic water quality monitoring and detection is promising. However, it has several limitations, including quality and quantity of data, complexity of environment variables, model interpretability, and computational requirements. ML models require large and high-quality datasets for training. In many cases, water quality data can be sparse, noisy, or incomplete (Liu et al., 2022a). Inconsistent data collection methods, missing values, or errors in sensor readings can compromise model accuracy and generalization. Additionally, imbalanced datasets can lead to biased predictions, where the model might perform poorly in detecting rare water quality events, such as pollution spikes or extreme contamination levels.

Another challenge is the complexity of environmental variables. Water quality is influenced by a multitude of dynamic factors, including weather conditions, seasonal changes, and anthropogenic activities (Akhtar et al., 2021). These variables are often interdependent and can introduce significant noise into the data. ML models may struggle to capture the intricate relationships between these factors, especially when dealing with nonlinear interactions or complex temporal patterns. Inaccurate modeling of these interactions can result in suboptimal predictions or misclassifications of water quality.

Furthermore, model interpretability is a significant concern in ML applications for environmental monitoring (Maloney et al., 2022). Many ML algorithms operate as black boxes. This makes it difficult to understand how they arrive at specific predictions. This lack of transparency can hinder trust in the model's decisions, particularly in regulatory or decision-making contexts where clear explanations are essential. Additionally, overfitting is another risk, where the model performs well on training data but fails to generalize to unseen data, leading to poor performance in real-world scenarios.

Finally, the scalability and computational requirements of ML models can pose challenges for real-time water quality monitoring. Training sophisticated models, such as deep learning networks, often requires significant computational power and time. Deploying these models in a real-time monitoring system may require substantial infrastructure and may not be feasible in resource-limited settings. Additionally, frequent updates to the model or retraining with new data can be computationally expensive, limiting the long-term sustainability of ML-based water quality monitoring systems.

10.6 Conclusion

In conclusion, the use of ML for automatic water quality monitoring and detection offers substantial potential to improve the accuracy and efficiency of environmental monitoring systems. However, the performance of ML models can vary significantly based on the quality, quantity, and characteristics of the data provided. Challenges such as imbalanced data, missing values, outliers, and the complexity of environmental factors can affect model accuracy and reliability. In this chapter, for instance, limited data on certain water quality categories led to the decision to shift from classification to regression, impacting the model's performance. Additionally, the preprocessing steps, including normalization and the removal of unnecessary columns, were crucial in improving model outcomes. While ML models can provide valuable insights into water quality trends, their performance is highly contingent on the data used. Continuous refinement and adaptation of the models are necessary to achieve optimal results. Addressing these limitations will be key to maximizing the potential of ML in water quality monitoring, ensuring that the models provide accurate and actionable insights for environmental management and public health.

References

Ahmad, T., Gupta, G., Sharma, A., Kaur, B., Alsahli, A. A., & Ahmad, P. (2020). Multivariate statistical approach to study spatiotemporal variations in water quality of a Himalayan Urban Fresh Water Lake. *Water*, 12(9), 2365. https://doi.org/10.3390/w12092365.

Akhlaq, M., Ellahi, A., Niaz, R., Khan, M., Sammen, S. S., & Scholz, M. (2024). Comparative analysis of machine learning algorithms for water quality prediction. *Tellus a Dynamic Meteorology and Oceanography*, 76(1), 177–192. https://doi.org/10.16993/tellusa.4069.

Akhtar, N., Syakir Ishak, M. I., Bhawani, S. A., & Umar, K. (2021). Various natural and anthropogenic factors responsible for water quality degradation: A review. *Water*, 13(19), 2660. https://doi.org/10.3390/w13192660.

Algaba, M. H., Huyghe, W., Van Leeuwen, K., Koop, S., & Eisenreich, S. (2023). Assessment and actions to support Integrated water resources management of Seville (Spain). *Environment Development and Sustainability*, 26(3), 7347–7375. https://doi.org/10.1007/s10668-023-03011-8.

Avramov, M., Thaivalappil, A., Ludwig, A., Miner, L., Cullingham, C. I., Waddell, L., & Lapen, D. R. (2023). Relationships between water quality and mosquito presence and abundance: A systematic review and meta-analysis. *Journal of Medical Entomology, 61*(1), 1–33. https://doi.org/10.1093/jme/tjad139.

Awad, M., Khanna, R., Awad, M., & Khanna, R. (2015). Support vector machines for classification. In *Efficient Learning Machines: Theories, Concepts, and Applications for Engineers and System Designers* (pp. 39–66). https://doi.org/10.1007/978-1-4302-5990-9_3.

Azrour, M., Mabrouki, J., Fattah, G., Guezzaz, A., & Aziz, F. (2022). Machine learning algorithms for efficient water quality prediction. *Modeling Earth Systems and Environment, 8*(2), 2793–2801. https://doi.org/10.1007/s40808-021-01266-6.

Boyd, C. E., Tucker, C. S., & Somridhivej, B. (2016). Alkalinity and hardness: Critical but elusive concepts in aquaculture. *Journal of the World Aquaculture Society, 47*(1), 6–41. https://doi.org/10.1111/jwas.12241.

Brown, R. M., McClelland, N. I., Deininger, R. A., & Tozer, R. G. (1970). A water quality index-do we dare. *Water and Sewage Works, 117*(10), 339–343.

Cao, Y., Zhang, X., Chen, Z., Zhang, Z., & Wei, H. (2022). Construction of pollution risk early warning model for urban drinking water supply chain. *Water Science & Technology Water Supply, 22*(12), 8540–8556. https://doi.org/10.2166/ws.2022.353.

Chen, H., Yang, J., Fu, X., Zheng, Q., Song, X., Fu, Z., … & Yang, X. (2022). Water quality prediction based on LSTM and attention mechanism: A case study of the Burnett River, Australia. *Sustainability, 14*(20), 13231. https://doi.org/10.3390/su142013231.

Dhebar, Y., & Deb, K. (2020). Interpretable rule discovery through bilevel optimization of split-rules of nonlinear decision trees for classification problems. *IEEE Transactions on Cybernetics, 51*(11), 5573–5584. https://doi.org/10.1109/TCYB.2020.3033003.

George, M., & Ngole-Jeme, V. M. (2022). An evaluation of the Khubelu Wetland and receiving stream water quality for community use. *Water, 14*(3), 442. https://doi.org/10.3390/w14030442.

Gopi, V. (2021). Potential of Cyanobacterium Spirulina platensis for Eutrophic Water Restoration (Doctoral dissertation, Université d'Ottawa/University of Ottawa).

Heisler, G. M., & Brazel, A. J. (2015). *The Urban Physical Environment: Temperature and Urban Heat Islands* (pp. 29–56). Hoboken, NJ: John Wiley & Sons, Ltd. https://doi.org/10.2134/AGRONMONOGR55.C2.

Jetoo, S., Grover, V., & Krantzberg, G. (2015). The toledo drinking water advisory: Suggested application of the water safety planning approach. *Sustainability, 7*(8), 9787–9808. https://doi.org/10.3390/su7089787.

Jo, T., & Jo, T. (2021). Instance based learning. In *Machine Learning Foundations: Supervised, Unsupervised, and Advanced Learning* (pp. 93–115). https://doi.org/10.1007/978-3-030-65900-4.

Juna, A., Umer, M., Sadiq, S., Karamti, H., Eshmawi, A. A., Mohamed, A., & Ashraf, I. (2022). Water quality prediction using KNN imputer and multilayer perceptron. *Water, 14*(17), 2592. https://doi.org/10.3390/w14172592.

Khaskheli, S. A., Ahmed Rahu, M., Siraj, S., Jamshed, H., & Iqbal, S. (2024). Optimized water quality forecasting using machine learning. *International Journal of Information Systems and Computer Technologies, 3*(2), 46–60. https://doi.org/10.58325/ijisct.003.02.0094.

Kheira, B., Khaled, M., & Hamed, B. (2024). Evaluation of water hardness treatment methods using sodium hydroxide and their impact on water quality. *Studies in Engineering and Exact Sciences, 5*(3), e12491. https://doi.org/10.54021/seesv5n3-037.

Kotecha, M. J., Bakori, D., Agarwal, S., Meraj, G., Kanga, S., Singh, S. K., & Farooq, M. (2024). Geoinformation for integrated urban water resource management. In *Earth Observation in Urban Monitoring* (pp. 93–111). Elsevier. https://doi.org/10.1016/B978-0-323-99164-3.00015-X.

Liu, Y., Liu, J., Zhao, Y., Wang, X., Song, S., Liu, H., & Yu, T. (2022a). Retrieving water quality parameters from noisy-label data based on instance selection. *Remote Sensing, 14*(19), 4742. https://doi.org/10.3390/rs14194742.

Liu, W., Fan, H., & Xia, M. (2022b). Credit scoring based on tree-enhanced gradient boosting decision trees. *Expert Systems with Applications, 189*, 116034. https://doi.org/10.1016/j.eswa.2021.116034.

Madhav, S., Ahamad, A., Singh, A. K., Kushawaha, J., Chauhan, J. S., Sharma, S., & Singh, P. (2020). Water pollutants: Sources and impact on the environment and human health. In *Sensors in Water Pollutants Monitoring: Role of Material* (pp. 43–62). https://doi.org/10.1007/978-981-15-0671-0_4.

Mai, Y., Zheng, J., Zeng, J., Wang, Z., Liu, F., Ma, L., Zhou, M., Zhao, S., Wu, B., Wang, C., Yan, Q., He, Z., & Shu, L. (2023). Protozoa as hotspots for potential pathogens in the drinking water of a subtropical megacity: Diversity, treatment, and health risk. In *Environmental Science & Technology.* https://doi.org/10.1021/acs.est.2c09139.

Maloney, K. O., Buchanan, C., Jepsen, R. D., Krause, K. P., Cashman, M. J., Gressler, B. P., ... & Schmid, M. (2022). Explainable machine learning improves interpretability in the predictive modeling of biological stream conditions in the Chesapeake Bay Watershed, USA. *Journal of Environmental Management, 322*, 116068. https://doi.org/10.1016/j.jenvman.2022.116068.

Nair, J. P., & Vijaya, M. S. (2021). Predictive models for river water quality using machine learning and big data techniques - A survey. In *Proceedings of the International Conference on Artificial Intelligence and Smart Systems (ICAIS-2021)* (pp. 1747–1753). https://doi.org/10.1109/icais50930.2021.9395832.

Nagaraju, T. V., Bala, G. S., Bonthu, S., & Mantena, S. (2023). Modelling biochemical oxygen demand in a large inland aquaculture zone of India: Implications and insights. *The Science of the Total Environment, 906*, 167386. https://doi.org/10.1016/j.scitotenv.2023.167386

Nallakaruppan, M. K., Gangadevi, E., Shri, M. L., Balusamy, B., Bhattacharya, S., & Selvarajan, S. (2024). Reliable water quality prediction and parametric analysis using explainable AI models. *Scientific Reports, 14*(1). https://doi.org/10.1038/s41598-024-56775-y.

Nguyen, H. Du, Nguyen, T. Q. D., Thi, H. N., Lap, B. Q., & Phan, T. T. H. (2022). The Use of machine learning algorithms for evaluating water quality index: A survey and perspective. In *2022 International Conference on Multimedia Analysis and Pattern Recognition, MAPR 2022- Proceedings.* https://doi.org/10.1109/MAPR56351.2022.9924736.

Pant, N., Toshniwal, D., & Gurjar, B. R. (2024). Short-term forecasting of dissolved oxygen based on spatial-temporal attention mechanism and kernel-based loss function. *Journal of Water Process Engineering, 69*, 106677. https://doi.org/10.1016/j.jwpe.2024.106677.

Peng, Q., Dong, Y., Chen, Y., Glidle, A., Kong, L., Yin, H., ... & Yang, K. (2024). Rapid profiling of fish cell nitrogen metabolism with single-cell Raman spectroscopy: Unveiling enzyme's role in ammonia detoxification. *Talanta, 277,* 126389. https://doi.org/10.1016/j.talanta.2024.126389.

Rahman, A., Syeed, M., Fatema, K., Karim, M. R., Khan, R. H., Shakhawat Hossain, M., & Uddin, M. F. (2025). Surface water quality index (WQI) forecasting dataset (Version 1). figshare. https://doi.org/10.6084/m9.figshare.28184252.v1.

Rahu, M. A., Chandio, A. F., Aurangzeb, K., Karim, S., Alhussein, M., & Anwar, M. S. (2023). Toward design of internet of things and machine learning-enabled frameworks for analysis and prediction of water quality. *IEEE Access, 11,* 101055–101086. https://doi.org/10.1109/ACCESS.2023.3315649.

Rahu, M. A., Shaikh, M. M., Karim, S., Chandio, A. F., Dahri, S. A., Soomro, S. A., & Ali, S. M. (2024). An IoT and machine learning solutions for monitoring agricultural water quality: A robust framework. *Mehran University Research Journal of Engineering and Technology, 43*(1), 192. https://doi.org/10.22581/muet1982.2401.2806.

Rajitha, A., K, A., Nagpal, A., Kalra, R., Maan, P., Kumar, A., & Abdul-Zahra, D. S. (2024). Machine Learning and AI-Driven water quality monitoring and treatment. *E3S Web of Conferences, 505,* 03012. https://doi.org/10.1051/e3sconf/202450503012.

Rane, N., Choudhary, S. P., & Rane, J. (2024). Ensemble deep learning and machine learning: Applications, opportunities, challenges, and future directions. *Studies in Medical and Health Sciences, 1*(2), 18–41. https://doi.org/10.48185/smhs.v1i2.122.

Shams, M. Y., Elshewey, A. M., El-kenawy, E. S. M., Ibrahim, A., Talaat, F. M., & Tarek, Z. (2024). Water quality prediction using machine learning models based on grid search method. *Multimedia Tools and Applications, 83*(12), 35307–35334. https://doi.org/10.1007/s11042-023-16737-4.

Siročić, A. P., Ojdanić, K., Dogančić, D., & Plantak, L. (2023). Water quality for human consumption from the public water supply system. *Environmental Sciences Proceedings, 25*(1), 21. https://doi.org/10.3390/ECWS-7-14230.

Srinivasulu, A. (2024). Urbanization in India: An evaluation from environmental perspectives. *EPRA International Journal of Multidisciplinary Research.* https://doi.org/10.36713/epra16519.

Wang, X., Li, Y., Qiao, Q., Tavares, A., & Liang, Y. (2023). Water quality prediction based on machine learning and comprehensive weighting methods. *Entropy, 25*(8). https://doi.org/10.3390/e25081186.

Water Science School. (2018, November 13). *Water Quality Information by Topic.* USGS. Retrieved January 24, 2025, from https://www.usgs.gov/special-topics/water-science-school/science/water-quality-information-topic.

West, A. O., Nolan, J. M., & Scott, J. T. (2016). Optical water quality and human perceptions: A synthesis. *Wiley Interdisciplinary Reviews: Water, 3*(2), 167–180. https://doi.org/10.1002/wat2.1127.

Xu, X., Lai, T., Jahan, S., Farid, F., & Bello, A. (2022). A machine learning predictive model to detect water quality and pollution. *Future Internet, 14*(11). https://doi.org/10.3390/fi14110324.

Zhang, P., Jia, Y., & Shang, Y. (2022). Research and application of XGBoost in imbalanced data. *International Journal of Distributed Sensor Networks, 18*(6). https://doi.org/10.1177/155013292211069.

11

Building Inclusive Smart Cities: The Role of Mathematical Models and AI Applications

Manee Sangaran Diagarajan, Chockalingam Aravind Vaithilingam, and Murugan Thangiah

11.1 Introduction

Artificial intelligence (AI) can be used to reduce manual workload such as automating tasks, making predictions, and providing practical solutions for a variety of fields. Over the last 40 years, AI has advanced from rule-based expert systems to generative AI (GenAI), which can create text, images, and videos. These systems are built on mathematical concepts, from matrix operations to various optimization methods. This chapter showcases a detailed understanding of the mathematical foundation that forms AI while including further details about its practical applications in building smart cities with their respecting AI development technologies and their future impact.

11.1.1 Evolution of the Artificial Intelligence Models Introduction

11.1.1.1 Expert Models

In the late 1980s, expert systems became a crucial aspect that aided in the growth of AI; it laid the foundation for further development by enabling the use of intelligent decision-making systems. These systems were created to mimic human competence and decision-making in various specialized disciplines, using rule-based programming languages like LISP and Prologue. The idea of constructing computers that might match or surpass human intelligence gained popularity during this period, as expert systems displayed their capacity to analyze massive volumes of domain-specific information and generate logical judgments. They were widely used in disciplines, such as medical diagnosis, financial analysis, and engineering design, representing a significant step toward constructing AI systems capable of emulating human thinking.

DOI: 10.1201/9781003630371-11

11.1.1.2 Machine Models

Machine intelligence began to gain prominence in 2010 with the learning process in categorization, segregation, and prediction, which was strongly based on the mathematical foundations of algebra, probability, and statistics. Deep learning (DL) also had exponential growth, where it replicated how the brain operates, which, in turn, resulted in varying outputs despite having the same input, whereas machine learning (ML) produces the same outcome every time. The unpredictability of DL causes the algorithm to be challenging, necessitating numerous layers of learning to produce appropriate decisions. Neural networks are the most prevalent DL principles that are used. The closest differences between the two are as shown in Figure 11.1.

These algorithms enabled Tesla to manufacture self-driving cars, Netflix to recommend shows that subscribers want to watch, and Facebook to curate user Feeds and share accurate tagging suggestions. Figure 11.2 shows three examples and the type of analysis used in their operations.

Despite its complexity and the integration of AI and ML, the Facebook News Feed algorithm is built around four core ranking factors. Facebook's algorithm

FIGURE 11.1
Learning models.

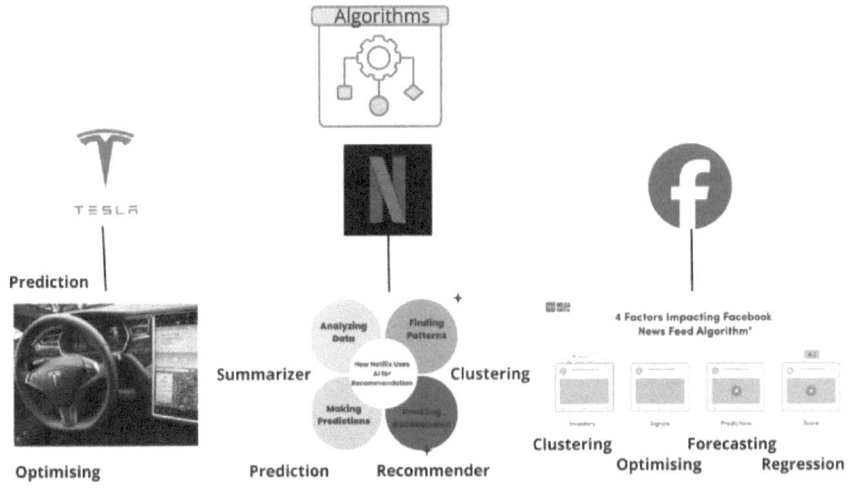

FIGURE 11.2
Real-world applications of learning models.

uses inventory, signals, predictions, and relevance to determine the most engaging content for users. Inventory includes all possible posts, while signals are data collected from users' behavior and interactions. Predictions are made based on past behavior and signals, estimating the likelihood of actions like clicking or sharing. Relevance is a score assigned to a post based on user preferences and predicted behaviors, pushing relevant content is more likely to appear at the top of the user's feed.

11.1.1.3 Functional Models

Language Models (LMs) are built upon probabilistic predictions of the most likely output. For example, when asked about the color of the sea, the most popular answer will be "blue," which is generally accurate. Large Language Models (LLMs) involve two key steps. First, they are trained on a very large sample of information from diverse sources (e.g., Wikipedia, books, Stack Overflow, Quora, public social media, GitHub, Reddit). Second, they predict the next word in a sentence by randomly truncating the input sentence and calculating the probability of the missing word based on context (Gkontzis et al., 2024). Figure 11.3 illustrates the reflective differences between these two model types. To ensure that the system generates accurate results, the input data can be specialized and more focused, leading to outcomes that are closer to the desired accuracy. These functional models form the foundation of generative artificial intelligence (GenAI), with common applications such as chatbots (text) and deepfakes (audio, video).

Figure 11.4 shows the process of fine-tuning a pretrained model to provide specified results. It begins with pretraining on generic data, which offers a basic awareness of general trends. The model is then further fine-tuned using field-specific data that fits it to the intricacies of a certain domain. The last stage is sued to produce particular outputs, such as a diagnosis based on a specialized report, demonstrating the model's capacity to use learned domain expertise to give focused outcomes.

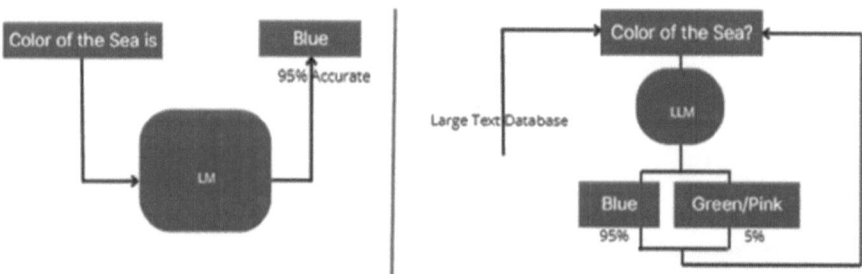

FIGURE 11.3
Language Models (LM) Vs. Large Language Models (LLM).

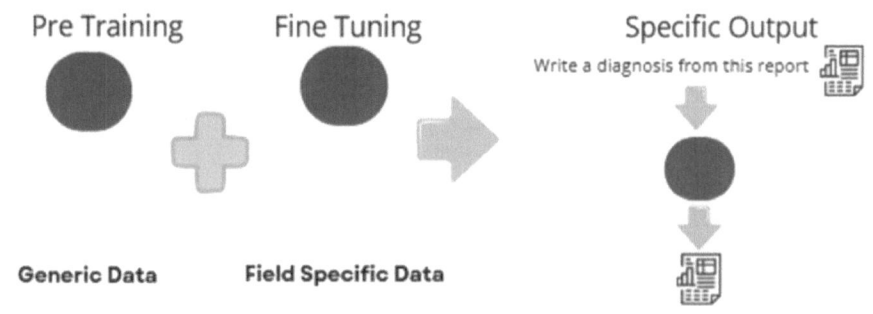

FIGURE 11.4
Process behind the Large Language Models (LLM).

11.2 Mathematical Foundations for Accessible AI

The foundation of AI lies in mathematical disciplines that enable algorithms to learn, adapt, and make decisions based on data. Mathematics is the foundation of current AI technologies, allowing for the creation, development, and optimization of intelligent systems. Linear algebra plays an important role in data representation, as vectors and matrices are the basic structures for operations such as neural network transformations. DL models, for example, use matrix multiplication to analyze incoming data and identify significant patterns. Calculus, particularly using methods such as gradient descent, is essential for training AI models. By computing partial derivatives of error functions, models iteratively modify parameters to improve its ability to make predictions, which makes optimization a critical component of the AI learning processes. Probability and statistics are vital for dealing with uncertainty and analyzing data. Probability allows AI systems to forecast the likelihood of occurrences, whereas statistics helps it with preparing and analyzing data for tasks like categorization and anomaly detection. Optimization techniques, such as stochastic gradient descent (SGD), minimize computational complexity and assure scalability, particularly for huge datasets, making them essential for AI algorithm creation. Graph theory also describes linkages and pathways in complicated networks, which helps with applications like routing algorithms and social network analysis. Meanwhile, information theory enables effective data compression and error control, which are essential for safe transmission and storage. These mathematical ideas work in cohesion to power the advanced operations and scalability of current AI systems. The key mathematical foundations required for intelligent models are as shown in Figure 11.5.

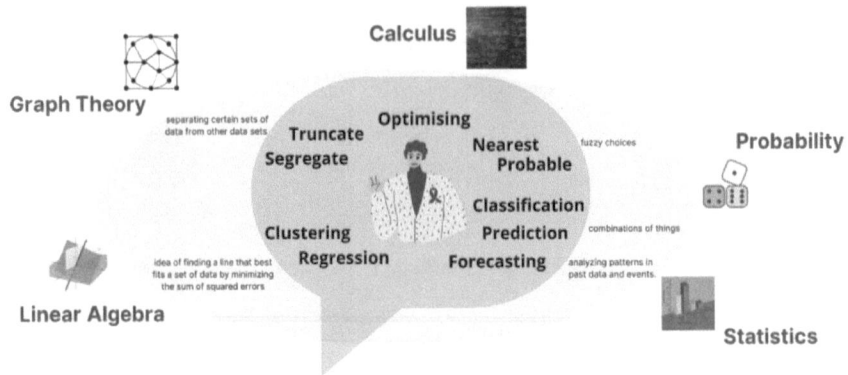

FIGURE 11.5
Key mathematical foundations used to build the functional models.

11.2.1 Mathematical Relational to Functional Model

ML is divided into four categories: supervised, unsupervised, semi-supervised, and reinforcement learning, each with a focus on certain data sets and tasks. Supervised learning uses labeled datasets to train algorithms for pattern identification and prediction. It covers classification algorithms like KNN, SVM, Naive Bayes, Decision Trees, and Random Forests, which are commonly used in diagnostics, customer retention, picture categorization, and fraud detection. Regression techniques like Linear and Logistic Regression are used to forecast advertising popularity, weather patterns, market trends, life expectancy, and population increase. Unsupervised learning, on the other hand, uses unlabeled data to allow computers to discover hidden patterns on their own. It supports dimensionality reduction techniques such as PCA, K-Means Clustering, and Mean Shift for data compression, structure identification, big data visualization, and feature extraction. Semisupervised learning combines labeled and unlabeled data to generalize from small, labeled datasets, using methods such as co-training and graph-based algorithms for classification, clustering, and regression, as demonstrated by Google Photos. Finally, reinforcement learning emphasizes interaction-based learning, optimizing performance through trial and error with neural networks and deep Q-networks, with applications in gaming AI, skill acquisition, robot navigation, and real-time decision-making. Figure 11.6 shows the overall framework representations of the mathematical foundations, and the type of learnings used (ML in this case) and the other side the application interface that is used for.

Supervised learning is particularly successful for tasks involving labeled data, with algorithms such as Logistic Regression and Decision Trees

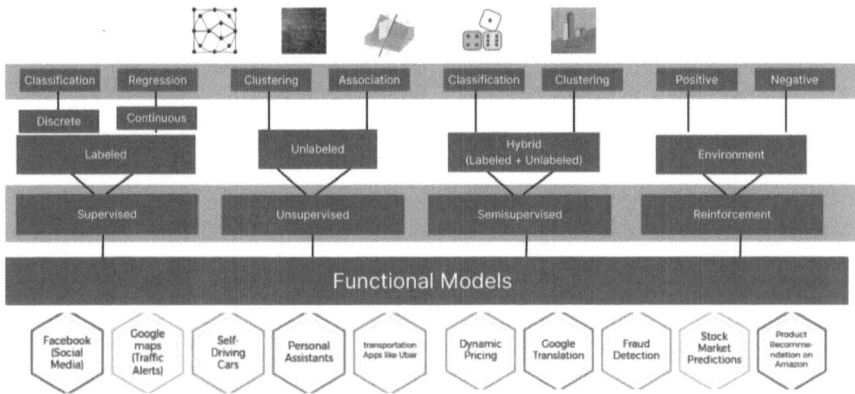

FIGURE 11.6
Framework representations of the mathematical foundations.

excelling in classification, and Linear Regression excelling at regression. Ensemble approaches like Random Forest and Gradient Boosting improve resilience and forecast accuracy, but they are computationally demanding. Unsupervised learning, on the other hand, seeks to find patterns or reduce complexity in unlabeled data by employing techniques such as K-Means Clustering and Dimensionality Reduction. Preprocessing methods like PCA are very useful for speeding feature selection. Random Forest and Boosting algorithms are examples of ensemble approaches, which increase accuracy by merging numerous models. From a computational standpoint, basic models like Linear Regression and Naive Bayes are lightweight and efficient, but sophisticated techniques like SVM and boosting require more resources.

The quickest algorithms include Linear Regression, K-Nearest Neighbors (KNN), Naive Bayes, SGD and Decision Trees. Linear and Logistic Regression, Random Forests and Decision Trees are popular approaches because to their variety and stability. While Decision Trees, Support Vector Machines (SVM), Neural Networks, and Gradient Boosting approaches are frequently regarded as the finest algorithms for handling complicated jobs. Random Forests, XGBoost, Linear Regression, and KNN are the most efficient because they balance accuracy and processing needs. Dimensionality reduction techniques like PCA are critical for lowering the number of features while retaining substantial information, but ensemble learning methods such as Gradient Boosting and AdaBoost are extremely successful at improving prediction accuracy by merging weak learners (Table 11.1).

TABLE 11.1

A Comparative Overview of Machine Learning Algorithms

Learning Methods	Fastest	Common	Effective	Efficient	Smartest	Accuracy
Linear regression K	Yes	Yes		Yes		
nearest neighbors (KNN)	Yes		Yes	Yes		
Stochastic Gradient Descent (SGD)	Yes		Yes	Yes	Yes	Yes
Naive Bayes	Yes					
Decision trees	Yes	Yes	Yes			
Logistic regression		Yes				
Random forests		Yes		Yes		
Support vector machines			Yes			

11.3 AI Applications across Smart Cities

Several sectors are rapidly being shaped around ML and AI as they enable various data-driven insights that significantly improve decision-making. In operations, ML algorithms analyze data to find inefficiencies, allowing organizations to simplify procedures, cut costs and increase productivity. Predictive capabilities enable businesses to examine, analyze, and respond proactively, such as forecasting equipment failures to guarantee timely maintenance, reducing downtime, and increasing machinery lifespans. AI-powered personalization curates client preferences by analyzing behavior and providing personalized options, hence increasing happiness and loyalty. In healthcare, AI speeds up drug discovery by analyzing massive datasets to find promising candidates, resulting in considerable time and cost savings. It also enhances genomics by analyzing genetic data, revealing insights into disease causes, and allowing for personalized therapy. Furthermore, AI improves the accuracy of climate models by digesting complicated environmental data. AI's real-world impact encompasses multiple industries and is driven by its ability to process vast amounts of data and obtain meaningful insights.

11.3.1 Retail

AI optimizes supply chains, demand forecasting, and customer personalization. Walmart employs predictive analytics to enhance inventory management, while Coca-Cola uses TensorFlow to streamline loyalty programs with optical character recognition (OCR).

Learning Type	Type	How It Operates	Type	Approach	Algorithm	Applications
Supervised	Labeled	Algorithms or models learn from a training dataset and improving through feedback	Task-driven	Classifications	KNN, SVM, Naive Bayes, Decision Tree, Random Forest	Diagnostics, Customer Retention, Image Classification, Identify fraud detection
				Regression	Linear, logistic	Advertising popularity prediction, weather forecasting, market forecasting, estimating life expectancy, population growth prediction
Unsupervised	Unlabeled	Algorithm explores the data to uncover underlying structures	Data driven	Dimensionality reduction	K-means clustering Principal component analysis (PCA) Mean Shift	Meaningful compression, structure discovery, Big data visualization, Feature Elicitation
				Clustering		Recommender systems, targeted marketing, Customer segmentation
Semi supervised	Labeled and unlabeled	Algorithm learns from the limited labeled dataset and applies insight to the larger dataset	Hybrid (task data) driven	Classifications, Clustering, Regression, Dimensionality reduction	Co-training Graph based methods Google photos	
Reinforcement	Learning by interaction	Algorithms use trial and error to determine optimal actions	Environment driven	Classifications, Control	Neural network, Deep Q networks	GameAI, Skill Acquisition, Learning Tasks, Robot Navigation, Real time decisions

Learning Type	Expand	Relational	Outcomes
Linear regression	Used for predicting continuous outcomes	Models the relationship between dependent and independent variables	Fits a linear equation to observed data
Logistic regression	Used for binary classification (yes/no)	Estimated probabilities using a logistic function	Often used in medical diagnosis and credit scoring
Decision tree	Classifies data based on feature values	Divides the population into homogenous sets based on significant attributes	East to interpret and visualize, but overfitting if not properly pruned.
Support vector machines	Used for classification tasks	Effective in high dimensional spaces, utilizes hyperplane to separate classes	Handle both linear and nonlinear classification through kernel trick
Naive Bayes algorithm	Used for classification tasks	Assumes independence among features when calculating probabilities	Often used in spam detection and sentiment analysis
K-means neighbors (KNN)	Used for classification and regression tasks	Classify new points from majority class of their nearest neighbors	Require distance normalization and computationally expensive
K-means clustering	Unsupervised for clustering tasks	Groups data into clusters iteratively assigns data points to the nearest centroid and recalculates	May converge to local minima
Random forest algorithm	Ensemble approach for classification and regression	combines decision trees for accuracy and prevent overfitting	Use major voting with robust to noise
Dimensionality reduction	Reduce number of features without losing information's	Principal Component Analysis help visualize data and improve model performance	Useful in preprocessing
Gradient boosting and Ad boosting	Enhance prediction accuracy through ensemble learning techniques	Combine multiple weak learners to create strong predictive model	Gradients minimize errors as it builds trees in a sequential manner

---

Challenge: Data-driven decision-making to optimize inventory management, pricing, and demand forecasting.

Analysis type	*Regression*: Predicting a continuous numerical value (e.g., sales). Classification: Predicting a categorical value (e.g., customer churn). Clustering: Grouping similar items or customers.
Mathematical foundation	*Linear Algebra*: For representing and manipulating data. *Statistics*: For probability distributions, hypothesis testing, and data analysis. *Calculus*: For optimization and gradient descent. *Time Series Analysis*: Forecasting future values based on historical data.
Tools:	*Pattern Recognition*: Identify hidden patterns in data that humans might miss. *Adaptability*: They can learn from new data and adjust their models accordingly. *Automation*: They can automate tasks and reduce manual effort.
Example	Walmart had issues with inventory management, pricing, and demand forecasts. The solution was to develop a predictive analytics platform that analyzes large volumes of data using ML techniques.
Impact	Improved inventory management, decreasing stockouts and overstocks while having optimized pricing tactics that maximized income. Accurately forecasted product demand, allowing for improved planning and allocation, resulting in increased sales and profitability.

11.3.2 Healthcare

From early disease detection to drug development, AI significantly improves patient care. Phamreasy utilizes ML to analyze medical images, enabling proactive healthcare solutions and improving patient outcomes.

Challenge: Include early disease detection and accelerated drug discovery processes.

Analysis type	*Regression*: Predicting a continuous outcome (e.g., blood pressure). *Classification*: Predicting a categorical outcome (e.g., disease diagnosis). *Survival Analysis*: Predicting time to an event (e.g., patient survival). *Time Series Analysis*: Forecasting based on historical data (e.g., hospital admissions).
Mathematical foundation	*Statistics*: Probability distributions, hypothesis testing, and data analysis. *Linear Algebra*: Representing and manipulating data. *Calculus*: Optimization and gradient descent.
Tools	Medical Imaging Analysis and Drug Discovery Platforms. *Pattern Recognition*: Identifying hidden patterns in complex medical data. *Predictive Power*: Accurately forecasting future health events. *Personalization*: Tailoring treatments to individual patients.
Example	Phamreasy is exploring the potential of using ML for analyzing medical images to identify potential health risks early on. This could lead to earlier intervention and improved patient outcomes.
Impact	

11.3.3 Finance

AI can be used to mitigate risks and enhances decision-making through fraud detection and credit scoring. Fintech platforms like Paytm use anomaly detection to secure transactions and provide personalized financial recommendations.

Challenge: Identifying fraudulent transactions and assessing creditworthiness in real-time	
Analysis type	*Regression*: Predicting a continuous outcome (e.g., credit risk score). *Classification*: Predicting a categorical outcome (e.g., default or no default). *Time Series Analysis*: Forecasting future trends (e.g., stock prices). *Neural Networks*: Complex models capable of learning from large datasets.
Mathematical foundation	*Statistics*: Probability distributions, hypothesis testing, and data analysis. *Linear Algebra*: Representing and manipulating data. *Calculus*: Optimization and gradient descent.
Tools:	Anomaly Detection and Risk Assessment Models are two tools. *Pattern Recognition*: Identifying hidden relationships in financial data. *Predictive Power*: Accurately forecasting potential risks. *Scalability*: Handling large datasets and complex models.
Example	Finology, a fintech business, uses machine learning to analyze financial data and detect fraudulent activities in loan applications which protects both the borrower and the lender.
Impact	Fraud Detection and Credit Scoring

11.3.4 Manufacturing

Challenge: Preventing equipment failures and ensuring product quality.	
Analysis type	*Regression*: Predicting continuous outcomes like product yield, energy consumption, or machine wear. *Classification*: Categorizing products based on quality, defects, or customer feedback. *Clustering*: Grouping similar products or manufacturing processes to identify patterns and optimize production. *Anomaly Detection*: Identifying outliers or abnormal events in production data to prevent defects or equipment failures.
Mathematical foundation	Statistics: Hypothesis testing, statistical process control, and data analysis. *Linear Algebra*: Representing and manipulating data, such as product features or process parameters. *Calculus*: Optimization of production processes, resource allocation, and quality control. *Optimization*: Solving complex problems like scheduling, inventory management, and supply chain optimization.

(Continued)

(Continued)

Tools	Predictive maintenance and AI-powered quality inspection systems.
	Pattern Recognition: Identifying hidden relationships in financial data.
	Predictive Power: Accurately forecasting potential risks.
	Scalability: Handling large datasets and complex models.
Example	Tata Motors is implementing ML for predictive maintenance in their factories. This helps them anticipate potential issues with machinery and prevent costly downtime.
Impact	*Quality Control*: Implementing automated inspection systems to detect defects and improve product quality.
	Predictive Maintenance: Predicting equipment failures to schedule maintenance proactively and reducing downtime.
	Process Optimization: Optimizing production processes to improve efficiency, reduce costs, and minimize waste.
	Product Design: Using generative design to create innovative and optimized product designs.

11.3.5 Agriculture

Precision agriculture leverages AI for resource optimization and yield improvement. John Deere's AI-powered sensors analyzes soil and weather data, enabling informed decisions for better farming yields.

Challenge: Optimizing crop yields and resource utilization in agriculture.

Analysis type	*Regression*: Predicting crop yields, soil nutrient levels, or weather patterns.
	Classification: Categorizing crops based on quality, disease, or pest infestation.
	Clustering: Grouping similar farms or regions based on soil type, climate, or crop patterns.
	Time Series Analysis: Forecasting crop prices, weather conditions, or market trends.
Mathematical foundation	*Statistics*: Hypothesis testing, statistical process control, and data analysis.
	Linear Algebra: Representing data, such as soil composition or weather data.
	Calculus: Optimization of agricultural practices, resource allocation, and yield maximization.
	Optimization: Solving complex problems like crop rotation, irrigation scheduling, and pest control.
Tools	Weather Prediction and Precision Agriculture Tools.
	Pattern Recognition: Identifying hidden relationships in financial data.
	Predictive Power: Accurately forecasting potential risks.
	Scalability: Handling large datasets and complex models.
Example	ITC uses ML to analyze weather data and predict potential crop threats. This allows farmers to take preventive measures and maximize their yields.
Impact	*Precision Agriculture*: Optimizing resource use (fertilizers, pesticides, water) based on real-time data to improve yields and reduce environmental impact.
	Disease Detection: Early detection of crop diseases to prevent significant losses and improve crop health.
	Yield Prediction: Predicting crop yields to optimize planting decisions and manage inventory.
	Market Analysis: Analyzing market trends and consumer preferences to optimize production and pricing.

11.3.6 Fashion

AI can be used to personalize shopping experiences, predict trends and streamline inventory management. Stitch Fix curates clothing recommendations tailored to user preferences using ML models.

Challenge: Product recommendations based on the preferences	
Analysis type	*Regression*: Predicting sales, customer satisfaction, or product demand.
	Classification: Categorizing customers based on demographics, preferences, or purchasing behavior.
	Clustering: Grouping similar products or customers to identify trends and optimize product offerings.
	Recommendation Systems: Suggesting products based on their preferences and purchase history
Mathematical foundation	*Statistics*: Hypothesis testing, data analysis, and market research.
	Linear Algebra: Representing and manipulating data, such as product features or customer information.
	Calculus: Optimization of inventory management, pricing, and marketing strategies.
	Optimization: Solving complex problems like supply chain optimization, demand forecasting, and personalized marketing.
Tools	Machine vision, clustering and classification tools
Example	*Nike (Athletic Apparel)*: Employs ML for product recommendations based on browsing behavior, purchase history, and athletic goals entered by users on their app. Nykaa (Beauty & Fashion E-commerce) uses ML to power virtual try-on experiences for cosmetics and eyewear, allowing customers to see how products look on their faces or address their vision needs.
Impact	*Personalized Recommendations*: Providing customers with highly relevant product recommendations to improve customer satisfaction and sales.
	Demand Forecasting: Predicting product demand to optimize inventory levels and reduce waste.
	Trend Analysis: Identifying emerging fashion trends to inform product design and marketing strategies.
	Customer Segmentation: Understanding customer preferences and behavior to tailor marketing campaigns and product offerings.

11.4 The Emergence of Generative AI and Advanced Technologies

11.4.1 Generative AI (GenAI)

GenAI represents a significant improvement in AI technology, enabling the creation of unique content such as text and images. Models like GPT (Generative Pretrained Transformer) and BERT (Bidirectional Encoder Representations from Transformers) are redefining natural language processing tasks, from translation to content generation (Figure 11.7).

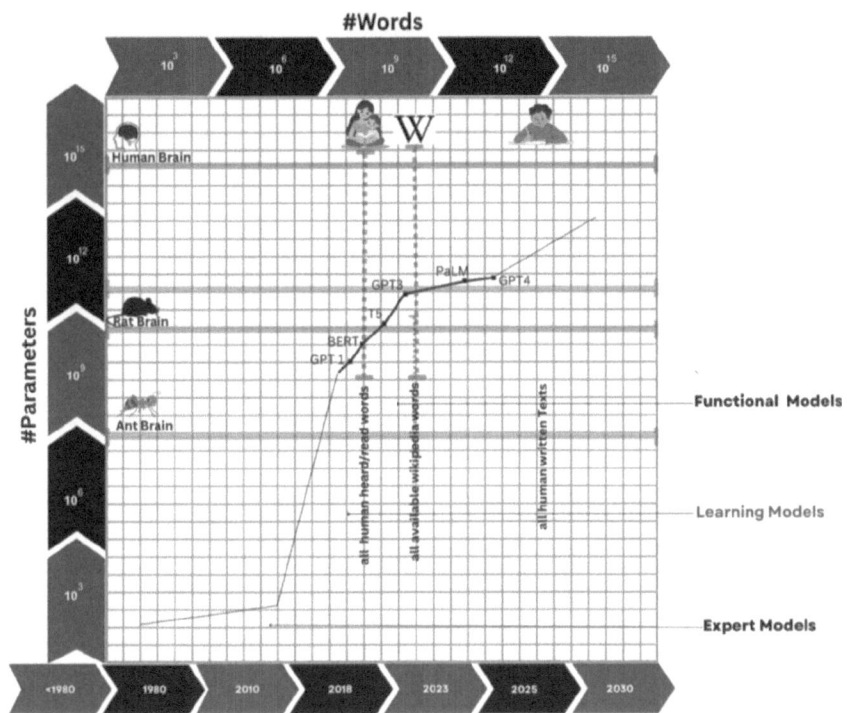

FIGURE 11.7
Evolution of Gen AI.

Challenge: Communication barriers between differently abled (deaf/mute) individuals and those novices of sign language.

Gap: Universal sign language standards complicate a particular way of developing solution (Figure 11.8)

11.4.2 Explainable AI (ExPAI)

Explainable artificial intelligence (XAI) comprises a collection of processes and techniques that enable human users to understand and trust the outputs produced by machine learning algorithms (Arrieta et al., 2020). The concept of explainable AI is used to simplify the specific purpose of an AI model, which includes its expected implications and potential biases. XAI aims to provide inside knowledge into the decision-making processes of these AI models, to ensure that stakeholders can confidently trust, validate, and effectively utilize these systems. It is crucial in assessing model accuracy, fairness, transparency, and the results of AI-enhanced decision-making (Dwivedi et al., 2023).

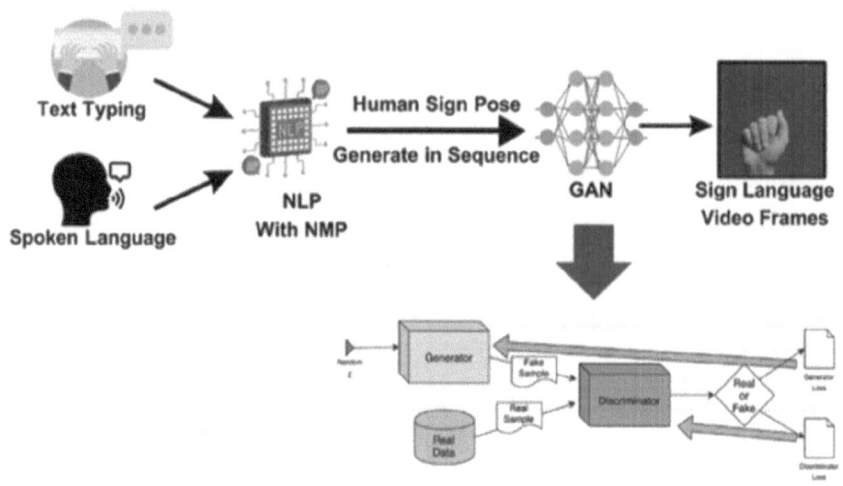

FIGURE 11.8
Transforming Text and Speech into Sign Language via NLP and GANs.

The framework of XAI techniques is comprised of three principal methods. The aspects of prediction accuracy and traceability cater to technological needs, while decision understanding addresses the requirements of human users. Prediction accuracy can be evaluated by executing simulations and contrasting the outputs of XAI with the training dataset results. A prominent method employed for this evaluation is Local Interpretable Model-Agnostic Explanations, which clarifies the predictions generated by machine learning algorithms. Traceability is another vital component in the realization of XAI, which can be achieved by restricting decision-making avenues and defining a more limited scope for machine learning rules and features. Decision understanding represents the human dimension; many individuals harbor doubts regarding AI, yet effective collaboration with AI systems necessitates a foundation of trust. This trust can be cultivated by providing education to the team that engages with the AI, allowing them to grasp the mechanisms behind the AI's decision-making processes (Figure 11.9).

11.4.3 Federated Learning (FedLearn)

Federated Learning (FL) is an innovative strategy that utilizes machine learning for distribution by allowing a central server to train a model across numerous decentralized devices or data sources while keeping the data on those devices. Instead of transferring raw data to a central server, only model updates such as gradients or weights are exchanged. This method of transfer enhances user privacy while reducing the overhead associated with communication. Launched by Google in 2016, FL is particularly prominent in environments where data sensitivity is of upmost importance, such as in healthcare, finance,

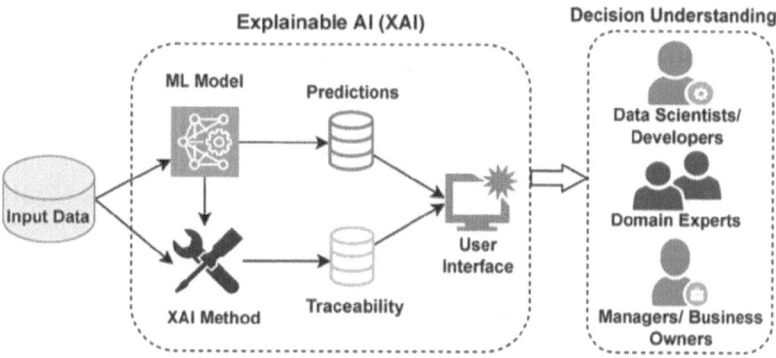

FIGURE 11.9
Explainable AI.

and mobile applications. Additionally, it addresses challenges related to data transfer that may arise from bandwidth restrictions or legal considerations.

FL fundamentally revolves around the concept of learning from data that is distributed across various locations. In contrast to traditional approaches that centralize data collection and processing, FL allows data to remain at its point of origin, which may include devices such as smartphones, servers in hospitals, or vehicles. This technique entails transmitting the model to the data source, where it undergoes training. Subsequently, only the model updates or gradients are sent back to a central server. These updates are then aggregated to enhance the global model, which is redistributed to all participants for additional training (Tan et al., 2022). This approach effectively addresses privacy issues that plagues conventional data science, providing a means to derive insights from data while upholding user privacy and data sovereignty within the realm of AI.

11.5 Ethical AI and Fairness in Smart Cities

While AI holds immense potential, its deployment poses challenges:

1. *Bias and Fairness*: Ensuring that algorithms are free from biases that could reinforce social inequalities.
2. *Data Privacy*: Balancing AI's data dependency with regulations like GDPR.
3. *Scalability*: Developing efficient models capable of handling growing data volumes and complexity.

Addressing these issues requires interdisciplinary efforts and a commitment to ethical AI practices.

11.6 Conclusion

With the goal of building inclusive and accessible smart cities, the integration of AI and the foundational mathematical behind it is undeniable. Theoretical principles such as optimization, probability, and data modeling are not just abstract concepts but are practical tools that can be used to create and further optimize real-world existing solutions. From enhancing digital accessibility to addressing infrastructural gaps, AI-enabled technologies have demonstrated their potential to solve problems across a wide range of fields which include issues like the digital divide, which could further promote inclusion.

However, achieving true inclusivity requires more than just technological advancements, it also demands a commitment to ethical AI practices, fairness in algorithm design and user-centric innovation. By leveraging AI-driven analysis and continuously optimizing systems through feedback, smart cities can encompass the diverse needs of their residents, ensuring true inclusivity.

Moving forward, collaboration between AI researchers, urban planners, policymakers, and stakeholders will be essential in facing challenges and discovering new opportunities. The synergy between mathematics, AI, and human-centered design is the key to ensuring sustainable, inclusive and accessible urban environments that fully utilize the power of technology.

References

Arrieta, A. B., Díaz-Rodríguez, N., Del Ser, J., Bennetot, A., Tabik, S., Barbado, A., García, S., Gil-López, S., Molina, D., Benjamins, R., & Chatila, R. (2020). Explainable Artificial Intelligence (XAI): Concepts, taxonomies, opportunities and challenges toward responsible AI. *Information Fusion*, 58, 82–115. https://doi.org/10.1016/j.inffus.2019.12.012

Batty, M. (2018). Artificial intelligence and smart cities. *Environment and Planning B: Urban Analytics and City Science*, 45(1), 3–6. https://doi.org/10.1177/2399808317751169

Bibri, S. E. (2020). Data-driven smart sustainable cities of the future: A comprehensive review of state-of-the-art literature. *Sustainable Cities and Society*, 61, 102360. https://doi.org/10.1016/j.scs.2020.102360.

Dwivedi, Y. K., Kshetri, N., Hughes, D. L., Baabdullah, A. M., Koohang, A., & Buhalis, D. (2023). Explainable artificial intelligence (XAI) in services: Extending the landscape of XAI through stakeholder engagement for responsible AI. *Information & Management*, 60(5), 103781. https://doi.org/10.1016/j.im.2023.103781

Giffinger, R., Fertner, C., Kramar, H., Kalasek, R., Pichler-Milanović, N., & Meijers, E. (2007). *Smart Cities – Ranking of European Medium-Sized Cities*. Vienna: Vienna University of Technology.

Gkontzis, A., Kotsiantis, S., Feretzakis, G., & Verykios, V. (2024). Enhancing urban resilience: Smart city data analyses, forecasts, and digital twin techniques at the neighborhood level. *Future Internet*, 16(2), 47. https://doi.org/10.3390/fi16020047

Kitchin, R. (2014). The real-time city? Big data and smart urbanism. *Geo Journal*, 79(1), 1–14. https://doi.org/10.1007/s10708-013-9516-8.

Kumar, N. M., & Mallick, P. K. (2021). Blockchain technology for smart cities: An overview. *Smart Cities*, 4(1), 182–210. https://doi.org/10.3390/smartcities4010011.

Lazer, D., & Radford, J. (2017). Data ex machina: Introduction to big data. *Annual Review of Sociology*, 43, 19–39. https://doi.org/10.1146/annurev-soc-060116-053457.

Lombardi, P., Giordano, S., Farouh, H., & Yousef, W. (2012). Modelling the smart city performance. *Innovation: The European Journal of Social Science Research*, 25(2), 137–149. https://doi.org/10.1080/13511610.2012.660325.

Lu, Y., Papagiannidis, S., & Alamanos, E. (2018). Internet of Things: A systematic review of the business literature from the user and organisational perspectives. *Technological Forecasting and Social Change*, 136, 285–297. https://doi.org/10.1016/j.techfore.2018.01.022.

McKinsey Global Institute. (2018). Smart cities: Digital solutions for a more livable future. https://www.mckinsey.com/business-functions/operations/our-insights/smart-cities-digital-solutions-for-a-more-livable-future.

Nam, T., & Pardo, T. A. (2011). Conceptualizing smart city with dimensions of technology, people, and institutions. In *Proceedings of the 12th Annual International Digital Government Research Conference*, 282–291. https://doi.org/10.1145/2037556.2037602.

Rahman, H., & Thakur, M. (2020). Artificial intelligence for sustainable smart cities: A review and future research agenda. *Sustainable Cities and Society*, 60, 102338. https://doi.org/10.1016/j.scs.2020.102338.

Tan, M., Wang, K., Zhang, C., Zhou, Z., & Yang, Q. (2022). Towards personalized federated learning. *IEEE Transactions on Neural Networks and Learning Systems*, 33(10), 4834–4849. https://doi.org/10.1109/TNNLS.2021.3116715

Zanella, A., Bui, N., Castellani, A., Vangelista, L., & Zorzi, M. (2014). Internet of things for smart cities. *IEEE Internet of Things Journal*, 1(1), 22–32. https://doi.org/10.1109/JIOT.2014.2306328.

12

Inclusive and Sustainable Urbanization Towards Sustainable Development Goals

Mazni Omar and Samsul Ariffin Abdul Karim

12.1 Introduction to Inclusiveness and SDGs

Urbanization plays a crucial role in advancing the United Nations' Sustainable Development Goals (SDGs), particularly in achieving Goal 11, which focuses on creating inclusive, safe, resilient, and sustainable cities and human settlements (United Nations, 2015). Urbanization is a phenomenon advancing globally, and as such, it integrates social, ecological, and economic dimensions, which are vital for achieving socially responsible and environmentally sustainable urbanization. However, when the focus is on economic activities, cities are now witnessing higher than 50% of the world's population living in cities, resulting in greater emissions of carbon, pollution, and health disparities between rich and poor. These facts bring to light the need that cities have to improve urban sustainability and inclusivity in order for them to play their part as effective contributions towards the achievement of SDGs (Krellenberg et al., 2019). Urban regions endure on socio-economic inequality since marginalized populations do not have access to basic social needs, adequate housing, and even the scope of economic participation. These issues reflect inadequate mechanisms to foster non-discriminative and environmentally sustainable urban development and governance. SDG 11 aims at promoting urbanization that is socially inclusive, as in the work by Gupta & Vegelin (2016). However, its implementation is much more focused on the idea of social inclusiveness rather than the required ecological and relational inclusiveness that adds to urban development sustainability.

Some scholars contend that, even though SDG 11 aims at promoting socially inclusive urbanization, in practice, it has been found that its dimensions are more inclined to the aspects of inclusiveness such as social inclusiveness and exclusionary inclusiveness of the integration of the ecological and relational dimensions, critical as they may be for sustainable urban development. In particular, Gupta and Vegelin (2016) emphasizes that sustainable urban development requires ecological inclusiveness, which ensures

DOI: 10.1201/9781003630371-12

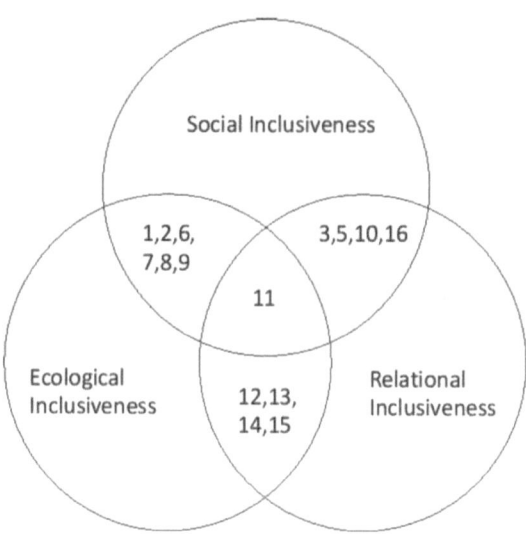

FIGURE 12.1
Applying Inclusiveness into the SDGs (Gupta & Vegelin, 2016).

that development is not only class-based, but also environment-friendly, and relational inclusiveness, which utilizes social governance designed for cities. Gupta and Vegelin (2016) has also formulated three inclusiveness dimensions: social, ecological, and relational, which are the key factors for urban sustainability. These are shown in Figure 12.1 showing the linkage of the inclusiveness dimension with different SDGs and hopes to achieve by 2030.

In terms of urbanization and inclusivity, the core SDGs are concentrated on SDG 11, which seeks to make urban areas or human settlements inclusive, safe, resilient, and sustainable. This goal focuses on the construction of smart cities that are able to face multiple environmental, social, and economic issues while protecting the well-being of their citizens. However, urbanization and inclusivity are not independent issues. They overlap with a broader spectrum of other SDGs, which focus on social and ecological sustainability.

Ecological and social inclusiveness also cover a number of other SDGs. SDG 1 (No poverty), SDG 2 (Zero Hunger), SDG 6 (Clean water and sanitation), SDG 7 (Affordable and clean energy), SDG 8 (Decent work and economic growth), and SDG 9 (Industry, innovation, and infrastructure) are all related with urbanization. Urbanization in these places anticipates fulfilling basic needs, providing economic opportunities, and developing infrastructure, which will help weaker segments of society. For instance, the urban growth of inclusiveness cities requires clean water, affordable energy, and decent work for all to provide an optimum standard of living.

Ecological sustainability and relational inclusiveness connect with SDG 12 (Responsible Consumption and Production), SDG 13 (Climate Action), SDG 14

(Life Below Water), and SDG 15 (Life On Land). These goals make it clear that urbanization should not come at the expense of nature. There has to be a particular way of approaching urbanization to reduce ecological impacts, combat changing climate, and conserve ecosystems. For instance, advanced techniques of sustainable urban planning reduce resource consumption, improve the use of renewable energy, and ensure the conservation of biodiversity, thereby actively aiding the health of the planet.

The social and relational dimension of urbanization is captured by SDG 3 (Good Health and Well-being), SDG 5 (Gender Equality), SDG 10 (Reduced Inequalities), and SDG 16 (Peace, Justice, And Strong Institutions). In a city designed for socio-economic inclusion, healthcare accessibility, gender inequality, social inequality, and violence have to be tackled. Moreover, strong governance is a requirement to ensure that urban policies are fair and appropriate multi-dimensionally, and they work.

Developing sustainable and inclusive cities, in the context of SDG 11, is linked to numerous other SDGs. This particular focus underlines the essence of a more integrated approach to urbanization, one that balances environmental, social, and economic factors. With proper targeting, cities can become engines of growth, resilience, and sustainability in meeting those interlinked goals, all of which would guarantee everyone's needs are met.

12.2 Enhancing Urban Inclusivity to Support SDGs

Urbanization integrates with the SDGs framework because cities are major determinants of a sustainable future. The SDGs imply a complex nexus between economic development, social equity, and environmental sustainability. The balance among urban sprawl, environmental protection, and economic growth is undoubtedly a challenge, especially in Hunan province, China, where urban sprawl is economically beneficial, but also severely damages the environment (Han et al., 2021).

Monitoring and achieving the SDGs with the aid of big data (BD) from urban areas is arguably risky. It implies the development of novel structures of measurements on different urban levels (Kharrazi et al., 2016). With SDG 11 set to achieve sustainable cities and communities, there is no doubt that cities play a crucial role in transforming sustainability. Nonetheless, the greatest hindrance to implementing integrated urban sustainability strategies highlighted from the case studies of four cities (Krellenberg et al., 2019).

To achieve the SDGs, Vardoulakis et al. (2020) have noted that the focus on the health of urban populations within cities is facilitated through certain interventions. These include zero-carbon housing and controlling air pollution. Embedding the SDGs at the local level, such as in the city of Bristol in the United Kingdom, could be achieved by integrating these goals into local policies and urban monitoring which could improve international city networks and demonstrate global intentions. Moreover, the 'Health in All Policies' framework ensures consultative processes that mainstream health into other sectors, in this case, urban planning, for as long as the process supports health and equity for all as defined in the SDGs (Ramirez-Rubio et al., 2019).

To achieve SDGs and improve urban outputs, benchmarking and monitoring of city planning policies are needed. Gaps in indicator frameworks tend to inhibit sustained evaluation of urban sustainability as well as health attainment (Giles-Corti et al., 2020). The examples of participatory urban planning processes in Chicago, Sao Paulo, and Delhi illustrate the effectiveness of public participation in sustainable urban development and social justice (Teklemariam, 2022).

The management of urban ecosystems is pivotal for the attainment of SDGs because it deals with the interplay synergies and trade-offs of urbanization against environmental sustainability. Effective urban ecosystem management requires consideration of economic growth and equality, as well as governance (Maes et al., 2019). Moreover, the co-production of urban knowledge, through city-university partnerships such as in South Africa, can assist in the localization of SDGs by enhancing context-specific collaborative urban governance (Croese & Duminy, 2023). For SDGs to be realizable, urbanization has to happen, which requires advances in information technologies, comprehensive planning, and multi-level coordination to meet the economic, environmental, and social goals simultaneously.

12.3 Emerging Technologies in Achieving SDGs

Artificial intelligence (AI) is a trendsetter in modern urban planning, serving as a cross-platform enabler that seamlessly integrates with other advanced technologies to tackle urban complexities and drive progress towards the SDGs. AI functions as a hybrid enabler, through machine learning algorithms enhancing the capabilities of BD analytics, Geographic Information Systems (GIS), blockchain, augmented reality (AR), virtual reality (VR), the IoT, and digital twin systems. By leveraging these integrations, urban planners can adopt a multidimensional approach to urban development, ensuring cities become more sustainable, resilient, and inclusive. The following section discusses each technology, highlighting its benefits, applications, and challenges, while also linking them to relevant SDGs.

12.3.1 Artificial Intelligence (AI)

The integration of artificial intelligence (AI) into urban systems promises to optimize resource utilization while elevating residents' living standards. However, this cannot be achieved without addressing the multitude of societal, technical, and ethical challenges posed by AI utilization. The ability of transforming AI holds to make cities more efficient resource utilizers while improving the standard of living. Although the approach towards this goal is not trivial, as challenges of an ethical, technical, and social merge with the implementation of AI, it can enhance effectiveness with urban planning goals by providing alternatives to predict-driven decision-making. There are several SDGs where AI is a major contributor to social and economic growth within a city.

AI, in conjunction with sensors and prediction models, allows for real-time air quality monitoring, assisting cities in curbing pollution and enhancing public health. Such advances support SDG 3 and SDG 11. AI systems can increase the effectiveness of recycling and optimize trash collection routes while simultaneously predicting the volume of waste created using advanced algorithms. All these methods are means of supporting SDG 12 and severe sustainability measures. The advancement of modernization aids AI in becoming a major contribution to disaster response efforts through the integration of correlating data sources to generate more predictive algorithms which directly contributes to SDG 11 and SDG 13. In addition, AI aids in enhancing public transportation and traffic, reducing congestion, and improving urban mobility through advanced algorithms. These improvements are in line with SDG 9, which pertains to industry, innovation, and infrastructure as well as SDG 11 (Yigitcanlar et al., 2020). AI-driven energy management systems optimize energy consumption in buildings and integrate renewable energy sources, contributing to SDG 7 and SDG 13 (Yigitcanlar et al., 2020).

Implementing AI in urban development requires several technical components. Among them are related to data infrastructure which high-quality, diverse datasets are essential for training AI models. This includes data from IoT sensors, satellite imagery, and government databases (Nosratabadi et al., 2020). In addition, computing power is needed to simulate and implement AI algorithms; particularly, deep learning models require significant computational resources, such as GPUs and cloud computing platforms (Fan et al., 2023). AI systems must integrate with existing urban infrastructure, such as transportation networks and energy grids, to ensure seamless operation and relate to the issue of interoperability (Si, 2022). Hence, a skilled workforce is important; thus, trained professionals are needed to develop, deploy, and maintain AI systems, ensuring their effective use in urban planning (Mhlanga, 2022).

Despite its potential, AI implementation in urban development faces several challenges such as AI systems can perpetuate biases if not designed and trained carefully, leading to unequal outcomes and unequal access (Supriya Kumari et al., 2024). The use of personal data in AI applications raises privacy concerns, requiring robust data protection measures (Mooradian et al., 2025). Moreover, ensuring transparency, safety, and ethical standards in AI deployment requires comprehensive regulatory frameworks (Díaz-Rodríguez et al., 2023).

To successfully confront the issues outlined, a human-centred, AI-based approach is necessary. This entails the creation of AI systems that guarantee inclusiveness, accountability, and transparency. For instance, the human-in-the-loop paradigm ensures that a person's input is factored into the decision-making processes of AI systems, minimizing bias and mistakes (Kumar et al., 2024). Also, integrating the efforts of government and the business sector with those of the general population will make it possible to develop AI solutions that address the needs of specific groups.

AI is involved in driving urbanization and the attainment of SDGs. It has the potential to revolutionize waste management, air quality measurement, disaster management, transportation systems, and energy consumption in cities. Nonetheless, meeting the technical requirements and challenges on ethical issues, data privacy, and the digital gap is essential to ensure fair and sustainable results. A human-centric focus combined with collaboration will allow cities to maximize their use of AI to fortify their urban ecosystems to be more resilient and inclusive.

12.3.2 Big Data Analytics

BD technology plays a transformative role in urban planning, enhancing forecasting, assessment, public participation, urban ecology, and public health (Balogun et al., 2020). By leveraging BD analytics and machine learning algorithms, smart city applications can be significantly improved, addressing key challenges such as crime forecasting, mobility trends, and epidemic prediction (Cesario, 2023). Moreover, he presents three case studies that illustrate BD's impact on data-driven, which are (1) Spatio-Temporal Crime Forecasting, using spatial analysis and auto-regressive models to predict crime patterns in Chicago; (2) Mobility Pattern Discovery, analyzing GPS data from Beijing taxis to identify mobility hotspots and trajectory trends; and (3) Epidemic forecasting, integrating mobility, and infection data to predict COVID-19 spread. In addition to predictive analytics, BD visualization enhances urban planning quality and efficiency by displaying real-time traffic and environmental data, facilitating human–computer interaction (Cao et al., 2020).

The integration of BD with spatial data expands its applications, particularly in GIS. Bovkir and Aydinoglu (2021) highlight the importance of GIS-based data visualization in smart cities, demonstrating how an open-source GIS-based dashboard using Apache Superset can effectively analyse air quality and traffic density for informed decision-making. The authors of the study have pointed out the importance of merging the IoT data capture with GIS system for better management of urban areas and planning smart cities.

A number of critical aspects must be noted in regard to the technical implementation of BD analytics. Urban data contain volume, variety, and velocity, which require a sophisticated technical infrastructure and resources to be processed. This does not end there, one of the most important primary requirements of advanced urban data collection systems is BD. Cities are taking advantage of a multitude of information sources such as IoT cameras, GPS units, satellites, and social media for real-time monitoring of the city's traffic, energy consumption, air quality, and regards public health (Bibri, 2018). As an example, the monitoring of building energy consumption by IoT-enabled sensors contributes to SDG 7. To do accurate analysis and help facilitate decision-making, these systems must be reliable and scalable for constant data processing and flow.

The processing of metropolitan datasets is a complex task that necessitates the existence of high-performance computing (HPC). Mobility analysis, crime pattern forecasting, and other urban issues can be addressed using machine learning algorithms with the aid of HPC (Casali et al., 2022). For instance, that HPC systems were used for processing taxi GPS data to develop transportation network models, which would contribute to SDG 9. Failure to use HPC technology in meeting the needs ranges from being unable to obtain actionable insights to quantifiable BD analytics, as the computational requirements could not be fulfilled.

Nevertheless, GIS, IoT, and social media all represent diverse mediums from which data must be collected, and that integration along with interoperability is crucial. Urban data are often incomplete because it exists in silos; therefore the availability of such data raises significant concerns (Glaeser et al., 2018). This could, for example, be the combination of air quality data captured from IoT sensors and environmental GIS which supports SDG 13. Comprehensive analysis and transparent decision-making are made possible through interoperability, which allows for effortless integration of data from dissimilar systems.

The remarkable scale of urban data generated on a daily basis necessitates scalable storage solutions, which are capable of providing real-time storage and retrieval using cloud computing while simultaneously ensuring data security and privacy (Yang et al., 2017). The storage must be scalable to facilitate applications like epidemic forecasting, which rely on the analysis of vast datasets relating to mobility and infections to project the spread of diseases. Without scalable storage, cities would be unable to efficiently manage and make use of their data.

At the core of BD analytics are advanced analytics and machine learning, which allow for productive modelling and decision-making. Large urban problems such as crime and traffic congestion are projected using spatial analysis techniques, auto-regressive models, and deep learning (Olaniyi et al., 2023). These predictive tools enable cities to resolve issues before they actually occur, thus contributing to SDG 11, Sustainable Cities, and Communities. Furthermore, machine learning algorithms automatically detect and analyse the weak patterns and trends in urban dynamics that are not normally associated with having significant impact.

The importance of data visualization tools is significant when it comes to showcasing the insights to urban planners and policymakers. Tools like GIS-based dashboards and interactive maps make complex data easier to interpret and put into action (Lata et al., 2022). For instance, visual representation of real-time traffic data can aid with transportation planning, which assists the achievement of SDG 9 and SDG 11. Understanding and visualization of information aids in harnessing the relevant portions of data to produce necessary insights that will help improve urban planning and governance.

Cybersecurity and privacy are equally important on a technical level. These measures ensure the protection of sensitive urban data. The use of personal and locational data brings forward privacy and security issues. To enable the use of data for urban development, there has to be protection by strong encryption, access controls, and anonymization techniques (Pratomo et al., 2023). Data security is important in guaranteeing adequate public confidence while pursuing SDG 16 (Peace, Justice and Strong Institutions). If left unchecked, these measures could result in data breaches and misappropriation that counter the benefits of BD analytics.

Purposeful usage of BD in the context of urban planning can be found in a few select countries, with China and the United States are studied for their practices. Boeing (2019) explores street network patterning and other urban morphology features of the U.S. cities through the usage of OpenStreetMap and computational lays within a bigger data analytics perspective. At the same time, Khan et al. (2022) have described the impediments in the application of BD analytics for sustainable smart city construction development. Such barriers include, but are not limited to, technological constraints, absence of established norms, intricacy of BD, and lack of sufficient analytical systems. These obstacles notwithstanding, BD have altered the face of urban planning by offering real-time data, smarter prediction models, and advanced analytics for modern-day faster decision-making to build smarter, more sustainable, and liveable cities.

12.3.3 Geographical Information System (GIS)

The concept of urbanization has brought about transformation among cities across the globe. Dense urban populations often lead to under-planned cities, overburdening infrastructure such as housing, transport, public utilities, and the environment. Planners are also challenged with new risks from disasters related to climate change. These challenges have increased the use of GIS in urban planning greatly. Urban planners analyse and make decisions from spatial data, improving the way resources are used (Chen et al., 2024). Furthermore, GIS allows for advanced geospatial integration, allowing to better facilitate urban structures, land usage, and public services which helps advance the concepts of modern urban sustainability and smart cities.

GIS extends its use in planning not just in mapping and visualization but as a decision-support system. It also enhances predictive modelling, simulation, and spatial analytics (Li et al., 2022). From developed countries to developing ones, GIS technologies are used for optimizing public transportation, health interventions, and environmental sustainability. While GIS provides numerous benefits, there are obstacles towards its adoption such as high technical and monetary requirements, issues with data standards, and threat to privacy (Diwan & Shukla, 2024).

The improvement of land-use planning, disaster management, and even urban mobility are ways in which GIS technology improves urban sustainability. A single feature that stands out when considering these changes is migration. The integration of urban data science and GIS also changes the landscape of urban governance by introducing newer ways to manage health care, transportation, economic planning, education, and even disasters (Tao, 2013).

As stated by Diwan and Shukla (2024), GIS improves strategic planning for urban land by preparing for housing, industrial, and green spaces. This fosters proper urban development while helping achieve sustainability. Furthermore, a targeted MCDM or multi-criteria decision-making means of decision-making aided by GIS can enhance the sustainability of urban land by 9%. This further encourages urban development and decreases environmental threats (Rahman & Szabó, 2022). In addition, the application of GIS-based assessment of land use aids in tracking urban expansion and helps achieve a healthy balance between ecological sustainability and infrastructure development, thereby attaining SDG 11 goals. The cities of today face a significant challenge when it comes to urban mobility. In this respect, GIS allows cities to map traffic, improve public transport structures, and lessen traffic congestion, which in turn increases access to mobility and the efficiency of transportation services (Droj et al., 2021). Similarly, GIS has been applied to manage traffic in pedestrian areas and improve public transport infrastructure in cities like Mumbai, thus working towards achieving SDG 9 and SDG 11.

In the realm of environmental sustainability, GIS also plays a significant role in real-time assessment of pollution, monitoring of deforestation, and measuring land degradation. Coupled with this, the technology assists in planning of urban green areas alongside climate change mitigation (Ouchra et al., 2022). Additionally, GIS combined with remote sensing data facilitates tracking of deforestation, carbon footprints, and natural disasters, which strengthens SDG 13 and SDG 15.

Urban sustainability relies heavily on resilience to disasters. For example, GIS is efficient in flood forecasting, monitoring wildfires, and assessing risks of earthquakes, all of which canvas emergency preparedness and disaster mitigation plans in more detail (Fang et al., 2023). The application of spatial data in aiding responses to emergencies leads to increased efficiency in evacuation, resource dispatching, and post-disaster recovery, all in relation to SDG 11 and SDG 13.

GIS technology has been effective in analyzing healthcare access, epidemiological mapping, and disease monitoring. During the COVID-19 pandemic, GIS analytics were used to assess hotspot infection zones, help optimize healthcare personnel and equipment usage, and even plan vaccination campaigns (Faisal et al., 2022). This goes hand in hand with SDG 3 through ensuring improved health outcomes from spatial data analysis.

Nonetheless, these benefits are accompanied by obstacles to the application of GIS in urban planning such as the need for adequate technical infrastructure and human capital. Thus, some of the most important needs are GIS software tools (ArcGIS, QGIS), sufficient resolution geospatial information (satellites, LiDAR, IoT sensors), and cloud processing devices. The successful implementation of GIS relies on proper data formatting and exchange, which provides compatibility between various urban planning applications (Liu et al., 2017).

However, the implementation of GIS faces a number of obstacles. The high economic costs tend to be a major constraint, with software licensing, satellite data purchase and computer equipment all needing considerable expenditure (James, 2002). In addition, using GIS technology for urban planning can pose risks to privacy and civil liberties regarding surveillance and intelligent monitoring systems employed in cities (Ni Loideain, 2017). Another challenge is that urban planners lack knowledge of GIS, hence the need for capacity building, training, and collaboration of the academic and business sector.

Urban planning has changed dynamically to have a data-mined approach, thanks to decision-support systems. This also includes GIS which offers predictive analytics and better decision-making. Their application to land-use planning, transportation, environmental control, disaster management, and even governance speaks volumes to their vast transformative potential for SDGs. GIS training, technical knowledge, expensive software, and data privacy are the main barriers to its wider adoption. As digital transformations are embraced by cities, this will require integrating GIS with policies aligned to SDG and smart city approaches for effective planning, making cities and urban regions sustainable, resilient, and liveable.

12.3.4 Internet of Things (IoT)

The IoT refers to a system of devices, sensors, and technologies that connect and interact with each other and exchange data over the Internet in a real-time. In an urban setting, IoT allows the building of 'smart cities' by adopting technology in infrastructure, transportation, energy systems, and public services. IoT provides real-time information and insights that empower cities to optimize resources, improve efficiency, and enhance overall living standards of citizens. Thus, IoT facilitates sustainable urban development and is instrumental in the attainment of the SDGs.

IoT sensors and applications are vital for core development of a sustainable urban environment in smart cities with respect to intelligent community, transportation, as well as disaster management, privacy, and security (Zeng et al., 2024). In fact, IoT enables data-driven decision-making and automation, which aids in the fulfilment of SDG 11, SDG 7, and SDG 13. Albeit, the implementation of IoT in urban infrastructures needs effective planning and collaboration between diverse sectors to reach the objectives of sustainability and efficiency (Son et al., 2023).

The use of IoT in city planning can enhance sustainability and effectiveness on a broader scale. For example, the advancement of Green-IoT (G-IoT) within the spheres of construction and smart cities allows for improvements in site safety, modern circularity, and sustainability. G-IoT technologies have further applications like smart drones, advanced 3D printing, green computing, and robotics. Policies that foster adoption will achieve SDG 9 and SDG 12 (Ullah et al., 2024). Moreover, the implementation of Cyber-Physical Systems (CPS) and IoT technologies in smart cities can lead to energy savings of over 25% and improved waste management of over 30%, translating into less carbon footprints (Umesh et al., 2024). As an example, smart streetlights are equipped with IoT sensors that are able to detect movement and ambient light. In the meantime, CPS controls dynamically adjust the brightness of the streetlight to reduce energy consumption while minimizing light pollution. In smart buildings, CPS uses IoT sensors to monitor occupancy, temperature, and air quality to optimize the HVAC and lighting systems for energy efficiency while maintaining the comfort of occupants. Likewise, in waste management, IoT sensors deployed in waste bins are able to track the fill levels. CPS platforms then schedule the collection and set the route to reduce fuel consumption while increasing operational efficiency.

Moreover, the proposed edge-based AI-IoT integrated energy-efficient intelligent transport system for smart cities aids in mitigations of greenhouse gas emissions, energy consumption, and traffic congestions while increasing the mileage of freight vehicles (Chavhan et al., 2022). These advancements not only benefit SDG 11 and SDG 13 but also reveal the IoT and CPS potential for transforming cities into smarter and more sustainable environments.

IoT is also essential in developing smart communities and increasing urban resilience. Real-time monitoring and data analytics enable IoT to manage disasters and provide emergency response, which contributes towards SDG 11 and SDG 13. For instance, cities can use IoT sensors to constantly monitor air and water quality in a bid to mitigate any future disasters (Rathore et al., 2016). In addition, IoT applications in smart traffic management systems and optimization of public transit systems help minimize congestion and emissions and hence fulfil SDG 11 alongside SDG 3.

There are many hurdles that hinder the widespread deployment of IoT in smart city development, such as data privacy, data security, and interdepartmental collaboration (Kaluarachchi, 2022). Moreover, its adoption in current urban environments entails a tremendous amount of technological integration and financial investment (Nam & Pardo, 2011). These challenges present an opportunity for municipalities to develop comprehensive policies that motivate IoT inclusion while considering potential breaches to privacy and security. The future development of IoT technologies such as smart 3D drones, smart 3D printers, and improvements in green computing will likely improve urban sustainability and resilience even further (Ullah et al., 2024).

IoT is a game-changing development that has the potential to foster urban development and the achieving of SDG goals. IoT is essential in the building of smart cities which are sustainable, efficient, resilient, inclusive, and safe. IoT applications in energy management, disaster response, transportation optimization, and waste reduction contribute directly to SDGs 7, 11, and 13. As cities continue to develop, the incorporation of IoT in the urban ecosystems must be conducted to ensure the cities are smarter, more sustainable, and more liveable in the years to come.

12.3.5 Digital Twin

Digital Twin is a representation of a physical entity, system, or procedure, which is continuously updated in real-time alongside the components that influence it. It depicts a self-modifying digital version replicating the traits, energy, as well as action of its tangible form. Within that framework, Urban Digital Twin (UDT) refers to a detailed construction of the digital version of any city or urban settlement combined with data acquired from different fields such as building infrastructure, energy supply, traffic, and ecology of the region. UDT can also use AI, cloud calculation, building information models (BIM), and geo-information systems (GIS), which in turn improve the life of a city by enabling the city to model, track, and control urban systems, providing a tremendous asset to sustainable growth.

Due to their unprecedented capacity to foster digital change in cities, Digital Twins technology is changing the way cities are built. UDTs promote enhanced decision-making with the help of real-time visuals and predictive analytics, enabling cities to match international sustainability standards. This technology has the potential to significantly contribute to the achievement of SDGs, particularly SDG 11, SDG 7, and SDG 9, by enabling smarter, more efficient, and inclusive urban ecosystems.

In response to the digital transformation, the UDTs is an initiative that seeks to develop intelligent and comprehensive solutions for the urbanization of the future. A UDT is an accurate electronic representation of a physical urban area at the level of a city or city region across multiple domains. A conceptual framework for UDT has been proposed identifying six main components and four key features as a starting point for urban planners, designers, and builders (Afif Supianto et al., 2024).

UDTs are instrumental in enhancing the sustainability of urban development and resilience. These twins improve inclusiveness pertaining to urban planning for all groups, including the marginalized, thus ensuring that nobody remains unaccounted for in the building of sustainable cities (Ziehl et al., 2023). This concerns of SDG 10 and SDG 11. In addition, UDTs also aid in urban decarbonization by offering management and planning tools for smart buildings, district heating networks, and micro-grids. For example, the DigiBUILD project evidences how UDTs optimize heat generation in the fourth generation District Heating and the smart charging of electric vehicles to increase energy consumption during periods of high renewable energy production while enhancing comfort through proactive building management and fault detection (Testasecca et al., 2023). These applications further support SDG 7 and SDG 13.

In combination with the green metrics regarding the sustainability goals of the urban development and the Digital Twins concept, a metric-based framework for sustainability planning of smart buildings and cities has been developed which will assist decision-makers at different tiers of urban planning and management system (Corrado et al., 2022). With this system, cities are able to monitor and track their development with regard to sustainability efforts, including SDG targets for urban development. With the use of UDTs, establishing full databases as well as answering the complex cross-domain questions improves both the efficacy and the quality of the decisions made by the urban planners in relation to the environmental, social, and economic indicators (Wu and Guan, 2024). This approach helps to achieve SDG 11 and SDG 17 (Partnerships for the Goals) by promoting inter-sectoral cooperation and information exchange.

Although promising, UDTs are hindered by their lack of a broader market adoption, these include data procurement processes, platform integration, and their coordination with other technologies (Mazzetto, 2024). Additionally, the maturity of City Digital Twins is still in its infancy where 90% of the conducted literature reviews are found within the initial development to mid-development range (Masoumi et al., 2023). More mature UDT systems need to incorporate contemporary technologies like AI, cloud computing, BIM, and GIS. These obstacles must be addressed to move forward with SDG 9 as well as ensuring that UDTs take an active part in fostering urban development that is sustainable.

UDTs constitute a powerful frontier for the promotion of sustainability in cities and in achieving the SDGs. Decarbonization and resilience are core challenges where UDTs can assist in transforming planning and management alongside their fostering of inclusivity and enhancing data informatics. Their development towards optimizing energy utilizations, improving infrastructures, and promoting socially balanced urban expansion directly serves the SDGs. However, without solution to the technological and operational challenges, many of their capabilities can remain untapped.

12.3.6 Blockchain

The emergence of new technologies, such as blockchain as a distributed ledger technology, has facilitated data transparency, security, and permanence which are essential towards enhancing urban integration. It has remarkable possibilities, especially in automating the governance systems like resources management using smart contracts, and improving stakeholder relations and collaborations in the urban areas. This emerging blockchain technology provides an opportunity for the cities to merge it with other technologies such as AI and IoT to develop intelligent and achieve sustainable urban systems. In this context, this initiative assesses the compatibility of blockchain technology with the SDGs, specifically SDG 9, SDG 11, and SDG 7.

The fundamental veracity of blockchains, which is the ability to automate governance systems with the use of smart contracts, enables new possibilities in automating urban management processes. Smart contracts are a digitally enabled self-executing contract that greatly improves processes such as land registry management, utility billing, or even providing public services. For example, once payment has been rendered, a smart contract can facilitate the transfer of ownership of property, thus eliminating the risk of deception and bureaucracy in business transactions (Alshahrani et al., 2023). The ability to achieve such automation enhances the trust accorded to these systems, while directly improving urban management systems which are vital towards achieving SDG 11.

A well-designed blockchain makes it an effective mechanism for asset management especially with regard to water and energy. The emergence of peer-to-peer trading mechanisms based on blockchain technology has permitted citizens to sell and purchase their surplus renewable energy without the use of middlemen (Mengelkamp et al., 2018). Lowering dependence on conventional energy sources and promoting the use of renewables lead to greater sustainability which contributes towards SDG 7. Furthermore, blockchain enables seamless interaction among urban stakeholders including the government, business, and public through secure and open data exchange. For instance, the infrastructure development planners can implement blockchain technology to monitor the progress of other projects in the same domain and effectively manage the resources (Khalfan et al., 2022).

As cities around the world continue to grow, the combination of blockchain and AI has the potential to make these systems more intelligent, and more effective. The supply chain, transport, governance, healthcare, and finance are just some of the areas that these technologies will improve. One area of mutual interest is guaranteeing AI training data integrity. Bias-sensitive areas such as social service allocation or predictive policing rely on using blockchains to eliminate any abusive tampering of the data used in creating AI models (Sion et al., 2019). This integration contributes to the achieving of SDG 9 through improvement of urban systems innovation.

AI and blockchain's conjoined effort can result in the emergence of autonomous governance over certain processes via smart contracts. To provide a scenario, an AI algorithm determining electricity consumption predicts increase in energy usage, and a companion smart contract implemented on the blockchain adjusts prices or reallocates resources (Wang et al., 2019). These advances in SDG 7 and SDG 11 will make it possible to manage urban resources much more effectively through the combination of AI and blockchain.

AI and blockchain technology can strengthening the security and safety aspects of self-driving cars in transportation and logistics. While optimizing sensitive information, blockchain guarantees an organized transaction history that helps keep vehicles secured from harmful cyberattacks (Bendiab et al., 2023). Furthermore, this technology adoption improves urban infrastructure as well as promotes creativity and innovation, which is in line with SDG 9. Also, price monitoring and anti-corruption can be integrated to combat against corruption in industries moving towards Industry 4.0 and Industry 5.0 with the help of Blockchain IoT models. These advancements will fundamentally change how governance and industry operate for the better (Hasan et al., 2022).

Blockchain's impact on financial systems is undeniable. Bhushan et al. (2020) explored its architecture, consensus protocols, and applications across diverse domains, including healthcare, transportation, energy grids, supply chain management, financial services, and data centre networks. They highlighted blockchain's potential to address trade-offs and challenges while offering innovative solutions. In the context of urban energy transitions, blockchain technology plays a crucial role by democratizing energy markets, enhancing service quality and reliability, and fostering civic engagement and governance. It provides insights into investment needs and supports the shift towards sustainable energy systems (Montakhabi et al., 2023), contributing to SDG 7 and SDG 11.

To address the technical and enterprise needs of smart cities, Fan et al. (2024) proposed a blockchain framework called SC-Chain. This framework implements a combination of access controls based on threshold signatures, and a BFT-type consensus to optimize the node enrolment and identification processes, which makes it possible to achieve higher efficiencies and greater system supports in enjoying decentralized advantages. This type of frameworks is a prerequisite to the urban application of blockchain because such technology is a must to accommodate the requirements of smart cities together with SDG 9 and SDG 11.

While blockchain has a huge potential, its application success will largely depend on a collective effort of other professionals in overcoming issues such as scalability, energy, and privacy. For these issues, careful monitoring should also be done to prevent stricter impositions of social inequality. Communities will benefit from increased security, trust, and transparency brought by the combination of blockchain and AI, which are the first steps towards more intelligent and sustainable urban environments. In conjunction with these technologies, IoT and 5G will be essential in developing Integrated Urban Solutions that prioritize social equity and inclusion.

12.3.7 Virtual Reality (VR) and Augmented Reality (AR)

Urban planners greatly benefit from immersive technologies such as VR, AR, and mixed reality (MR). These technologies, alongside BIM, make it easier to run public engagement campaigns, decision-making, and simulations (Liu et al., 2024). The application of VR and AR technology integrated with BIM has become a hot topic within the focus of collaborative construction and urban planning. More and more studies on construction management are relying on VR and AR technologies, especially focusing on BIM applications (Seyman Guray & Kismet, 2023). With this development, urban planners can more efficiently model urban features by making sophisticated modelling measures and managing resources more efficiently. For instance, VR simulations of buildings that are enabled with BIM have the potential to minimize energy consumption which supports SDG 7 and SDG 12. The application of VR, AR, and BIM enables enhanced public engagement, as it allows urban planners to easily run campaigns and improve decision-making and simulations. In the construction of sustainable smart cities, modern civilization is now seeking the integration of smart technologies as solutions. This is possible as the addition of VR technology enables urban planners to easily create and model smart city systems.

According to Jamei et al. (2017), planners can use VR to visualize the impact of their decisions in real-time and engage with different scenarios before putting them into action. For planners collaborating towards building resilient cities to achieve SDG 11, VR can model the urban infrastructure needed for climate change. In the same manner, AR allows for increased innovation and imagination when it comes to designs in architecture and urban planning. Such tools help make decisions faster since these experiences occur in real-time, permitting stakeholders to work together more freely and quickly. As an example, planners can use AR to place proposed designs of structures into a real space and see how they might look, allowing citizens to experience the design changes firsthand.

VR technology also strengthens urban landscape planning by allowing the realistic processing of information and active simulation of design results (Liu et al., 2024). This capability is particularly useful for achieving SDG 9 and SDG 15, as these planners will be able to integrate green spaces and sustainable infrastructure within the natural context. By integrating the real and digital world, AR and VR technologies enhance the ability of planners to preserve the environment while developing urban areas.

Apart from visualization and planning, urban planning can use immersive technologies to improve public participation. Integrated with physical elements, AR and VR can foster citizen engagement by transforming passive phenomena into active and interactive ones (Katika et al., 2022). Like, AR can be used to display proposed urban developments in vantage points, which the public is to critique or suggest modifications. This strategy promotes all-rounded growth by making sure developments in urban areas meet the expectations of the locals. Furthermore, immersive technologies make it possible for city planners to obtain feedback from stakeholders and the general population in a timely manner, including sensitive respondents such as older people. Planners can present designs in digital form to the people and receive opinions and suggestions, which can help them during the construction planning process. With regard to SDG 10, this is a better approach for urban modernization since it aids in reducing the constructed barriers.

Regardless of the promise that VR and AR technologies have in urban planning, their wide-scale implementation is being hindered by purchasing costs, technical difficulties, and the need for user training. It is equally as important to ensure that these technologies do not further enable social discrimination. More attention should be directed towards methods of implementation that are less capital intensive, user-friendly interfaces, and the combination of VR/AR with AI and IoT. At the same time, policymakers and urban planners should ensure that immersive technologies development and implementation is undertaken with an ethical mindset.

Effective urban planning can greatly benefit from VR and AR as they provide additional leverage in fostering the SDGs. Vivid representation of data, boosting civic interest and using this information to make decisions enhance the chance of creating extractive, inclusive, and sustainable cities. The future of urbanization is heavily reliant on how new immersive technologies will be fused into the existing systems such as BIM (Table 12.1).

The integration of various technologies, such as AI, BD, and IoT, can create more robust and efficient urban solutions. Blockchain technology can

TABLE 12.1

Depicts the Summary of Technology Applied and Example of Application Supporting SDGs

Technology	Example Application	References	Supporting SDGs
Artificial intelligence (AI)	Optimizing waste collection routes, predicting waste generation, real-time air quality monitoring, disaster response, traffic optimization, and energy management.	Gupta and Degbelo (2023, Yigitcanlar et al. (2020), Nosratabadi et al. (2020), Fan et al. (2023)	SDG 3, SDG 7, SDG 9, SDG 11, SDG 12, SDG 13
Big data analytics	Crime forecasting, mobility pattern discovery, epidemic prediction, GIS-based data visualization for smart cities.	Cesario (2023), Bovkir and Aydinoglu (2021), Cao et al. (2020), Khan et al. (2022)	SDG 7, SDG 9, SDG 11, SDG 13, SDG 16

(Continued)

TABLE 12.1 (*Continued*)

Depicts the Summary of Technology Applied and Example of Application Supporting SDGs

Technology	Example Application	References	Supporting SDGs
Geographical Information System (GIS)	Urban land-use planning, transportation optimization, environmental monitoring, disaster resilience, healthcare accessibility analysis.	Chen et al. (2024), Li et al. (2022), Diwan and Shukla (2024), Rahman, and Szabó (2022)	SDG 3, SDG 9, SDG 11, SDG 13, SDG 15
Internet of Things (IoT)	Smart energy management, waste reduction, disaster response, traffic management, smart transportation.	Zeng et al. (2024), Sharma et al. (2024), Ullah et al. (2024), Khadka et al. (2024), Chavhan et al. (2022)	SDG 3, SDG 7, SDG 9, SDG 11, SDG 13
Digital twin	Urban planning simulation, real-time city monitoring, optimizing urban energy use, digital mapping of infrastructure.	Afif Supianto et al. (2024), Ziehl et al. (2023), Testasecca et al. (2023), Wu and Guan (2024), Masoumi (2023)	SDG 7, SDG 9, SDG 10, SDG 11, SDG 13, SDG 17
Blockchain	Decentralized urban governance, peer-to-peer energy trading, transparent infrastructure tracking, AI-Blockchain integration for secure data.	Mengelkamp et al. (2018), Wang et al. (2019), Montakhabi et al. (2023), Hasan et al. (2022)	SDG 7, SDG 9, SDG 11
Virtual reality (VR) and augmented reality (AR)	Urban planning visualization, climate and disaster impact simulation, interactive citizen engagement, immersive urban modelling.	Jishtu and Yadav (2021), Sabah et al. (2023),	SDG 7, SDG 9, SDG 10, SDG 11, SDG 12, SDG 15

address data privacy concerns by ensuring secure and transparent data transactions. Meanwhile, AR/VR and digital twins enable realistic simulations that enhance usability and user experience. GIS technology, combined with IoT sensors, facilitates accurate spatial data collection, while AI and machine learning leverage BD for advanced process mining, real-time monitoring, and predictive analytics.

12.4 Challenges and Mitigation Strategies in Urban Development

Urban development is a critical component supporting the United Nations' SDGs. Cities are hubs of innovation, economic activity, and cultural exchange, but they also face significant challenges in implementing sustainable and inclusive systems. These challenges include high implementation costs, data privacy and security concerns, and technological disparities. Addressing these issues requires innovative solutions such as public–private partnerships (PPPs), robust data governance frameworks, and capacity-building initiatives.

12.4.1 Challenges in Urban Development and SDGs

In the efforts to foster inclusiveness in urban development to promote the SDGs, several key challenges must be addressed, as discussed in the following sections.

12.4.1.1 High Implementation Costs

Significant funding is required for building and maintaining urban structures for a city to be termed as sustainable. Smart city infrastructure, renewable resources of energy as well as efficient public transport is costly to build and maintain. There are several costs for the deployment of IoT devices, sensors, and data analytics platforms, which could be expensive, for example Kitchin (2014), mentions these upfront costs. Moreover, many IoT devices are placed on existing assets as a strategy to gather data. Most cities, especially the underdeveloped ones, may find it difficult to bear the costs incurred when transforming old assets to new sustainable standards.

Insufficient implementation causes integration divides in the urban landscapes as a result of its profound costs. Rich cities are capable to support investment in high-end technologies, while underdeveloped ones find it hard to fulfil basic infrastructure development. This indeed creates a gap among the cities in regards to the quality of life and service provisions, which goes against one of the SDG goals of 'leaving no one behind' (United Nations, 2015).

12.4.1.2 Data Privacy and Security

The use of IoT and BD as analytics in urban systems boosts the concern towards the issue of data protection. Smart cities heavily rely on the use of data obtained through sensors, cameras, and various connected devices. This data aids in traffic management, improving the distribution of energy, and enhancing public safety. Unfortunately, this data often contains highly confidential information such as the individual's location, behaviour, and preferences.

As depicted by Hilbert (2016), the sensitive data is likely to face risks of breach and access without authorization. Without robust data governance frameworks, cities risk violating citizens' privacy and eroding public trust in smart city initiatives. Furthermore, cyberattacks on critical urban infrastructure, such as power grids and transportation systems, could have devastating consequences for public safety and economic stability.

12.4.1.3 Technological Disparities

Adoption of smart city technologies is greatly hindered by the imbalance in the availability of digital infrastructure. On one hand, there are cities with modern digital networks and high-speed internet, while on the other hand, many do not even have basic access to the internet. This inequality makes it difficult to harness the benefits of smart city technology solutions for all residents.

The absence of integration and standardization of these systems within the city also poses significant technical issues. A number of different smart city initiatives are launched independently, resulting in the use of different technologies and incompatible standards in different departments. As a consequence, coordination is compromised, which limits the flow of data between the systems and affects the productivity of urban systems (Batty, 2018). For instance, some sections of the transportation system that are not linked to energy or waste management systems may not properly utilize resources and decrease negative environmental effects.

12.4.2 Mitigation Strategies

To mitigate these challenges, the following recommendations should be considered: fostering cooperation across all levels of stakeholders, enhancing data governance, providing training, and improving digital skills—all while upholding human values.

12.4.2.1 Public–Private Partnerships

A viable solution for private and public sector cooperation to sustain urban development projects is through PPPs. For example, C40 Cities (2020) emphasizes the role of PPPs in financing renewable energy projects and improving public transportation systems. In this situation, private partners invest in and manage infrastructure and service provision along with creating value in public goods. By doing so, the governments can improve public services without disproportionately increasing their budgetary allocations.

This approach allows a city to capitalize on the private sector's technological and project management skills through the help of, for example, consultants engaging in the design and implementation of the IoT networks with regulatory assistance and service provision consistency guaranteed by the government. This approach is a step towards better management of public funds and more efficient realization of smart city technologies.

12.4.2.2 Robust Data Governance

Establishing adequate frameworks to address the issues pertained to data privacy and security is crucial for cities in rationalizing the governance of data. Thus, there ought to be mechanisms such as regulatory frameworks for data collection, storage, and usage that define how information is shared, including how accountability and transparency will be ensured. The EU GDPR bears an example of detail that provides for the protection of personal data and rights of the citizens (Tikkinen-Piri et al., 2018).

Local governments have to ensure that cybersecurity protocols are established to prevent cyberattacks aimed at essential infrastructure. This may include setting up firewalls, vulnerability management, and personnel training. With enhanced technology development, urbanization will be more ethical, supported by civilians, and publicly trusted (Haou et al., 2025).

12.4.2.3 Capacity Building

Building capacity sustainably is of critical component in addressing the technology gap and enabling the practical realization of smart city projects. Urban planners, policymakers, and other relevant participants need to be trained on how to utilize newer technologies and assimilate them into existing frameworks. This encompasses the knowledge of technological components of the IoT, BD, and AI, as well as the ethical and social boundaries that exist in the usage of these technologies.

Building capacity to strengthen education and digital literacy among citizens should also be prioritized. Training and educational material can easily enable them to become part of the many smart city initiatives and use the tools provided to them, which improves the performance of urban systems ecosystem. This allows the citizens to feel incorporated and included to positively impact the system.

12.5 Conclusion and the Way Forward

Technology integration plays a pivotal role as a key enabler in the development of smart, sustainable cities. By leveraging vast amounts of data generated from sensor networks, IoT devices, and digital infrastructure, cities can enhance decision-making, optimize resource utilization, and drive meaningful progress towards achieving the SDGs. However, for urban development to be truly sustainable and inclusive, three core components must be emphasized: equitable access to technology, social and economic inclusivity, and environmental sustainability.

Despite being a fundamental pillar of the SDGs, urban development faces significant challenges, including high implementation costs, data privacy concerns, and technological disparities. Addressing these challenges requires innovative solutions such as PPPs, robust data governance frameworks, and capacity-building initiatives. By adopting these approaches, cities can establish sustainable, inclusive, and resilient urban systems that benefit all residents, ensuring that technological advancements do not exacerbate existing inequalities.

Moreover, while the integration of emerging technologies—such as AI, BD analytics, IoT, blockchain, and digital twins—can transform urban landscapes, it must be grounded in human values, ethical considerations, and inclusivity. The success of smart cities depends not only on technological efficiency but also on their ability to enhance human well-being, protect fundamental rights, and foster equitable growth. Achieving this vision necessitates strong collaboration among governments, private sector stakeholders, and citizens, ensuring that technology serves as a tool for social progress rather than a source of division.

References

Afif Supianto, A., Nasar, W., Margrethe Aspen, D., Hasan, A., Karlsen, A. S. T., & Torres, R. D. S. (2024). An urban digital twin framework for reference and planning. *IEEE Access*, *12*, 152444–152465. https://doi.org/10.1109/ACCESS.2024.3478379.

Alshahrani, N. M., Mat Kiah, M. L., Zaidan, B. B., Alamoodi, A. H., & Saif, A. (2023). A review of smart contract blockchain based on multi-criteria analysis: Challenges and motivations. *Computers, Materials & Continua*, *75*(2), 2833–2858. https://doi.org/10.32604/cmc.2023.036138.

Balogun, A.-L., Marks, D., Sharma, R., Shekhar, H., Balmes, C., Maheng, D., Arshad, A., & Salehi, P. (2020). Assessing the potentials of digitalization as a tool for climate change adaptation and sustainable development in urban centres. *Sustainable Cities and Society*, *53*, 101888. https://doi.org/10.1016/j.scs.2019.101888.

Batty, M. (2018). Artificial intelligence and smart cities. *Environment and Planning B: Urban Analytics and City Science*, *45*(1), 3–6. https://doi.org/10.1177/2399808317751169.

Bendiab, G., Hameurlaine, A., Germanos, G., Kolokotronis, N., & Shiaeles, S. (2023). Autonomous vehicles security: Challenges and solutions using blockchain and artificial intelligence. *IEEE Transactions on Intelligent Transportation Systems*, *24*(4), 3614–3637. https://doi.org/10.1109/TITS.2023.3236274.

Bhushan, B., Khamparia, A., Sagayam, K. M., Sharma, S. K., Ahad, M. A., & Debnath, N. C. (2020). Blockchain for smart cities: A review of architectures, integration trends and future research directions. *Sustainable Cities and Society*, *61*, 102360. https://doi.org/10.1016/j.scs.2020.102360.

Bibri, S. E. (2018). The IoT for smart sustainable cities of the future: An analytical framework for sensor-based big data applications for environmental sustainability. *Sustainable Cities and Society*, *38*, 230–253. https://doi.org/10.1016/j.scs.2017.12.034.

Boeing, G. (2019). Urban spatial order: Street network orientation, configuration, and entropy. *Applied Network Science*, *4*(1), 67. https://doi.org/10.1007/s41109-019-0189-1.

Bovkir, R., & Aydinoglu, A. C. (2021). Big urban data visualization approaches within the smart city: Gis-based open-source dashboard example. *The International Archives of the Photogrammetry, Remote Sensing and Spatial Information Sciences*, *XLVI-4/W5-2021* (pp. 125–130). https://doi.org/10.5194/isprs-archives-XLVI-4-W5-2021-125-2021.

Cao, X., Wang, M., & Liu, X. (2020). Application of big data visualization in urban planning. *IOP Conference Series: Earth and Environmental Science, 440*(4), 042066. https://doi.org/10.1088/1755-1315/440/4/042066.

Casali, Y., Aydin, N. Y., & Comes, T. (2022). Machine learning for spatial analyses in urban areas: A scoping review. *Sustainable Cities and Society, 85,* 104050. https://doi.org/10.1016/j.scs.2022.104050

Cesario, E. (2023). Big data analytics and smart cities: Applications, challenges, and opportunities. *Frontiers in Big Data, 6.* https://doi.org/10.3389/fdata.2023.1149402.

Chavhan, S., Gupta, D., Gochhayat, S. P., N., C. B., Khanna, A., Shankar, K., & Rodrigues, J. J. P. C. (2022). Edge computing AI-IoT integrated energy-efficient intelligent transportation system for smart cities. *ACM Transactions on Internet Technology, 22*(4), 1–18. https://doi.org/10.1145/3507906.

Chen, L., Li, J., Xu, M., & Xing, W. (2024). Navigating urban complexity: The role of GIS in spatial planning and urban development. *Applied and Computational Engineering, 65*(1), 282–287. https://doi.org/10.54254/2755-2721/65/20240519.

Corrado, C. R., DeLong, S. M., Holt, E. G., Hua, E. Y., & Tolk, A. (2022). Combining green metrics and digital twins for sustainability planning and governance of smart buildings and cities. *Sustainability, 14*(20), 12988. https://doi.org/10.3390/su142012988.

Croese, S., & Duminy, J. (2023). Co-producing urban expertise for SDG localization: The history and practices of urban knowledge production in South Africa. *Urban Geography, 44*(3), 538–557. https://doi.org/10.1080/02723638.2022.2079868.

Díaz-Rodríguez, N., Del Ser, J., Coeckelbergh, M., López de Prado, M., Herrera-Viedma, E., & Herrera, F. (2023). Connecting the dots in trustworthy artificial intelligence: From AI principles, ethics, and key requirements to responsible AI systems and regulation. *Information Fusion, 99,* 101896. https://doi.org/10.1016/j.inffus.2023.101896.

Diwan, A. A., & Shukla, Ar. S. (2024). Utilization of GIS technology in urban land-use planning: A Mumbai case study. *Interantional Journal of Scientific Research in Engineering and Management, 8*(008), 1–15. https://doi.org/10.55041/IJSREM37322.

Droj, G., Droj, L., & Badea, A.-C. (2021). GIS-based survey over the public transport strategy: An instrument for economic and sustainable urban traffic planning. *ISPRS International Journal of Geo-Information, 11*(1), 16. https://doi.org/10.3390/ijgi11010016.

Faisal, K., Alshammari, S., Alotaibi, R., Alhothali, A., Bamasag, O., Alghanmi, N., & Bin Yamin, M. (2022). Spatial analysis of COVID-19 vaccine centers distribution: A case study of the city of Jeddah, Saudi Arabia. *International Journal of Environmental Research and Public Health, 19*(6), 3526. https://doi.org/10.3390/ijerph19063526.

Fan, K., Lu, H., Bai, Y., Luo, Y., Yang, Y., Zhang, K., & Li, H. (2024). SC-chain: An efficient blockchain framework for smart city. *IEEE Internet of Things Journal, 11*(5), 7863–7877. https://doi.org/10.1109/JIOT.2023.3317451.

Fan, Z., Yan, Z., & Wen, S. (2023). Deep learning and artificial intelligence in sustainability: A review of SDGs, Renewable Energy, and Environmental Health. *Sustainability, 15*(18), 13493. https://doi.org/10.3390/su151813493.

Fang, Z., Yue, P., Zhang, M., Xie, J., Wu, D., & Jiang, L. (2023). A service-oriented collaborative approach to disaster decision support by integrating geospatial resources and task chain. *International Journal of Applied Earth Observation and Geoinformation, 117*, 103217. https://doi.org/10.1016/j.jag.2023.103217.

Giles-Corti, B., Lowe, M., & Arundel, J. (2020). Achieving the SDGs: Evaluating indicators to be used to benchmark and monitor progress towards creating healthy and sustainable cities. *Health Policy, 124*(6), 581–590. https://doi.org/10.1016/j.healthpol.2019.03.001.

Glaeser, E. L., Kominers, S. D., Luca, M., & Naik, N. (2018). Big data and big cities: The promises and limitations of improved measures of urban life. *Economic Inquiry, 56*(1), 114–137. https://doi.org/10.1111/ecin.12364.

Gupta, S., & Degbelo, A. (2023). An empirical analysis of AI contributions to sustainable cities (SDG 11). In F. Mazzi & L. Floridi (Eds.), *The ethics of artificial intelligence for the Sustainable Development Goals* (Vol. 152, pp. 401–416). Springer. https://doi.org/10.1007/978-3-031-21147-8_25

Gupta, J., & Vegelin, C. (2016). Sustainable development goals and inclusive development. *International Environmental Agreements: Politics, Law and Economics, 16*(3), 433–448. https://doi.org/10.1007/s10784-016-9323-z.

Han, Z., Jiao, S., Zhang, X., Xie, F., Ran, J., Jin, R., & Xu, S. (2021). Seeking sustainable development policies at the municipal level based on the triad of city, economy and environment: Evidence from Hunan province, China. *Journal of Environmental Management, 290*, 112554. https://doi.org/10.1016/j.jenvman.2021.112554.

Haou, E., Allarané, N., Aholou, C. C., & Bondoro, O. (2025). Integrating sustainable development goals into urban planning to advance sustainability in Sub-Saharan Africa: Barriers and practical solutions from the case study of Moundou, Chad. *Urban Science, 9*(2), 22. https://doi.org/10.3390/urbansci9020022.

Hasan, M. K., Akhtaruzzaman, Md., Kabir, S. R., Gadekallu, T. R., Islam, S., Magalingam, P., Hassan, R., Alazab, M., & Alazab, M. A. (2022). Evolution of industry and blockchain era: Monitoring price hike and corruption using BIoT for smart government and industry 4.0. *IEEE Transactions on Industrial Informatics, 18*(12), 9153–9161. https://doi.org/10.1109/TII.2022.3164066.

Hilbert, M. (2016). Big data for development: A review of promises and challenges. *Development Policy Review, 34*(1), 135–174. https://doi.org/10.1111/dpr.12142.

Jamei, E., Mortimer, M., Seyedmahmoudian, M., Horan, B., & Stojcevski, A. (2017). Investigating the role of virtual reality in planning for sustainable smart cities. *Sustainability, 9*(11), 2006. https://doi.org/10.3390/su9112006.

James, J. (2002). Low-cost information technology in developing countries: Current opportunities and emerging possibilities. *Habitat International, 26*(1), 21–31. https://doi.org/10.1016/S0197-3975(01)00030-3.

Jishtu, P., & Yadav, M. (2021). Futuristic technology in architecture & planning – Augmented and virtual reality: An overview. *International Journal on Soft Computing, Artificial Intelligence and Applications (IJSCAI), 10*, 1–13. https://doi.org/10.5121/IJSCAI.2021.10101

Kaluarachchi, Y. (2022). Implementing data-driven smart city applications for future cities. *Smart Cities, 5*(2), 455–474. https://doi.org/10.3390/smartcities5020025.

Katika, T., Karaseitanidis, I., Tsiakou, D., Makropoulos, C., & Amditis, A. (2022). Augmented reality (AR) supporting citizen engagement in circular economy. *Circular Economy and Sustainability*, 2(3), 1077–1104. https://doi.org/10.1007/s43615-021-00137-7.

Khalfan, M., Azizi, N., Haass, O., Maqsood, T., & Ahmed, I. (2022). Blockchain technology: Potential applications for public sector e-procurement and project management. *Sustainability*, 14(10), 5791. https://doi.org/10.3390/su14105791.

Khan, M. A., Siddiqui, M. S., Rahmani, M. K. I., & Husain, S. (2022). Investigation of big data analytics for sustainable smart city development: An emerging country. *IEEE Access*, 10, 16028–16036. https://doi.org/10.1109/ACCESS.2021.3115987.

Kharrazi, A., Qin, H., & Zhang, Y. (2016). Urban big data and sustainable development goals: Challenges and opportunities. *Sustainability*, 8(12), 1293. https://doi.org/10.3390/su8121293.

Khadka, U., Hossain, S., Sarkar, S., & Khan, N. (2024). Cyber-physical systems and IoT: Transforming smart cities for sustainable development. *Advanced International Journal of Multidisciplinary Research*, 2(5). https://doi.org/10.62127/aijmr.2024.v02i05.1106

Kitchin, R. (2014). The real-time city? Big data and smart urbanism. *GeoJournal*, 79(1), 1–14. https://doi.org/10.1007/s10708-013-9516-8.

Krellenberg, K., Bergsträßer, H., Bykova, D., Kress, N., & Tyndall, K. (2019). Urban sustainability strategies guided by the SDGs—A tale of four cities. *Sustainability*, 11(4), 1116. https://doi.org/10.3390/su11041116.

Kumar, S., Datta, S., Singh, V., Datta, D., Kumar Singh, S., & Sharma, R. (2024). Applications, challenges, and future directions of human-in-the-loop learning. *IEEE Access*, 12, 75735–75760. https://doi.org/10.1109/ACCESS.2024.3401547.

Lata, K., Sood, A., Kaur, K., Benipal, A. K., & Pateriya, B. (2022). Web-GIS based dashboard for real-time data visualization & analysis using open source technologies. *Journal of Geomatics*, 16(2), 134–146. https://doi.org/10.58825/jog.2022.16.2.42.

Li, Y., Zhao, Q., & Zhong, C. (2022). GIS and urban data science. *Annals of GIS*, 28(2), 89–92. https://doi.org/10.1080/19475683.2022.2070969.

Liu, X., Wang, X., Wright, G., Cheng, J., Li, X., & Liu, R. (2017). A state-of-the-art review on the integration of building information modeling (BIM) and geographic information system (GIS). *ISPRS International Journal of Geo-Information*, 6(2), 53. https://doi.org/10.3390/ijgi6020053.

Liu, Z., He, Y., Demian, P., & Osmani, M. (2024). Immersive technology and building information modeling (BIM) for sustainable smart cities. *Buildings*, 14(6), 1765. https://doi.org/10.3390/buildings14061765.

Maes, M. J. A., Jones, K. E., Toledano, M. B., & Milligan, B. (2019). Mapping synergies and trade-offs between urban ecosystems and the sustainable development goals. *Environmental Science & Policy*, 93, 181–188. https://doi.org/10.1016/j.envsci.2018.12.010.

Masoumi, H., Shirowzhan, S., Eskandarpour, P., & Pettit, C. J. (2023). City digital twins: Their maturity level and differentiation from 3D city models. *Big Earth Data*, 7(1), 1–36. https://doi.org/10.1080/20964471.2022.2160156

Mazzetto, S. (2024). A review of urban digital twins integration, challenges, and future directions in smart city development. *Sustainability*, 16(19), 8337. https://doi.org/10.3390/su16198337.

Mengelkamp, E., Gärttner, J., Rock, K., Kessler, S., Orsini, L., & Weinhardt, C. (2018). Designing microgrid energy markets. *Applied Energy, 210*, 870–880. https://doi.org/10.1016/j.apenergy.2017.06.054.

Mhlanga, D. (2022). Human-centered artificial intelligence: The superlative approach to achieve sustainable development goals in the fourth industrial revolution. *Sustainability, 14*(13), 7804. https://doi.org/10.3390/su14137804.

Montakhabi, M., Madhusudan, A., Mustafa, M. A., Vanhaverbeke, W., Almirall, E., & van der Graaf, S. (2023). Leveraging blockchain for energy transition in urban contexts. *Big Data & Society, 10*(2). https://doi.org/10.1177/20539517231205503.

Mooradian, N., Franks, P. C., & Srivastav, A. (2025). The impact of artificial intelligence on data privacy: A risk management perspective. *Records Management Journal*. https://doi.org/10.1108/RMJ-06-2024-0013.

Nam, T., & Pardo, T. A. (2011). Smart city as urban innovation. In *Proceedings of the 5th International Conference on Theory and Practice of Electronic Governance*, (pp. 185–194). https://doi.org/10.1145/2072069.2072100.

Ni Loideain, N. (2017). Cape Town as a smart and safe city: Implications for governance and data privacy. *International Data Privacy Law, 7*(4), 314–334. https://doi.org/10.1093/idpl/ipx018.

Nosratabadi, S., Mosavi, A., Keivani, R., Ardabili, S., & Aram, F. (2020). State of the art survey of deep learning and machine learning models for smart cities and urban sustainability. In *Engineering for Sustainable Future* (pp. 228–238). https://doi.org/10.1007/978-3-030-36841-8_22.

Olaniyi, O. O., Okunleye, O. J., & Olabanji, S. O. (2023). Advancing data-driven decision-making in smart cities through big data analytics: A comprehensive review of existing literature. *Current Journal of Applied Science and Technology, 42*(25), 10–18. https://doi.org/10.9734/cjast/2023/v42i254181.

Ouchra, H., Belangour, A., & Erraissi, A. (2022). Satellite data analysis and geographic information system for urban planning: A systematic review. In *2022 International Conference on Data Analytics for Business and Industry (ICDABI)* (pp. 558–564). https://doi.org/10.1109/ICDABI56818.2022.10041487.

Pratomo, A. B., Mokodenseho, S., & Aziz, A. M. (2023). Data encryption and anonymization techniques for enhanced information system security and privacy. *West Science Information System and Technology, 1*(01), 1–9. https://doi.org/10.58812/wsist.v1i01.176.

Rahman, Md. M., & Szabó, G. (2022). Sustainable urban land-use optimization using GIS-based multicriteria decision-making (GIS-MCDM) approach. *ISPRS International Journal of Geo-Information, 11*(5), 313. https://doi.org/10.3390/ijgi11050313.

Ramirez-Rubio, O., Daher, C., Fanjul, G., Gascon, M., Mueller, N., Pajín, L., Plasencia, A., Rojas-Rueda, D., Thondoo, M., & Nieuwenhuijsen, M. J. (2019). Urban health: An example of a "health in all policies" approach in the context of SDGs implementation. *Globalization and Health, 15*(1), 87. https://doi.org/10.1186/s12992-019-0529-z.

Rathore, M. M., Ahmad, A., Paul, A., & Rho, S. (2016). Urban planning and building smart cities based on the internet of things using big data analytics. *Computer Networks, 101*, 63–80. https://doi.org/10.1016/j.comnet.2015.12.023.

Seyman Guray, T., & Kismet, B. (2023). VR and AR in construction management research: Bibliometric and descriptive analyses. *Smart and Sustainable Built Environment*, 12(3), 635–659. https://doi.org/10.1108/SASBE-01-2022-0015.

Sharma, P., Bamini, J., Vijayalakshmi, S., N, V., Meenambika, A., & Singh, V. (2024). Exploring the implications of IoT integration in urban infrastructures for sustainable smart cities. In *2024 International Conference on Intelligent and Innovative Technologies in Computing, Electrical and Electronics (IITCEE)* (pp. 1–5). IEEE. https://doi.org/10.1109/IITCEE59897.2024.10468019

Si, D. (2022). A Framework to analyze the impacts of AI with the sustainable development goals. *Highlights in Science, Engineering and Technology*, 17, 313–323. https://doi.org/10.54097/hset.v17i.2621.

Sion, L., Dewitte, P., Van Landuyt, D., Wuyts, K., Emanuilov, I., Valcke, P., & Joosen, W. (2019). An architectural view for data protection by design. In *2019 IEEE International Conference on Software Architecture (ICSA)* (pp. 11–20). https://doi.org/10.1109/ICSA.2019.00010.

Son, T. H., Weedon, Z., Yigitcanlar, T., Sanchez, T., Corchado, J. M., & Mehmood, R. (2023). Algorithmic urban planning for smart and sustainable development: Systematic review of the literature. *Sustainable Cities and Society*, 94, 104562. https://doi.org/10.1016/j.scs.2023.104562.

Kumari, S., Kumari, A., & Waoo, A. A. (2024). AI For sustainable development: Innovations & applications. *ShodhKosh: Journal of Visual and Performing Arts*, 5(5). https://doi.org/10.29121/shodhkosh.v5.i5.2024.1896.

Sabah, S., Hossain, I., Weiss, D., & Tillmann, A. (2023). A fusion of XR technology and physical objects to increase citizens participation in urban planning. In *Proceedings of DeLFI 2023 – Die 21. E-Learning Fachtagung Informatik* (p. 57). https://doi.org/10.18420/delfi2023-57

Tao, W. (2013). Interdisciplinary urban GIS for smart cities: Advancements and opportunities. *Geo-Spatial Information Science*, 16(1), 25–34. https://doi.org/10.1080/10095020.2013.774108.

Teklemariam, N. (2022). Sustainable development goals and equity in urban planning: A comparative analysis of Chicago, São Paulo, and Delhi. *Sustainability*, 14(20), 13227. https://doi.org/10.3390/su142013227.

Testasecca, T., Lazzaro, M., & Sirchia, A. (2023). Towards digital twins of buildings and smart energy networks: Current and future trends. In *2023 IEEE International Workshop on Metrology for Living Environment (MetroLivEnv)* (pp. 96–101). https://doi.org/10.1109/MetroLivEnv56897.2023.10164035.

Tikkinen-Piri, C., Rohunen, A., & Markkula, J. (2018). EU general data protection regulation: Changes and implications for personal data collecting companies. *Computer Law & Security Review*, 34(1), 134–153. https://doi.org/10.1016/j.clsr.2017.05.015.

United Nations. (2015). *Transforming our world: The 2030 Agenda for Sustainable Development*. Retrieved from https://www.un.org/sustainabledevelopment.

Ullah, F., Olatunji, O., & Qayyum, S. (2024). A scoping review of green Internet of Things in construction and smart cities: Current applications, adoption strategies and future directions. *Smart and Sustainable Built Environment*. https://doi.org/10.1108/SASBE-11-2023-0349.

Umesh, K., Sarowar, H., Shifa, S., & Nahid, K. (2024). Cyber-physical systems and IoT: Transforming smart cities for sustainable development. *Advanced International Journal of Multidisciplinary Research*, 2(5). https://doi.org/10.62127/aijmr.2024.v02i05.1106.

Vardoulakis, S., Salmond, J., Krafft, T., & Morawska, L. (2020). Urban environmental health interventions towards the Sustainable Development Goals. *Science of The Total Environment, 748*, 141530. https://doi.org/10.1016/j.scitotenv.2020.141530.

Wang, S., Ouyang, L., Yuan, Y., Ni, X., Han, X., & Wang, F.-Y. (2019). Blockchain-enabled smart contracts: Architecture, applications, and future trends. *IEEE Transactions on Systems, Man, and Cybernetics: Systems, 49*(11), 2266–2277. https://doi.org/10.1109/TSMC.2019.2895123.

Wu, T. G., & Guan, C. (2024). Advancing intra and inter-city urban digital twins: An updated review. *Journal of Planning Education and Research.* https://doi.org/10.1177/0739456X241260887.

Yang, C., Huang, Q., Li, Z., Liu, K., & Hu, F. (2017). Big Data and cloud computing: Innovation opportunities and challenges. *International Journal of Digital Earth, 10*(1), 13–53. https://doi.org/10.1080/17538947.2016.1239771.

Yigitcanlar, T., Desouza, K., Butler, L., & Roozkhosh, F. (2020). Contributions and risks of artificial intelligence (AI) in building smarter cities: Insights from a systematic review of the literature. *Energies, 13*(6), 1473. https://doi.org/10.3390/en13061473.

Zeng, F., Pang, C., & Tang, H. (2024). Sensors on internet of things systems for the sustainable development of smart cities: A systematic literature review. *Sensors, 24*(7), 2074. https://doi.org/10.3390/s24072074.

Ziehl, M., Herzog, R., Degkwitz, T., Niggemann, M. H., Ziemer, G., & Thoneick, R. (2023). Transformative research in digital twins for integrated urban development: Two real-world experiments on unpaid care workers. *International Journal of E-Planning Research, 12*(1), 1–18. https://doi.org/10.4018/IJEPR.333851.

Index